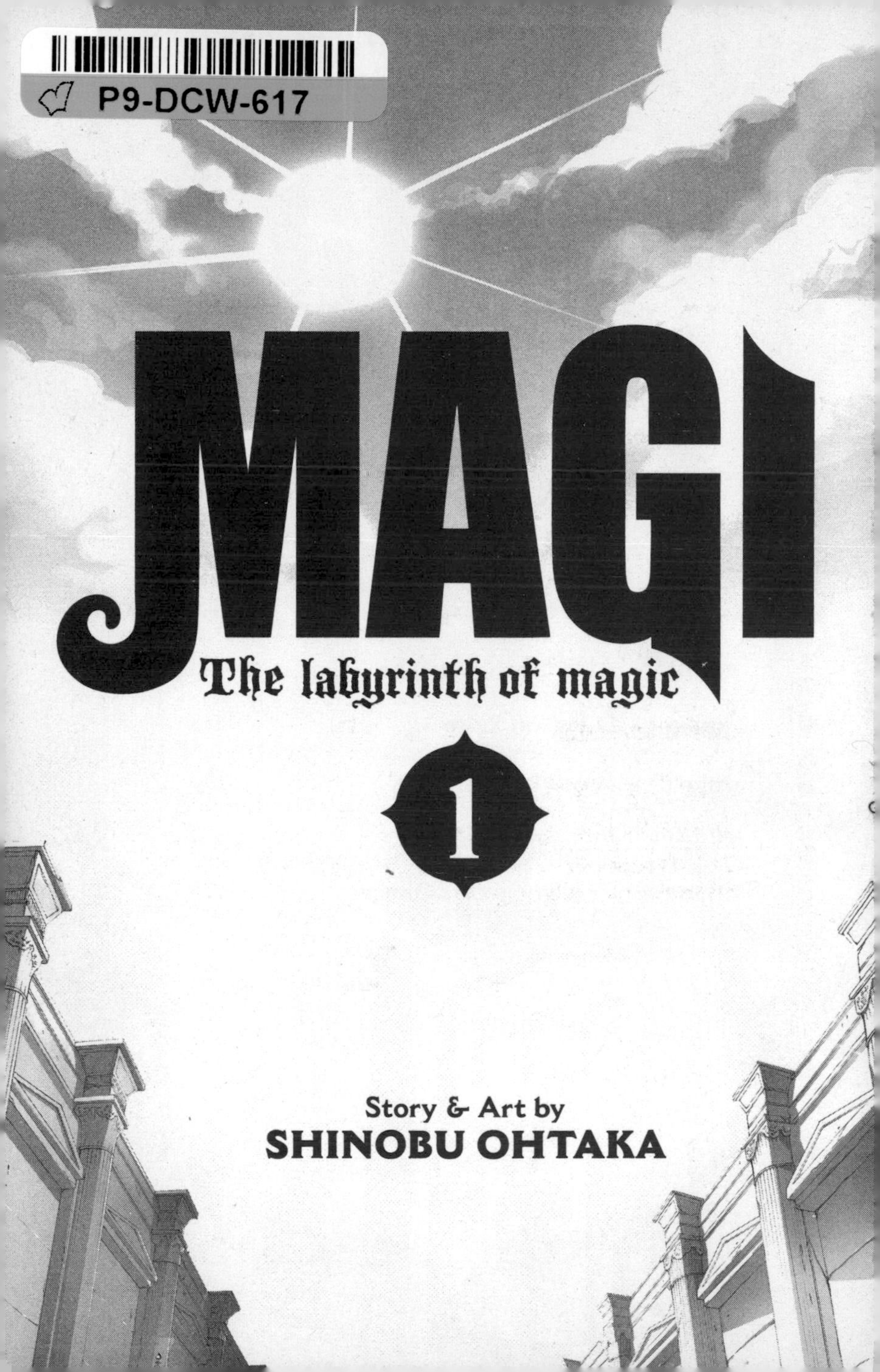
MAGI
The labyrinth of magic
1
Story & Art by
SHINOBU OHTAKA

MAGI
The labyrinth of magic

CONTENTS

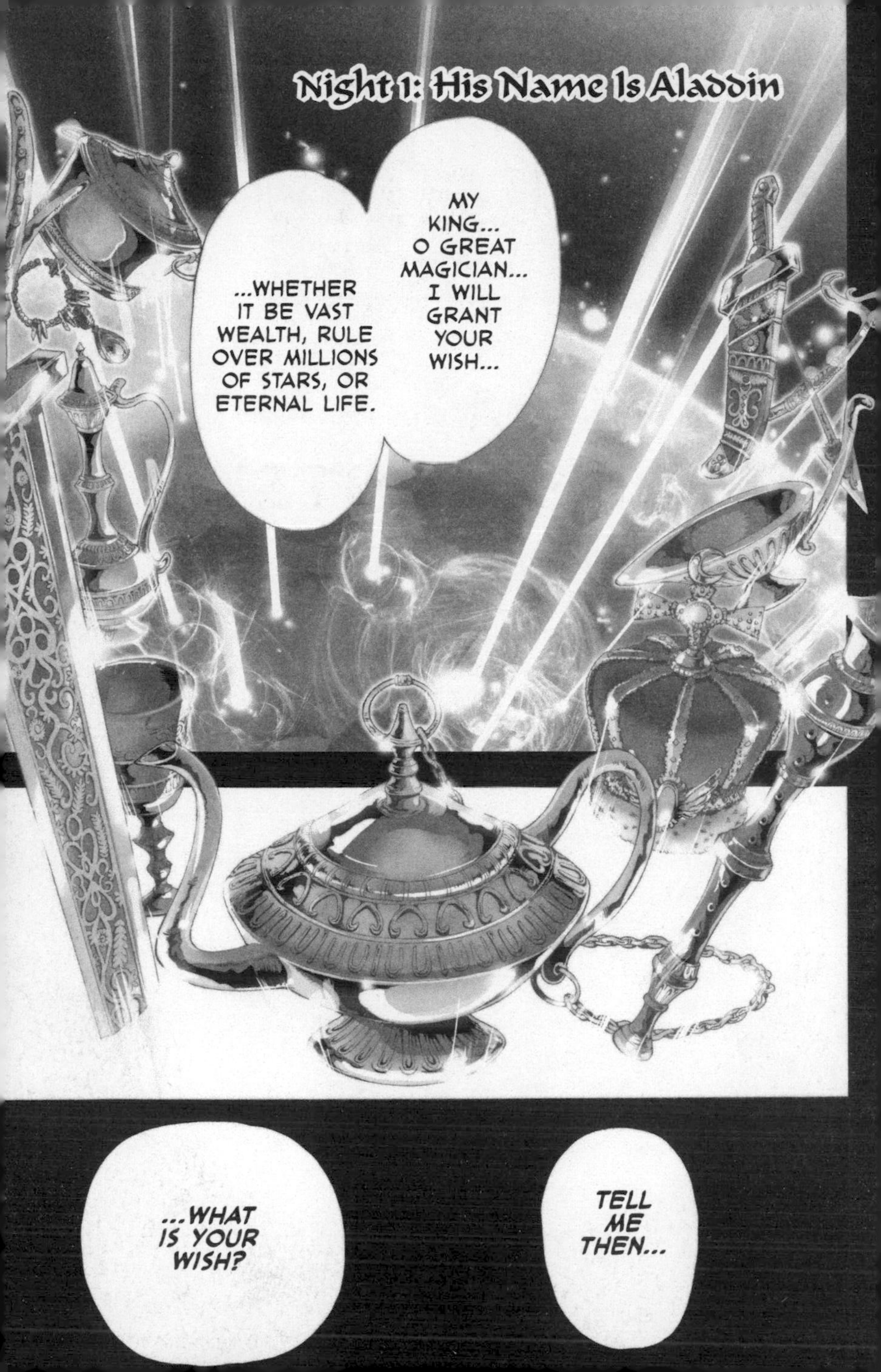
Night 1: His Name Is Aladdin
MY KING... O GREAT MAGICIAN... I WILL GRANT YOUR WISH...
...WHETHER IT BE VAST WEALTH, RULE OVER MILLIONS OF STARS, OR ETERNAL LIFE.
TELL ME THEN...
...WHAT IS YOUR WISH?

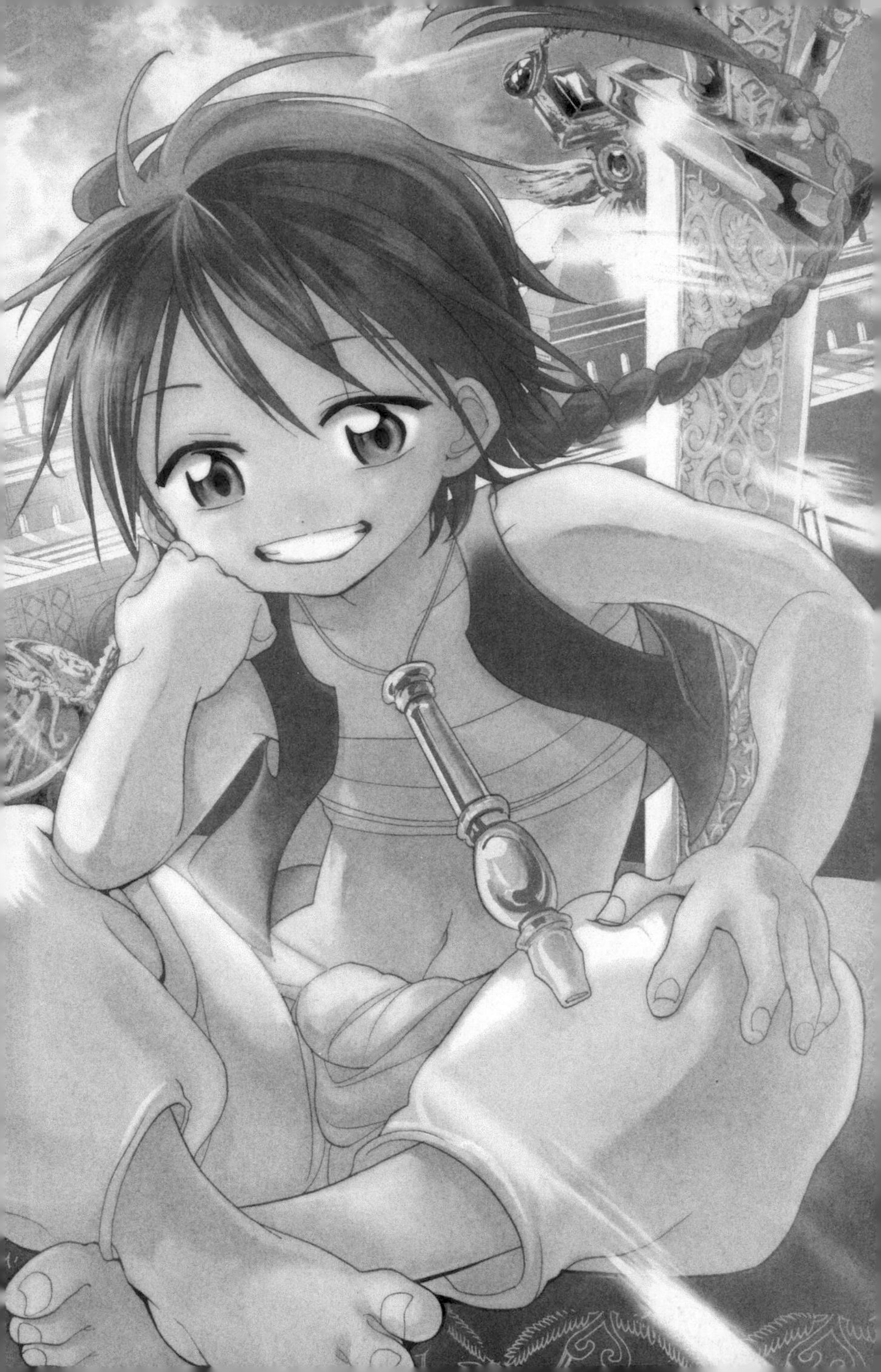

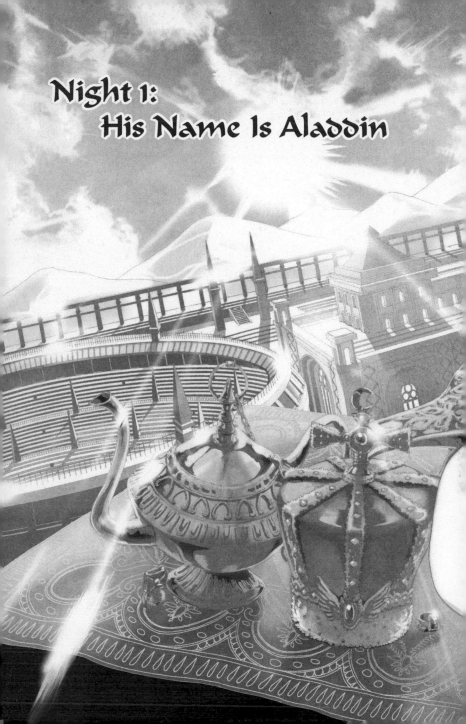

Night 1:
His Name Is Aladdin

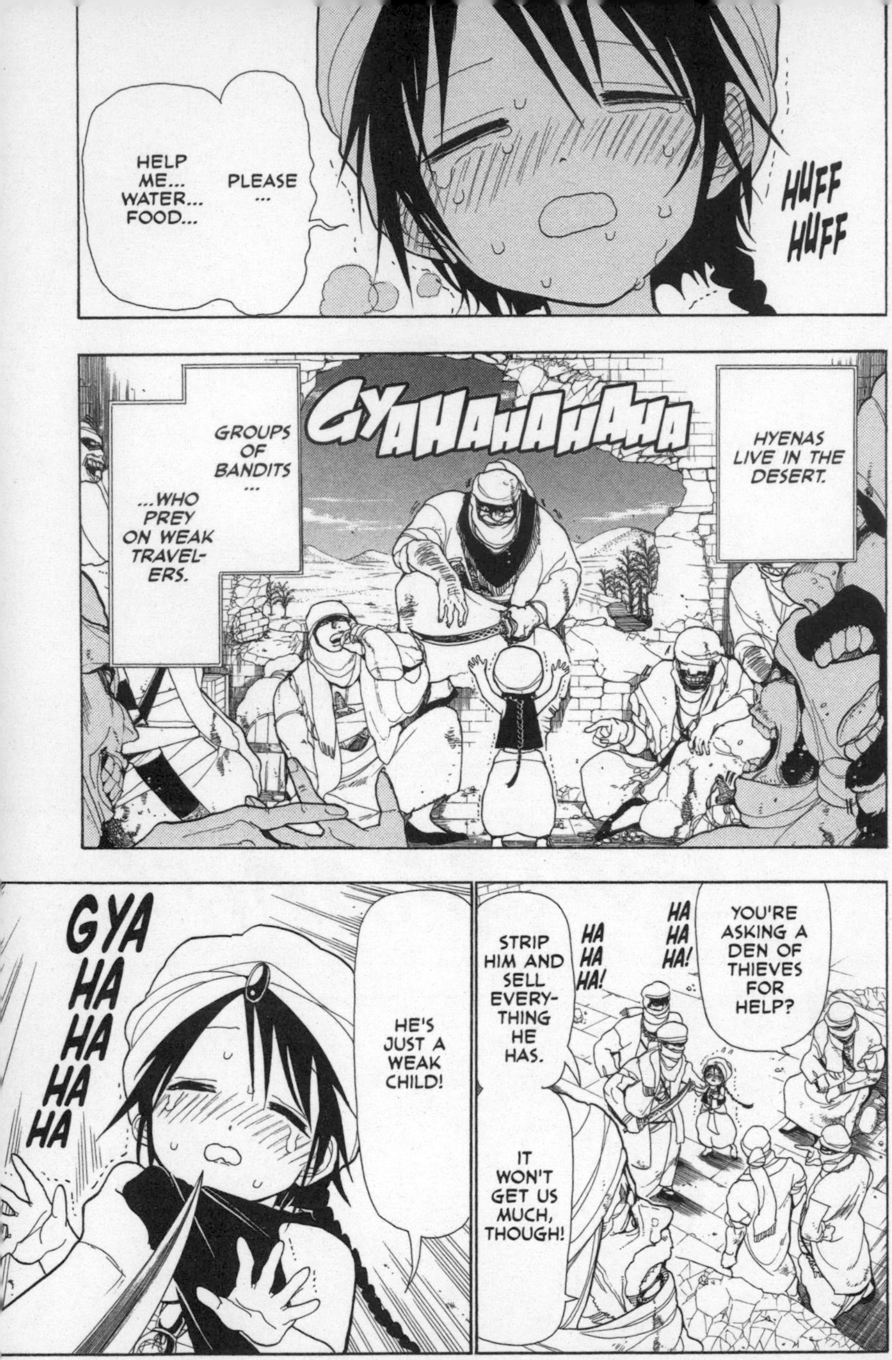
HELP ME... WATER... FOOD...
PLEASE ...
HUFF HUFF
HYENAS LIVE IN THE DESERT.
GYAHAHAHAHAHA
GROUPS OF BANDITS ...
...WHO PREY ON WEAK TRAVEL-ERS.
YOU'RE ASKING A DEN OF THIEVES FOR HELP?
HA HA HA!
HA HA HA!
STRIP HIM AND SELL EVERY-THING HE HAS.
IT WON'T GET US MUCH, THOUGH!
HE'S JUST A WEAK CHILD!
GYA HA HA HA HA HA

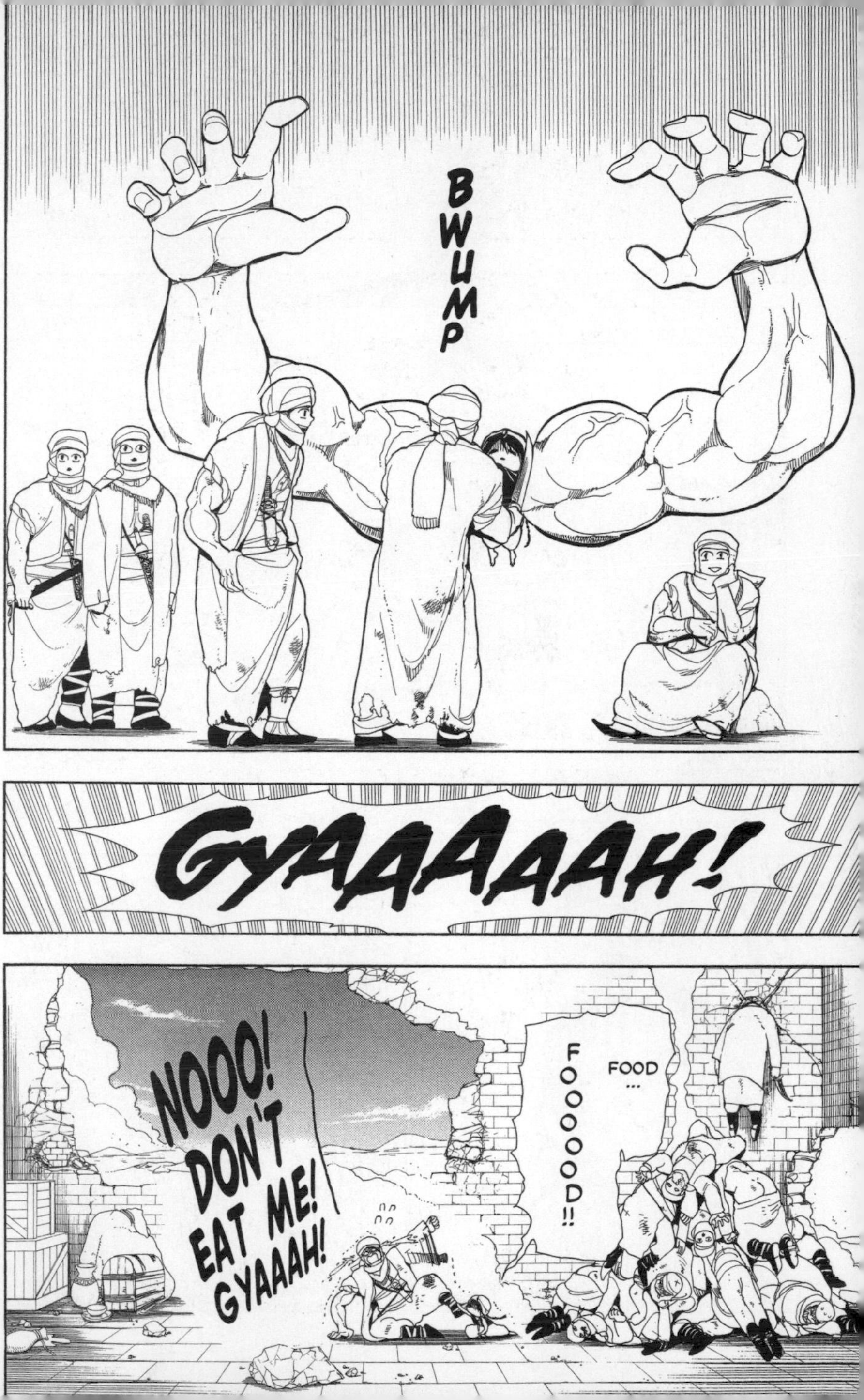
BWUMP
GYAAAAAH!
FOOD...
FOOOOOOD!!
NOOO! DON'T EAT ME! GYAAAH!

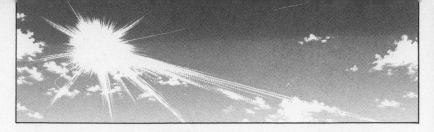

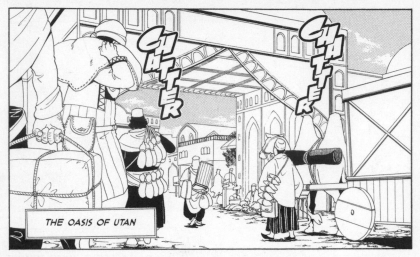

CHATTER

CHATTER

THE OASIS OF UTAN

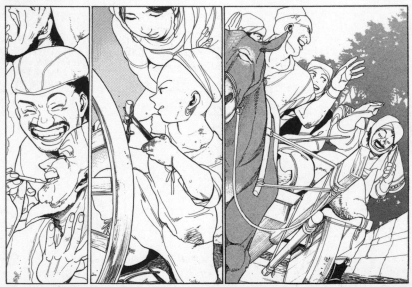

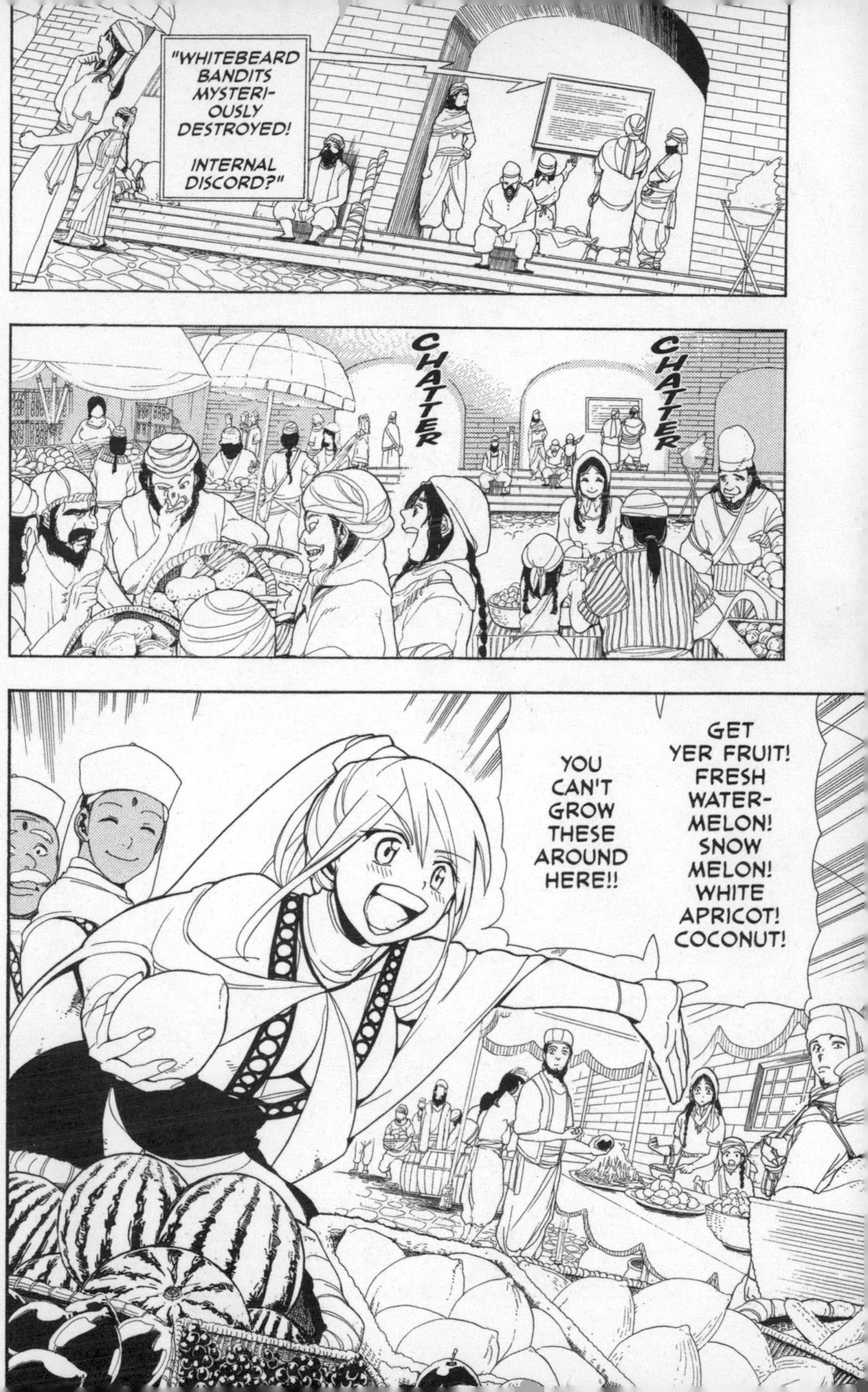

"WHITEBEARD BANDITS MYSTERIOUSLY DESTROYED! INTERNAL DISCORD?"
CHATTER
CHATTER
GET YER FRUIT! FRESH WATERMELON! SNOW MELON! WHITE APRICOT! COCONUT!
YOU CAN'T GROW THESE AROUND HERE!!

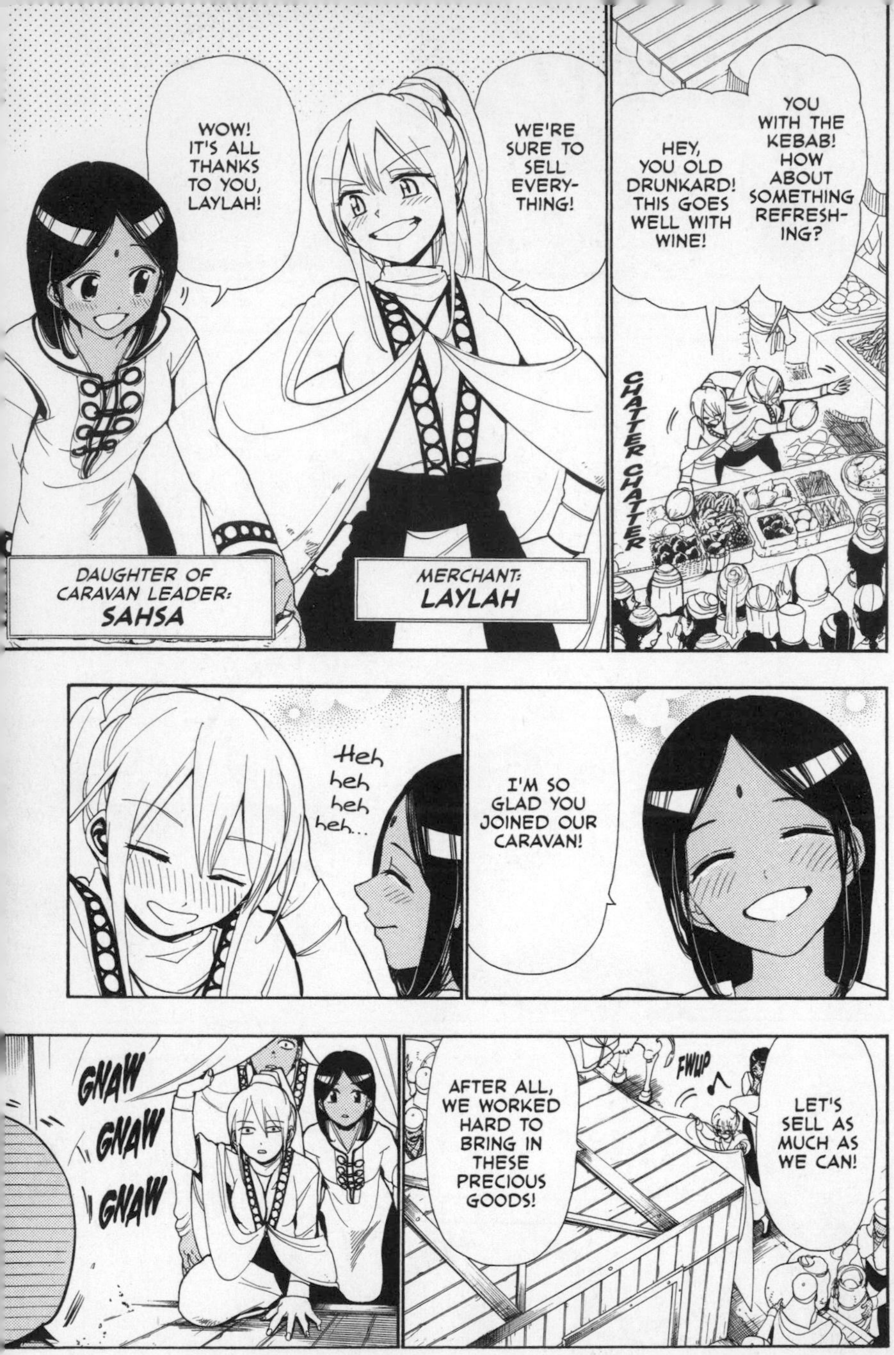
YOU WITH THE KEBAB! HOW ABOUT SOMETHING REFRESHING?
HEY, YOU OLD DRUNKARD! THIS GOES WELL WITH WINE!
CHATTER CHATTER
WE'RE SURE TO SELL EVERYTHING!
WOW! IT'S ALL THANKS TO YOU, LAYLAH!
MERCHANT: LAYLAH
DAUGHTER OF CARAVAN LEADER: SAHSA
I'M SO GLAD YOU JOINED OUR CARAVAN!
Heh heh heh heh...
LET'S SELL AS MUCH AS WE CAN!
FWUP ♪
AFTER ALL, WE WORKED HARD TO BRING IN THESE PRECIOUS GOODS!
GNAW GNAW GNAW

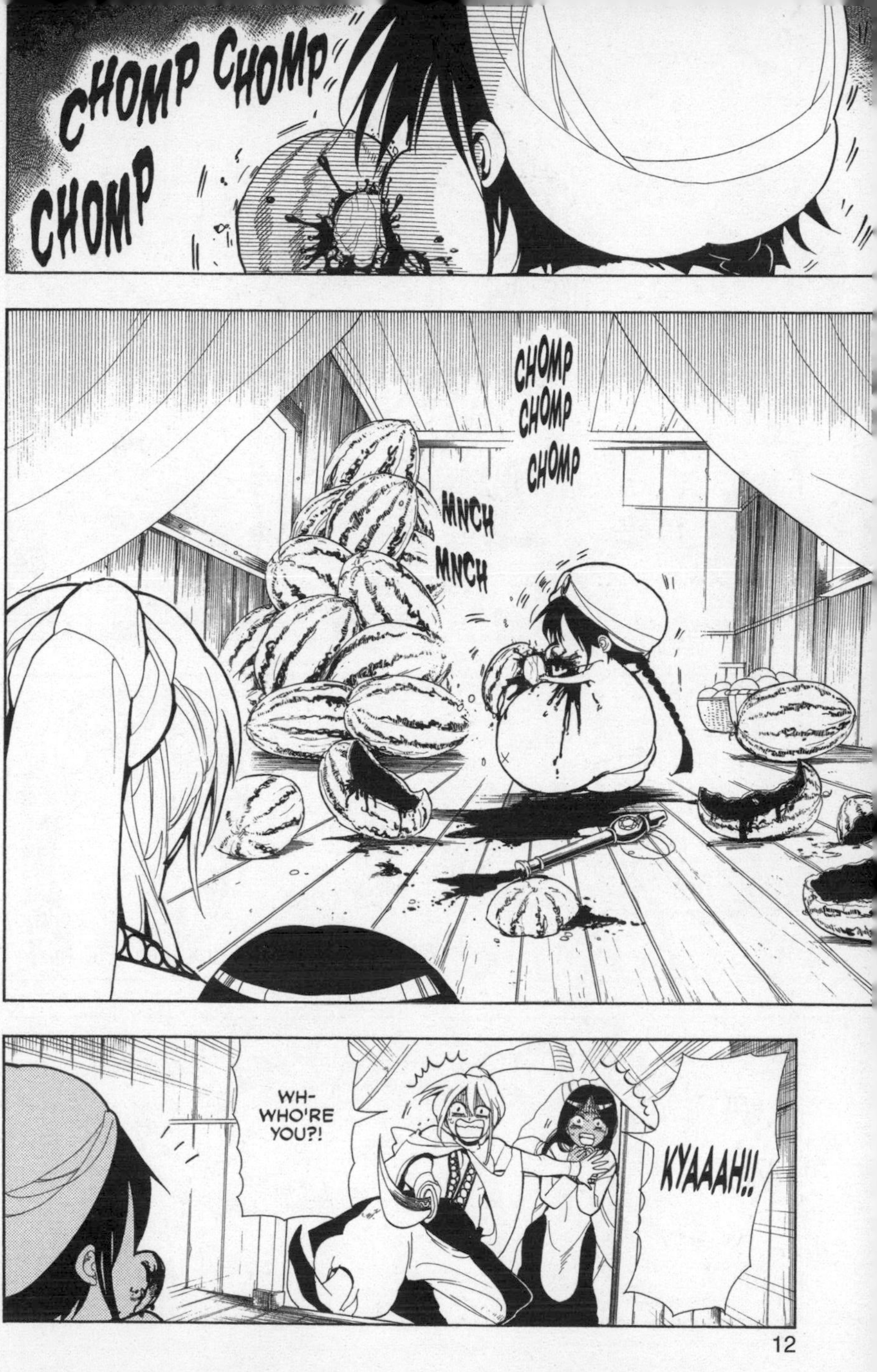
CHOMP CHOMP
CHOMP
CHOMP
CHOMP
CHOMP
MNCH
MNCH
KYAAAH!!
WH-WHO'RE YOU?!

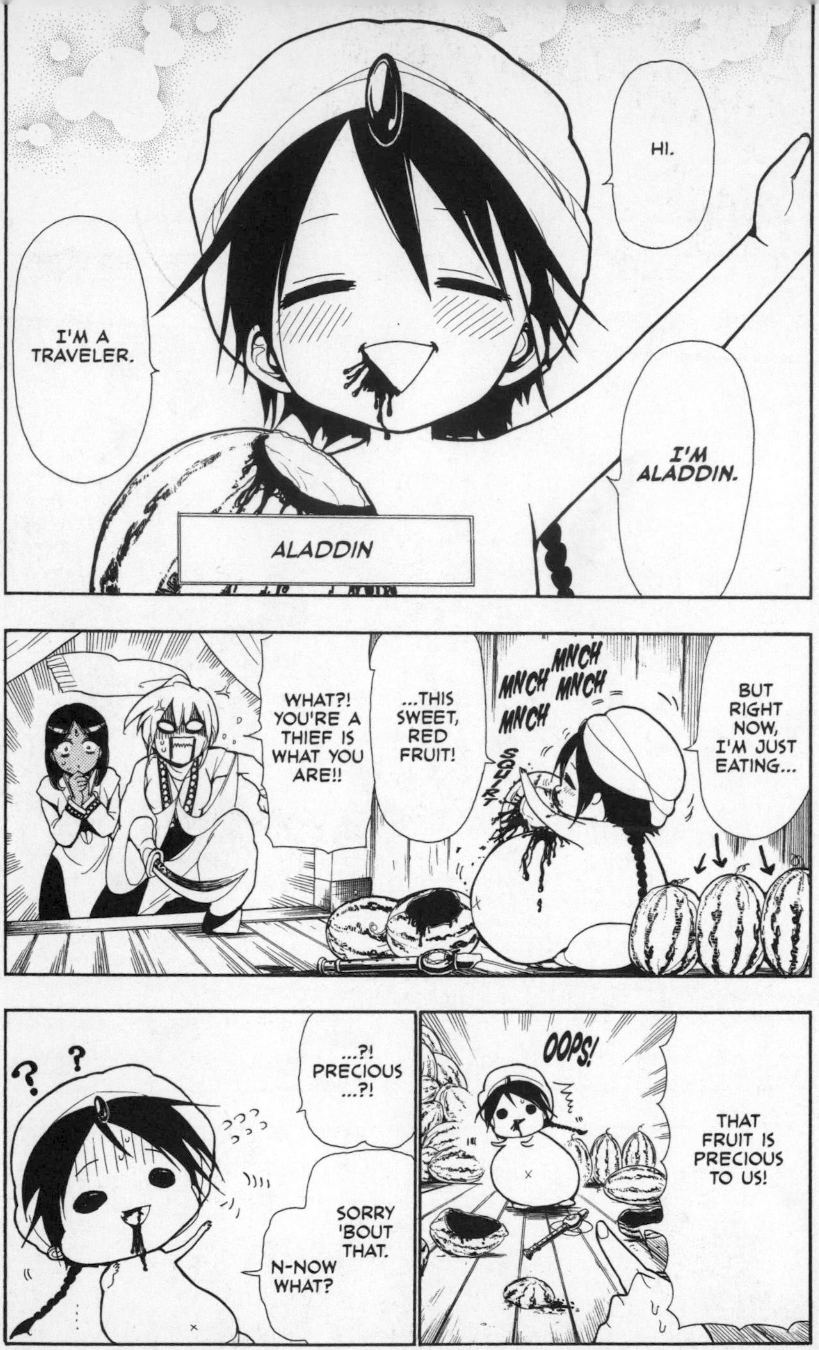
HI.
I'M ALADDIN.
I'M A TRAVELER.
ALADDIN
BUT RIGHT NOW, I'M JUST EATING...
MNCH MNCH MNCH MNCH
SQUIRT
...THIS SWEET, RED FRUIT!
WHAT?! YOU'RE A THIEF IS WHAT YOU ARE!!
OOPS!
THAT FRUIT IS PRECIOUS TO US!
...?! PRECIOUS ...?!
SORRY 'BOUT THAT.
N-NOW WHAT?

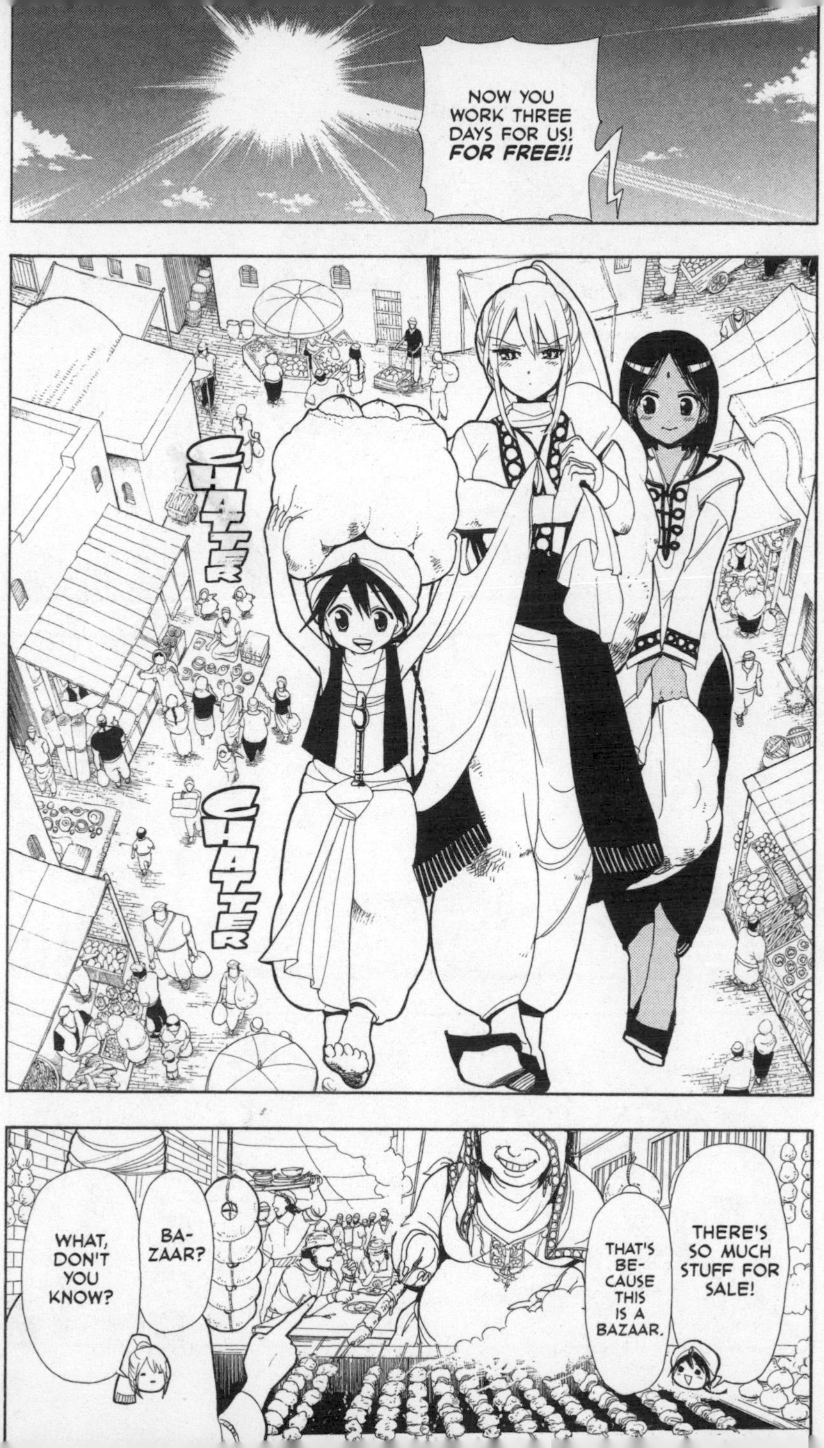
NOW YOU WORK THREE DAYS FOR US! FOR FREE!!
CHATTER
CHATTER
THERE'S SO MUCH STUFF FOR SALE!
THAT'S BE-CAUSE THIS IS A BAZAAR.
BA-ZAAR?
WHAT, DON'T YOU KNOW?

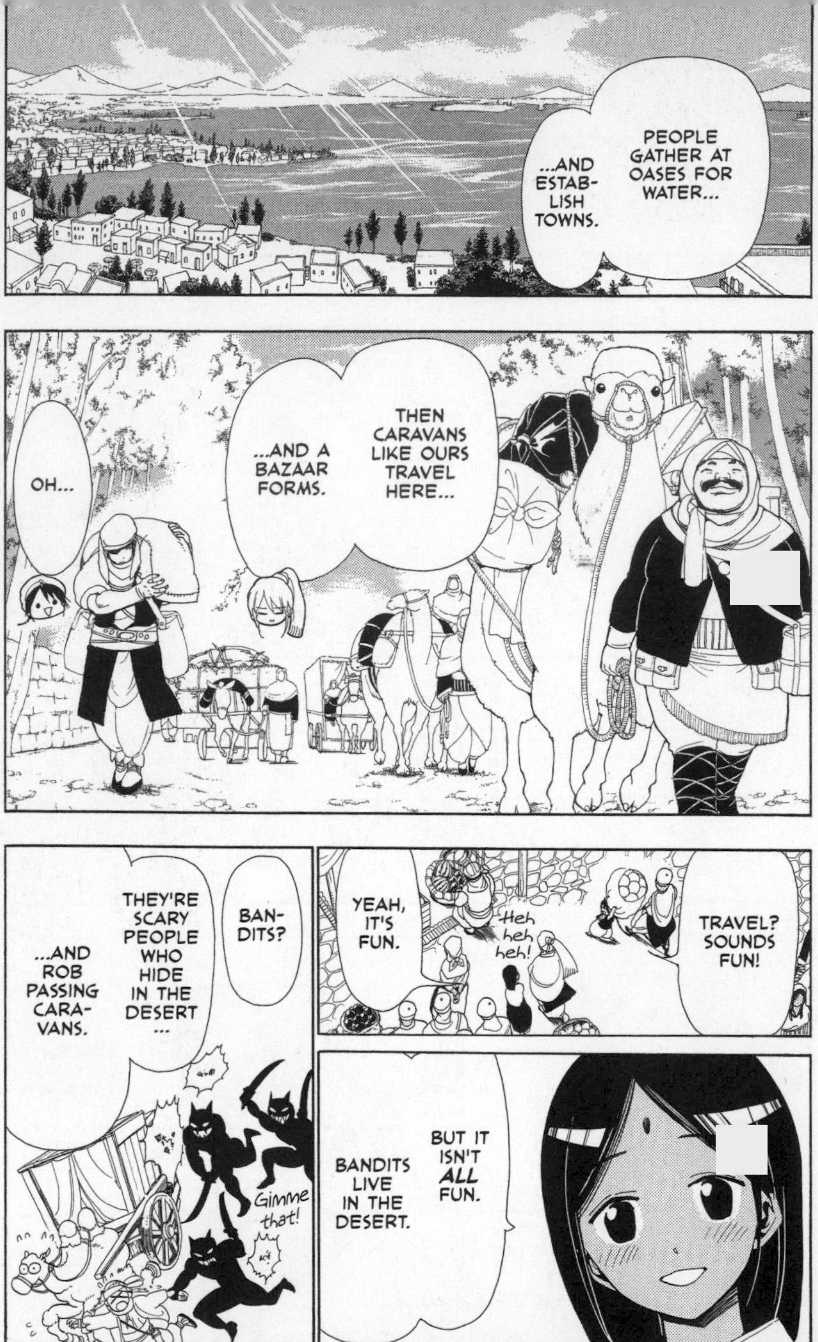
PEOPLE GATHER AT OASES FOR WATER...
...AND ESTAB-LISH TOWNS.
THEN CARAVANS LIKE OURS TRAVEL HERE...
...AND A BAZAAR FORMS.
OH...
TRAVEL? SOUNDS FUN!
YEAH, IT'S FUN.
Heh heh heh!
BUT IT ISN'T *ALL* FUN.
BANDITS LIVE IN THE DESERT.
BAN-DITS?
THEY'RE SCARY PEOPLE WHO HIDE IN THE DESERT...
...AND ROB PASSING CARA-VANS.
Gimme that!

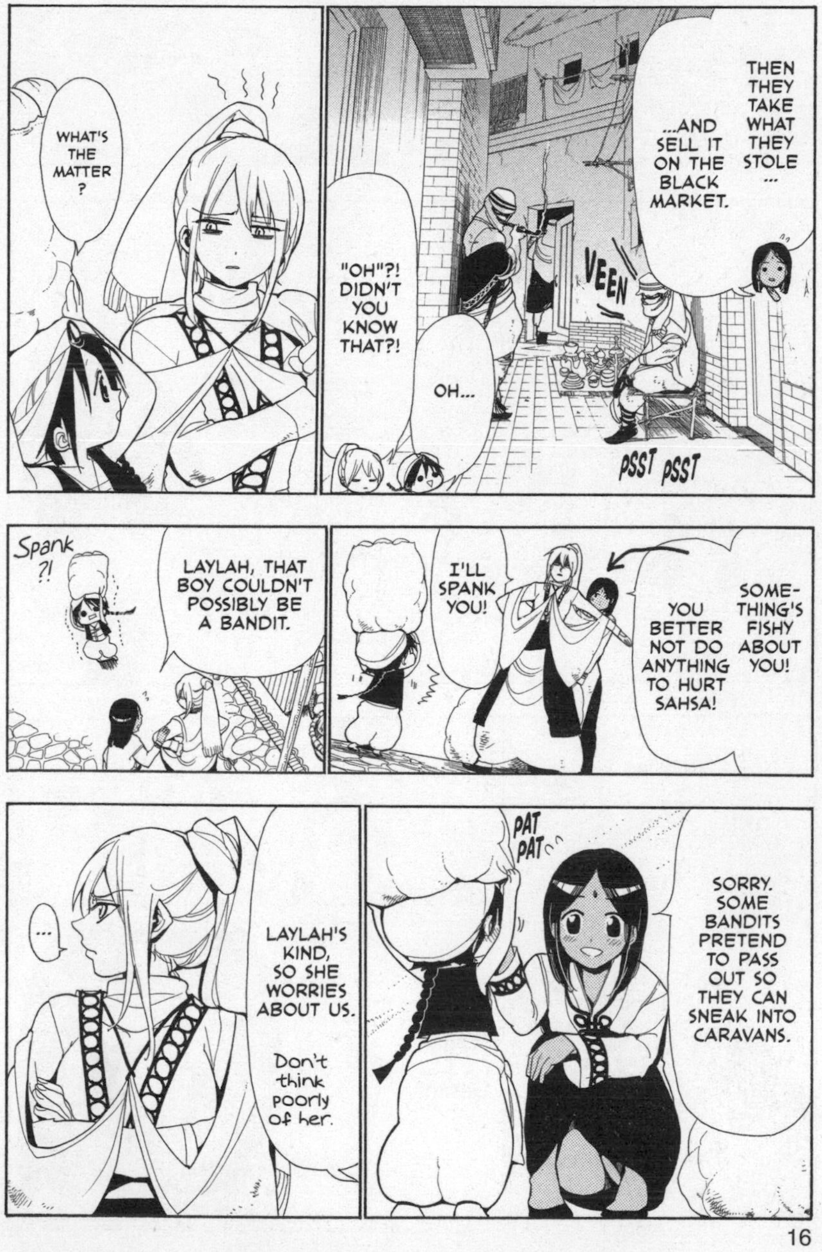
THEN THEY TAKE WHAT THEY STOLE ...
...AND SELL IT ON THE BLACK MARKET.
VEEN
OH...
"OH"?! DIDN'T YOU KNOW THAT?!
PSST PSST
WHAT'S THE MATTER?
SOME-THING'S FISHY ABOUT YOU!
YOU BETTER NOT DO ANYTHING TO HURT SAHSA!
I'LL SPANK YOU!
LAYLAH, THAT BOY COULDN'T POSSIBLY BE A BANDIT.
Spank ?!
PAT PAT
SORRY. SOME BANDITS PRETEND TO PASS OUT SO THEY CAN SNEAK INTO CARAVANS.
LAYLAH'S KIND, SO SHE WORRIES ABOUT US.
Don't think poorly of her.
...

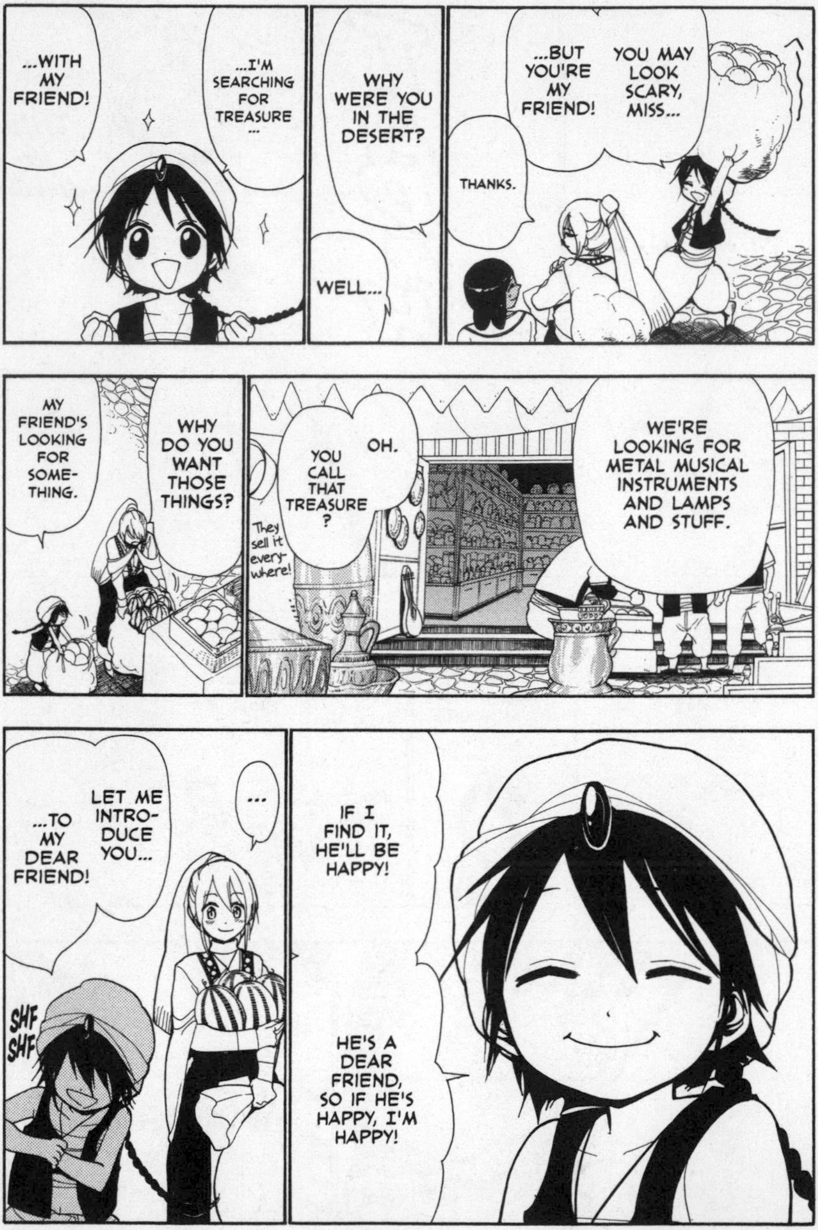
YOU MAY LOOK SCARY, MISS...
...BUT YOU'RE MY FRIEND!
THANKS.
WHY WERE YOU IN THE DESERT?
WELL...
...I'M SEARCHING FOR TREASURE...
...WITH MY FRIEND!
WE'RE LOOKING FOR METAL MUSICAL INSTRUMENTS AND LAMPS AND STUFF.
OH.
YOU CALL THAT TREASURE?
They sell it everywhere!
WHY DO YOU WANT THOSE THINGS?
MY FRIEND'S LOOKING FOR SOMETHING.
IF I FIND IT, HE'LL BE HAPPY!
HE'S A DEAR FRIEND, SO IF HE'S HAPPY, I'M HAPPY!
...
LET ME INTRODUCE YOU...
...TO MY DEAR FRIEND!
SHF SHF

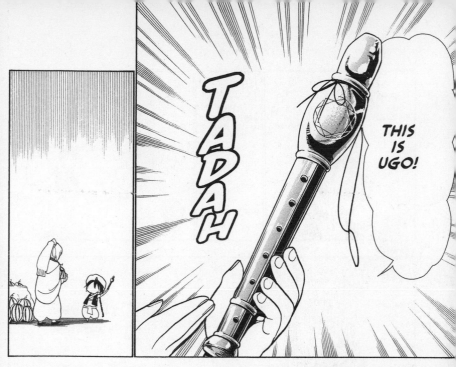

THIS IS UGO!

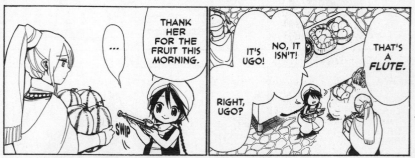

...

THANK HER FOR THE FRUIT THIS MORNING.

SWIP

IT'S UGO!

NO, IT ISN'T!

RIGHT, UGO?

THAT'S A FLUTE.

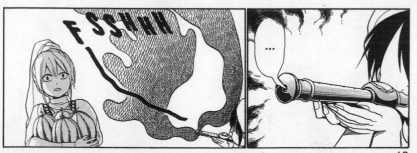

FSSHHH

...

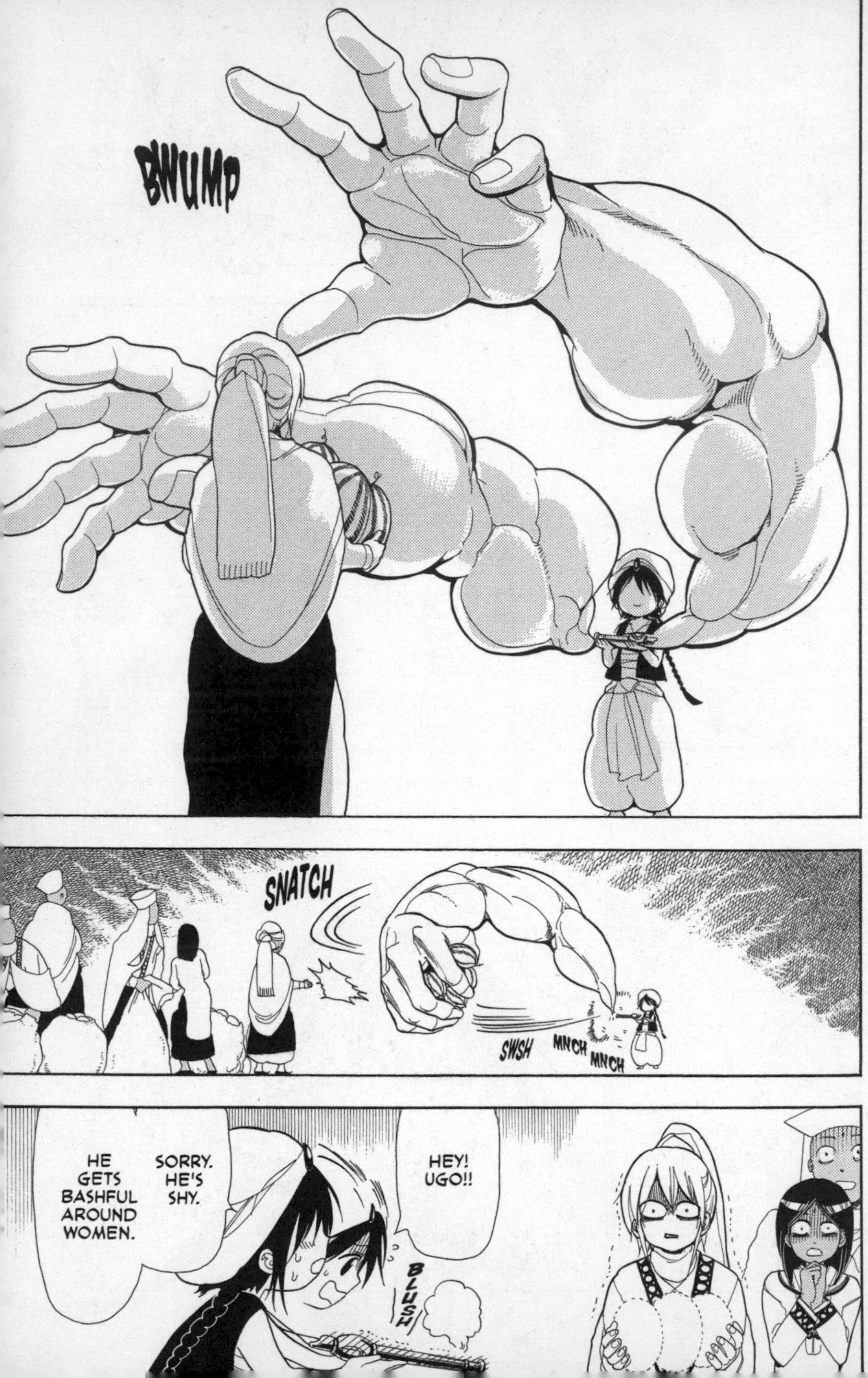
BWUMP
SNATCH
SWSH
MNCH MNCH
HEY! UGO!!
SORRY. HE'S SHY.
HE GETS BASHFUL AROUND WOMEN.
BLUSH

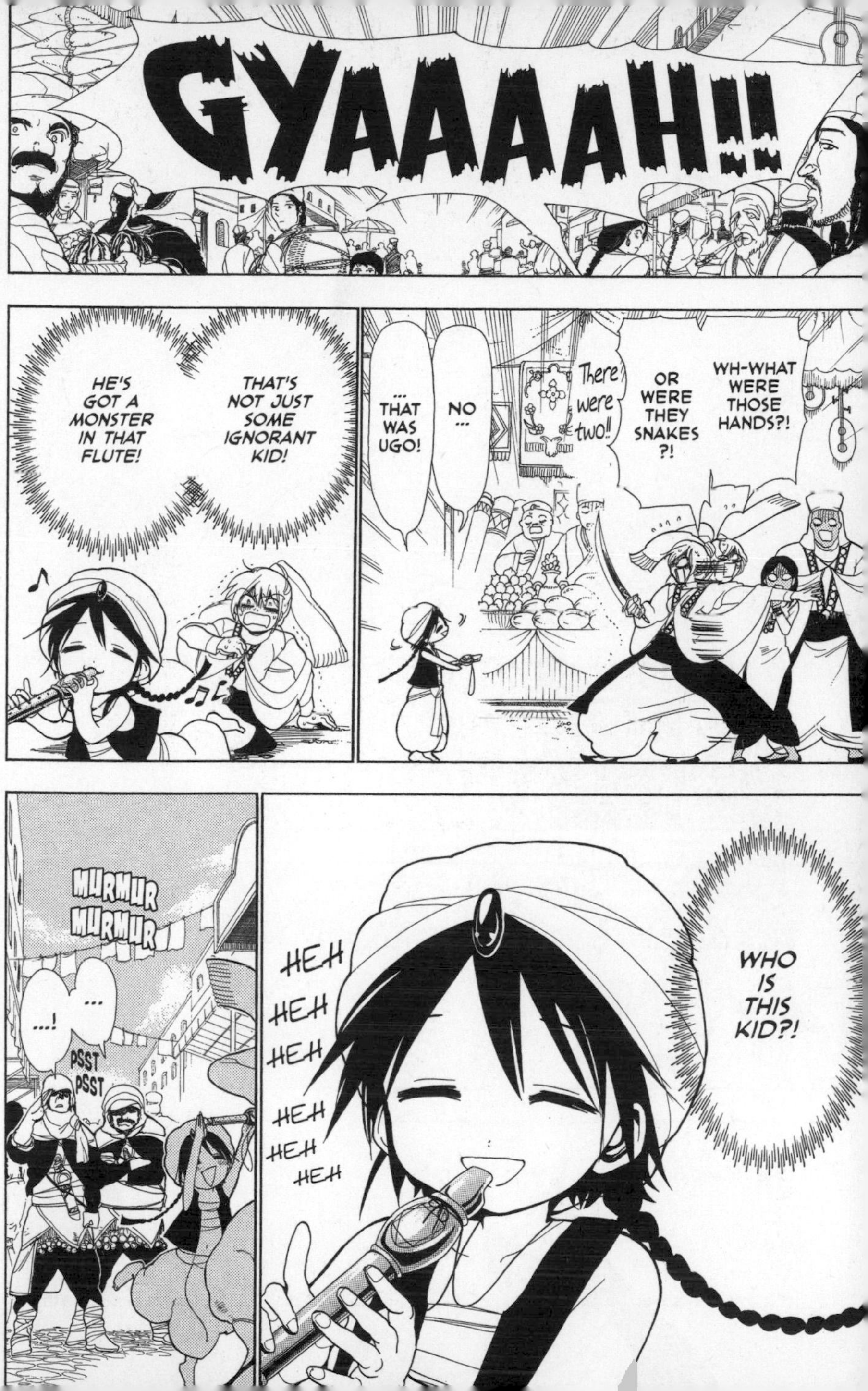
GYAAAAH!!
WH-WHAT WERE THOSE HANDS?!
OR WERE THEY SNAKES ?!
There were two!!
NO ...
... THAT WAS UGO!
THAT'S NOT JUST SOME IGNORANT KID!
HE'S GOT A MONSTER IN THAT FLUTE!
WHO IS THIS KID?!
HEH HEH HEH HEH HEH HEH
MURMUR MURMUR
...
...!
PSST PSST

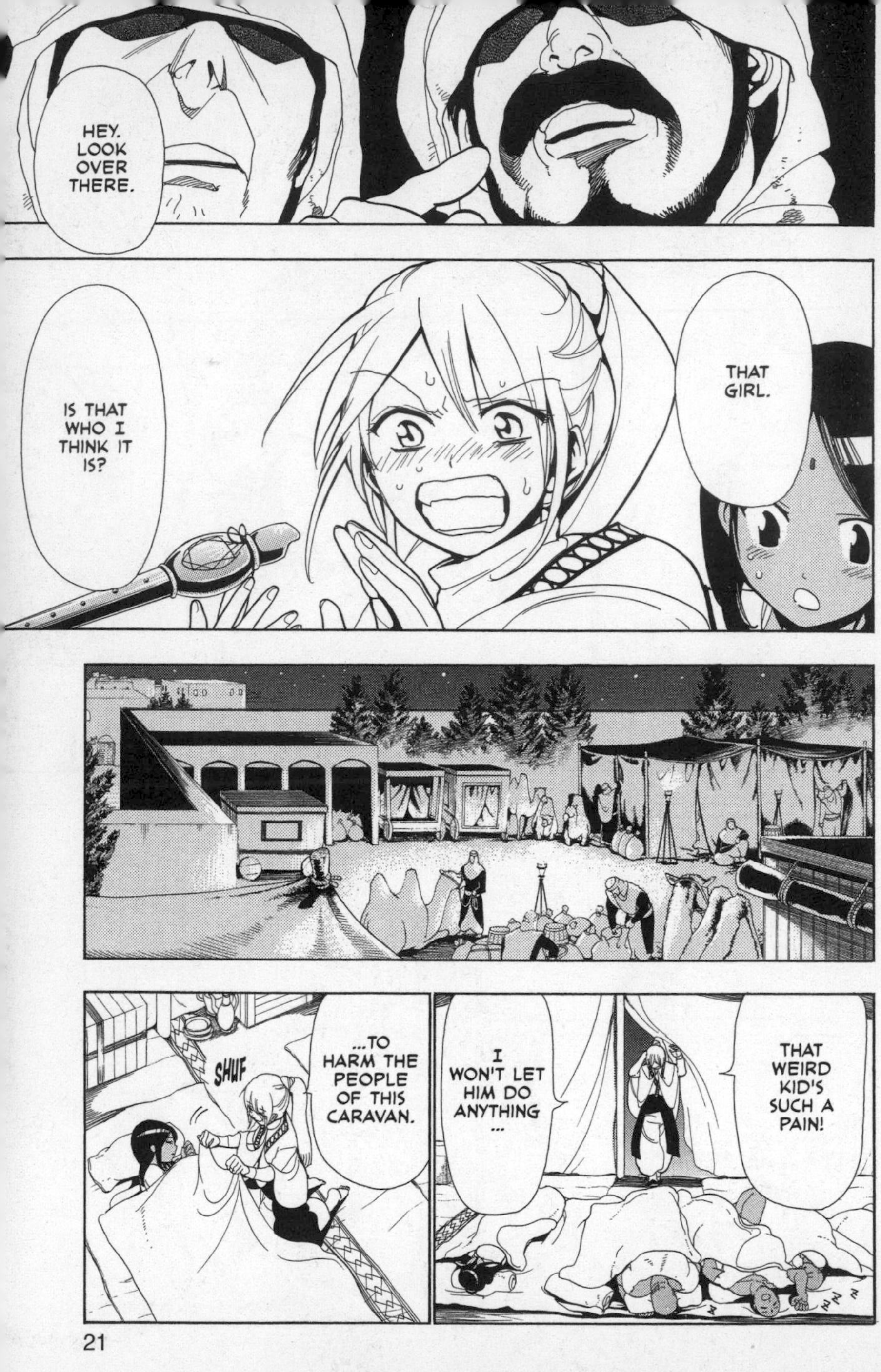
HEY. LOOK OVER THERE.
THAT GIRL.
IS THAT WHO I THINK IT IS?
THAT WEIRD KID'S SUCH A PAIN!
I WON'T LET HIM DO ANYTHING ...
...TO HARM THE PEOPLE OF THIS CARAVAN.
SHUF

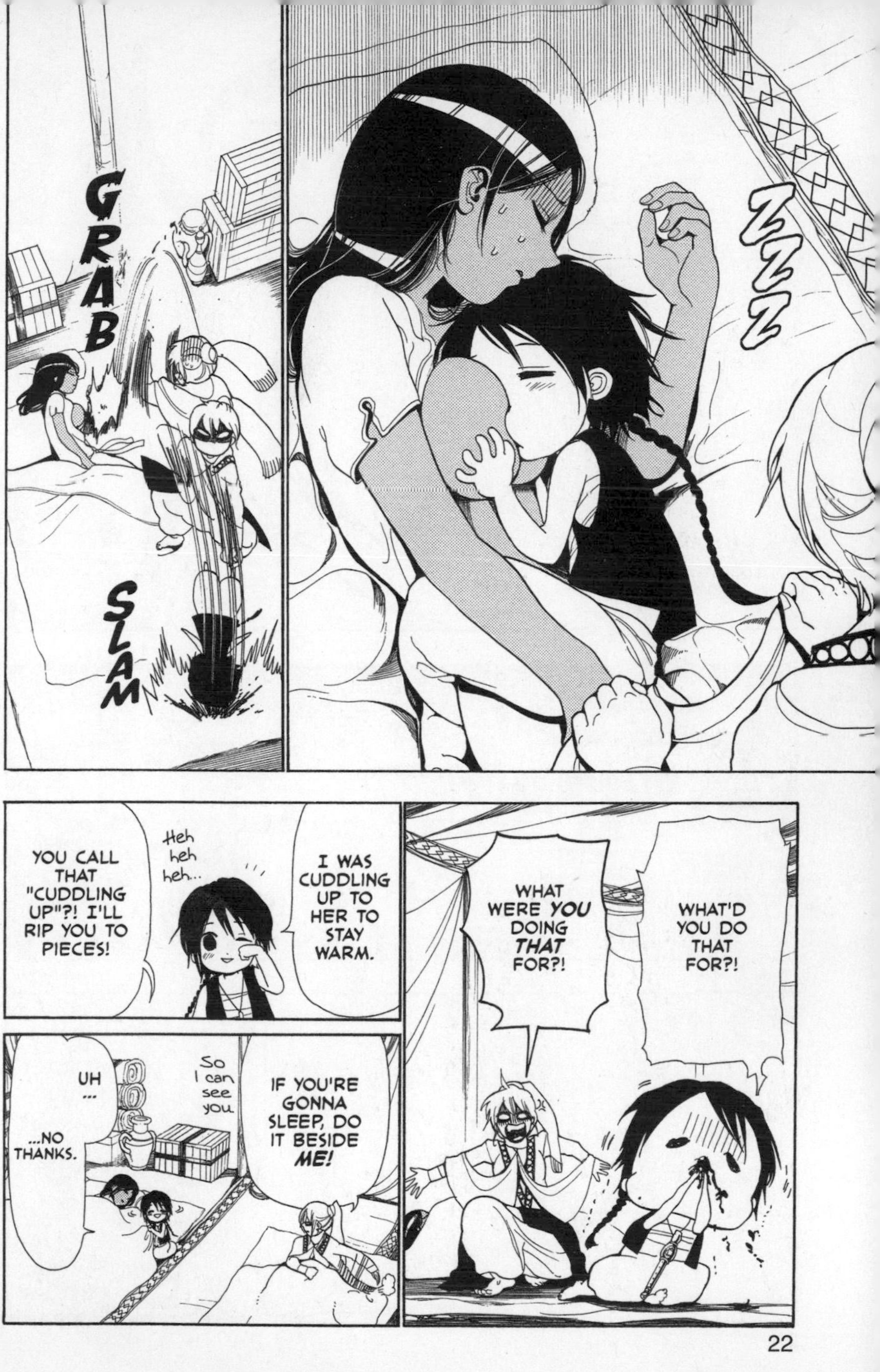
ZZZ
GRAB
SLAM
WHAT'D YOU DO THAT FOR?!
WHAT WERE *YOU* DOING *THAT* FOR?!
I WAS CUDDLING UP TO HER TO STAY WARM.
Heh heh heh...
YOU CALL THAT "CUDDLING UP"?! I'LL RIP YOU TO PIECES!
IF YOU'RE GONNA SLEEP, DO IT BESIDE *ME!*
So I can see you.
UH ...
...NO THANKS.

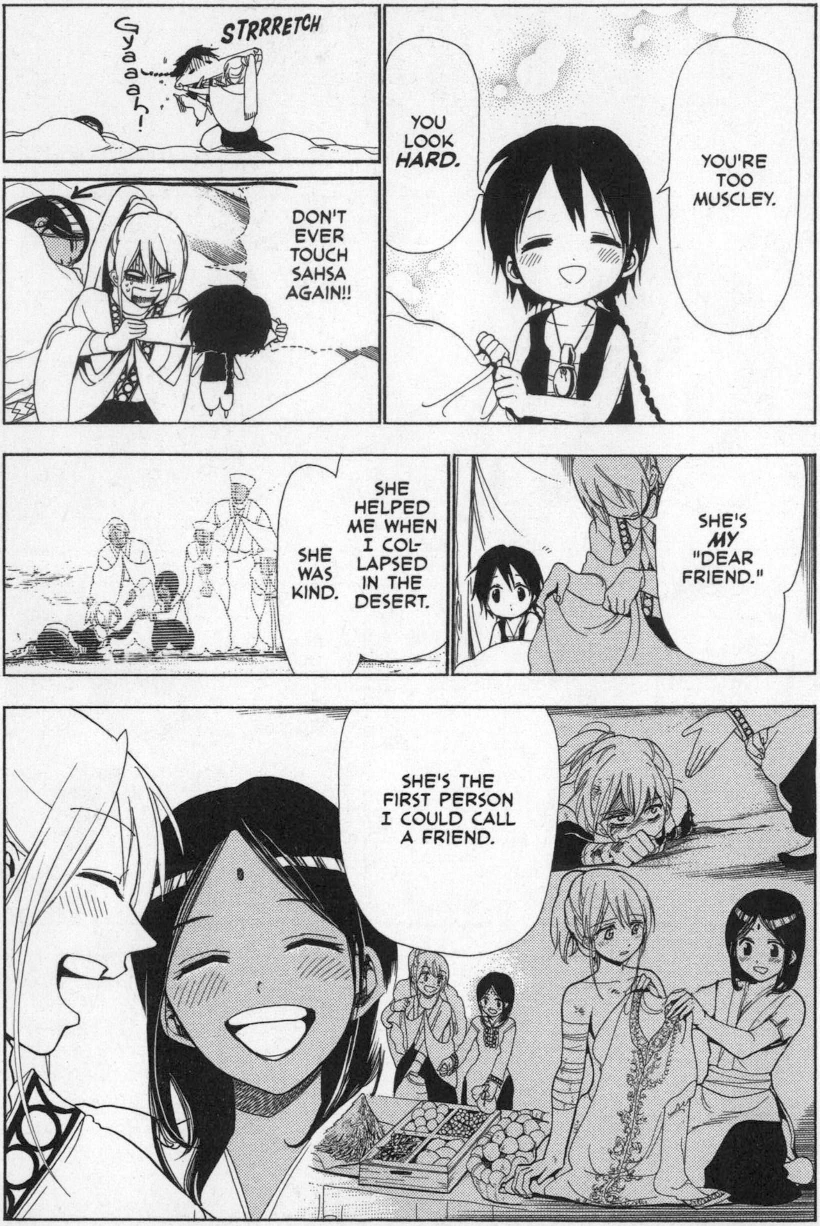
YOU'RE TOO MUSCLEY.
YOU LOOK HARD.
STRRRETCH
Gyaaah!
DON'T EVER TOUCH SAHSA AGAIN!!
SHE'S MY "DEAR FRIEND."
SHE HELPED ME WHEN I COL-LAPSED IN THE DESERT.
SHE WAS KIND.
SHE'S THE FIRST PERSON I COULD CALL A FRIEND.

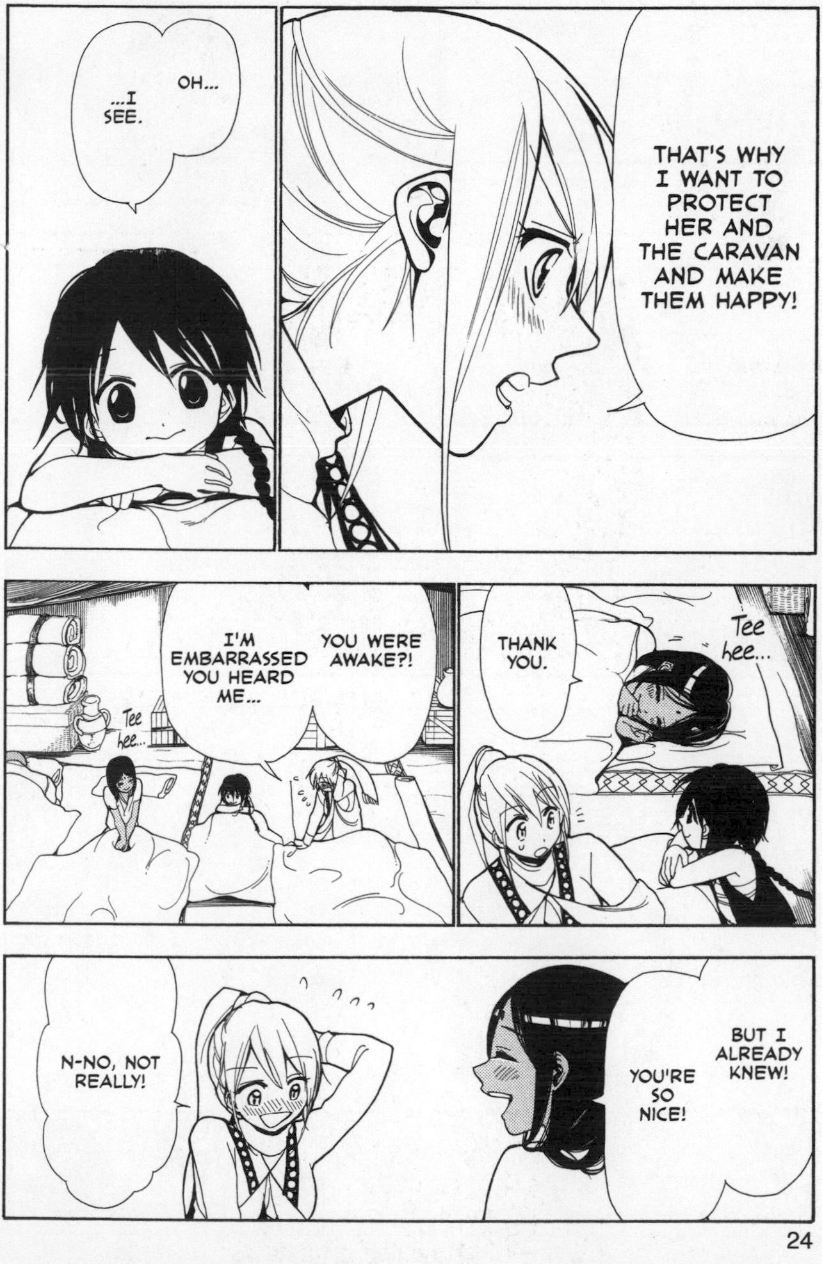
THAT'S WHY I WANT TO PROTECT HER AND THE CARAVAN AND MAKE THEM HAPPY!
OH...
...I SEE.
Tee hee...
THANK YOU.
YOU WERE AWAKE?!
I'M EMBARRASSED YOU HEARD ME...
Tee hee...
BUT I ALREADY KNEW!
YOU'RE SO NICE!
N-NO, NOT REALLY!

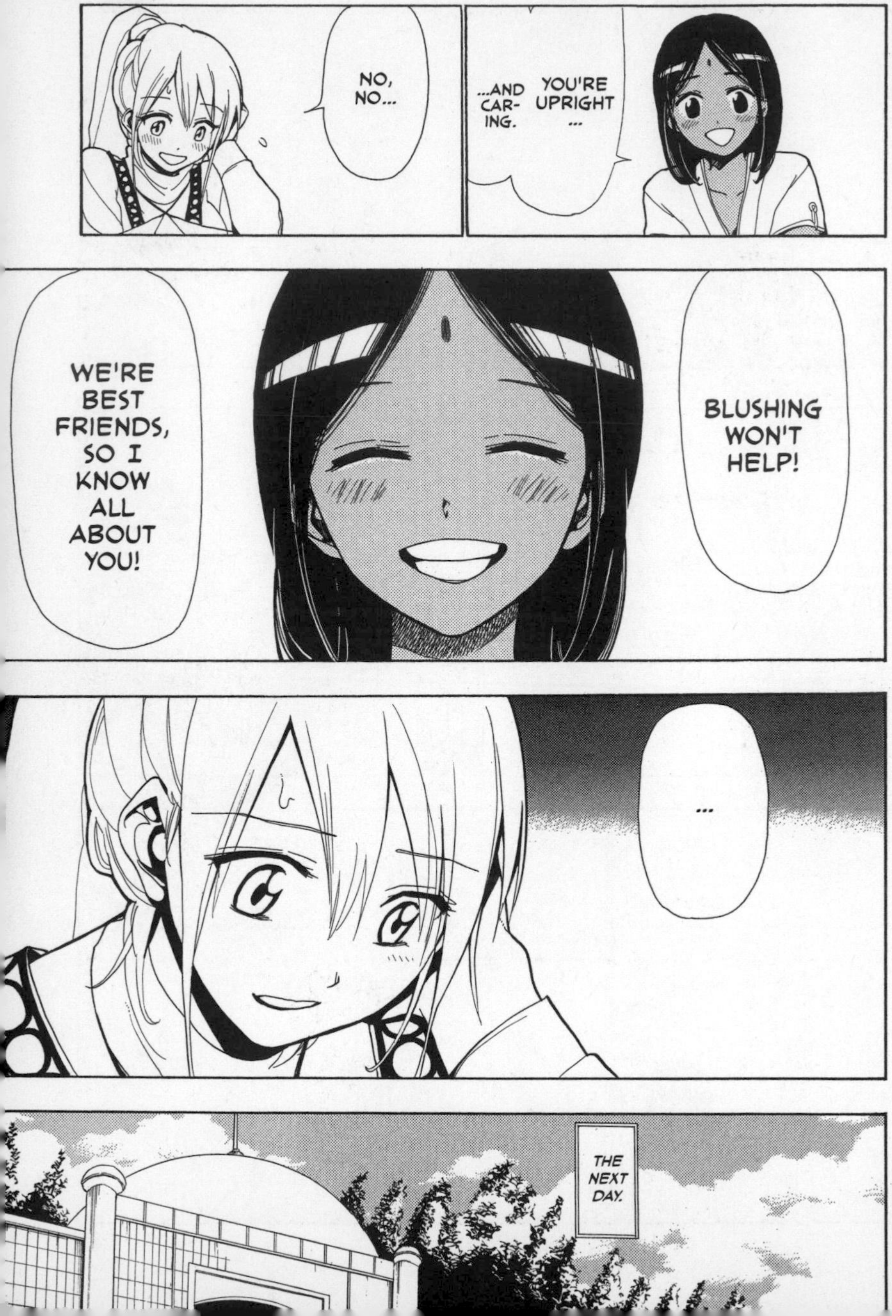
YOU'RE UPRIGHT ...
...AND CARING.
NO, NO...
BLUSHING WON'T HELP!
WE'RE BEST FRIENDS, SO I KNOW ALL ABOUT YOU!
...
THE NEXT DAY.

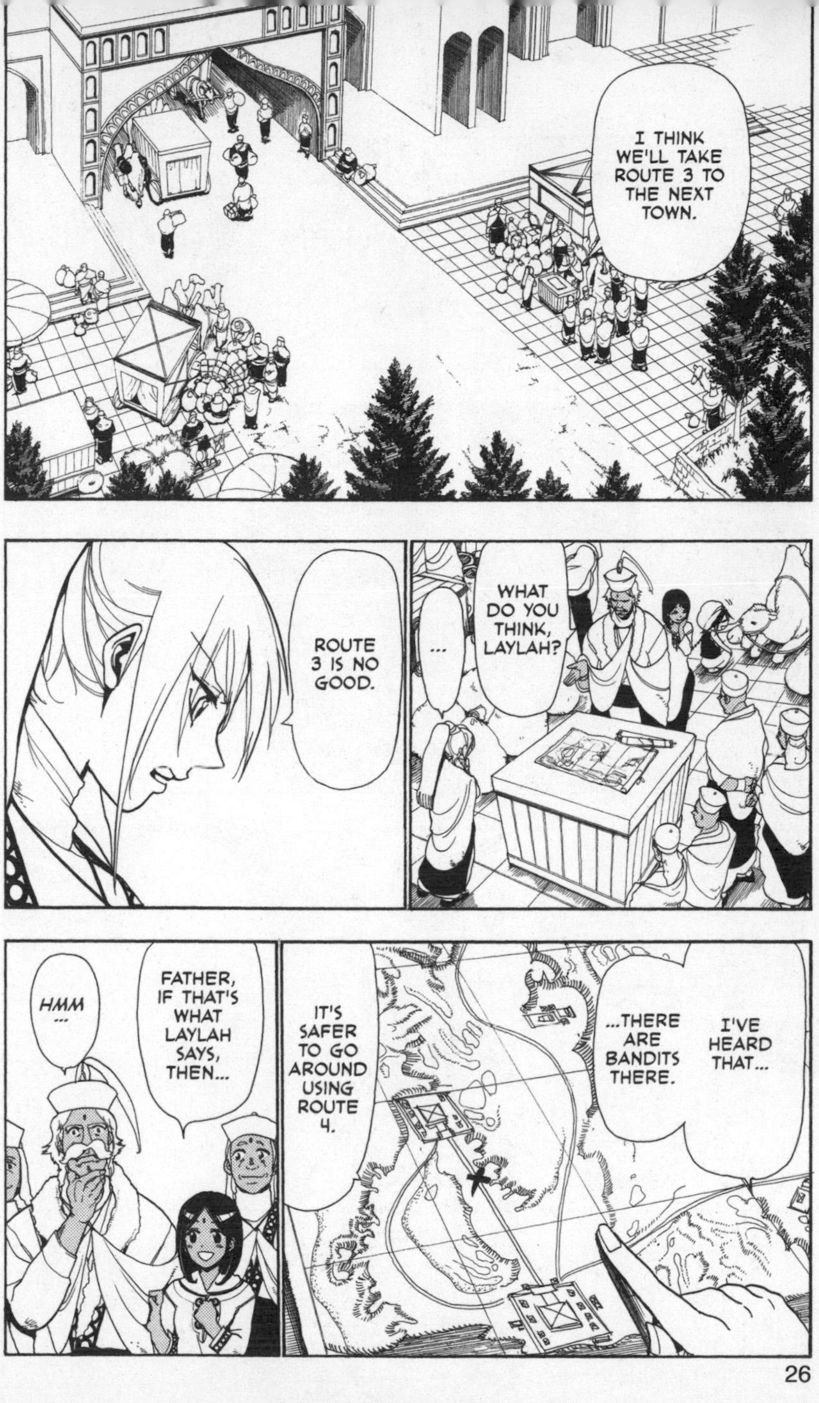
I THINK WE'LL TAKE ROUTE 3 TO THE NEXT TOWN.
WHAT DO YOU THINK, LAYLAH?
...
ROUTE 3 IS NO GOOD.
I'VE HEARD THAT...
...THERE ARE BANDITS THERE.
IT'S SAFER TO GO AROUND USING ROUTE 4.
FATHER, IF THAT'S WHAT LAYLAH SAYS, THEN...
HMM...

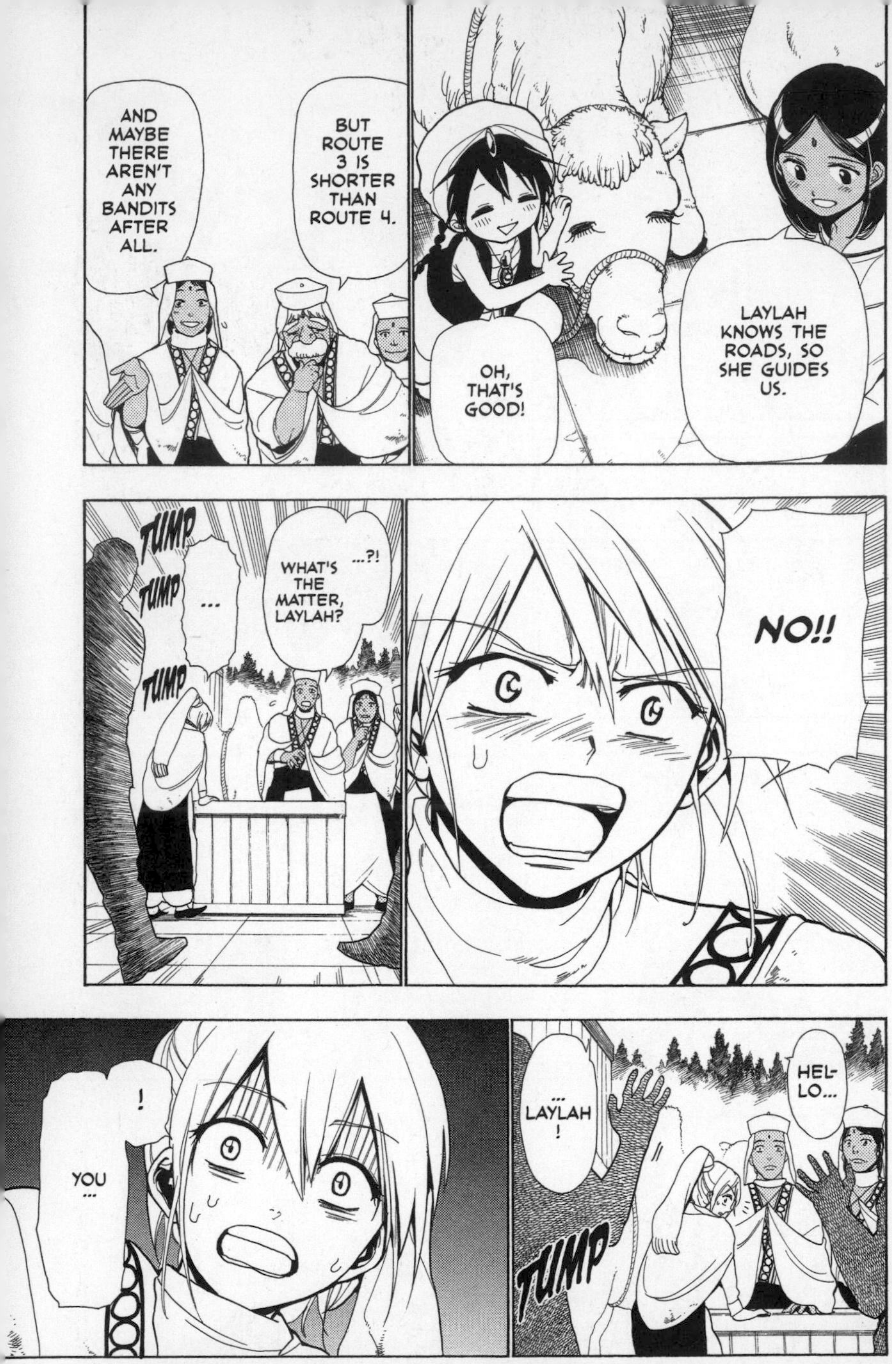
LAYLAH KNOWS THE ROADS, SO SHE GUIDES US.
OH, THAT'S GOOD!
BUT ROUTE 3 IS SHORTER THAN ROUTE 4.
AND MAYBE THERE AREN'T ANY BANDITS AFTER ALL.
NO!!
...?!
WHAT'S THE MATTER, LAYLAH?
TUMP
TUMP
...
TUMP
HEL-LO...
... LAYLAH!
TUMP
!
YOU ...

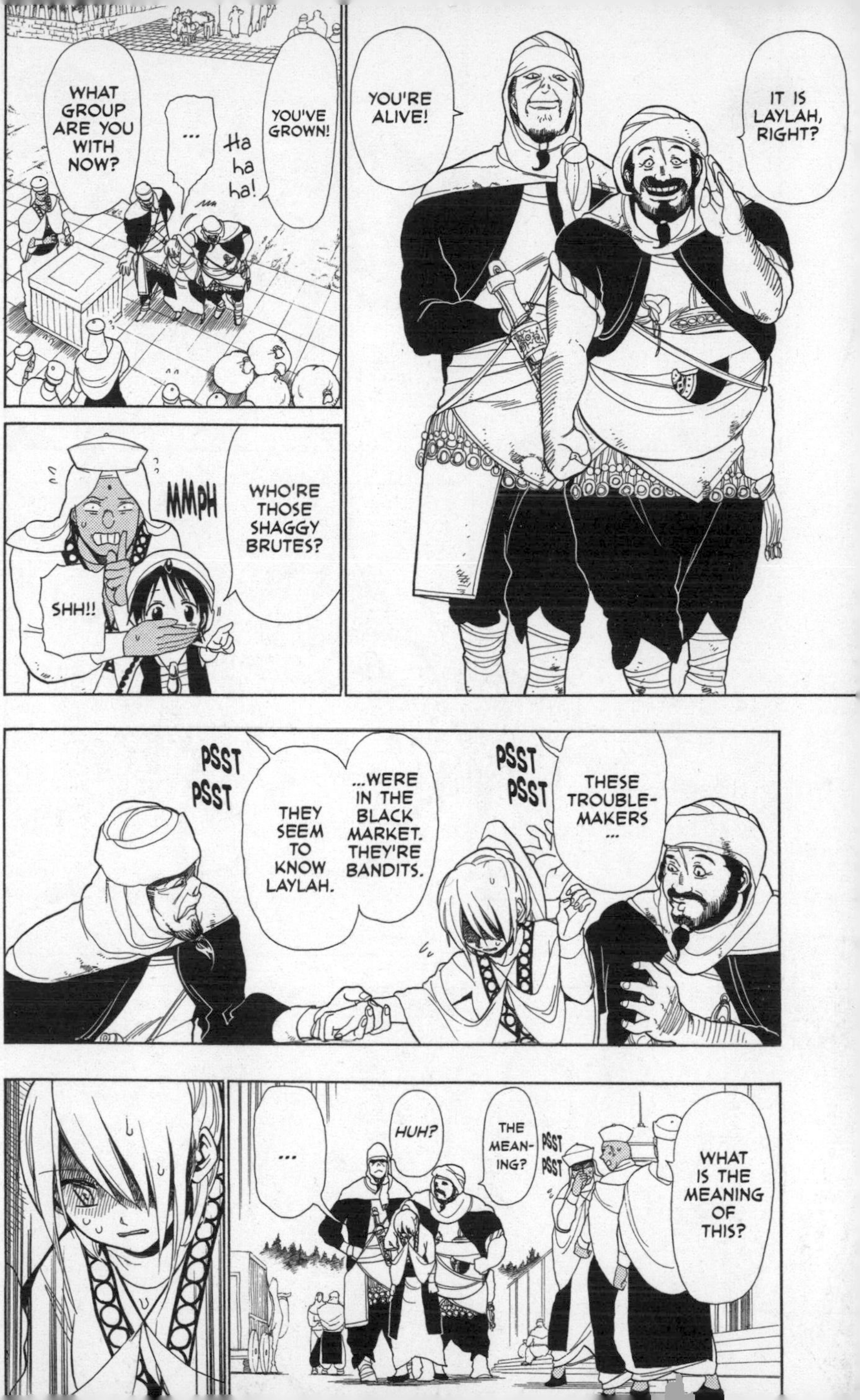
IT IS LAYLAH, RIGHT?
YOU'RE ALIVE!
YOU'VE GROWN!
Ha ha ha!
...
WHAT GROUP ARE YOU WITH NOW?
WHO'RE THOSE SHAGGY BRUTES?
MMPH
SHH!!
PSST PSST
THESE TROUBLE-MAKERS...
...WERE IN THE BLACK MARKET. THEY'RE BANDITS.
PSST PSST
THEY SEEM TO KNOW LAYLAH.
WHAT IS THE MEANING OF THIS?
PSST PSST
THE MEANING?
HUH?
...

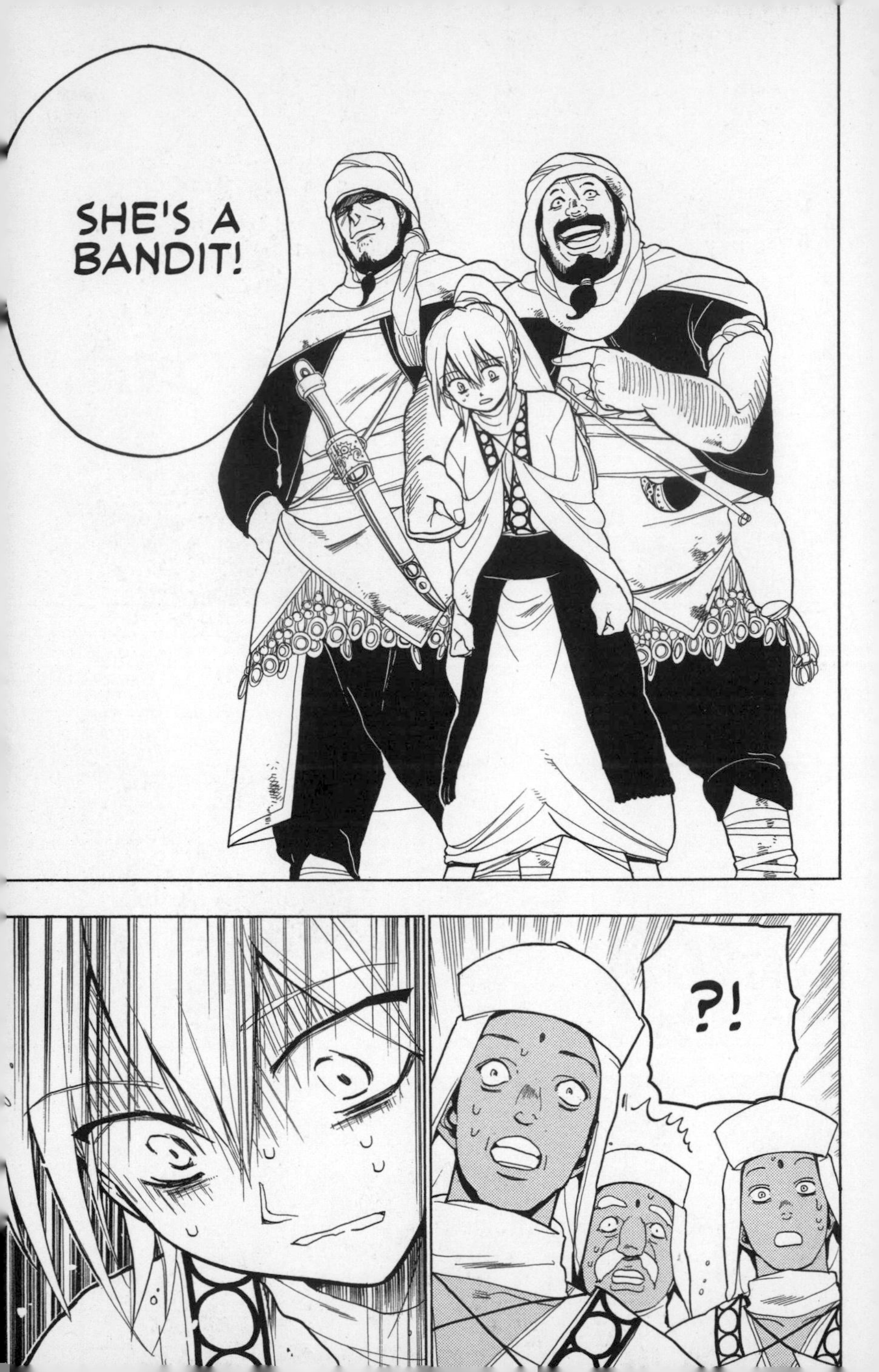
SHE'S A BANDIT!
?!

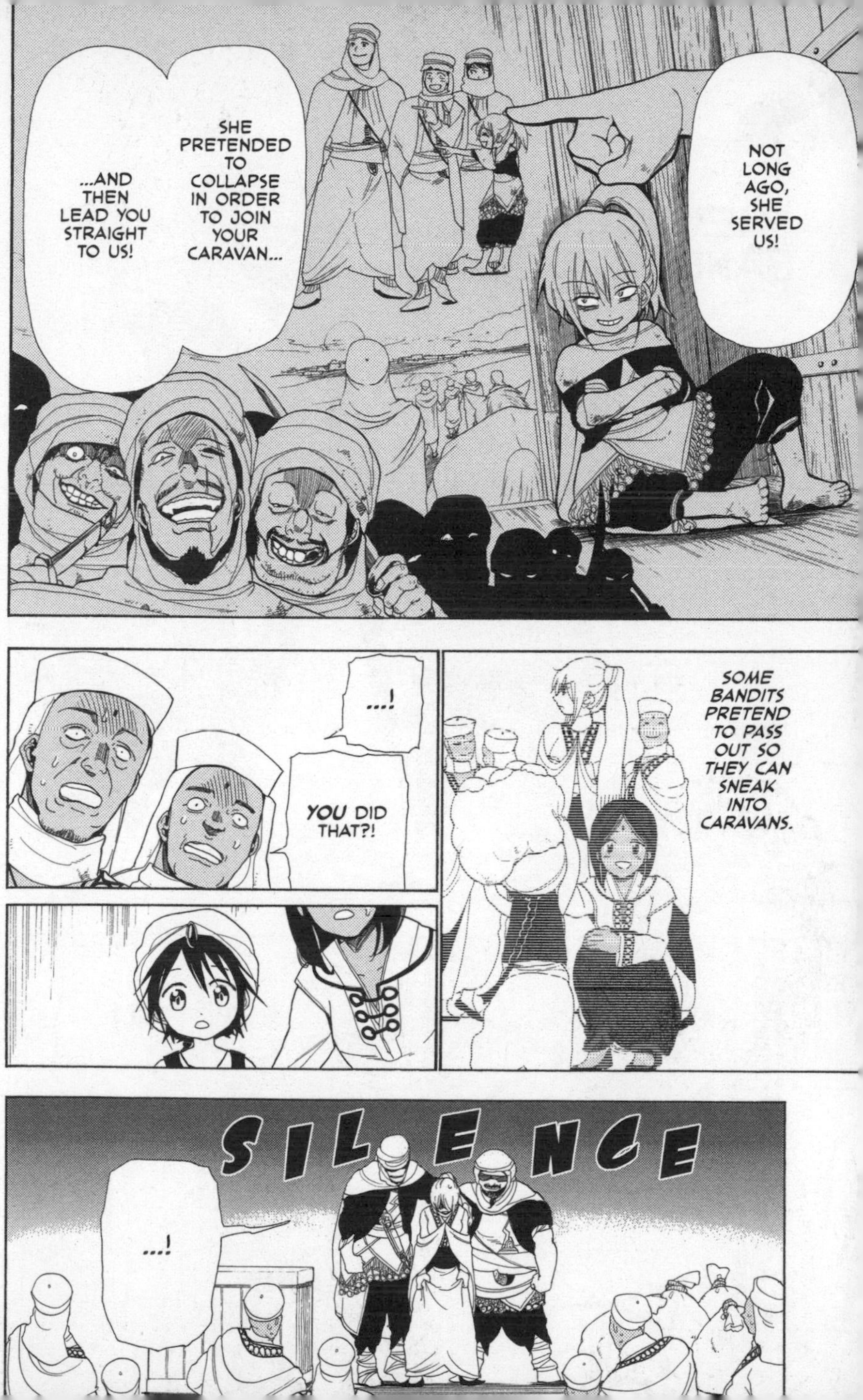
NOT LONG AGO, SHE SERVED US!
SHE PRETENDED TO COLLAPSE IN ORDER TO JOIN YOUR CARAVAN...
...AND THEN LEAD YOU STRAIGHT TO US!
SOME BANDITS PRETEND TO PASS OUT SO THEY CAN SNEAK INTO CARAVANS.
...!
YOU DID THAT?!
SILENCE
...!

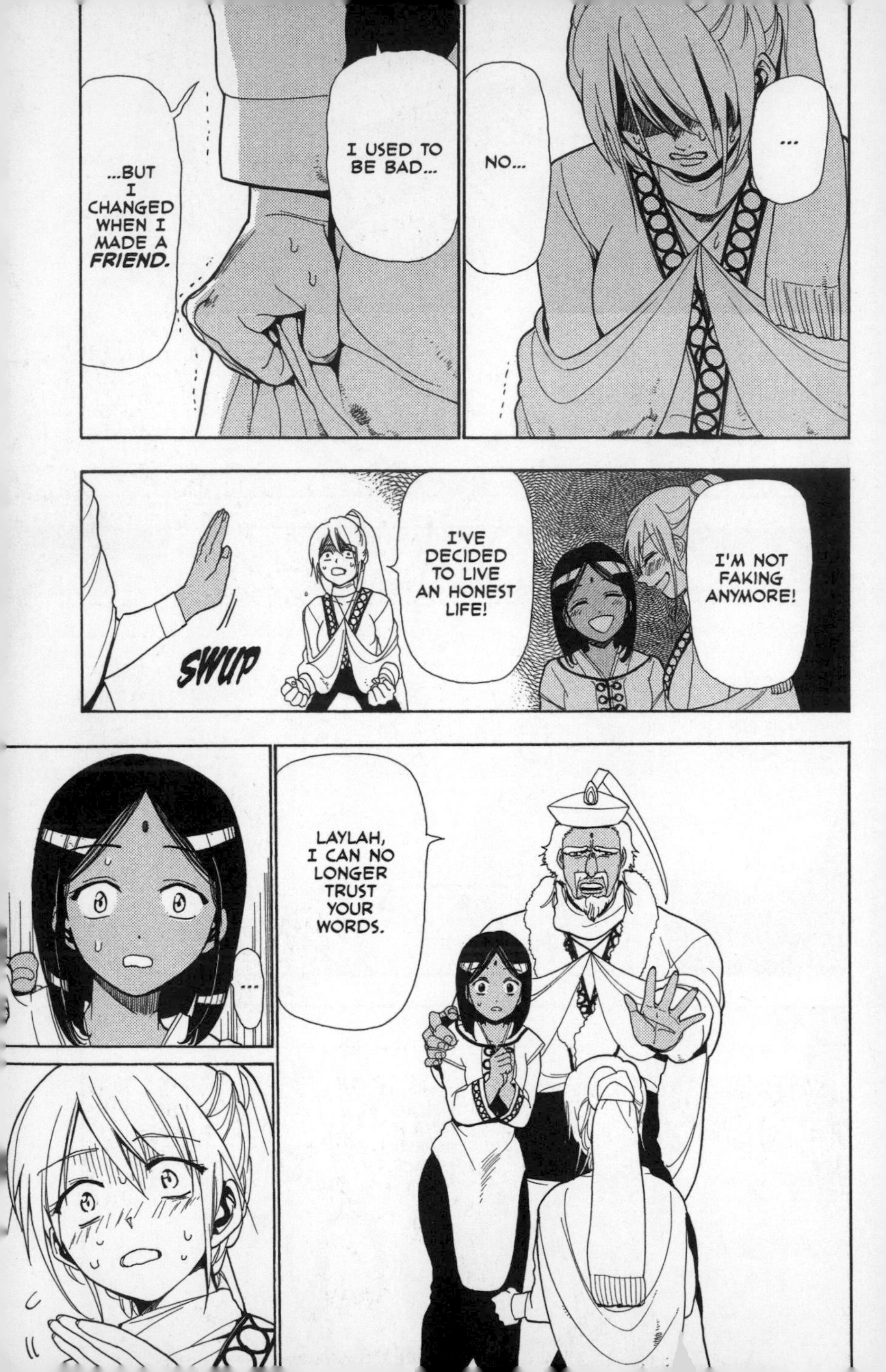
...
NO...
I USED TO BE BAD...
...BUT I CHANGED WHEN I MADE A FRIEND.
I'M NOT FAKING ANYMORE!
I'VE DECIDED TO LIVE AN HONEST LIFE!
SWUP
LAYLAH, I CAN NO LONGER TRUST YOUR WORDS.
...

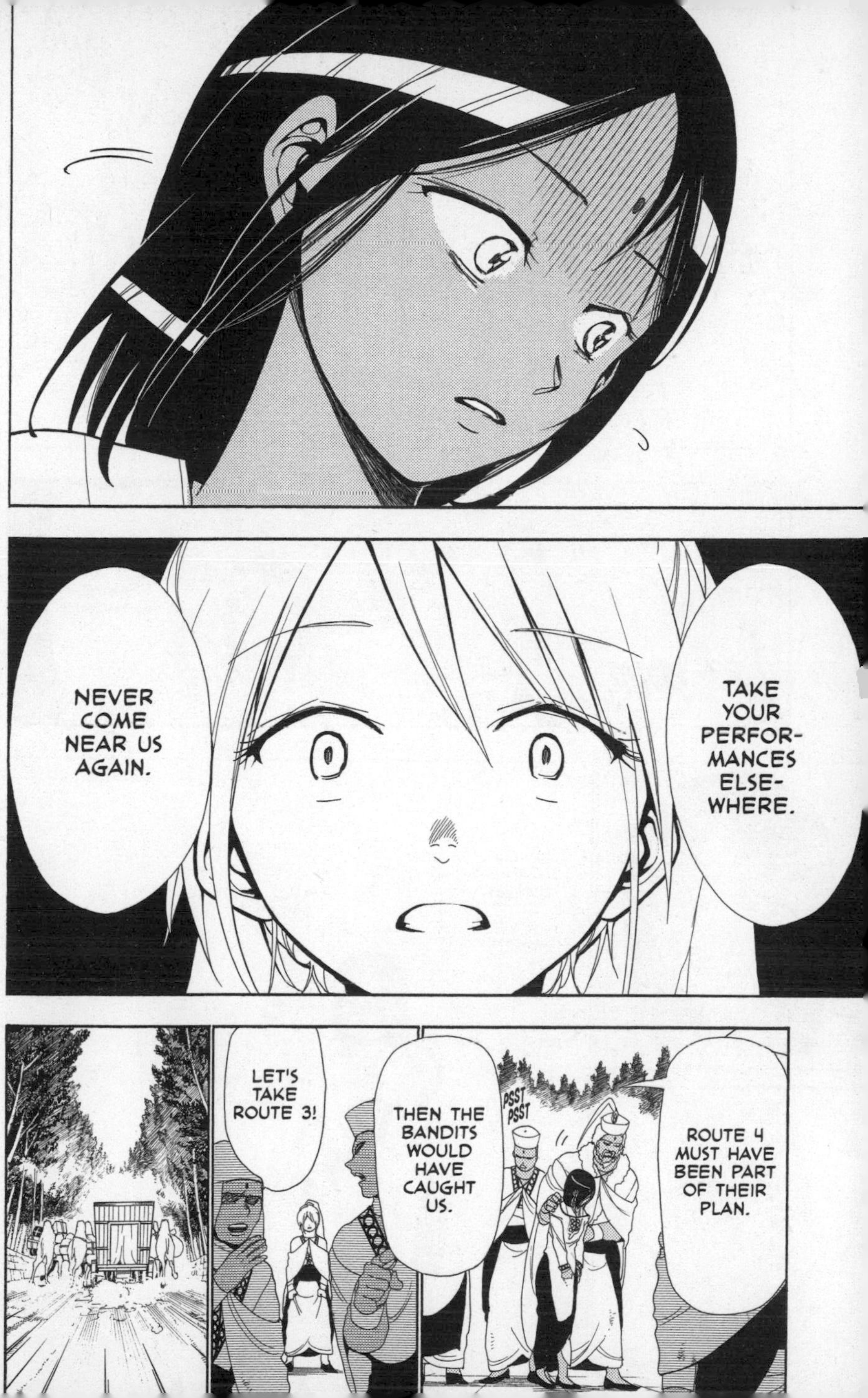
TAKE YOUR PERFOR-MANCES ELSE-WHERE.
NEVER COME NEAR US AGAIN.
ROUTE 4 MUST HAVE BEEN PART OF THEIR PLAN.
PSST PSST
THEN THE BANDITS WOULD HAVE CAUGHT US.
LET'S TAKE ROUTE 3!

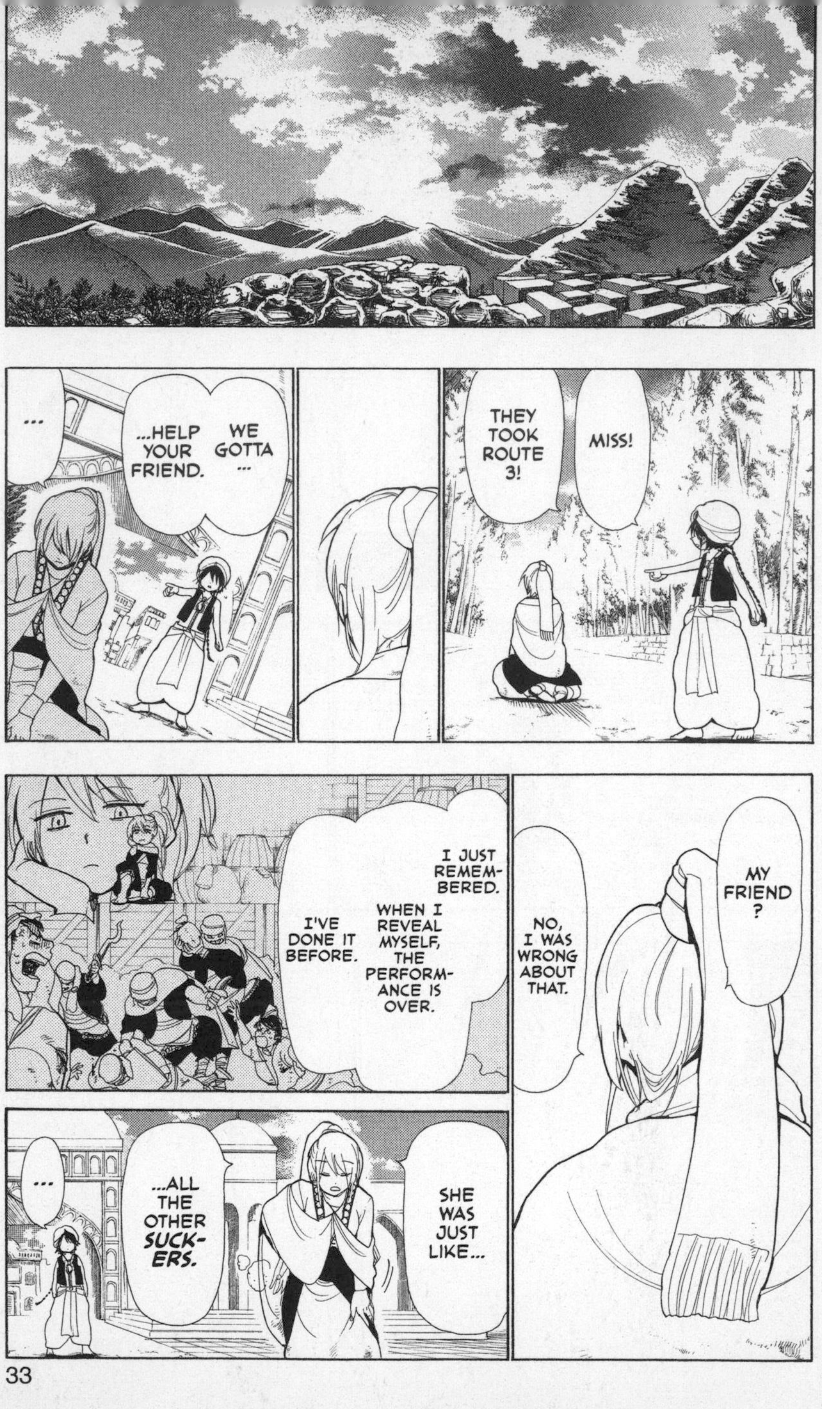
MISS!
THEY TOOK ROUTE 3!
WE GOTTA ...
...HELP YOUR FRIEND.
...
MY FRIEND?
NO, I WAS WRONG ABOUT THAT.
I JUST REMEMBERED.
WHEN I REVEAL MYSELF, THE PERFORMANCE IS OVER.
I'VE DONE IT BEFORE.
SHE WAS JUST LIKE...
...ALL THE OTHER *SUCKERS.*
...

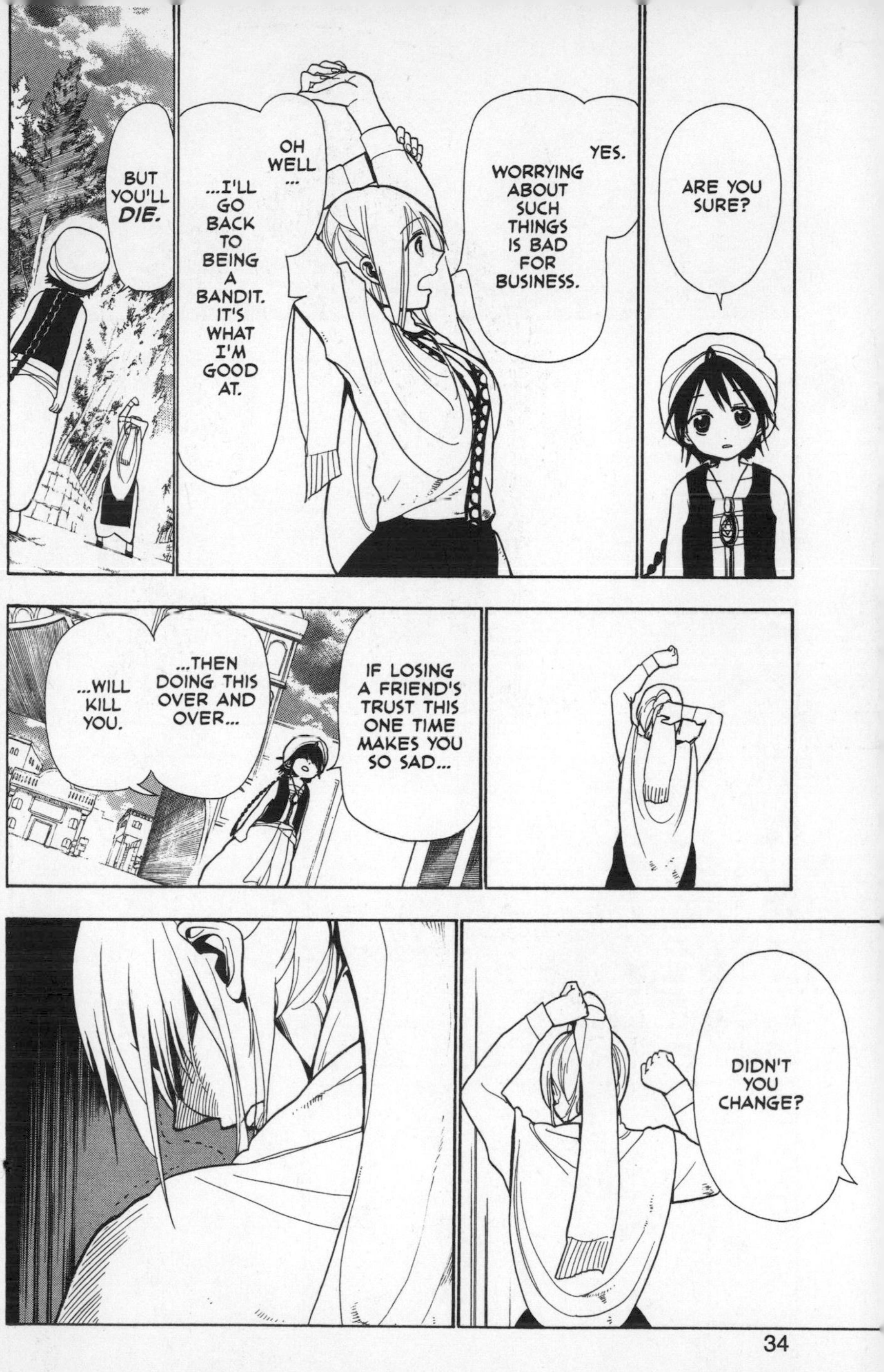
ARE YOU SURE?
YES.
WORRYING ABOUT SUCH THINGS IS BAD FOR BUSINESS.
OH WELL ...
...I'LL GO BACK TO BEING A BANDIT. IT'S WHAT I'M GOOD AT.
BUT YOU'LL *DIE.*
IF LOSING A FRIEND'S TRUST THIS ONE TIME MAKES YOU SO SAD...
...THEN DOING THIS OVER AND OVER...
...WILL KILL YOU.
DIDN'T YOU CHANGE?

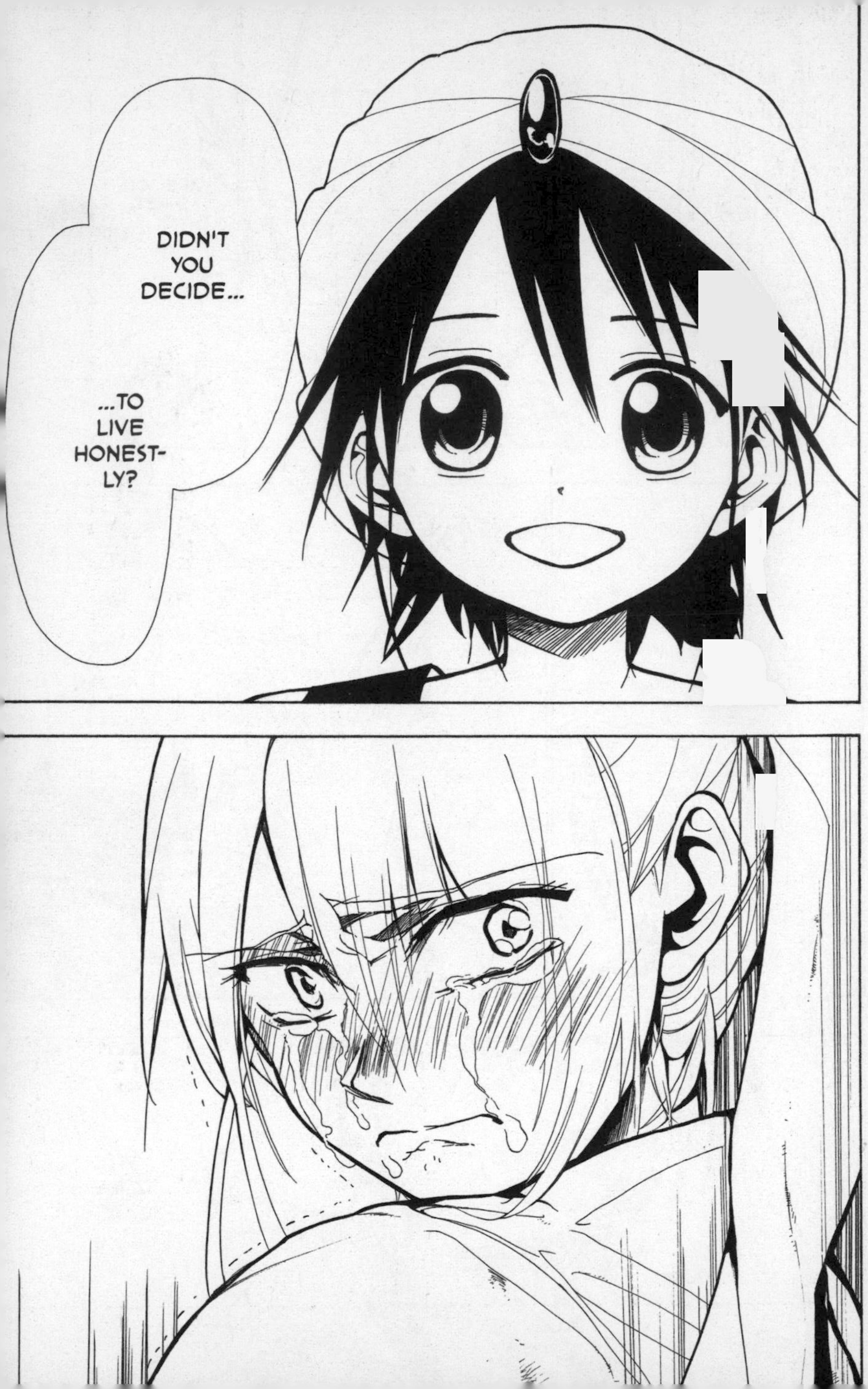
DIDN'T YOU DECIDE...
...TO LIVE HONEST-LY?

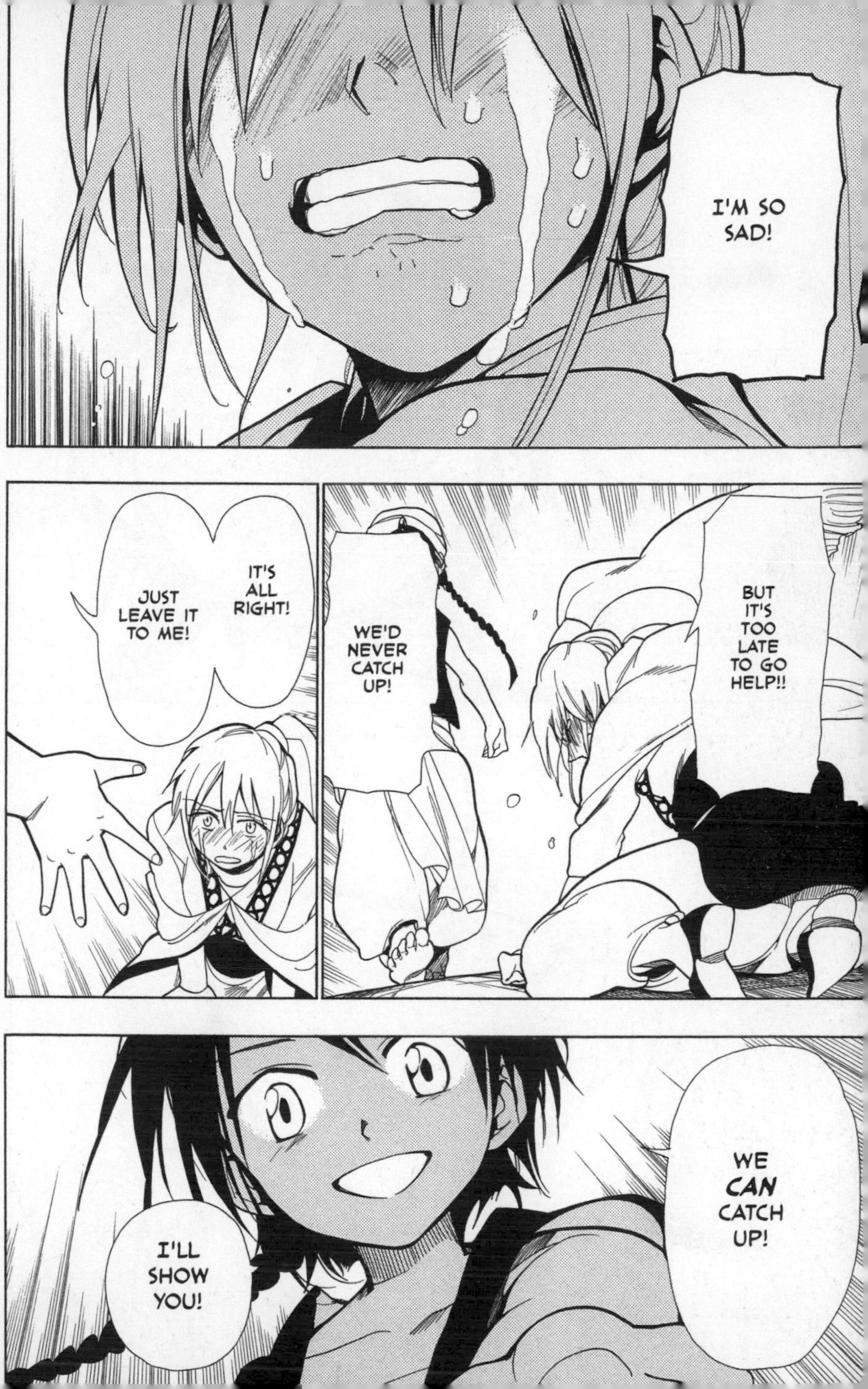
I'M SO SAD!
BUT IT'S TOO LATE TO GO HELP!!
WE'D NEVER CATCH UP!
IT'S ALL RIGHT!
JUST LEAVE IT TO ME!
WE *CAN* CATCH UP!
I'LL SHOW YOU!

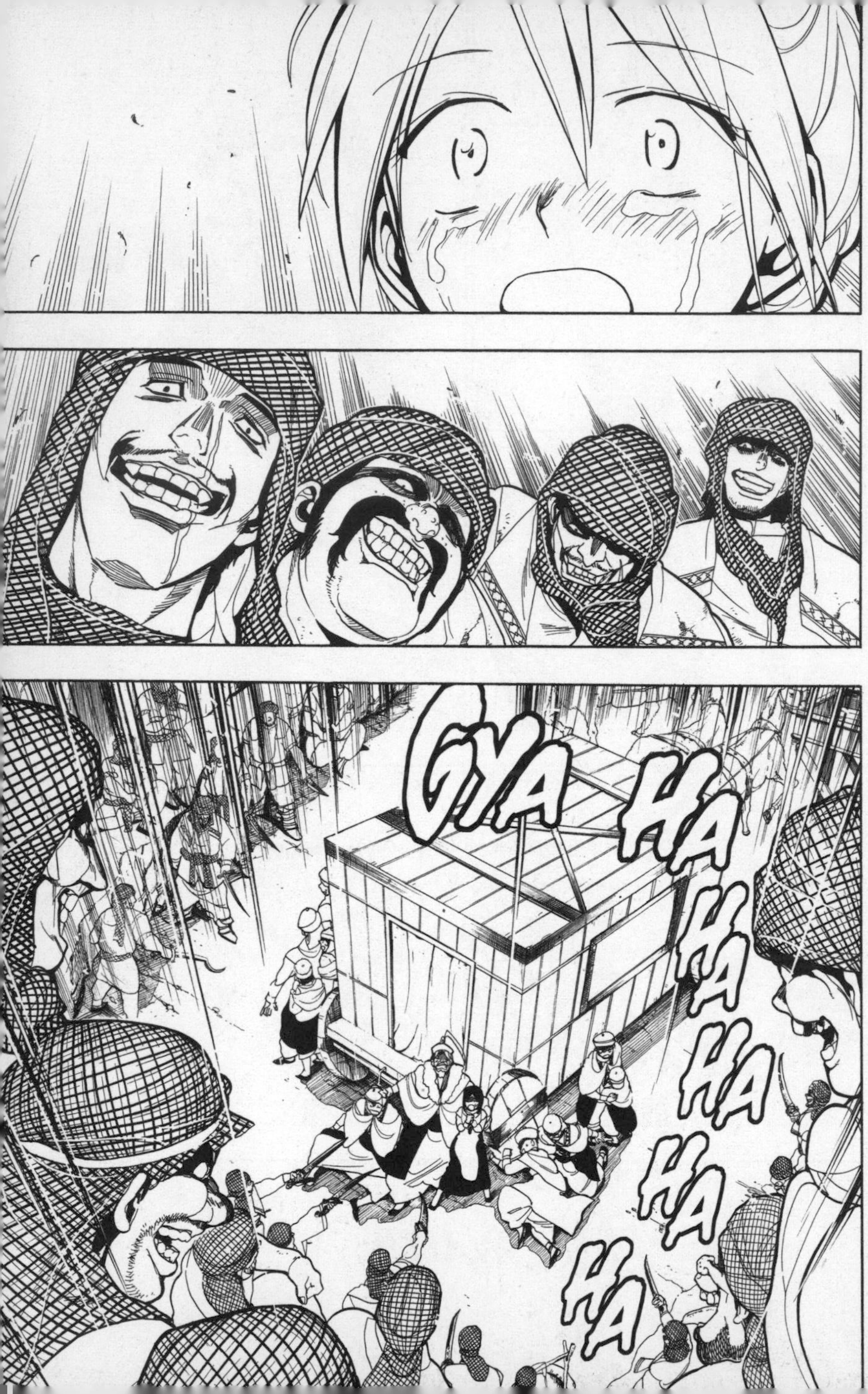
GYA HA HA HA HA HA HA HA

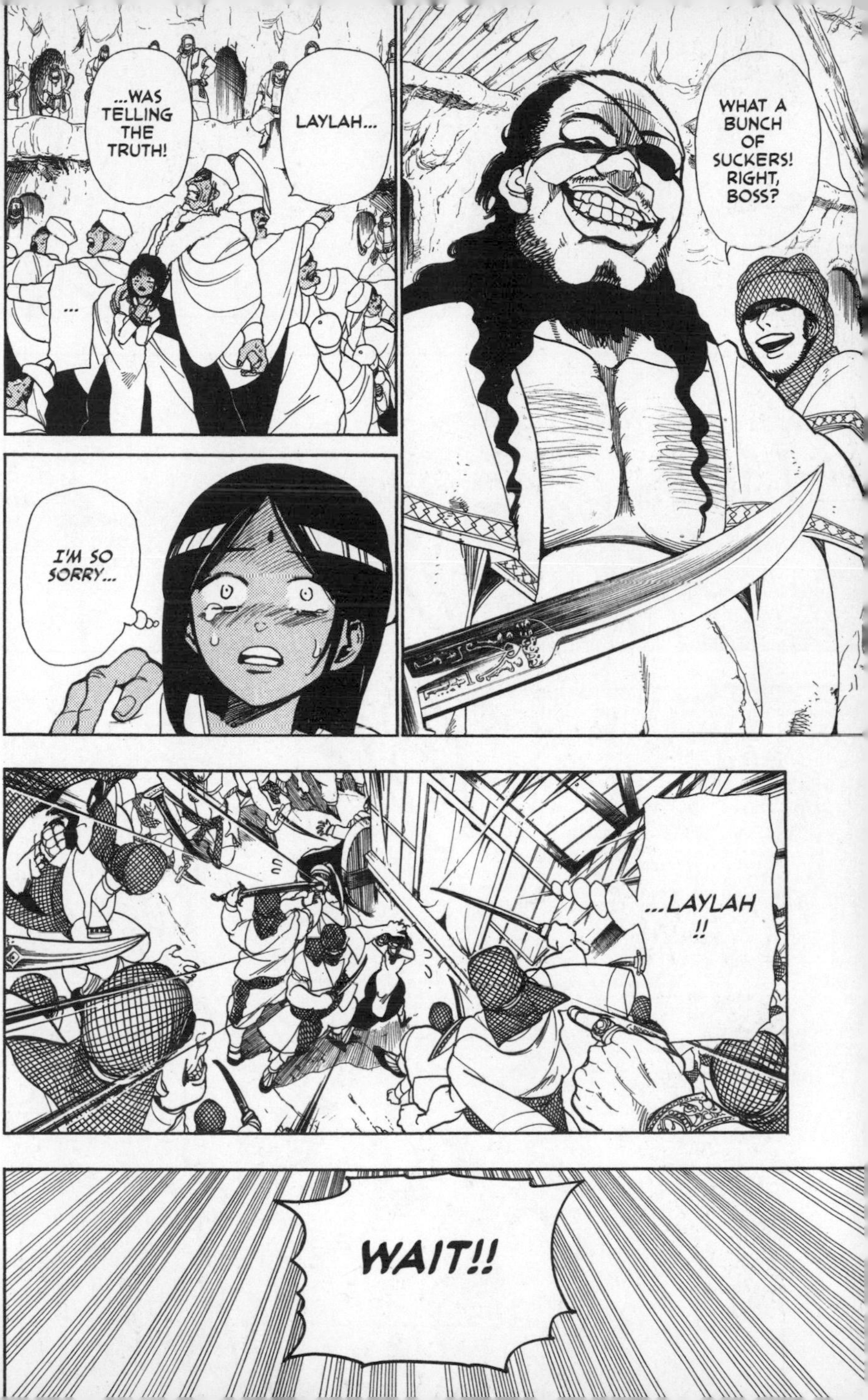
WHAT A BUNCH OF SUCKERS! RIGHT, BOSS?
LAYLAH...
...WAS TELLING THE TRUTH!
...
I'M SO SORRY...
...LAYLAH !!
WAIT!!

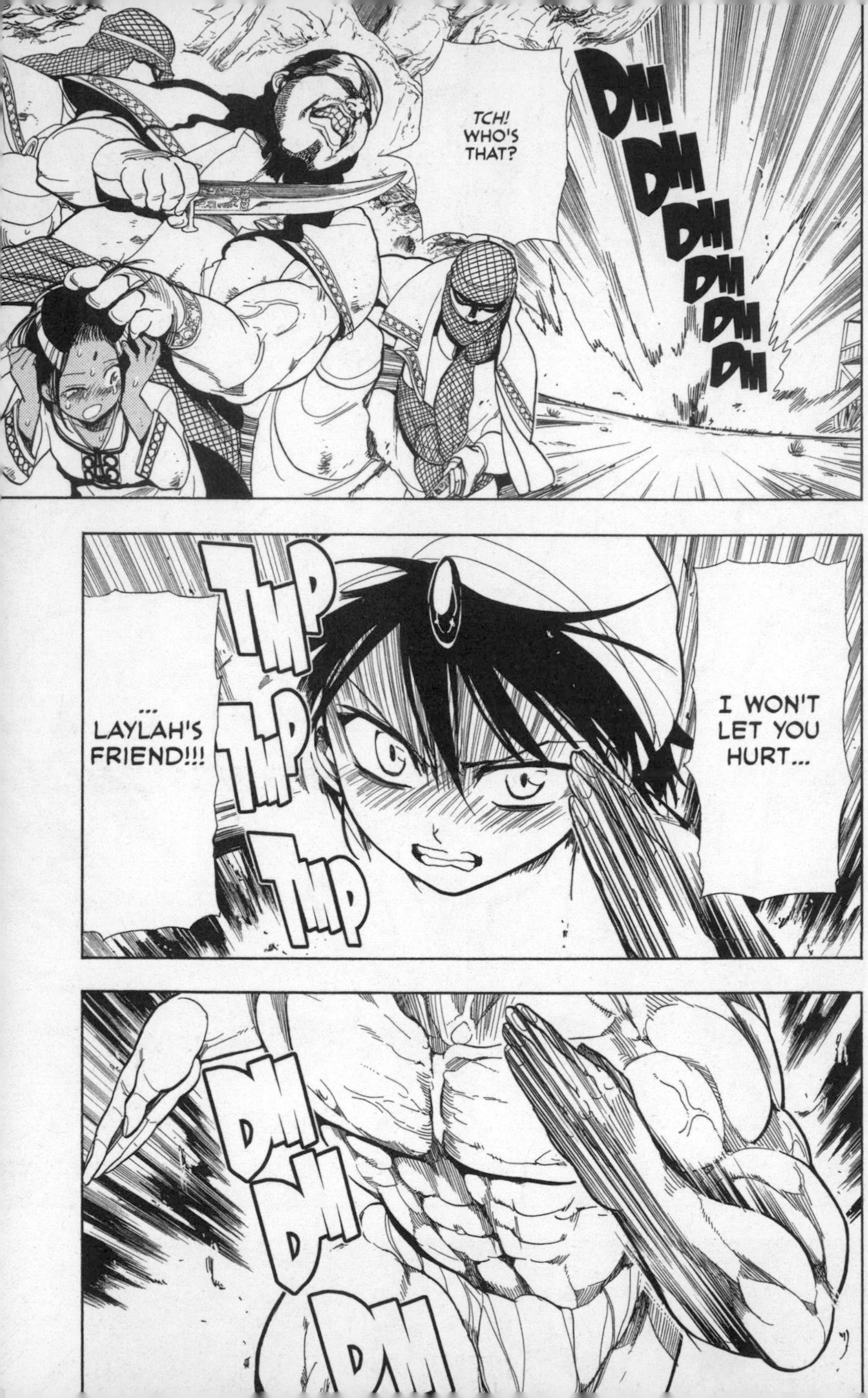
TCH! WHO'S THAT?
DM DM DM DM DM DM DM
I WON'T LET YOU HURT...
... LAYLAH'S FRIEND!!!
TMP TMP TMP
DM DM DM

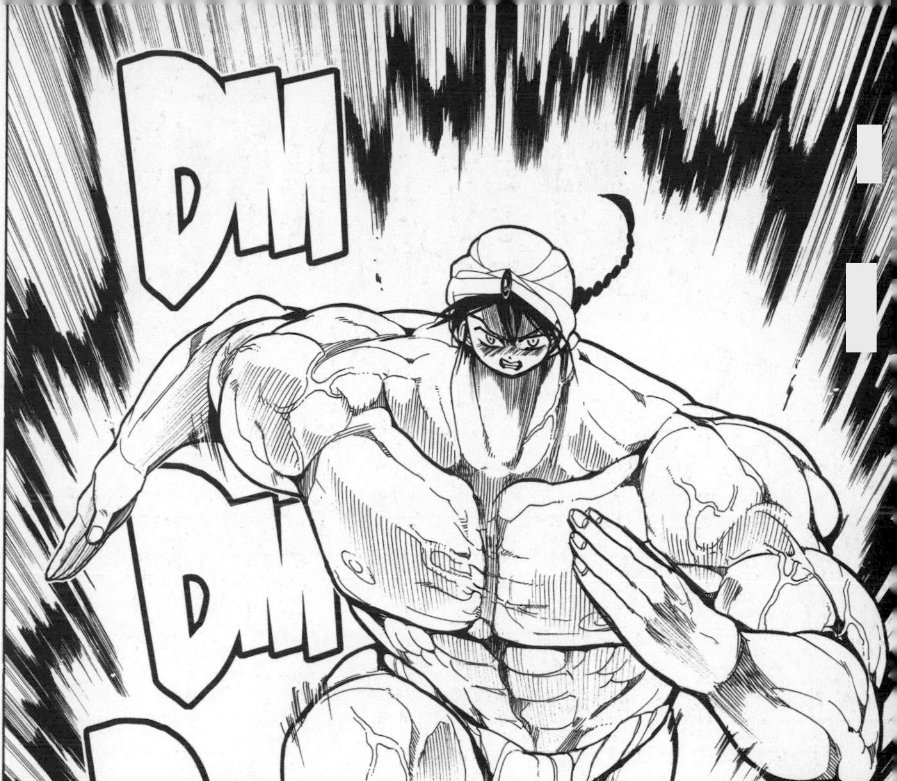
DM
DM
DM
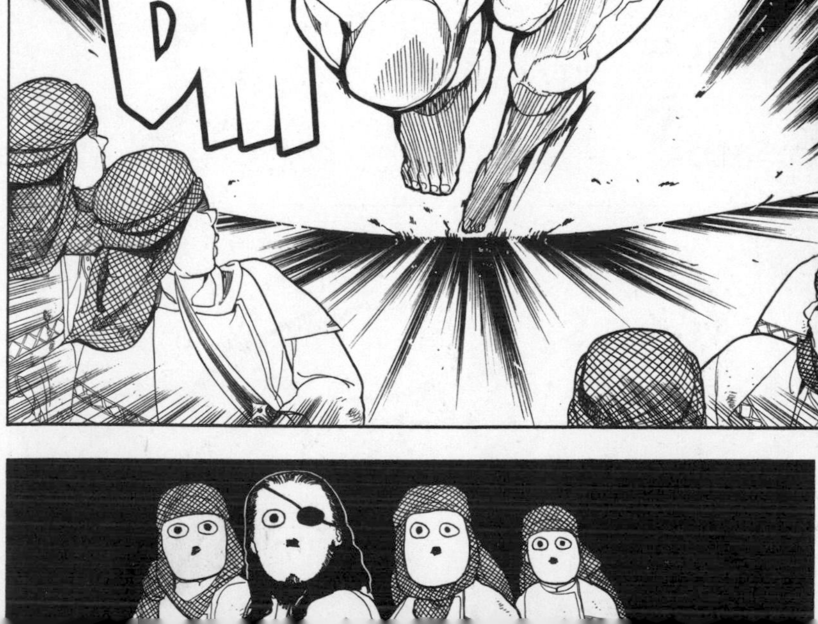

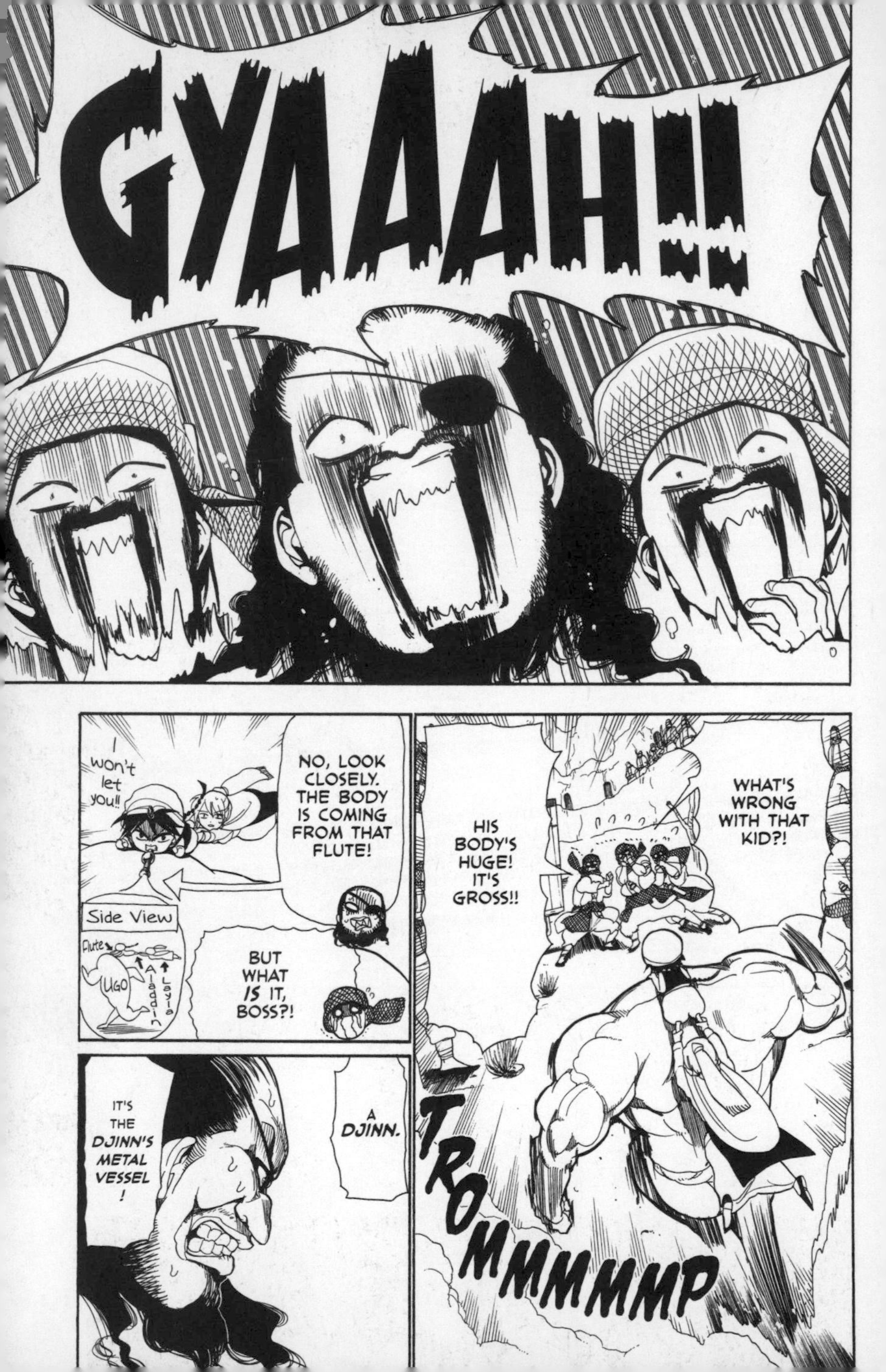
GYAAAH!!
WHAT'S WRONG WITH THAT KID?!
HIS BODY'S HUGE! IT'S GROSS!!
TROMMMMMMP
NO, LOOK CLOSELY. THE BODY IS COMING FROM THAT FLUTE!
I won't let you!!
Side View
Flute
UGO
Aladdin
Layla
BUT WHAT *IS* IT, BOSS?!
A *DJINN.*
IT'S THE *DJINN'S METAL VESSEL*!

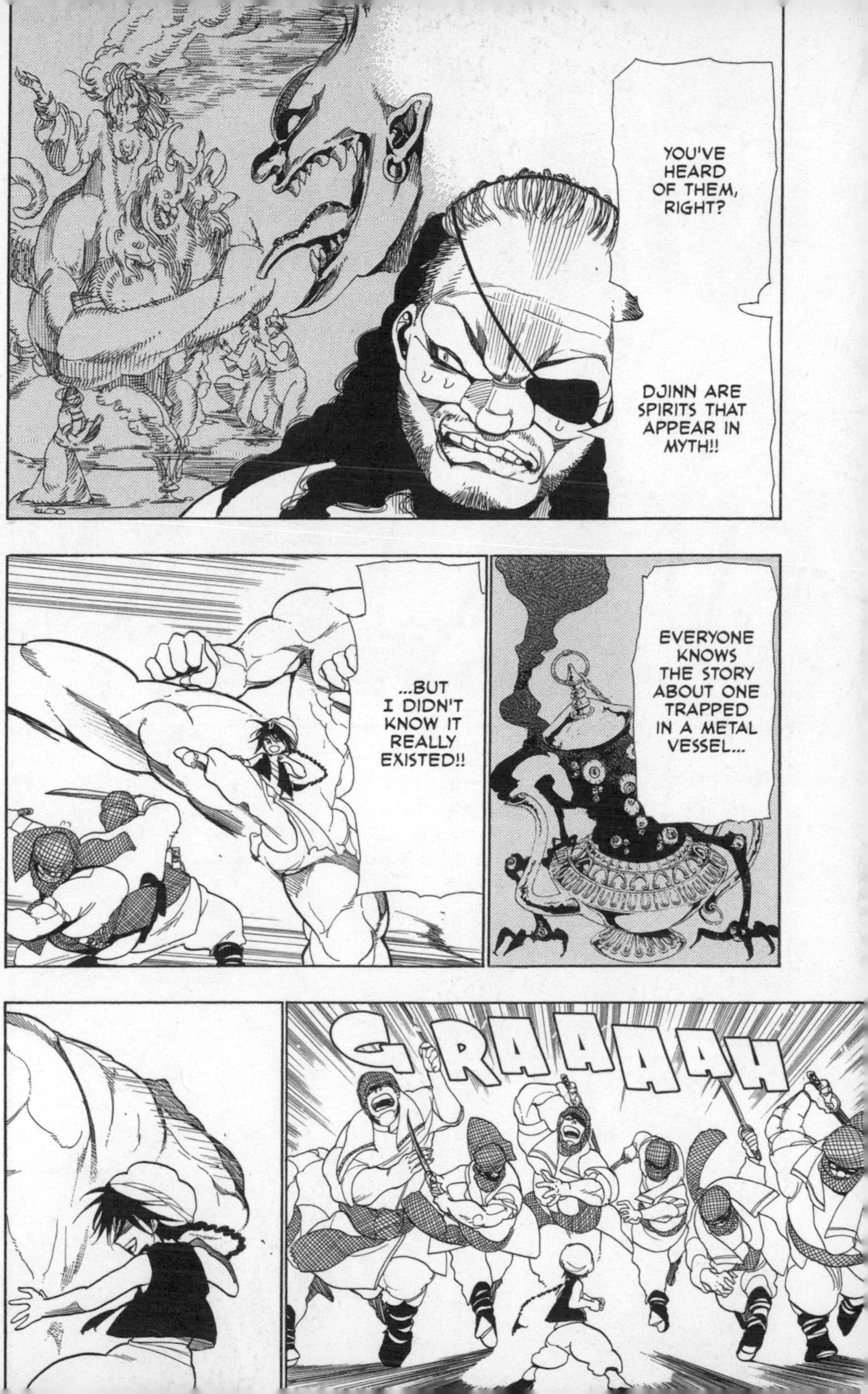
YOU'VE HEARD OF THEM, RIGHT?
DJINN ARE SPIRITS THAT APPEAR IN MYTH!!
EVERYONE KNOWS THE STORY ABOUT ONE TRAPPED IN A METAL VESSEL...
...BUT I DIDN'T KNOW IT REALLY EXISTED!!
GRAAAAH

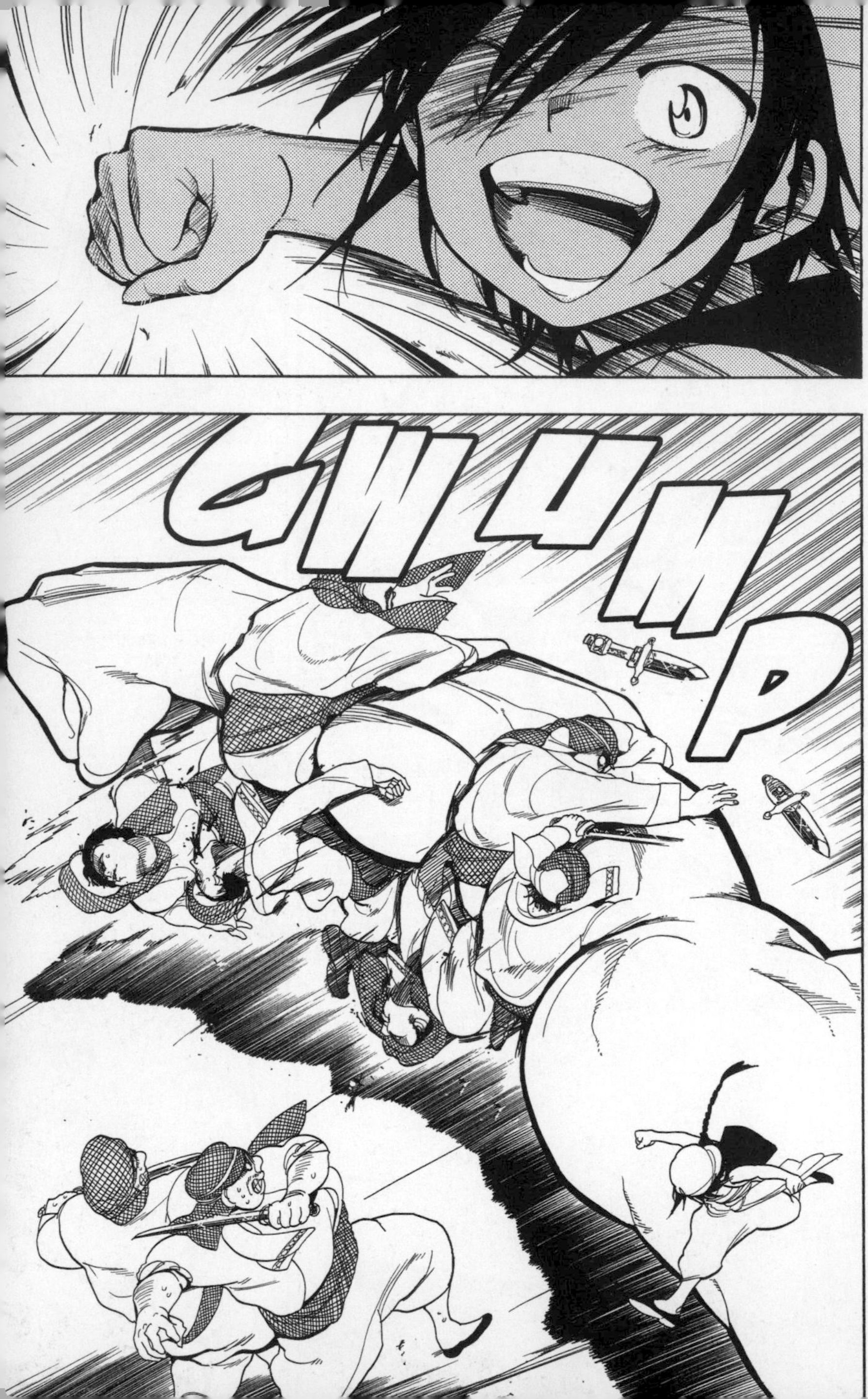
GWUMP

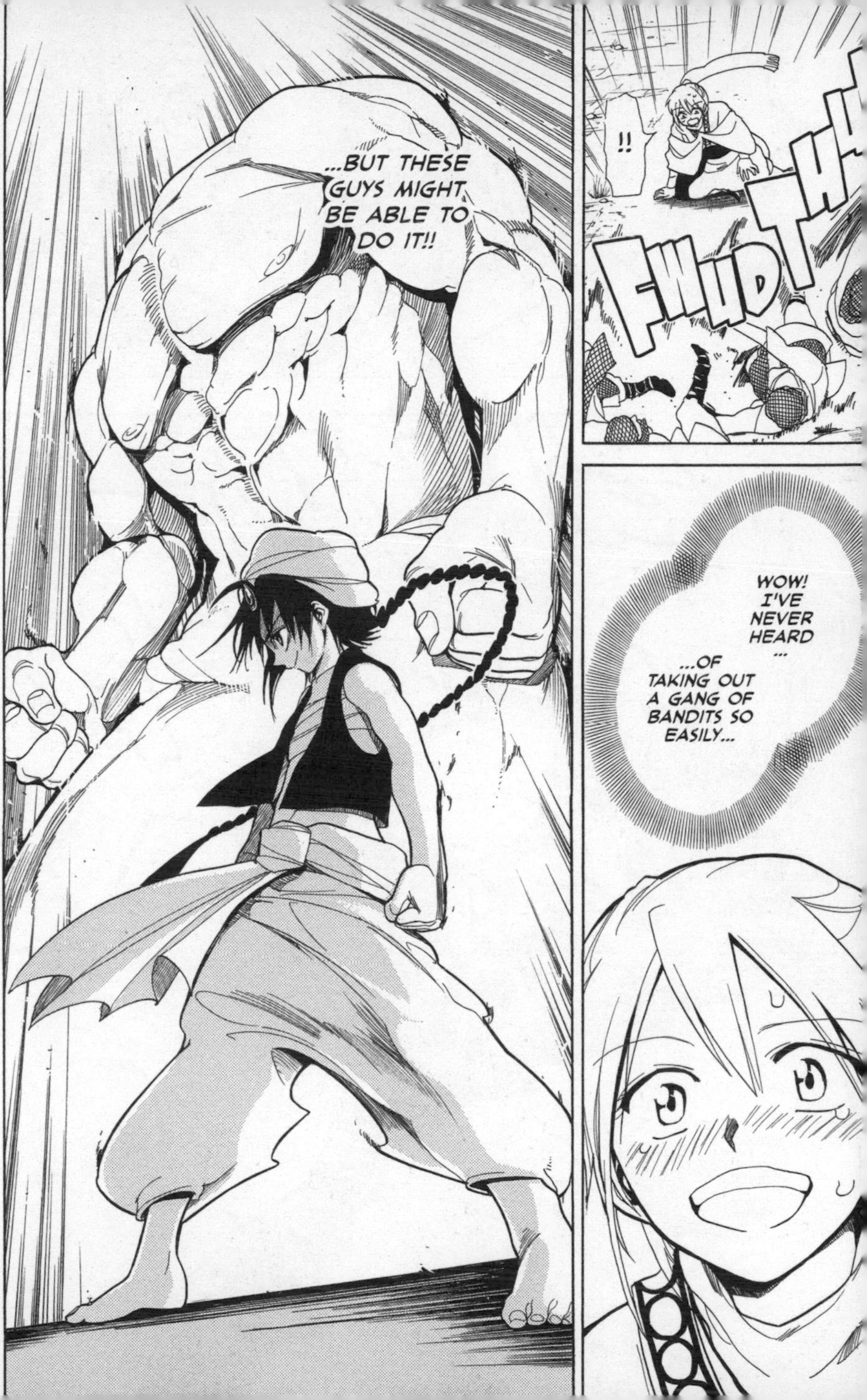
!!
FWUD
THU
WOW! I'VE NEVER HEARD...
...OF TAKING OUT A GANG OF BANDITS SO EASILY...
...BUT THESE GUYS MIGHT BE ABLE TO DO IT!!

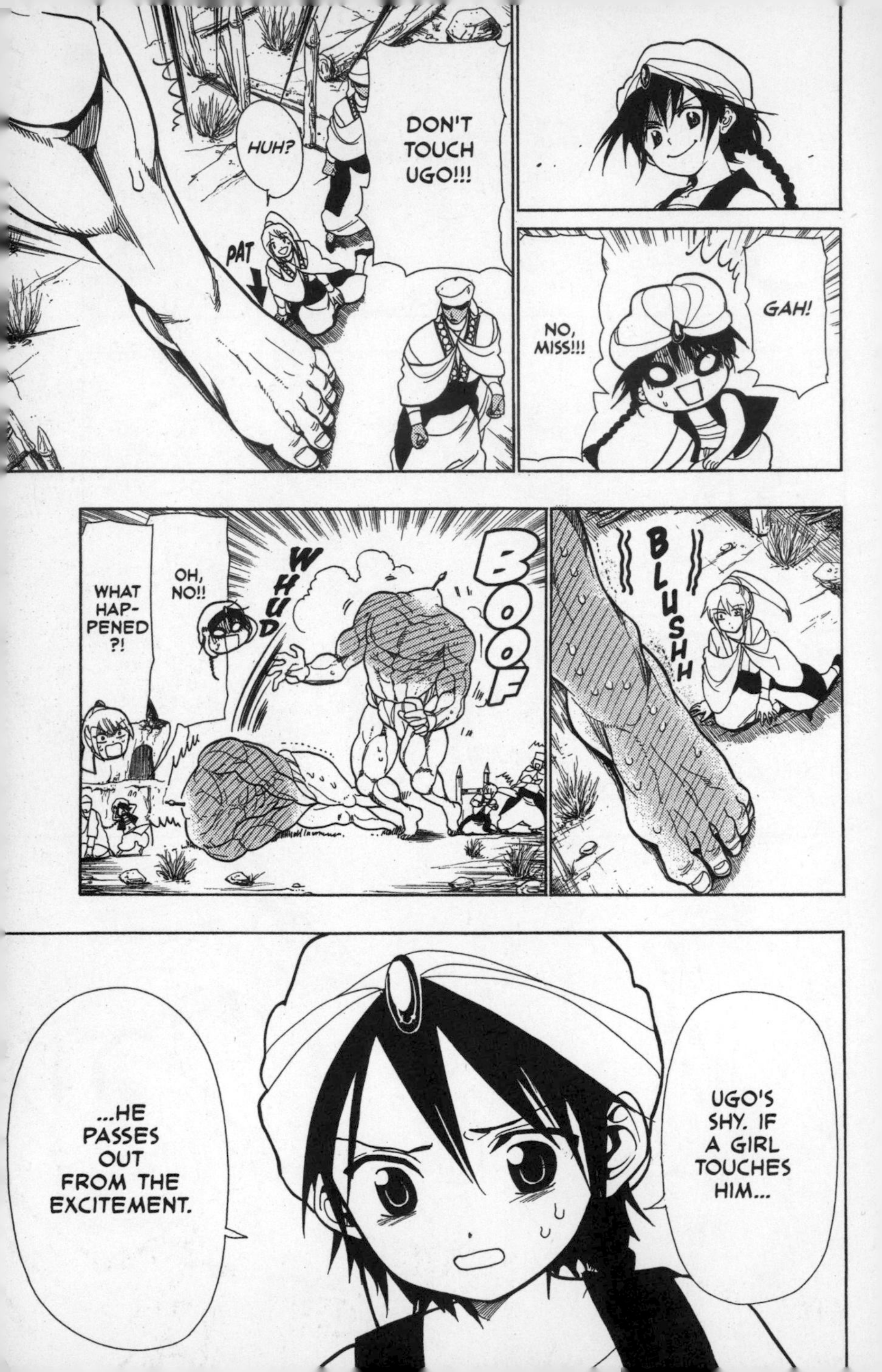
GAH!
NO, MISS!!!
DON'T TOUCH UGO!!!
HUH?
PAT
BLUSHH
BOOOF
WHUD
OH, NO!!
WHAT HAP-PENED?!
UGO'S SHY. IF A GIRL TOUCHES HIM...
...HE PASSES OUT FROM THE EXCITEMENT.

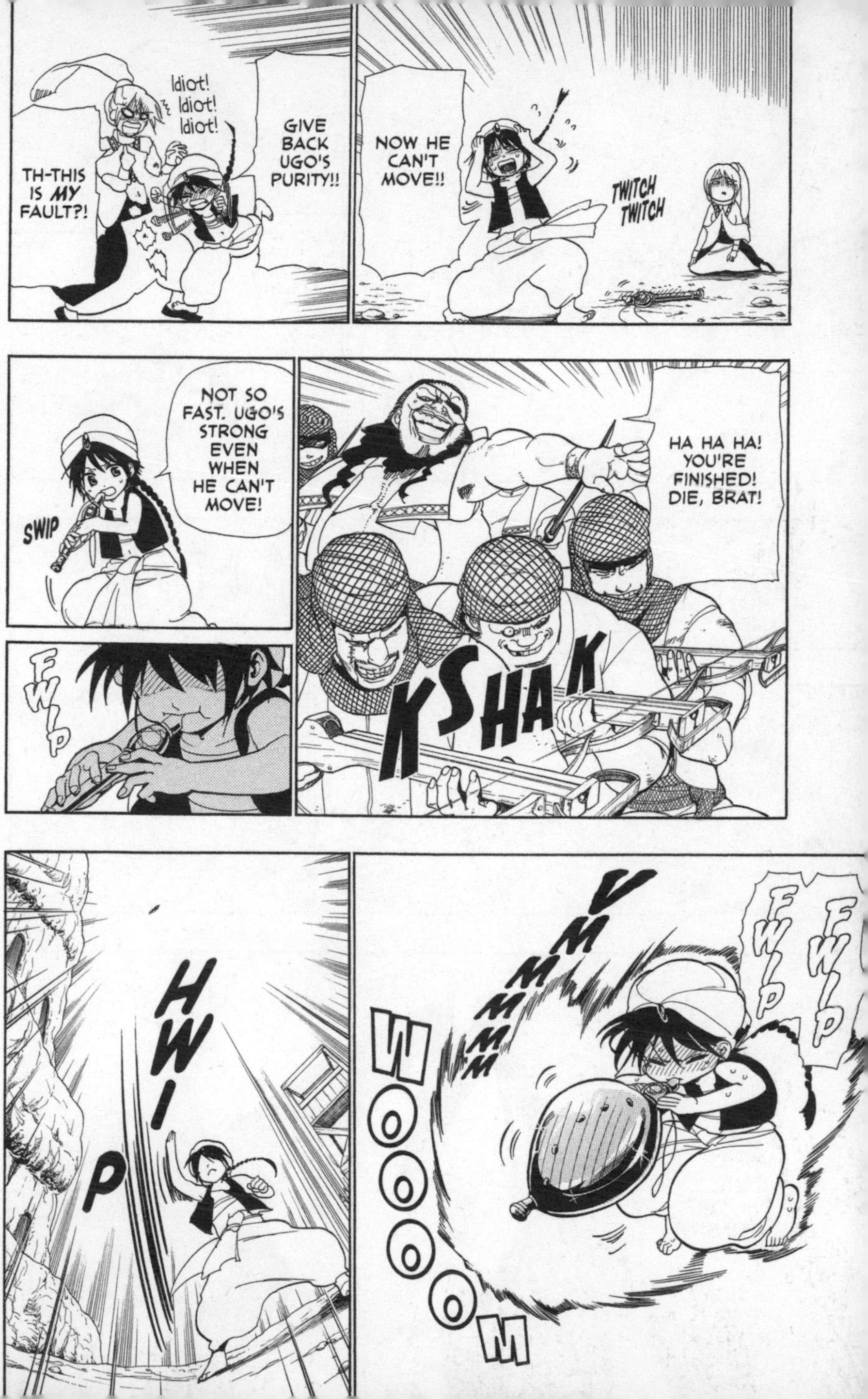
NOW HE CAN'T MOVE!!
TWITCH TWITCH
GIVE BACK UGO'S PURITY!!
Idiot! Idiot! Idiot!
TH-THIS IS MY FAULT?!
HA HA HA! YOU'RE FINISHED! DIE, BRAT!
KSHAK
NOT SO FAST. UGO'S STRONG EVEN WHEN HE CAN'T MOVE!
SWIP
FWIP
FWIP FWIP
VMMMMMMM
WOOOOOOOM
HWIP

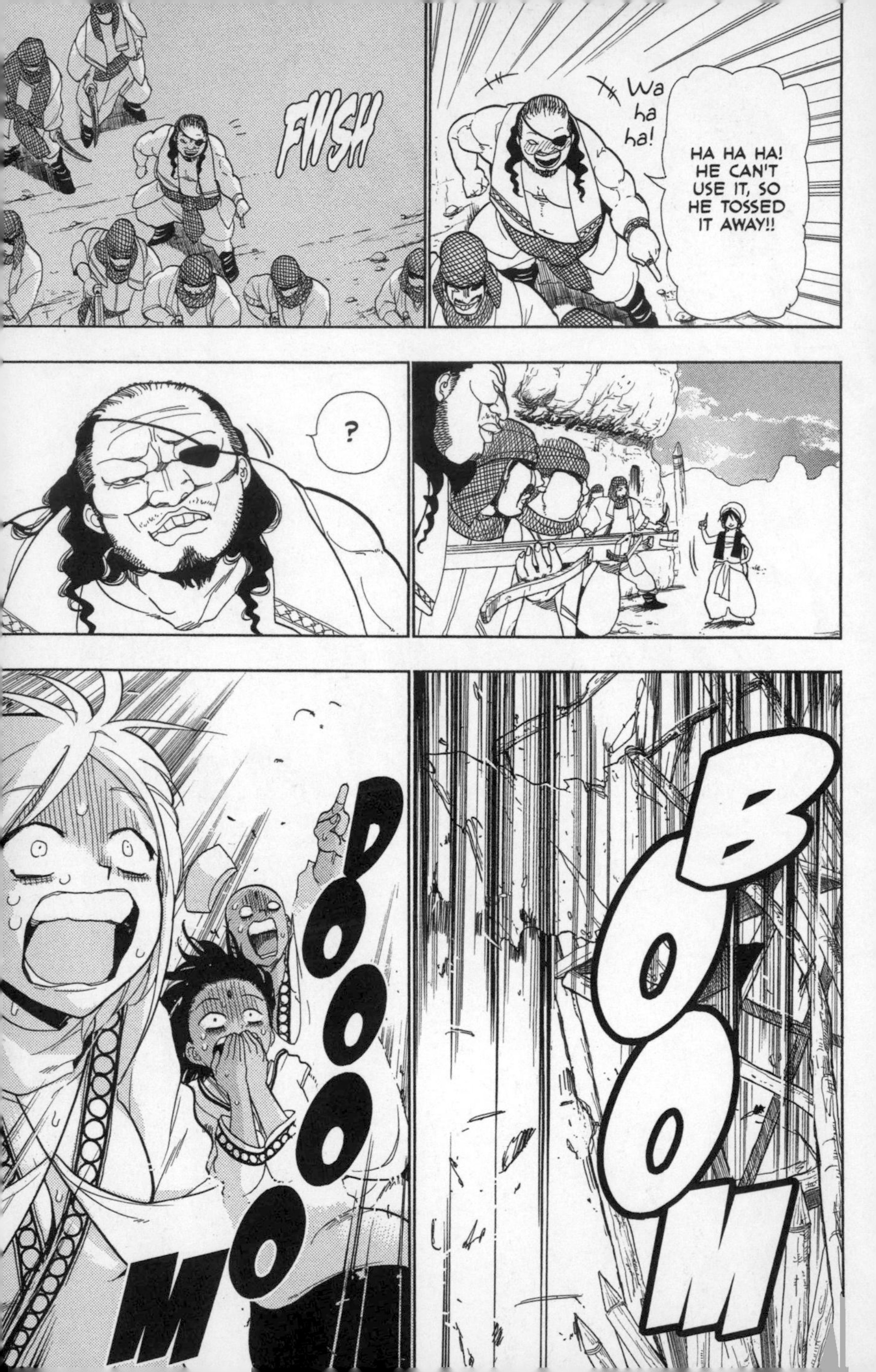
Wa ha ha!
HA HA HA! HE CAN'T USE IT, SO HE TOSSED IT AWAY!!
FWSH
?
BOOOOM
DOOOOOM

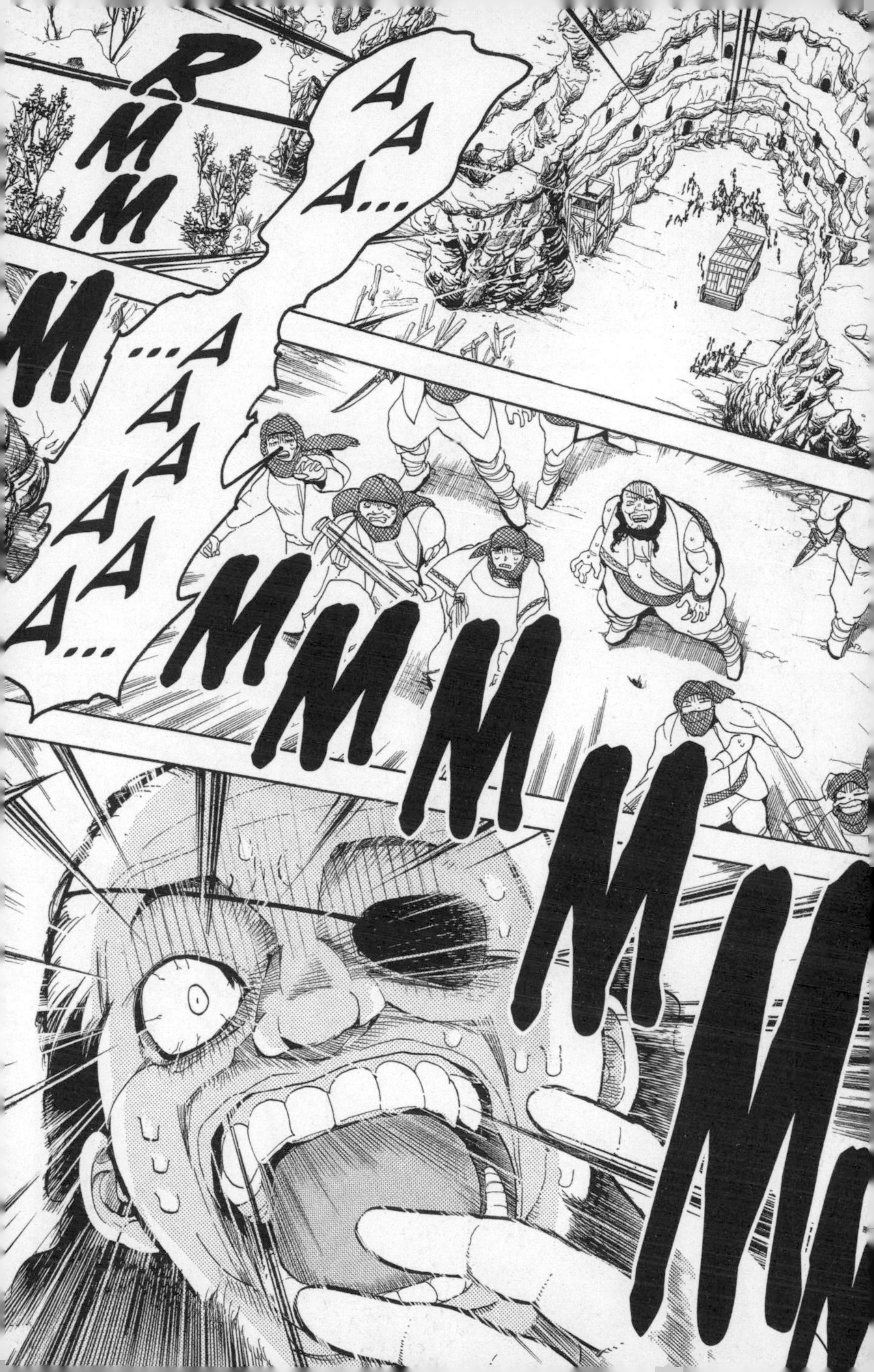
RMMMM...
AAA...AAAAAA...
MMMMMMM

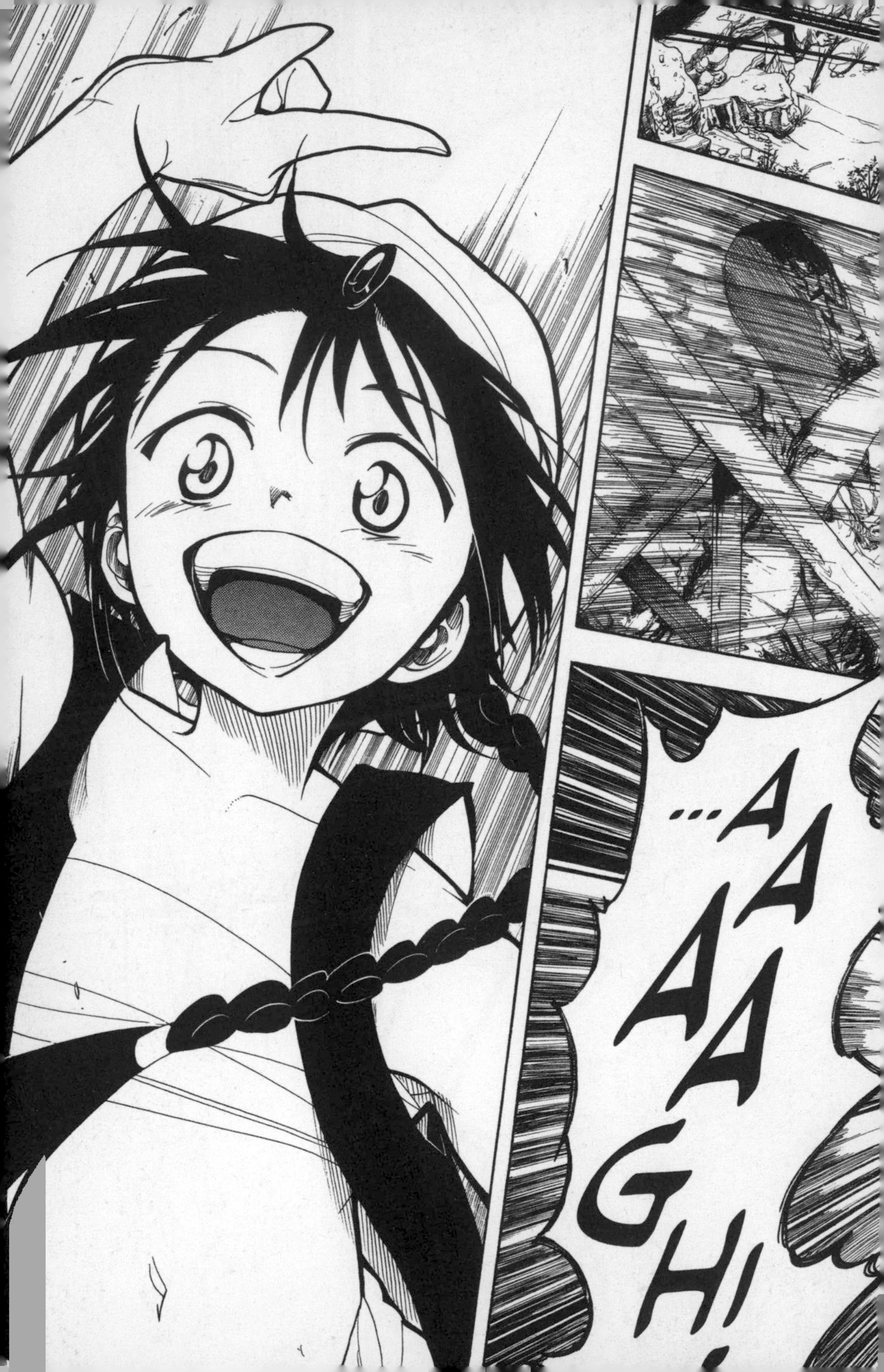
...AAAAAGH!

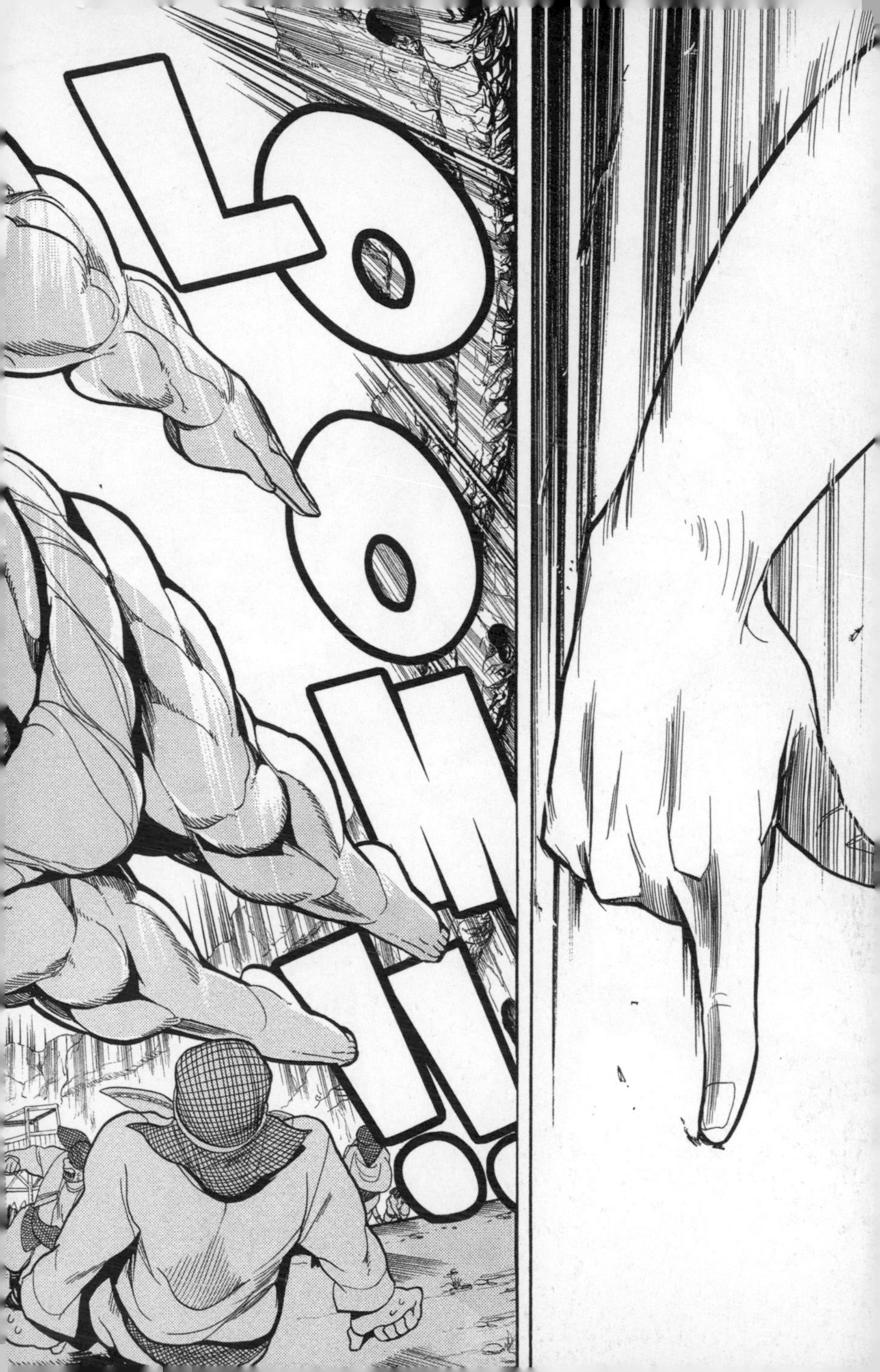
LOOM..

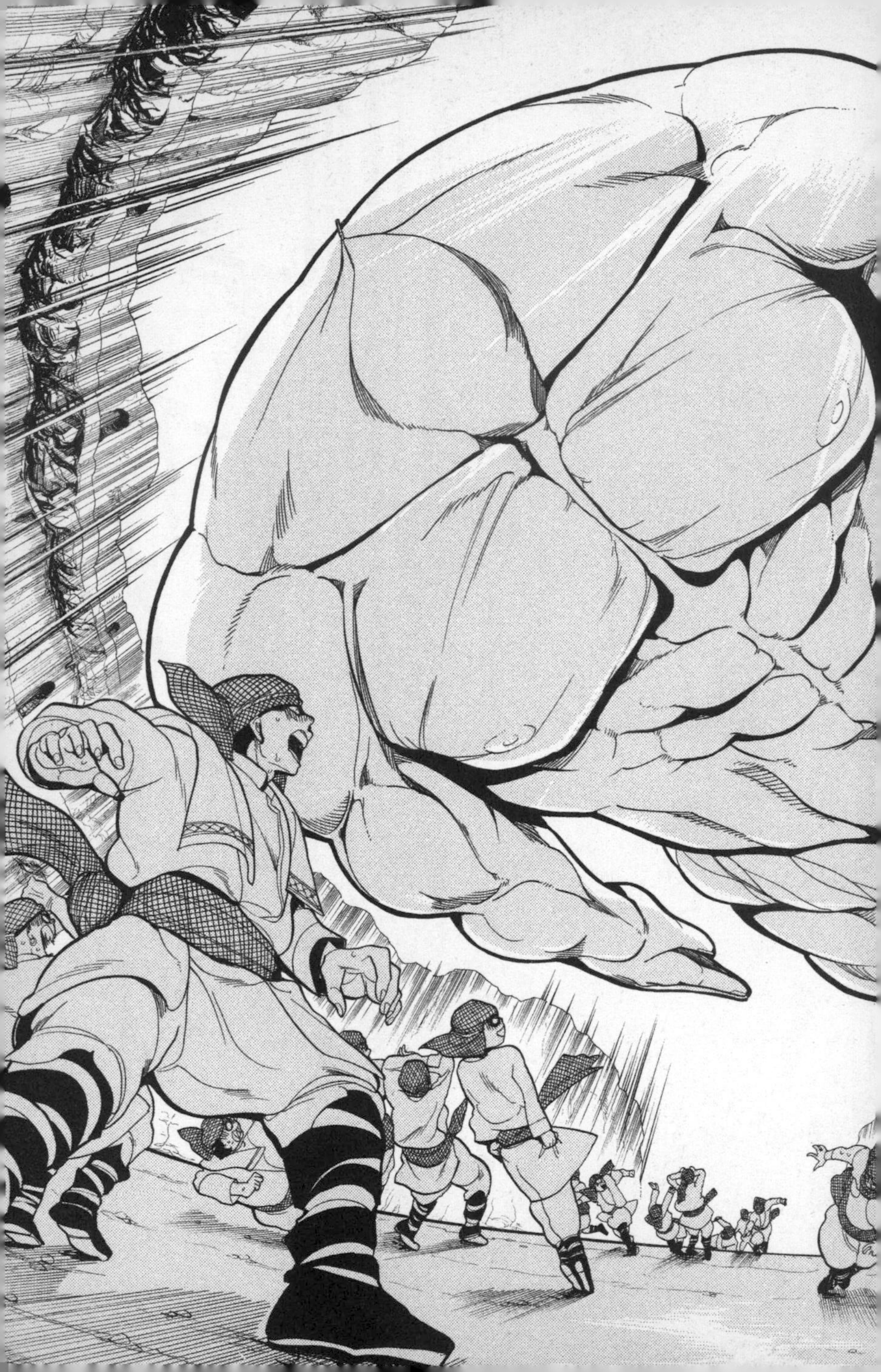

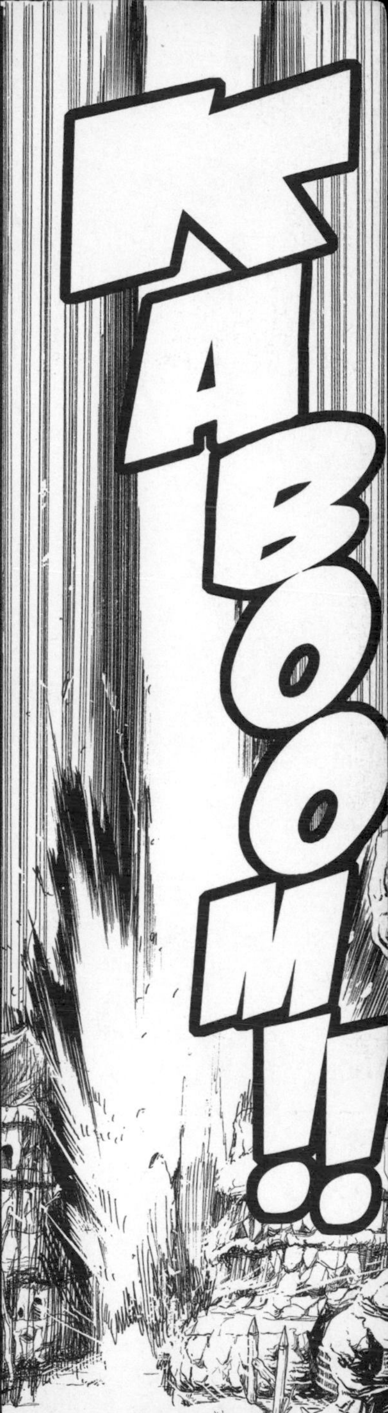
KABOOM!!
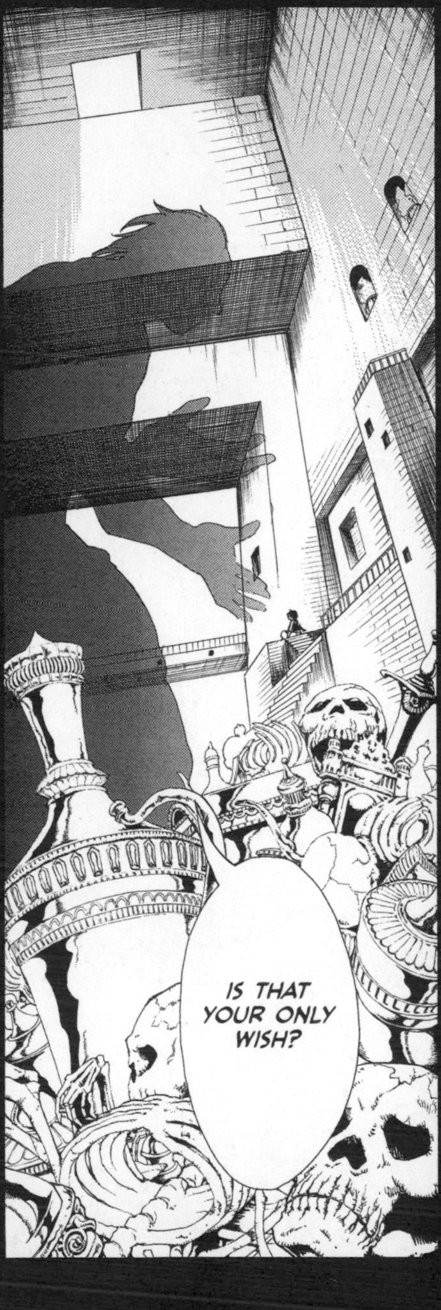
IS THAT YOUR ONLY WISH?

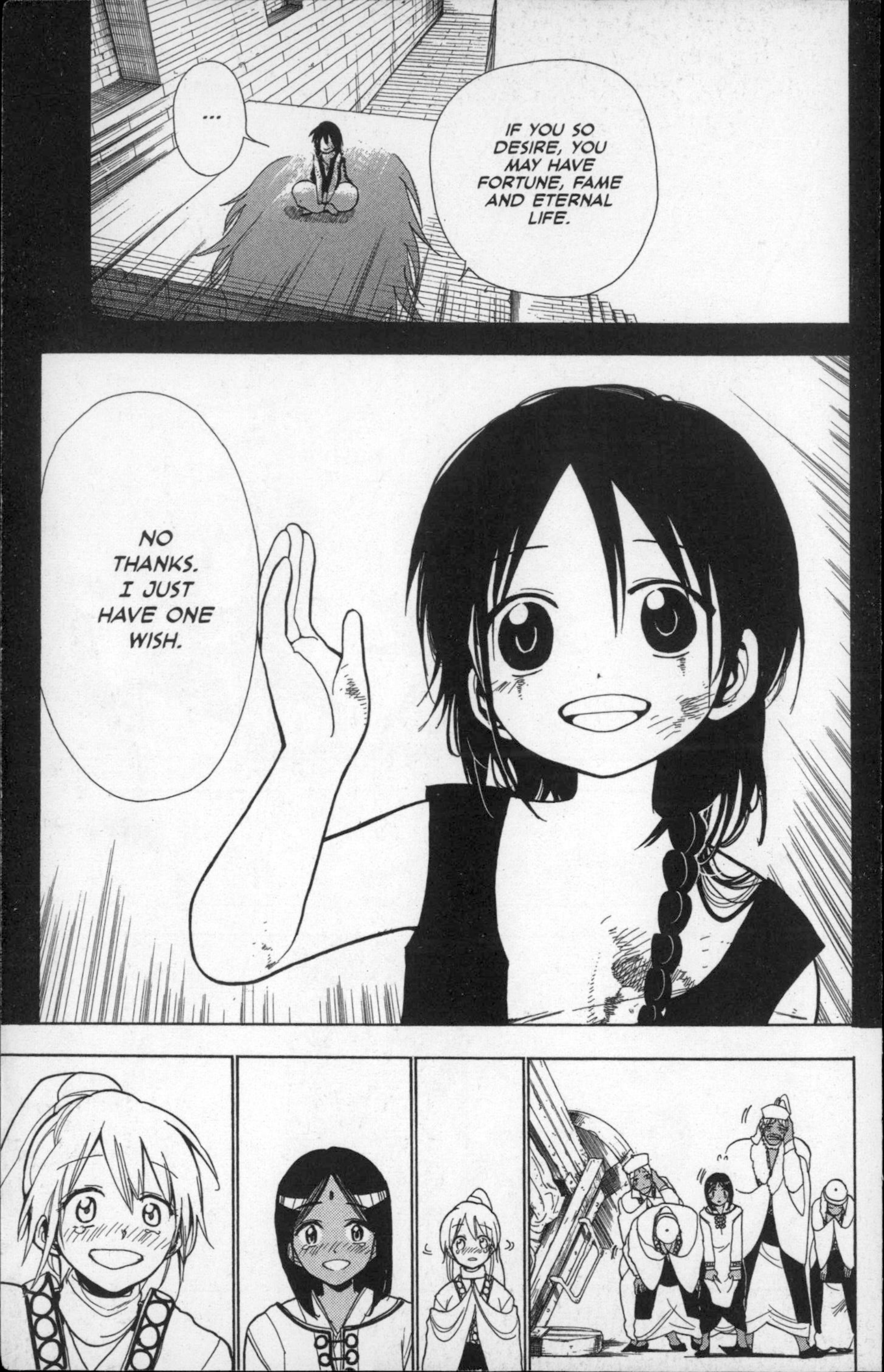
IF YOU SO DESIRE, YOU MAY HAVE FORTUNE, FAME AND ETERNAL LIFE.
...
NO THANKS. I JUST HAVE ONE WISH.

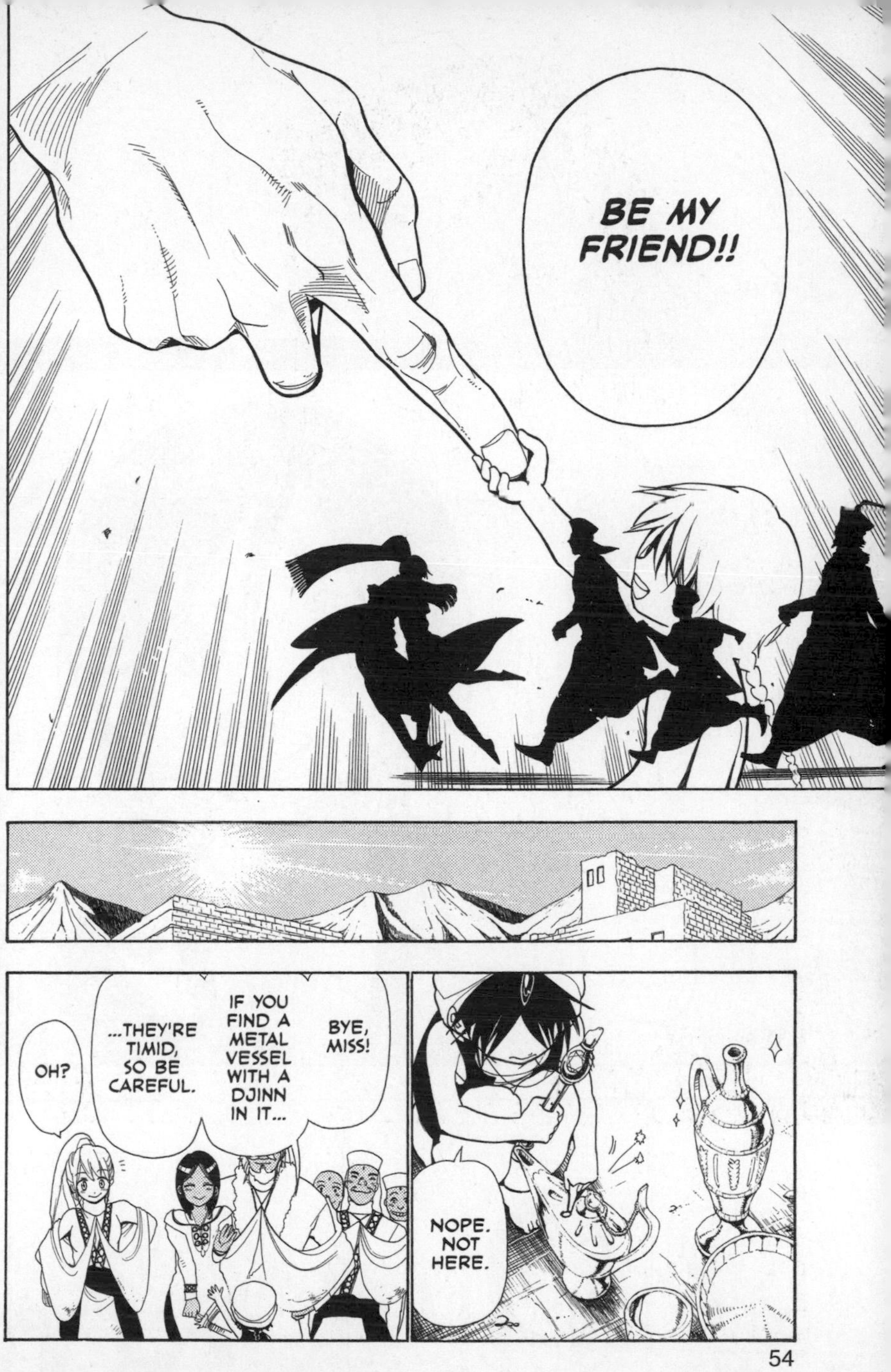
BE MY FRIEND!!
NOPE. NOT HERE.
BYE, MISS!
IF YOU FIND A METAL VESSEL WITH A DJINN IN IT...
...THEY'RE TIMID, SO BE CAREFUL.
OH?

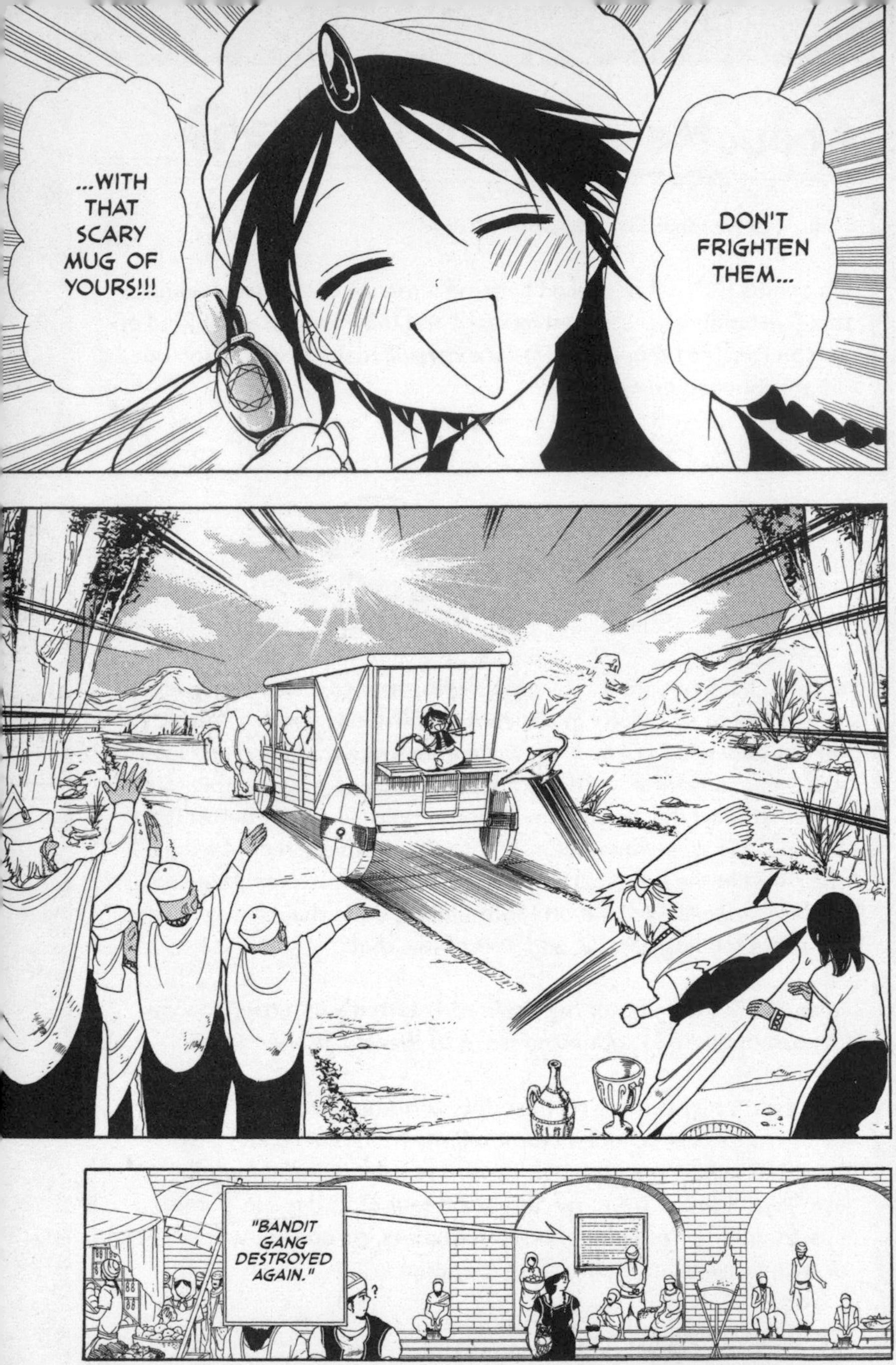
DON'T FRIGHTEN THEM...
...WITH THAT SCARY MUG OF YOURS!!!
"BANDIT GANG DESTROYED AGAIN."

About Me—Shinobu Ohtaka ❶

Hello! I draw *Magi*. I'm ***Shinobu Ohtaka!***

It's been a little while since I became a manga author, but I realized that I've hardly ever stepped forward and talked about what kind of person I am, so I think I'll ***introduce myself,*** making sure to include what happened ***up until Magi.***

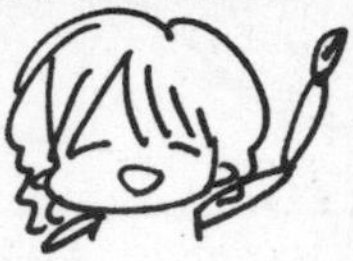

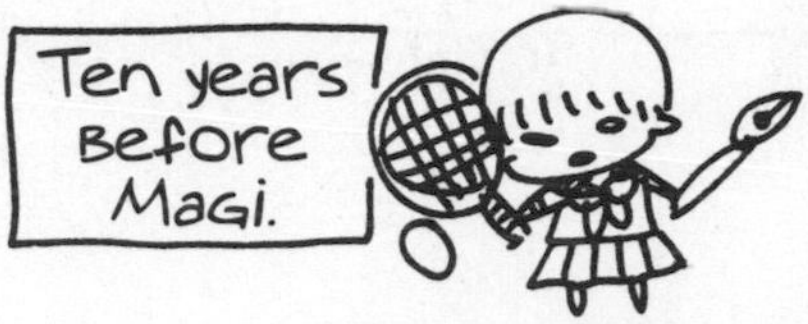
Ten years Before Magi.

Let's go back to before I started drawing manga. I was ***the type of student to sit quietly in the corner of the classroom.*** I wasn't particularly good at anything, my grades were middling, and I was just a bench warmer in the tennis club. I played a supporting role in everything I did, but the one thing I could do a little better than anyone else was ***draw pictures.*** With the motivation of playing a main role in the future as someone who drew pictures, ***I started drawing manga.*** Well, I didn't formulate it quite that clearly at the time, but looking back, it was sort of like that.

In about my ***first year of high school,*** I started submitting manga manuscripts. And I submitted them to ***Weekly Shonen Jump!***

Night after night I drew manuscripts at home, and then I snoozed away my days at school. I ***didn't tell my friends*** at school that I wanted to be a manga author and was submitting my work. I also ***kept it secret from my family.*** All four of us lived in a small apartment in an old complex. Nonetheless, ***no one knew*** that I was drawing manga and submitting my scripts.

Continued on page 154.

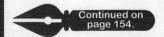

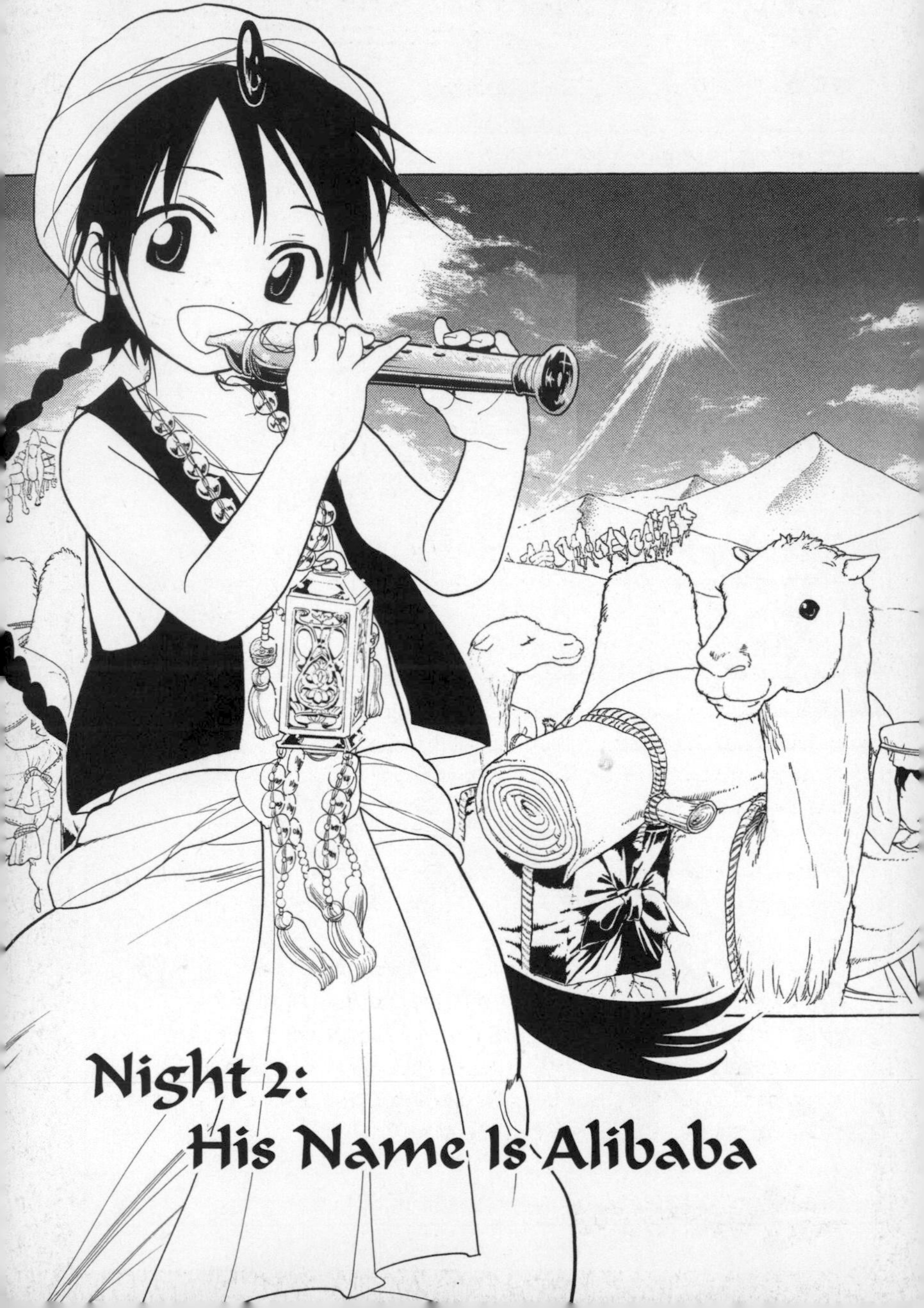
Night 2:
His Name Is Alibaba

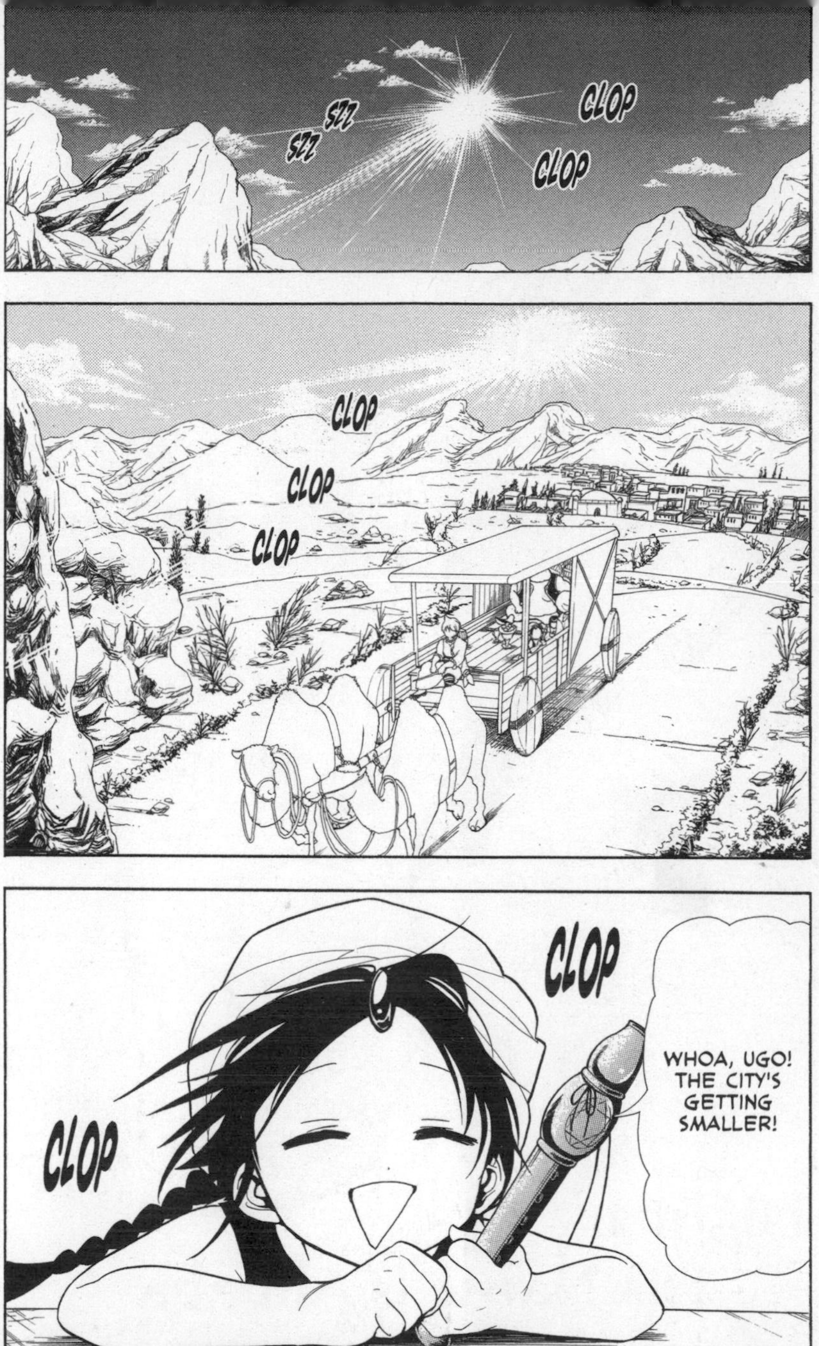
CLOP
CLOP
SZZ
SZZ
CLOP
CLOP
CLOP
WHOA, UGO! THE CITY'S GETTING SMALLER!
CLOP
CLOP

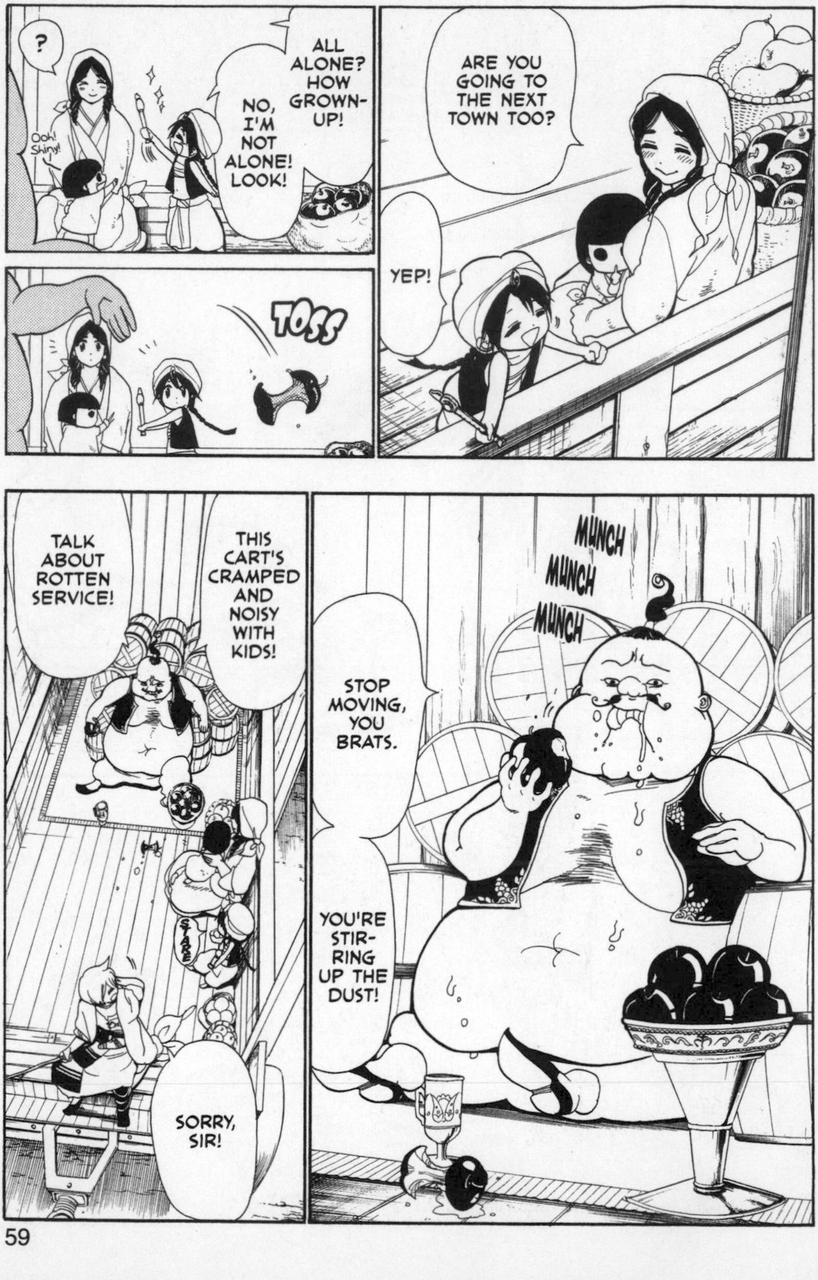
ARE YOU GOING TO THE NEXT TOWN TOO?
YEP!
ALL ALONE? HOW GROWN-UP!
NO, I'M NOT ALONE! LOOK!
?
Ooh! Shiny!
TOSS
MUNCH
MUNCH
MUNCH
STOP MOVING, YOU BRATS.
YOU'RE STIR-RING UP THE DUST!
THIS CART'S CRAMPED AND NOISY WITH KIDS!
TALK ABOUT ROTTEN SERVICE!
STARE
SORRY, SIR!

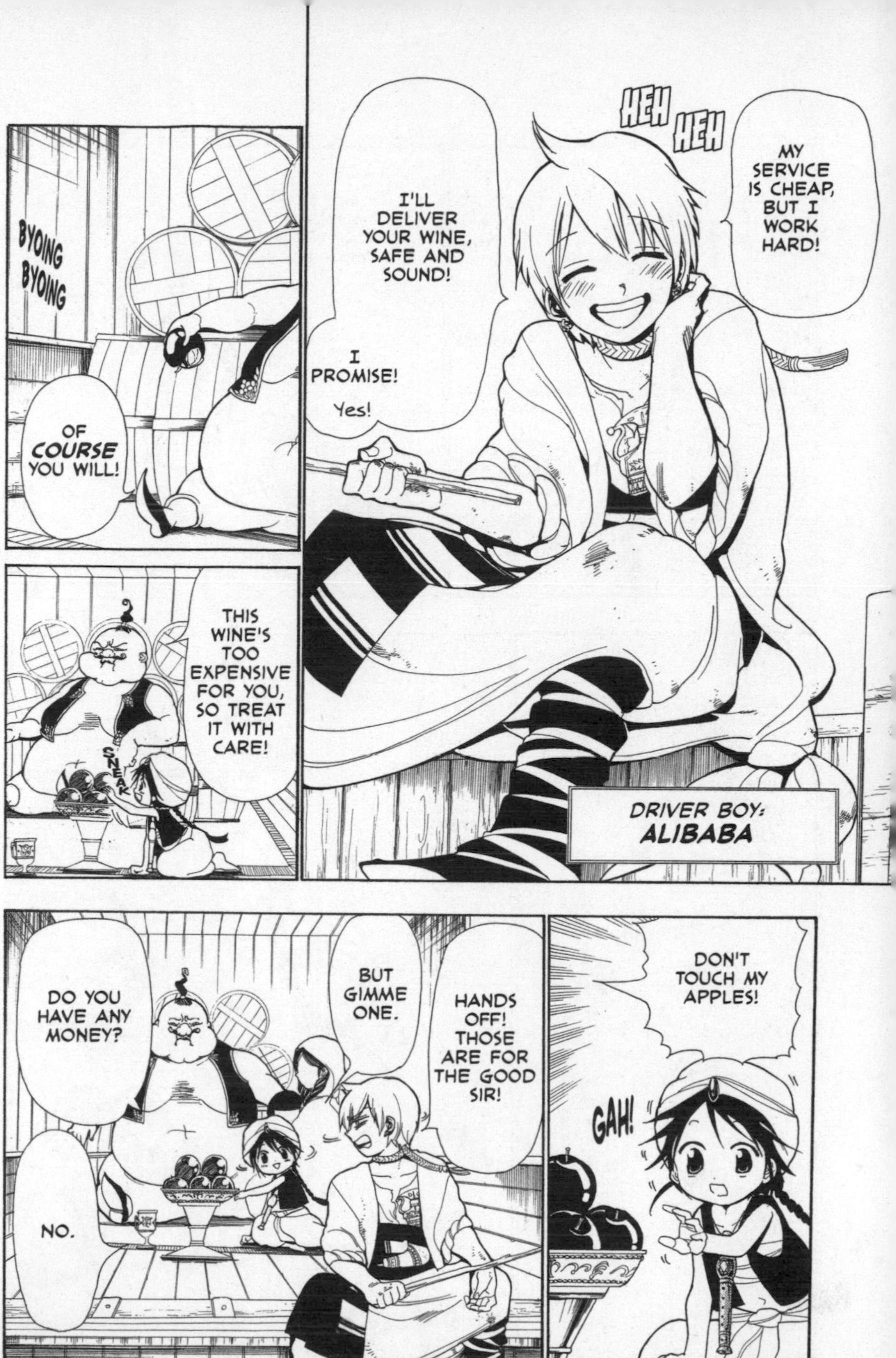
HEH HEH
MY SERVICE IS CHEAP, BUT I WORK HARD!
I'LL DELIVER YOUR WINE, SAFE AND SOUND!
I PROMISE!
Yes!
DRIVER BOY: ALIBABA
BYOING BYOING
OF COURSE YOU WILL!
THIS WINE'S TOO EXPENSIVE FOR YOU, SO TREAT IT WITH CARE!
SNEAK
DON'T TOUCH MY APPLES!
GAH!
HANDS OFF! THOSE ARE FOR THE GOOD SIR!
BUT GIMME ONE.
DO YOU HAVE ANY MONEY?
NO.

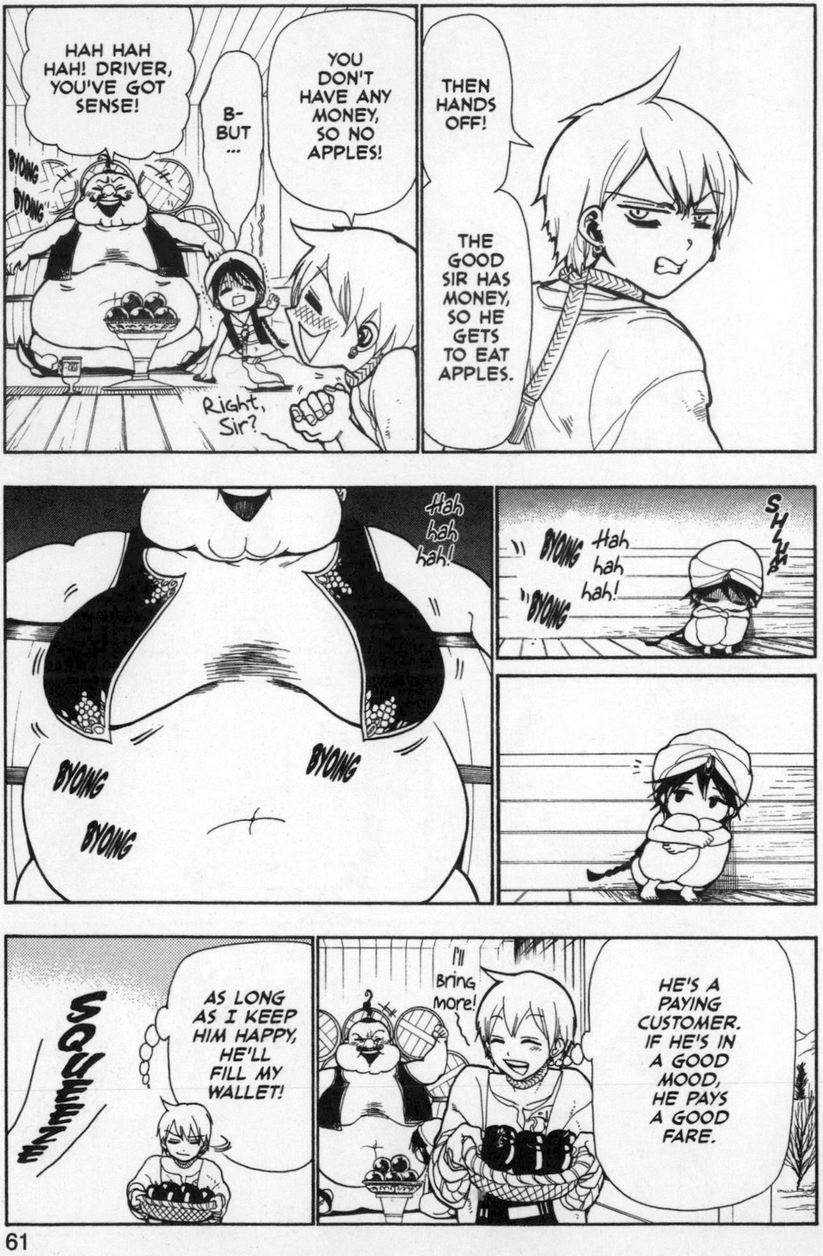
THEN HANDS OFF!
THE GOOD SIR HAS MONEY, SO HE GETS TO EAT APPLES.
YOU DON'T HAVE ANY MONEY, SO NO APPLES!
B-BUT ...
HAH HAH HAH! DRIVER, YOU'VE GOT SENSE!
BYOING
BYOING
Right, Sir?
SHLUMP
Hah hah hah!
BYOING
BYOING
Hah hah hah!
BYOING
BYOING
BYOING
HE'S A PAYING CUSTOMER. IF HE'S IN A GOOD MOOD, HE PAYS A GOOD FARE.
I'll Bring more!
AS LONG AS I KEEP HIM HAPPY, HE'LL FILL MY WALLET!
SQUEEEZE

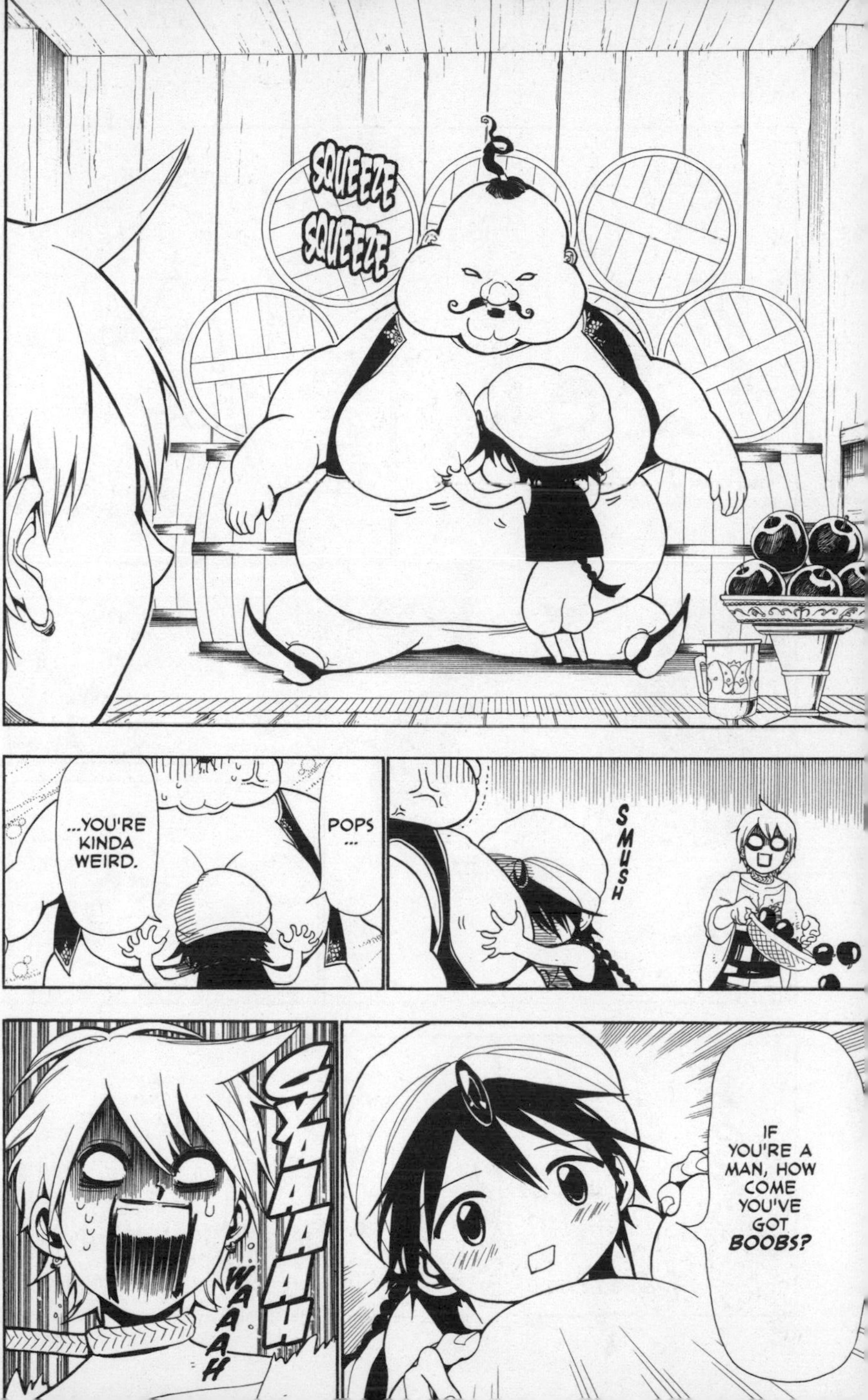
SQUEEZE
SQUEEZE
SMUSH
POPS...
...YOU'RE KINDA WEIRD.
IF YOU'RE A MAN, HOW COME YOU'VE GOT BOOBS?
GYAAAAH
WAAAAH

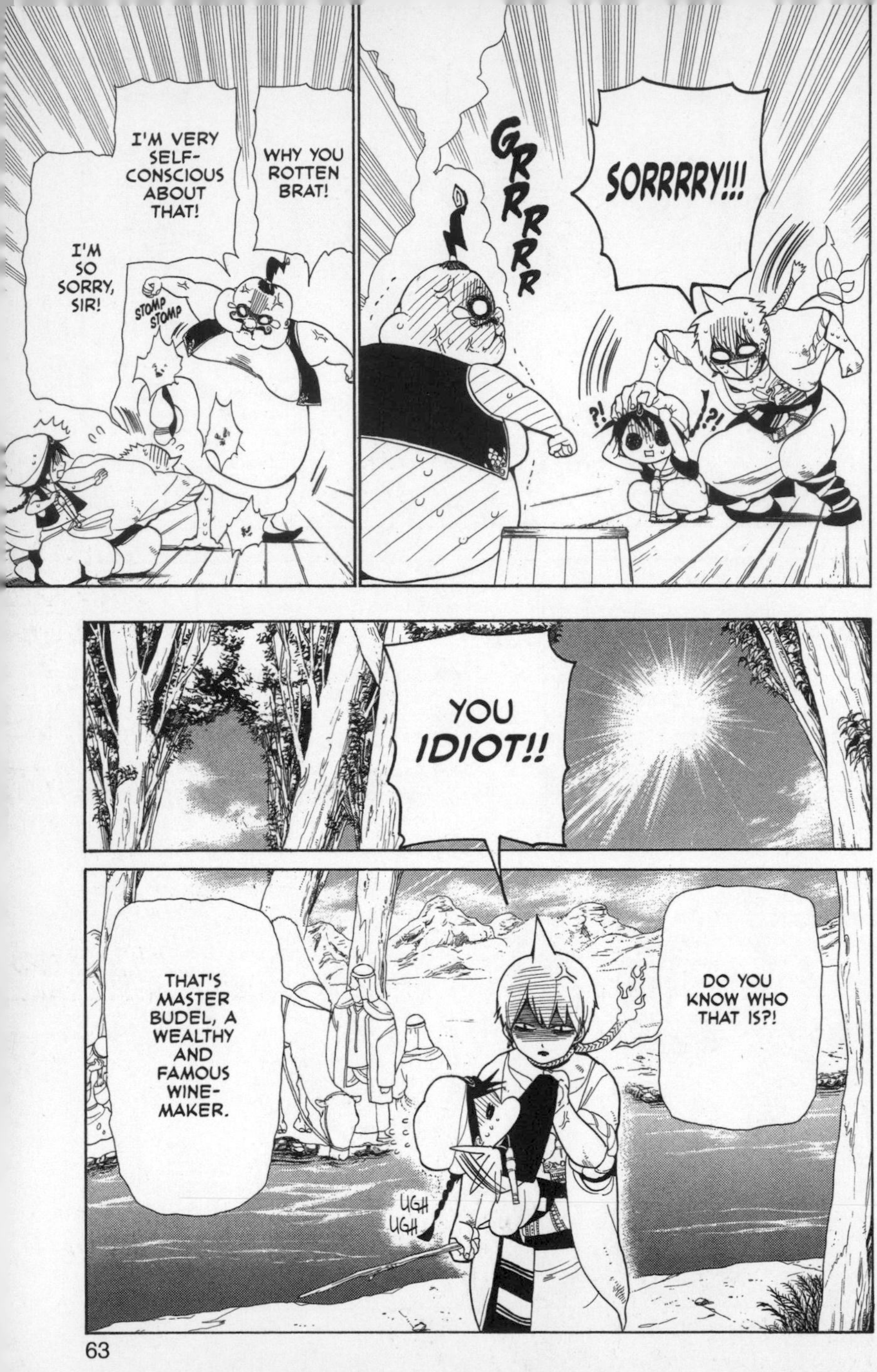
SORRRRY!!!
GRRRRR
?!
?!
WHY YOU ROTTEN BRAT!
I'M VERY SELF-CONSCIOUS ABOUT THAT!
I'M SO SORRY, SIR!
STOMP STOMP
YOU IDIOT!!
DO YOU KNOW WHO THAT IS?!
THAT'S MASTER BUDEL, A WEALTHY AND FAMOUS WINE-MAKER.
UGH UGH

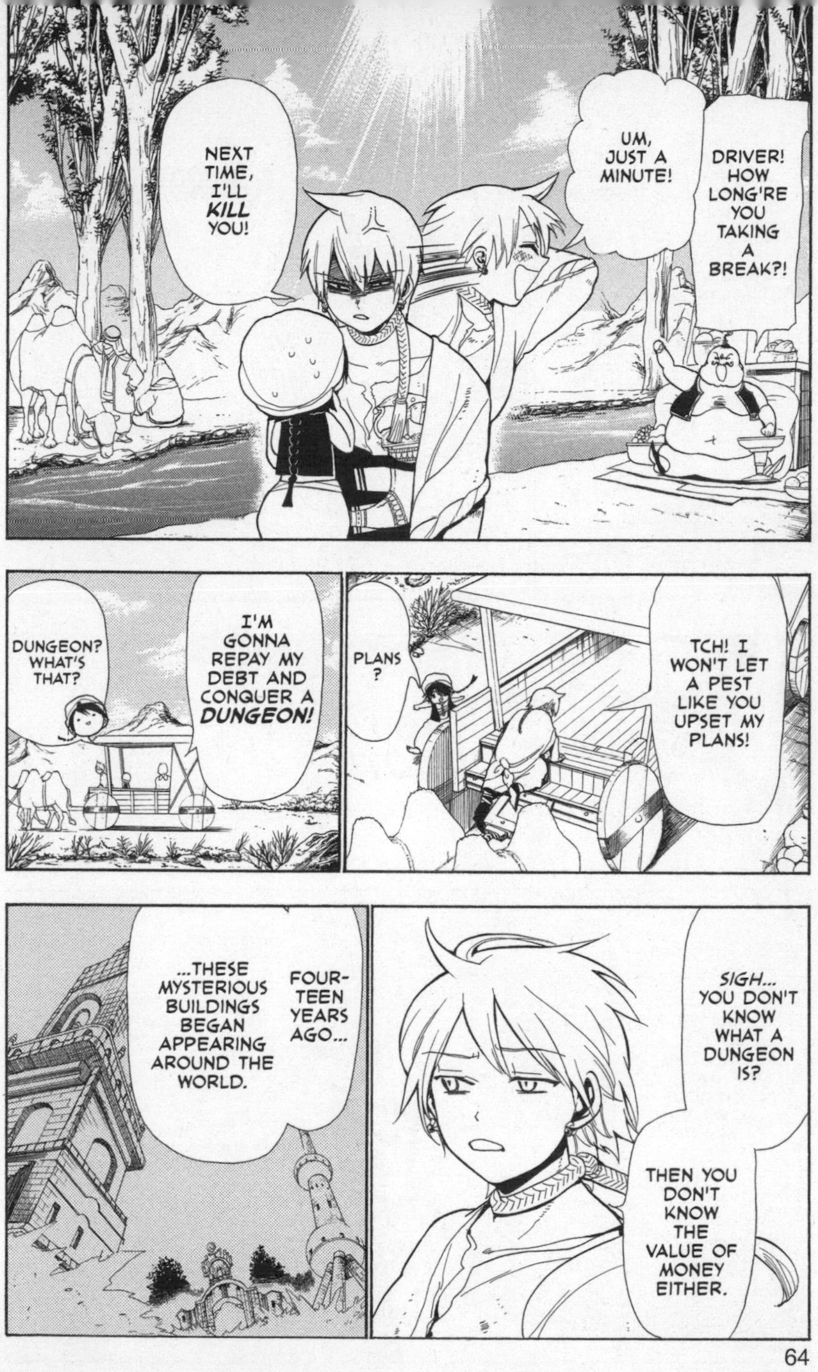
DRIVER! HOW LONG'RE YOU TAKING A BREAK?!
UM, JUST A MINUTE!
NEXT TIME, I'LL *KILL* YOU!
TCH! I WON'T LET A PEST LIKE YOU UPSET MY PLANS!
PLANS ?
I'M GONNA REPAY MY DEBT AND CONQUER A *DUNGEON!*
DUNGEON? WHAT'S THAT?
SIGH... YOU DON'T KNOW WHAT A DUNGEON IS?
THEN YOU DON'T KNOW THE VALUE OF MONEY EITHER.
FOURTEEN YEARS AGO...
...THESE MYSTERIOUS BUILDINGS BEGAN APPEARING AROUND THE WORLD.

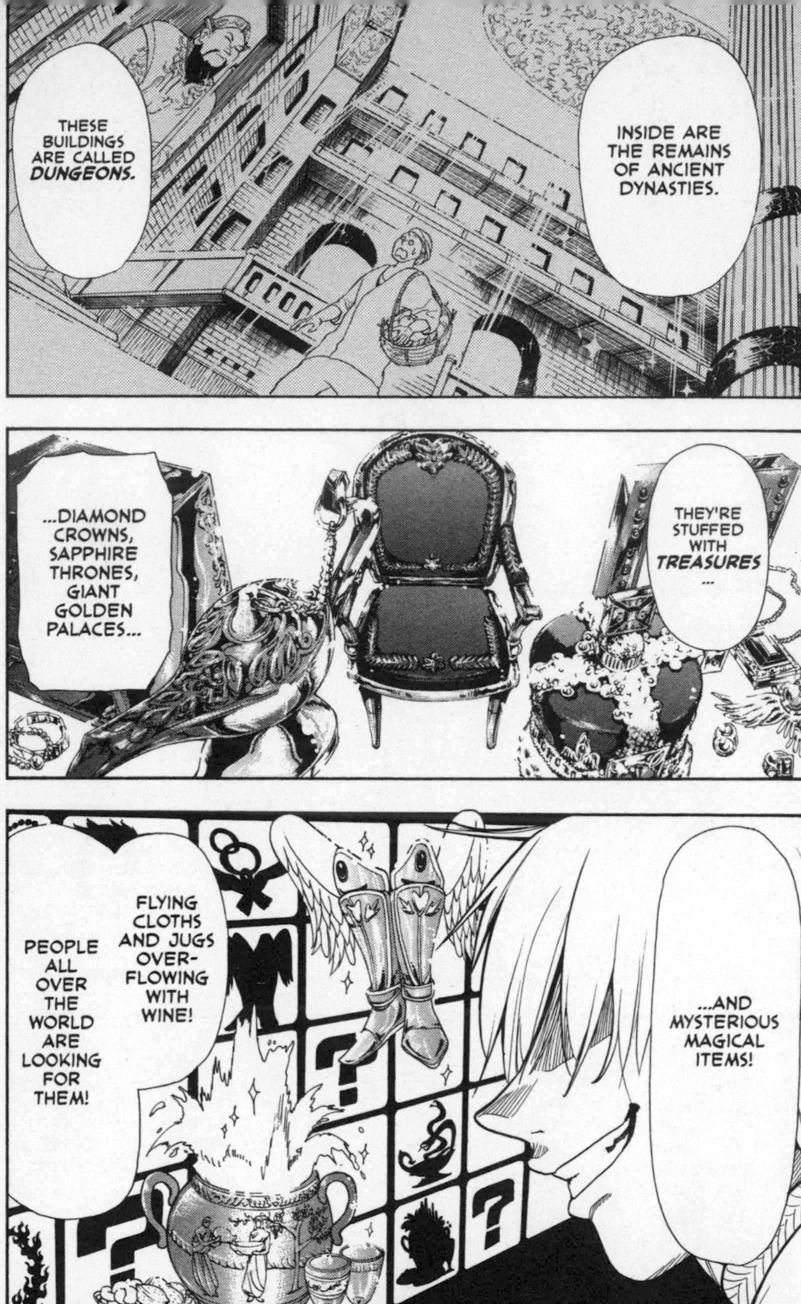
INSIDE ARE THE REMAINS OF ANCIENT DYNASTIES.
THESE BUILDINGS ARE CALLED *DUNGEONS.*
THEY'RE STUFFED WITH *TREASURES* ...
...DIAMOND CROWNS, SAPPHIRE THRONES, GIANT GOLDEN PALACES...
...AND MYSTERIOUS MAGICAL ITEMS!
FLYING CLOTHS AND JUGS OVER-FLOWING WITH WINE!
PEOPLE ALL OVER THE WORLD ARE LOOKING FOR THEM!

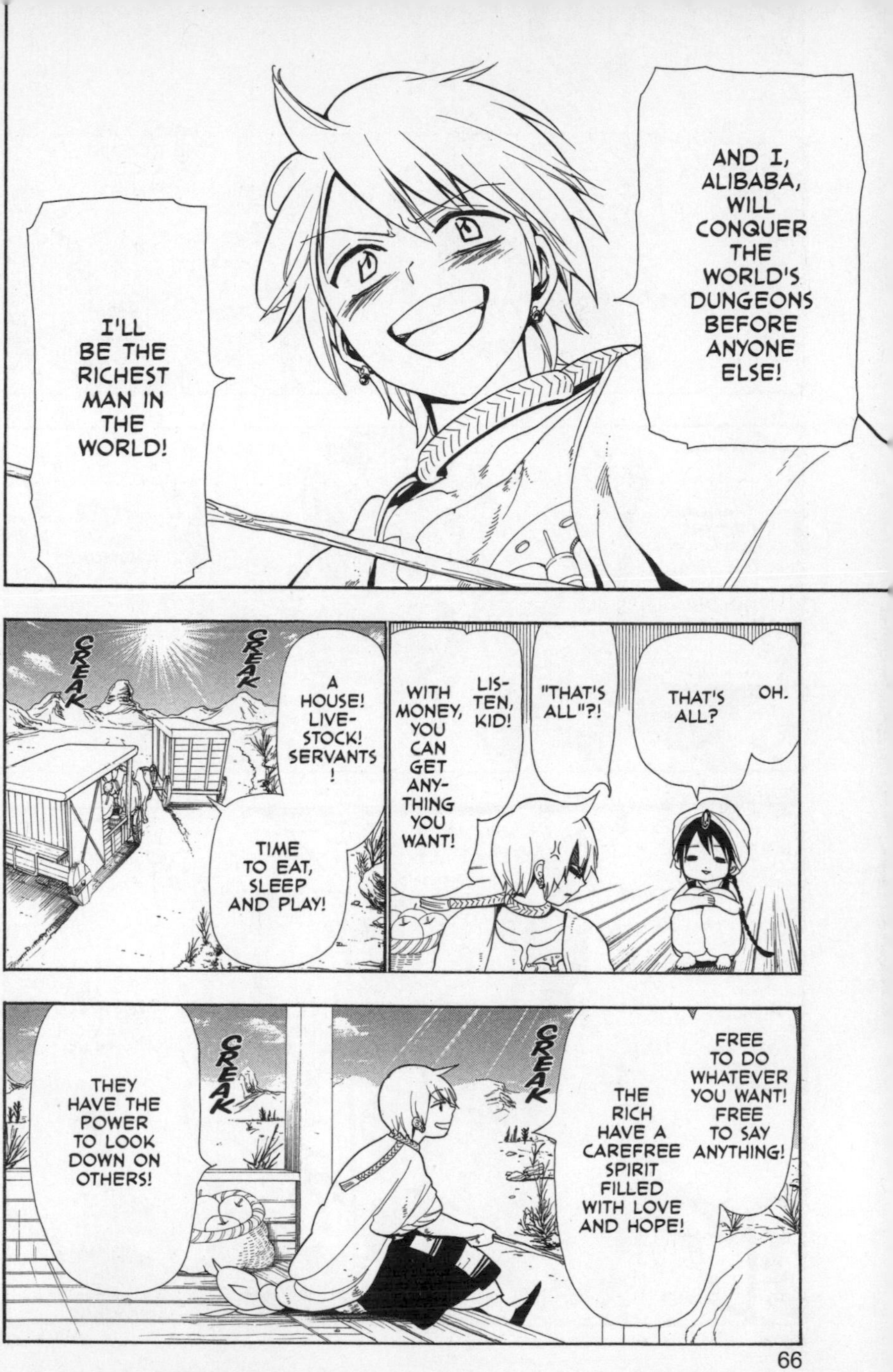
AND I, ALIBABA, WILL CONQUER THE WORLD'S DUNGEONS BEFORE ANYONE ELSE!
I'LL BE THE RICHEST MAN IN THE WORLD!
OH.
THAT'S ALL?
"THAT'S ALL"?!
LIS-TEN, KID!
WITH MONEY, YOU CAN GET ANY-THING YOU WANT!
CREAK
CREAK
A HOUSE! LIVE-STOCK! SERVANTS!
TIME TO EAT, SLEEP AND PLAY!
CREAK
FREE TO DO WHATEVER YOU WANT! FREE TO SAY ANYTHING!
THE RICH HAVE A CAREFREE SPIRIT FILLED WITH LOVE AND HOPE!
CREAK
THEY HAVE THE POWER TO LOOK DOWN ON OTHERS!

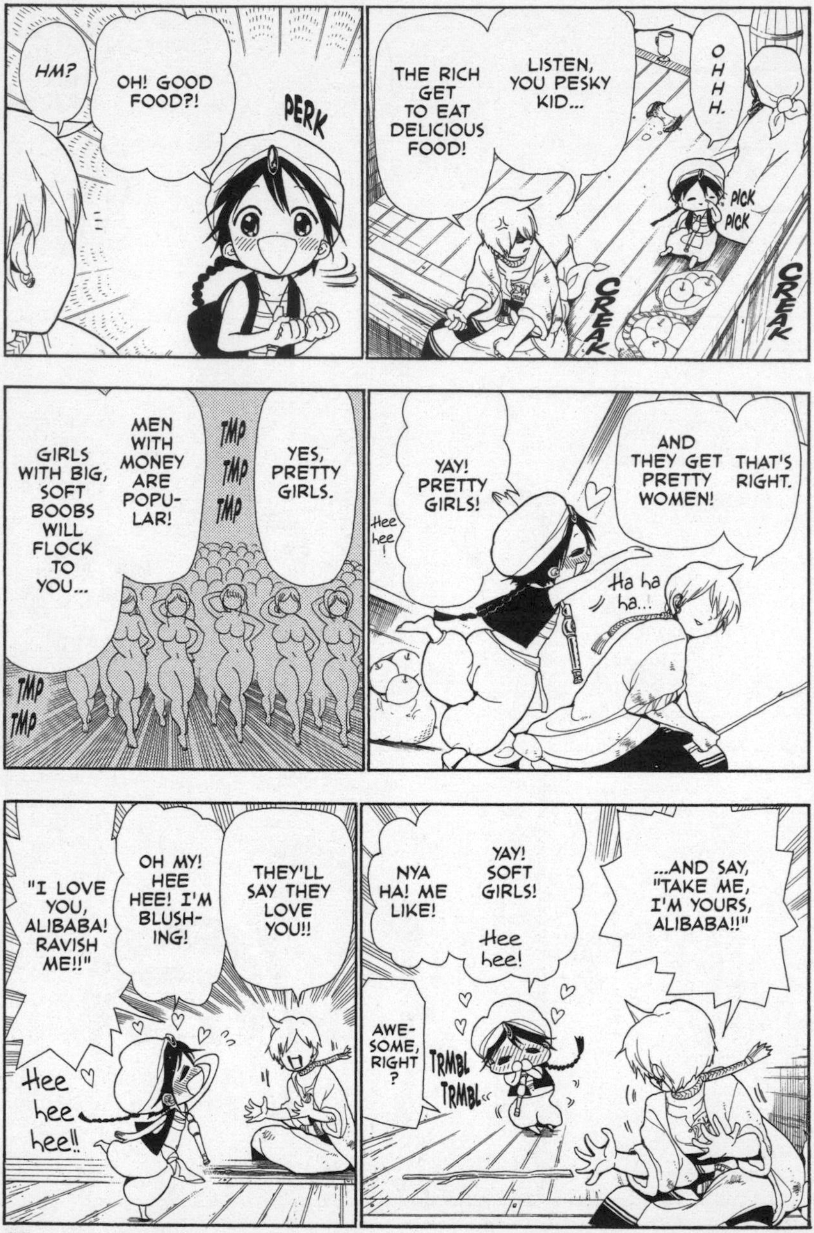
OHHH.
LISTEN, YOU PESKY KID...
THE RICH GET TO EAT DELICIOUS FOOD!
PICK PICK
CREAK
CREAK
HM?
OH! GOOD FOOD?!
PERK
THAT'S RIGHT.
AND THEY GET PRETTY WOMEN!
YAY! PRETTY GIRLS!
Hee hee!
Ha ha ha...!
YES, PRETTY GIRLS.
TMP TMP TMP
MEN WITH MONEY ARE POPU-LAR!
GIRLS WITH BIG, SOFT BOOBS WILL FLOCK TO YOU...
TMP TMP
...AND SAY, "TAKE ME, I'M YOURS, ALIBABA!!"
YAY! SOFT GIRLS!
Hee hee!
NYA HA! ME LIKE!
AWE-SOME, RIGHT?
TRMBL TRMBL
THEY'LL SAY THEY LOVE YOU!!
OH MY! HEE HEE! I'M BLUSH-ING!
"I LOVE YOU, ALIBABA! RAVISH ME!!"
Hee hee hee!!

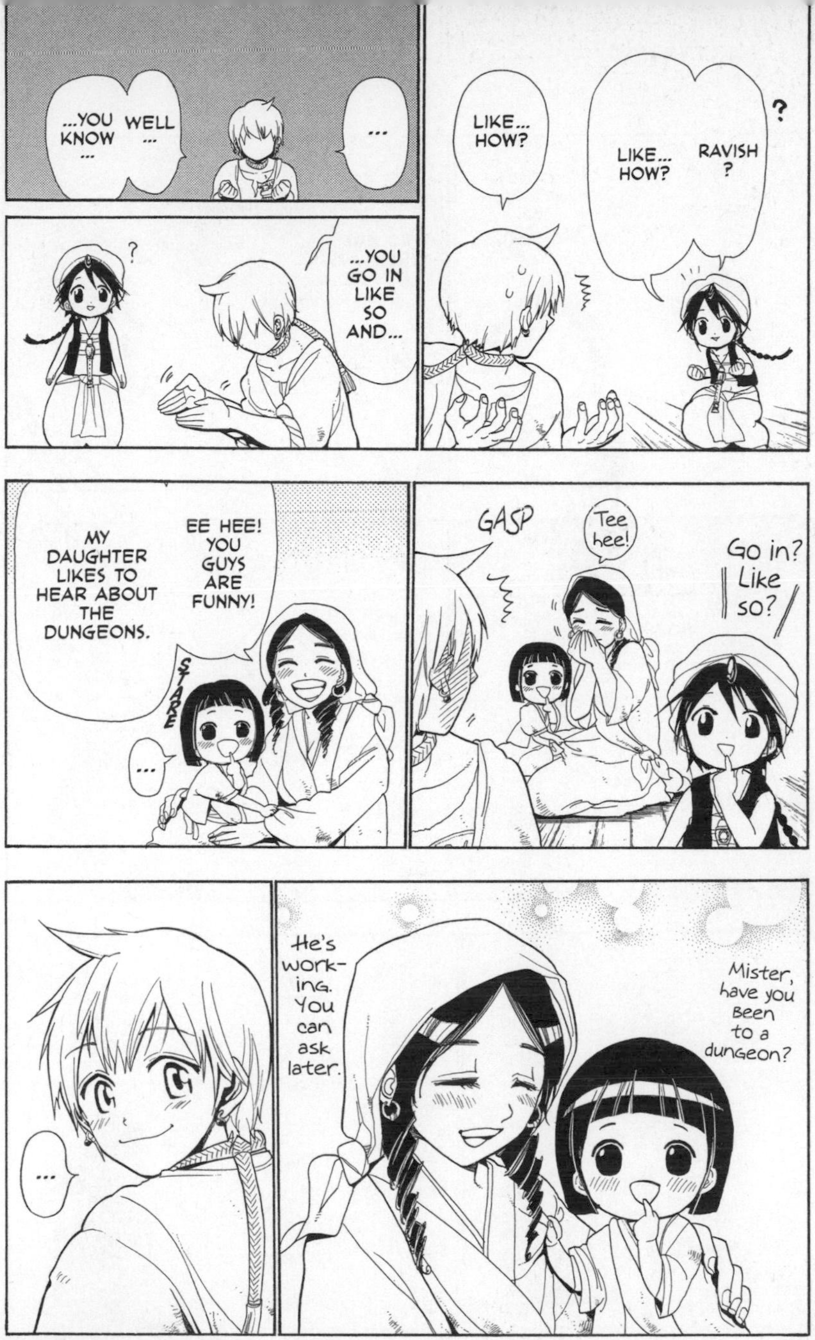
LIKE... HOW?
LIKE... HOW? RAVISH?
...YOU KNOW... WELL...
...
...YOU GO IN LIKE SO AND...
GASP
Tee hee!
Go in? Like so?
EE HEE! YOU GUYS ARE FUNNY!
MY DAUGHTER LIKES TO HEAR ABOUT THE DUNGEONS.
STARE
...
Mister, have you Been to a dungeon?
He's work-ing. You can ask later.
...

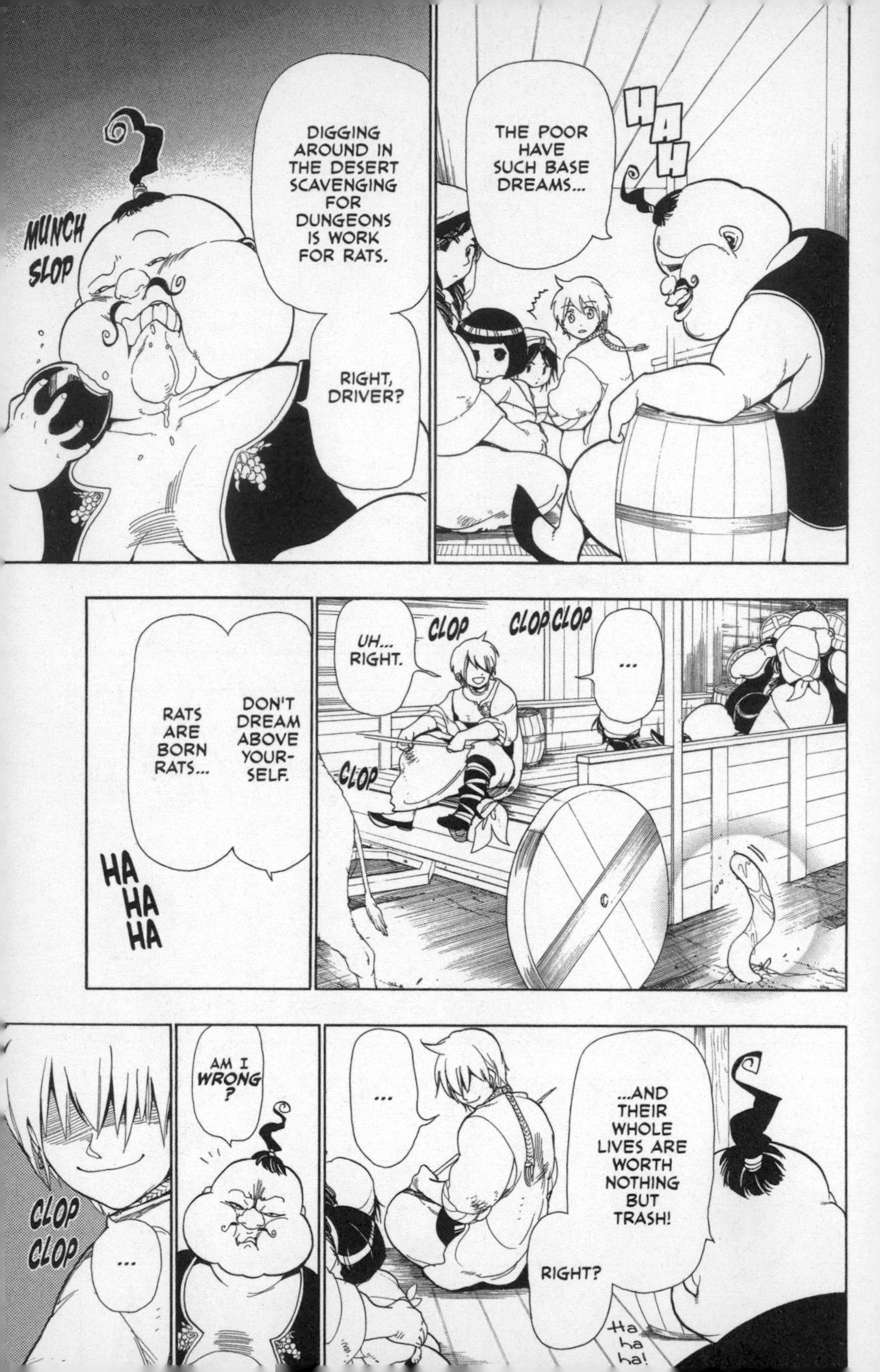
HAHAH
THE POOR HAVE SUCH BASE DREAMS...
DIGGING AROUND IN THE DESERT SCAVENGING FOR DUNGEONS IS WORK FOR RATS.
RIGHT, DRIVER?
MUNCH SLOP
CLOP CLOP
...
CLOP
UH... RIGHT.
CLOP
DON'T DREAM ABOVE YOUR-SELF.
RATS ARE BORN RATS...
HA HA HA
...AND THEIR WHOLE LIVES ARE WORTH NOTHING BUT TRASH!
RIGHT?
Ha ha ha!
...
AM I WRONG?
CLOP CLOP
...

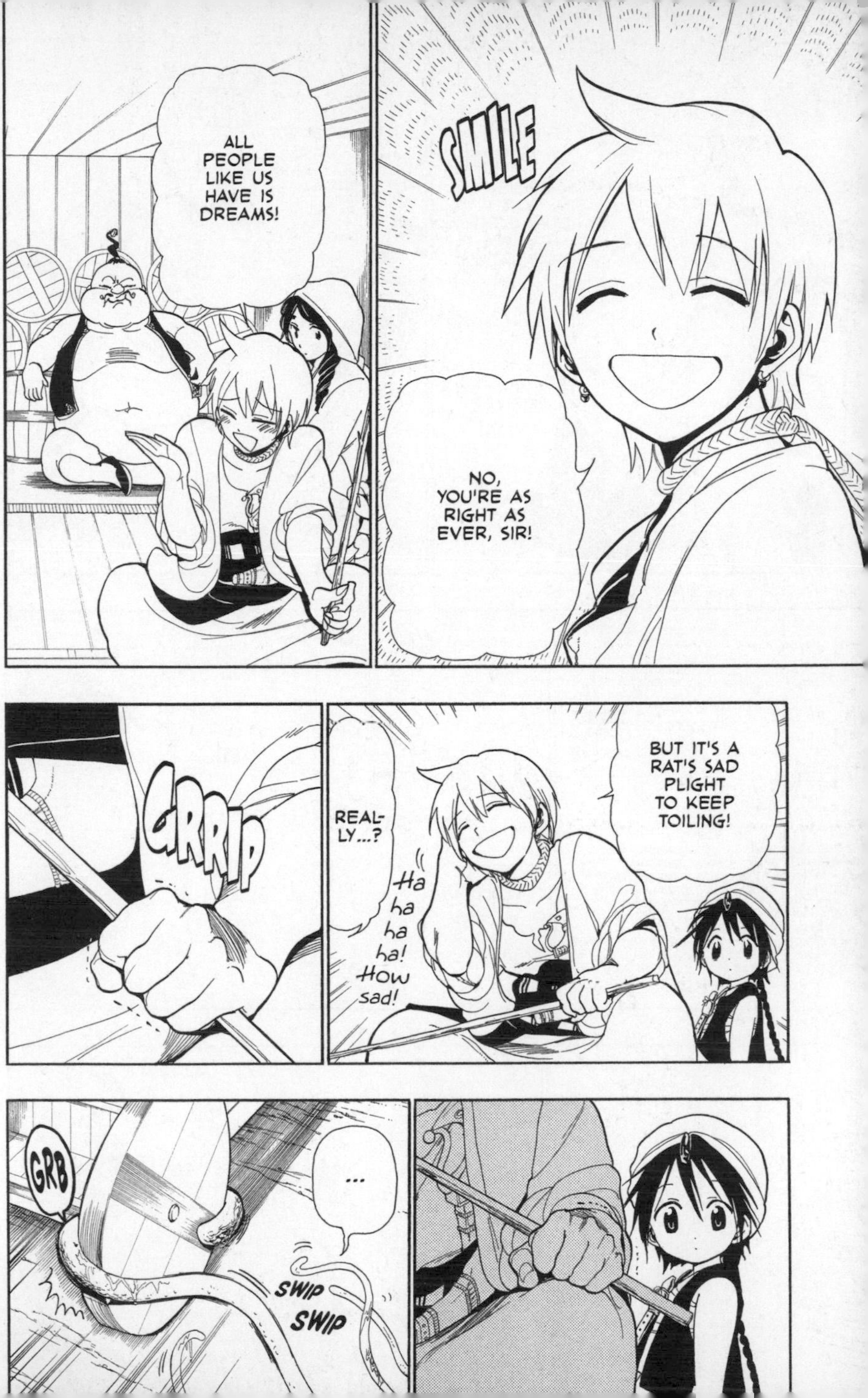
SMILE
NO, YOU'RE AS RIGHT AS EVER, SIR!
ALL PEOPLE LIKE US HAVE IS DREAMS!
BUT IT'S A RAT'S SAD PLIGHT TO KEEP TOILING!
REAL-LY...?
Ha ha ha ha! How sad!
GRRIP
...
GRB
SWIP SWIP

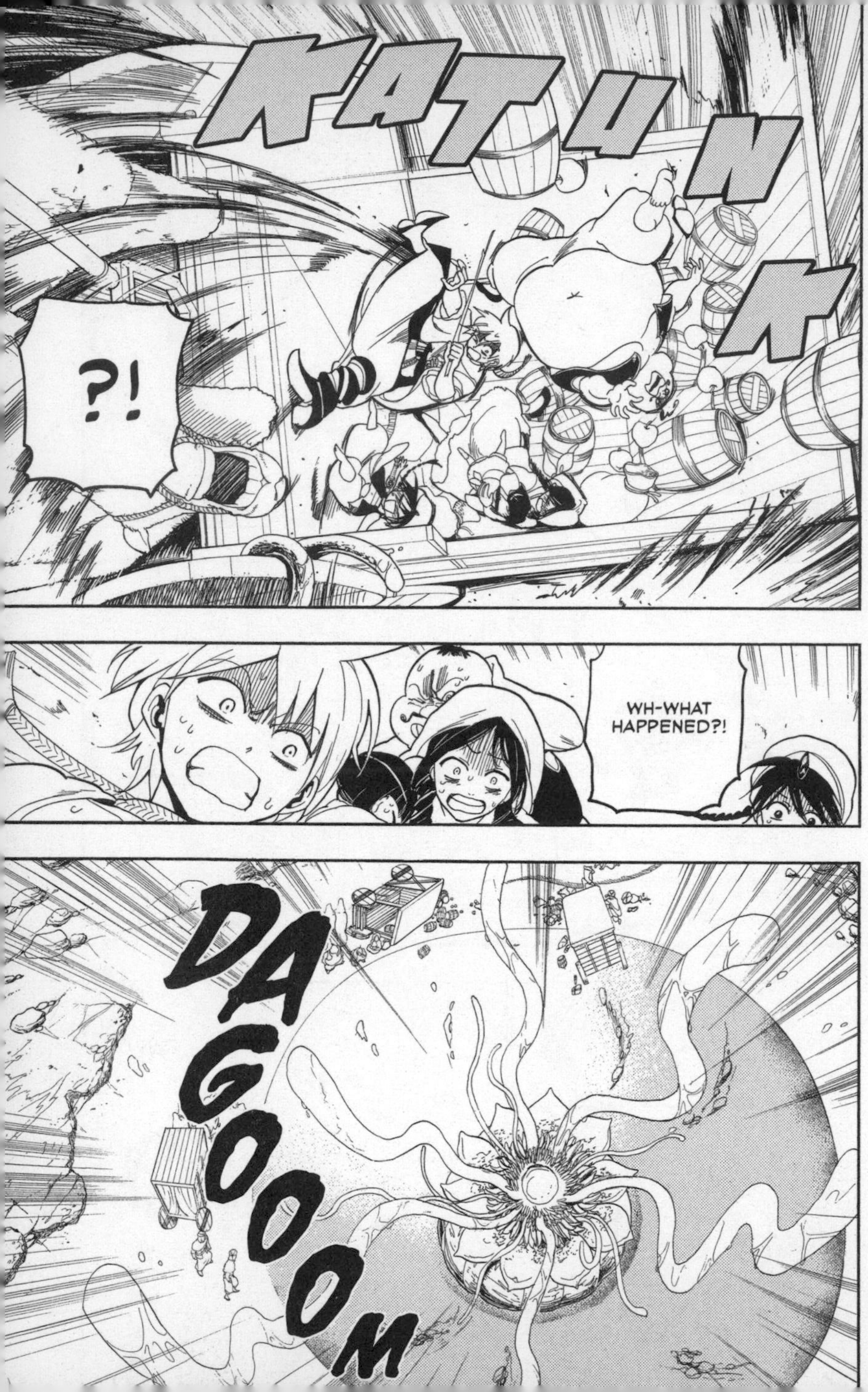
KATUNK
?!
WH-WHAT HAPPENED?!
DAGOOOM

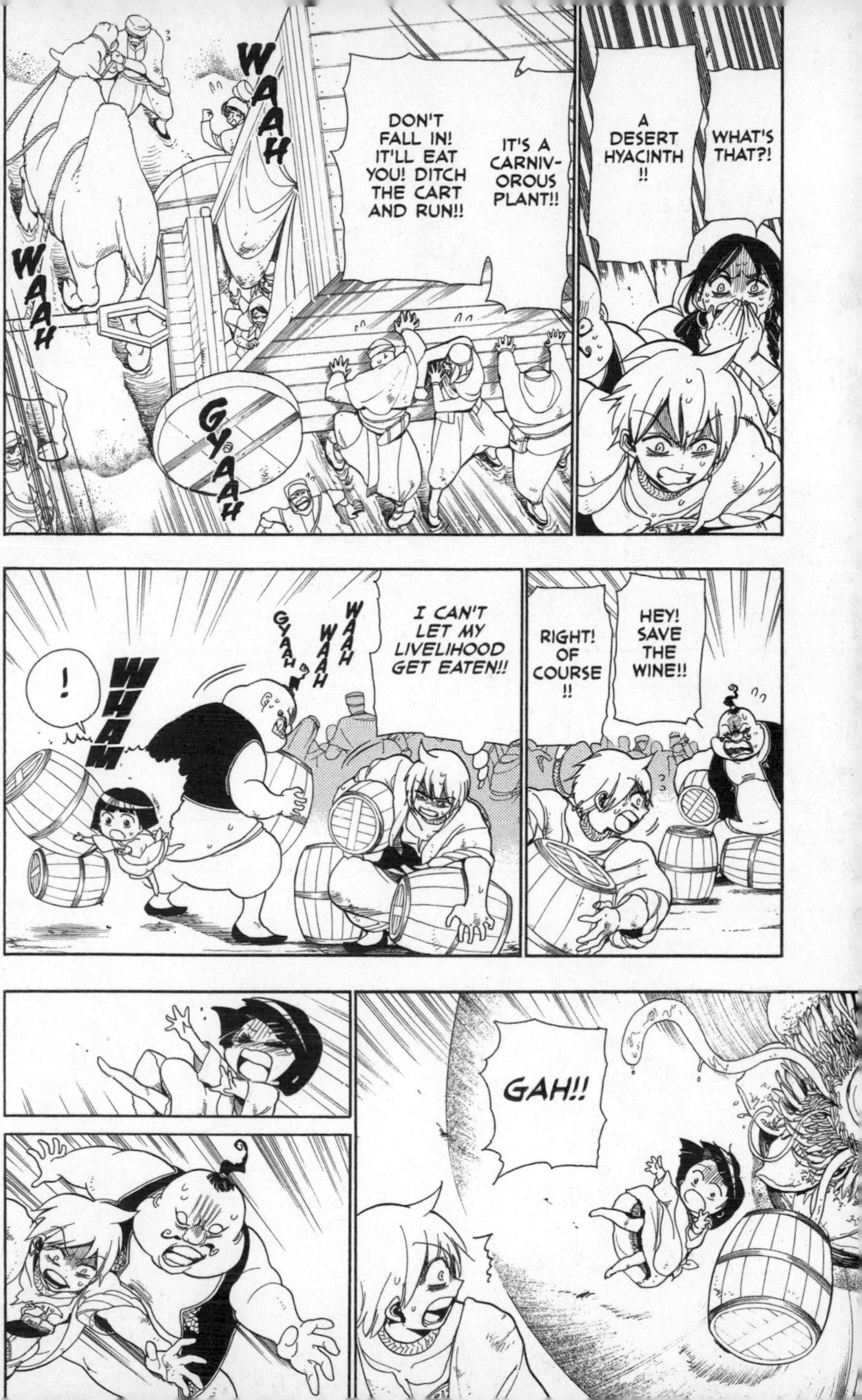
WHAT'S THAT?!
A DESERT HYACINTH !!
IT'S A CARNIVOROUS PLANT!!
DON'T FALL IN! IT'LL EAT YOU! DITCH THE CART AND RUN!!
WAAH
WAAH
GYAAAH
HEY! SAVE THE WINE!!
RIGHT! OF COURSE !!
I CAN'T LET MY LIVELIHOOD GET EATEN!!
WAAH
WAAH
GYAAH
WHAM
!
GAH!!

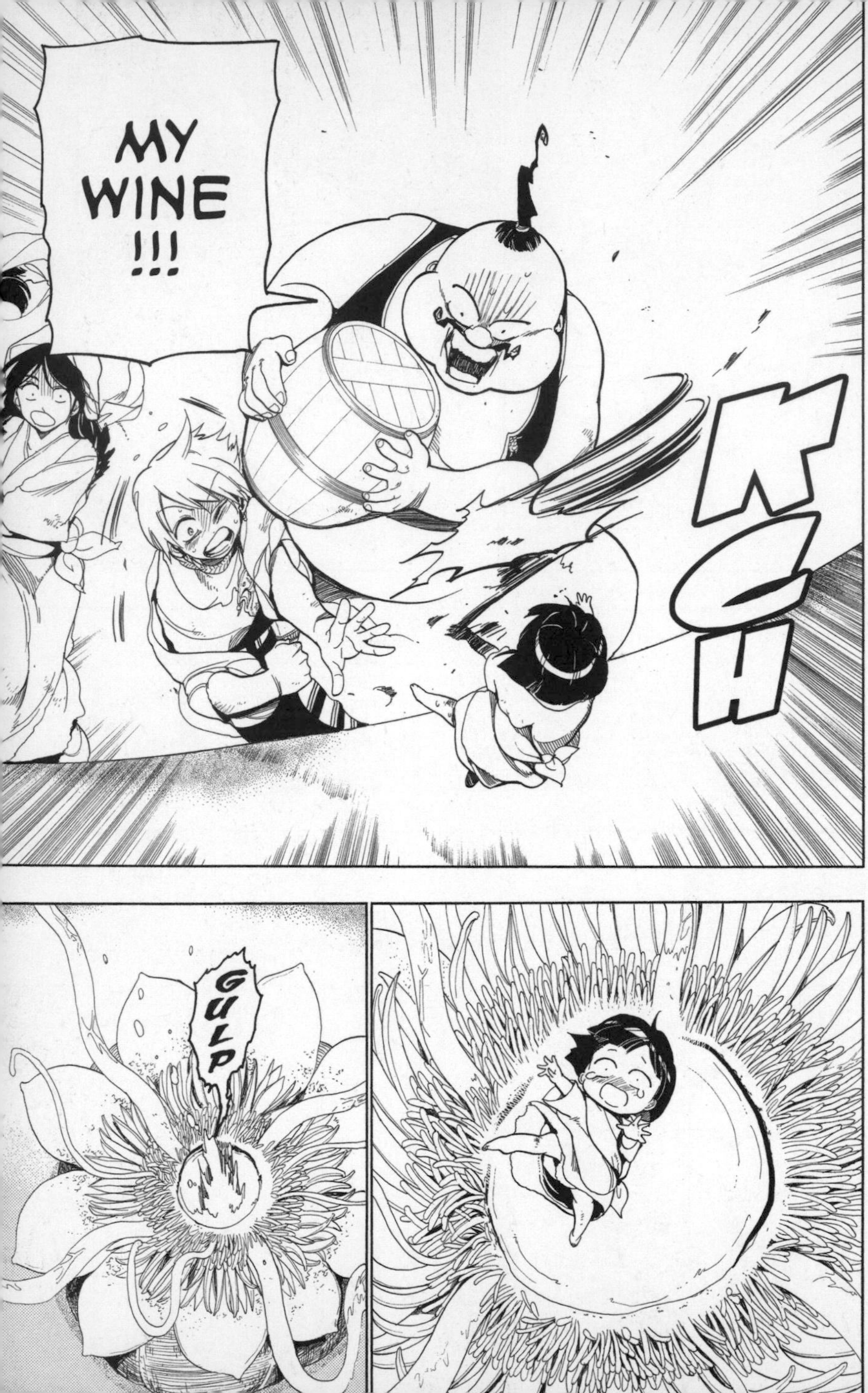
MY WINE !!!
KRCH
GULP

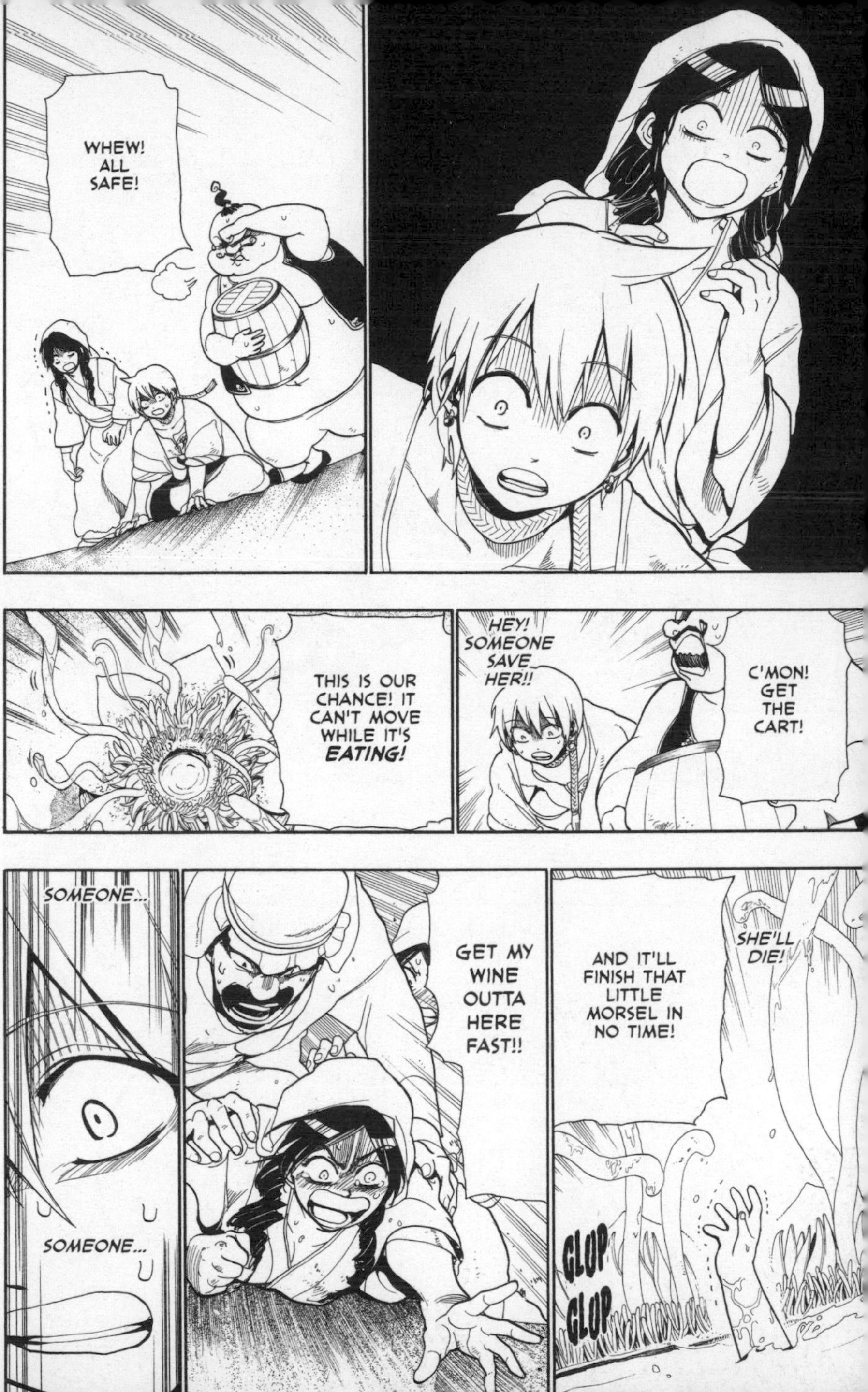
WHEW! ALL SAFE!
C'MON! GET THE CART!
HEY! SOMEONE SAVE HER!!
THIS IS OUR CHANCE! IT CAN'T MOVE WHILE IT'S *EATING!*
SHE'LL DIE!
AND IT'LL FINISH THAT LITTLE MORSEL IN NO TIME!
GLUP
GLUP
GET MY WINE OUTTA HERE FAST!!
SOMEONE...
SOMEONE...

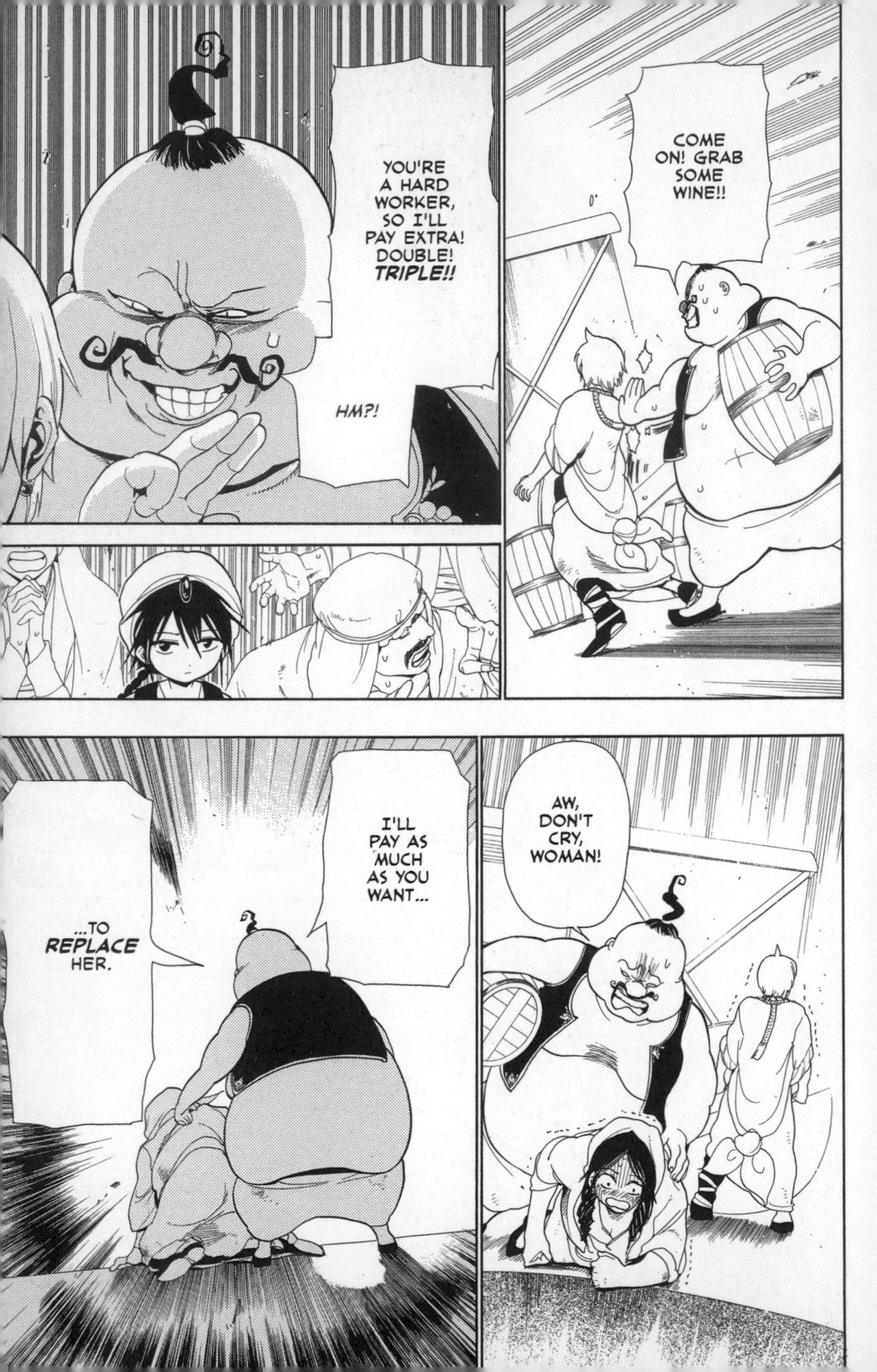
COME ON! GRAB SOME WINE!!
YOU'RE A HARD WORKER, SO I'LL PAY EXTRA! DOUBLE! *TRIPLE!!*
HM?!
AW, DON'T CRY, WOMAN!
I'LL PAY AS MUCH AS YOU WANT...
...TO *REPLACE* HER.

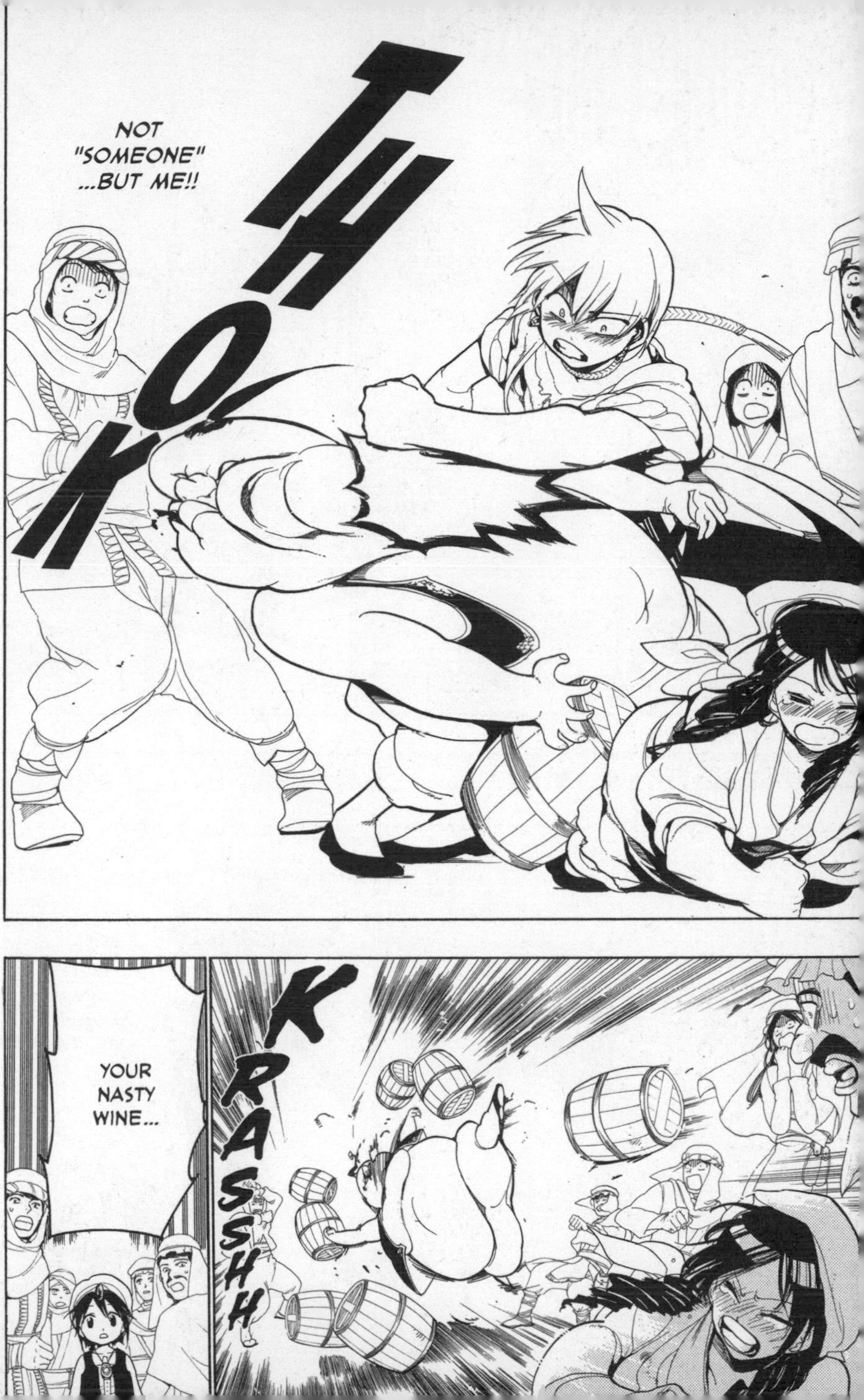
THOK
NOT "SOMEONE" ...BUT ME!!
KRASSHH
YOUR NASTY WINE...

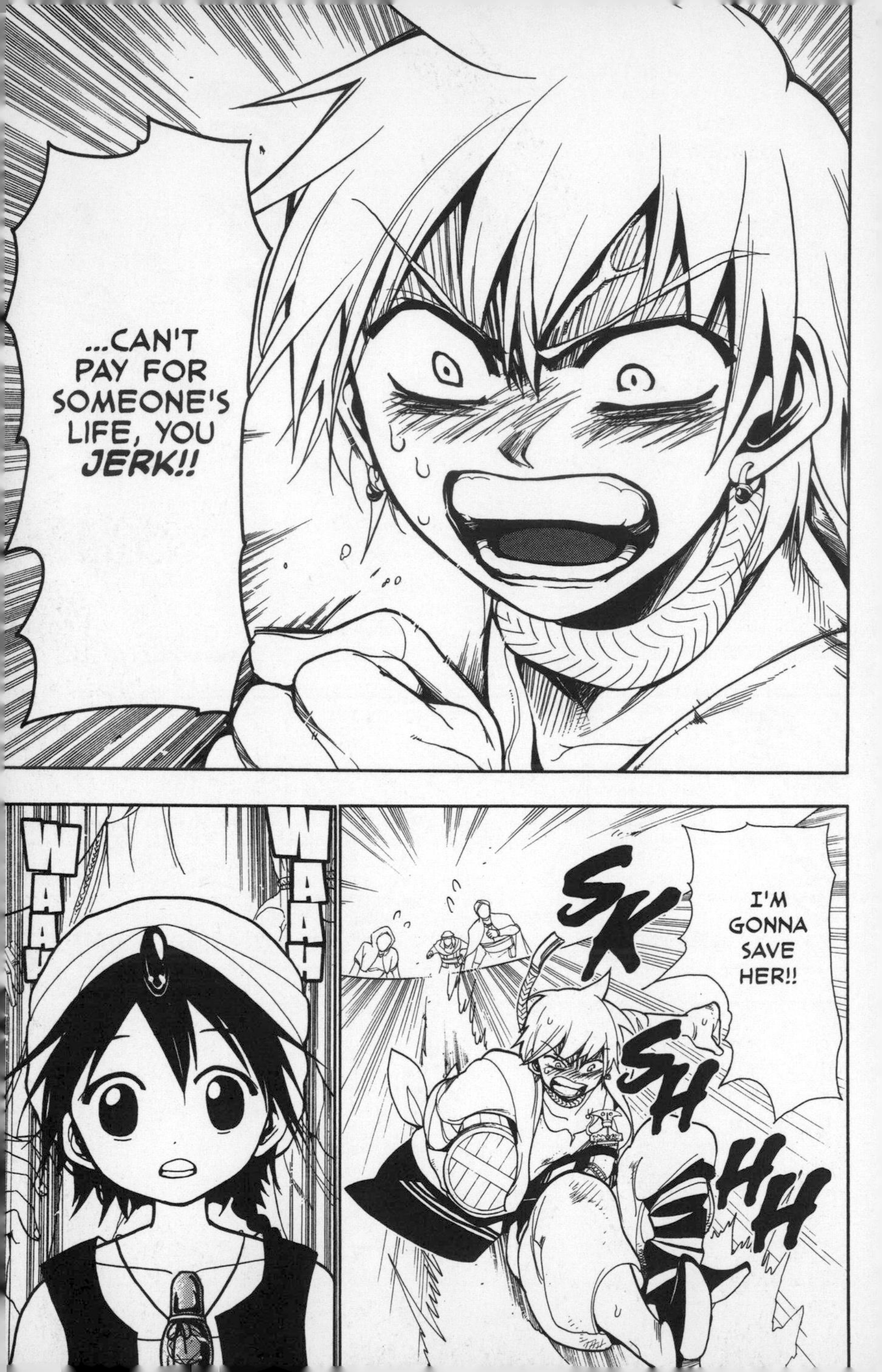
...CAN'T PAY FOR SOMEONE'S LIFE, YOU JERK!!
I'M GONNA SAVE HER!!
SKSHHHH
WAAAH
WAAA

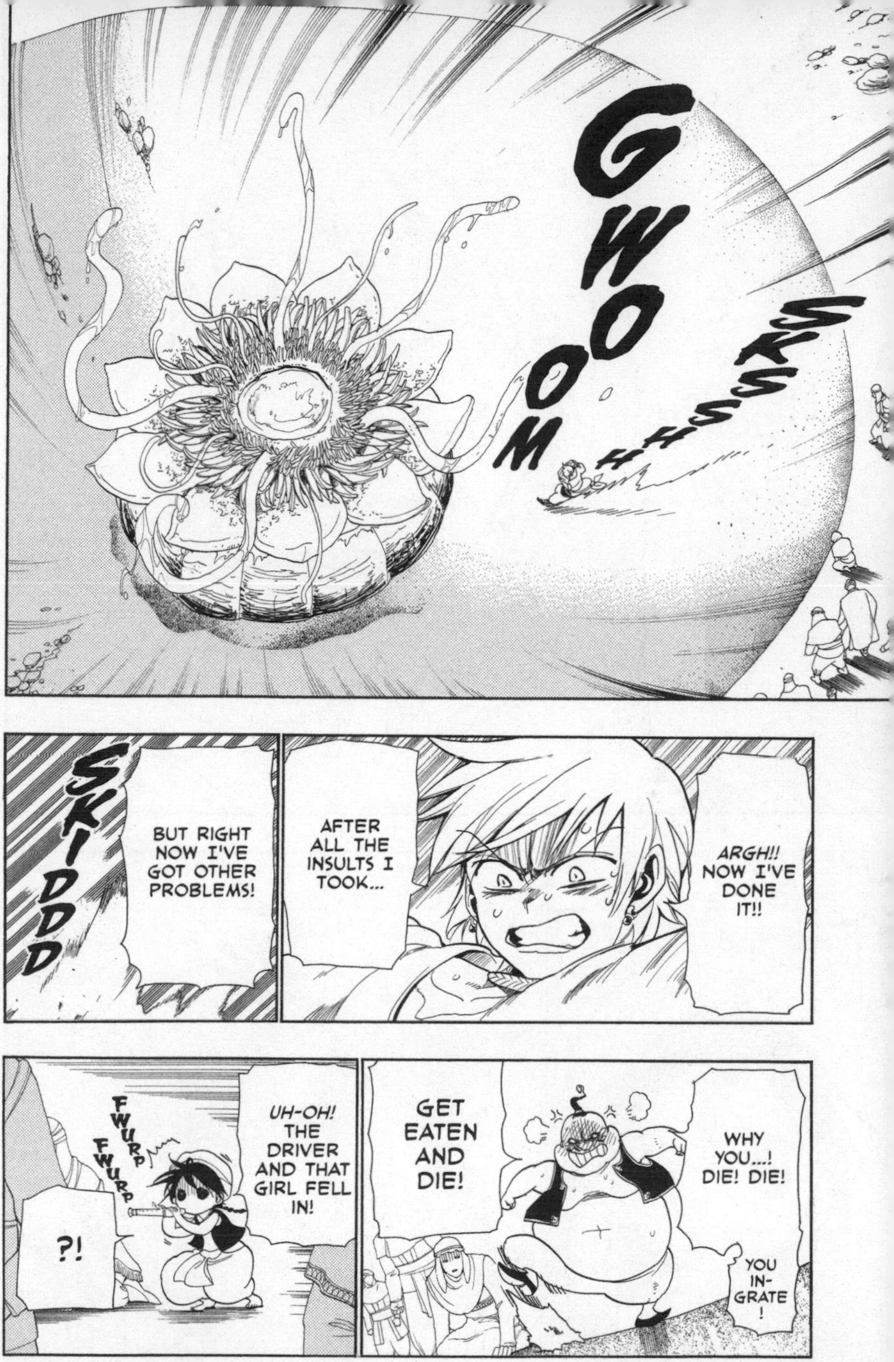
GWOOOM
SKSSSHH
ARGH!! NOW I'VE DONE IT!!
AFTER ALL THE INSULTS I TOOK...
BUT RIGHT NOW I'VE GOT OTHER PROBLEMS!
SKIDDDD
WHY YOU...! DIE! DIE!
YOU IN-GRATE!
GET EATEN AND DIE!
UH-OH! THE DRIVER AND THAT GIRL FELL IN!
FWURP FWURP
?!

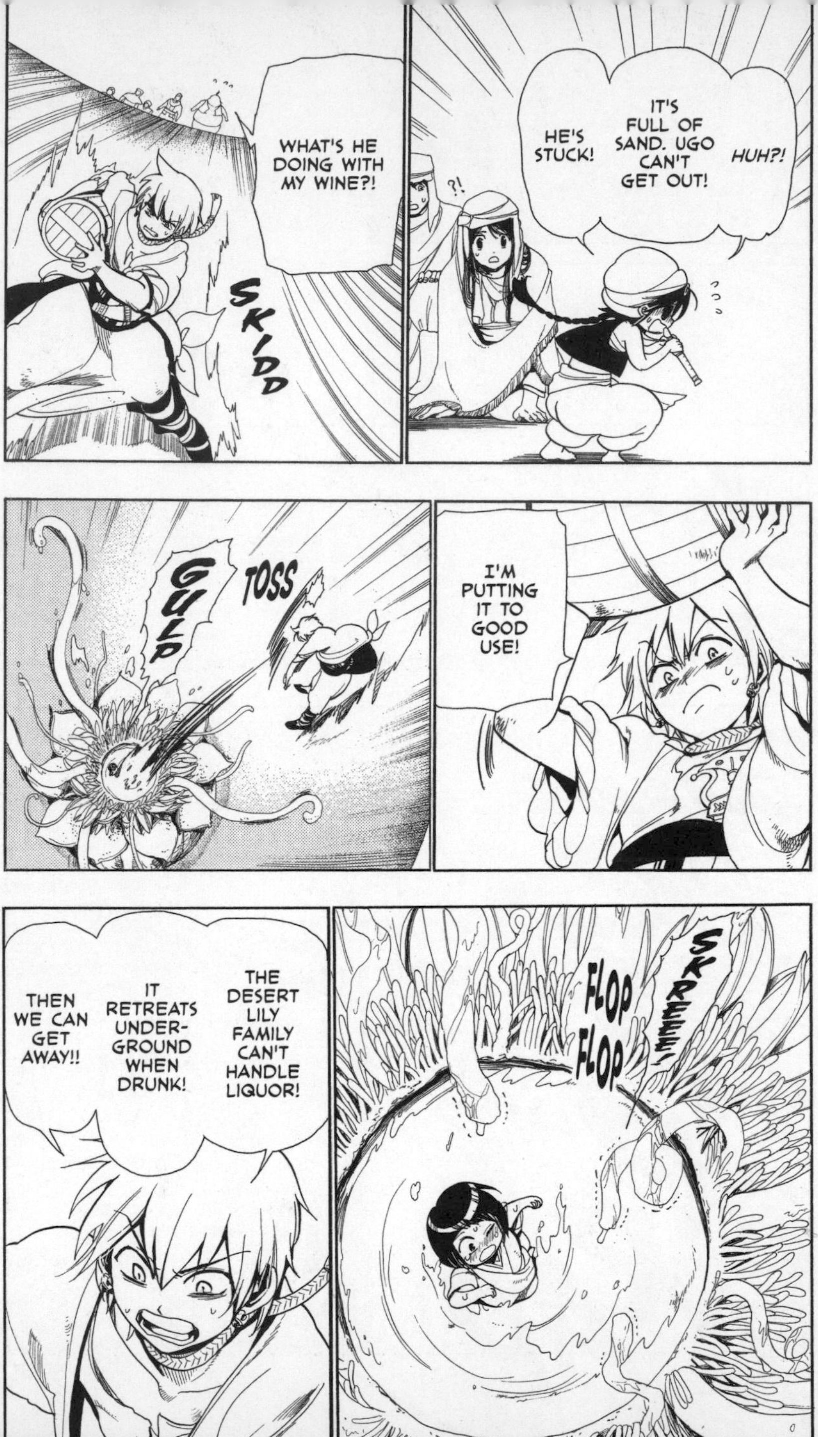
HUH?!
IT'S FULL OF SAND. UGO CAN'T GET OUT!
HE'S STUCK!
?!
WHAT'S HE DOING WITH MY WINE?!
SKIDD
I'M PUTTING IT TO GOOD USE!
TOSS
GULP
SKREEE!
FLOP FLOP
THE DESERT LILY FAMILY CAN'T HANDLE LIQUOR!
IT RETREATS UNDER-GROUND WHEN DRUNK!
THEN WE CAN GET AWAY!!

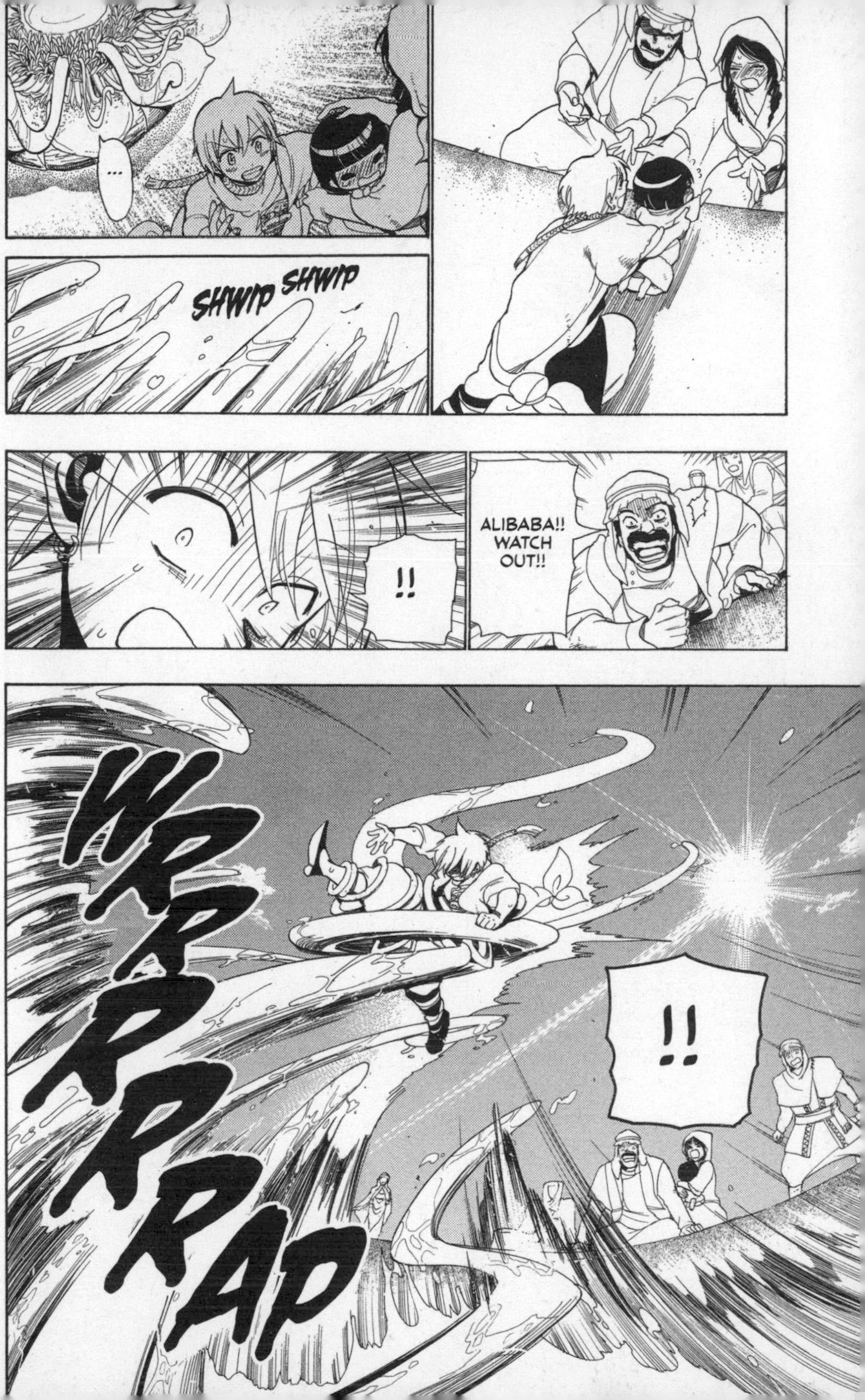
...
SHWIP SHWIP
ALIBABA!! WATCH OUT!!
!!
!!
WRRRRRAP

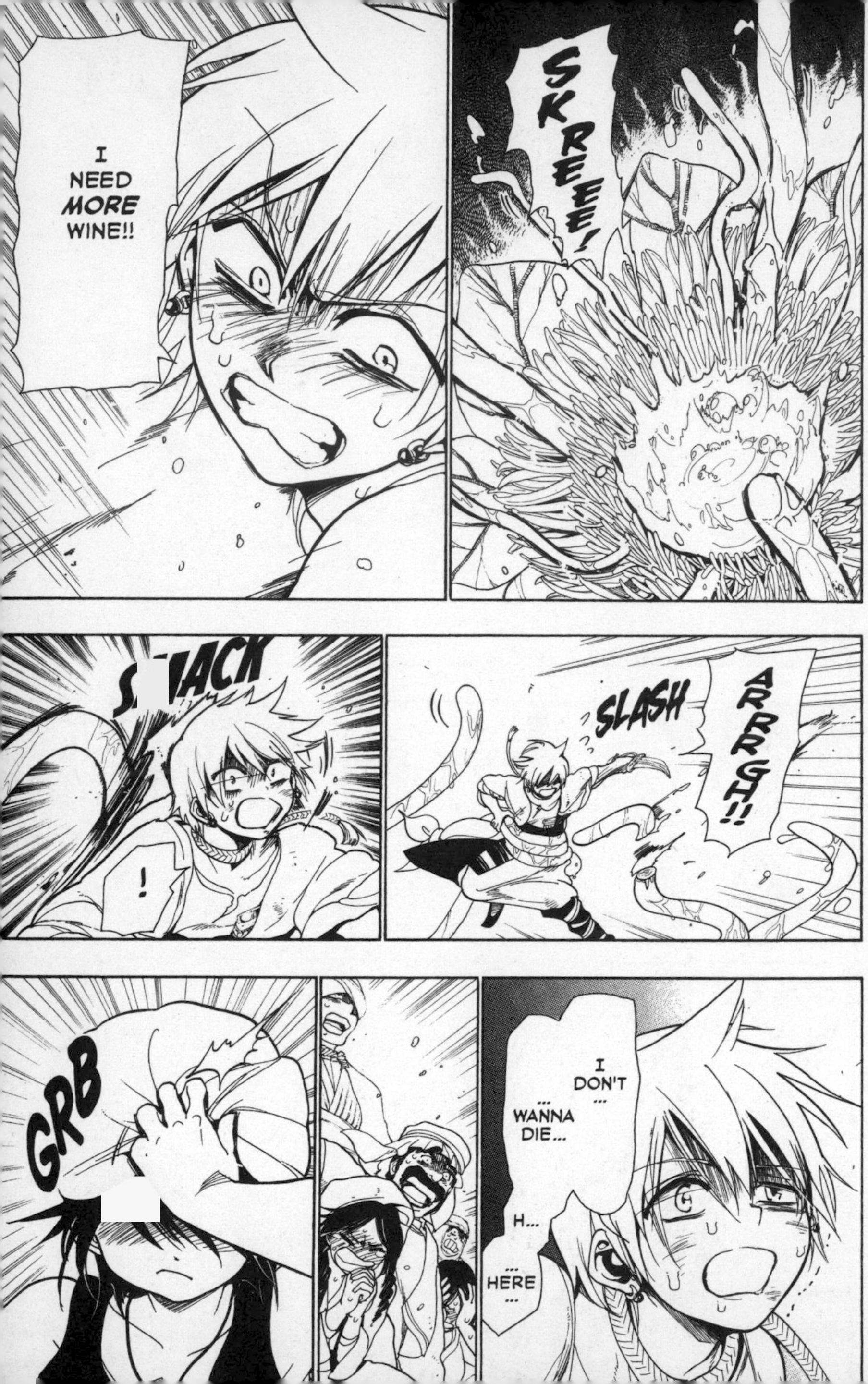

SKREEE!
I NEED MORE WINE!!
ARRRGH!!
SLASH
S ACK
!
I DON'T ... ... WANNA DIE...
H... ... HERE ...
GRB

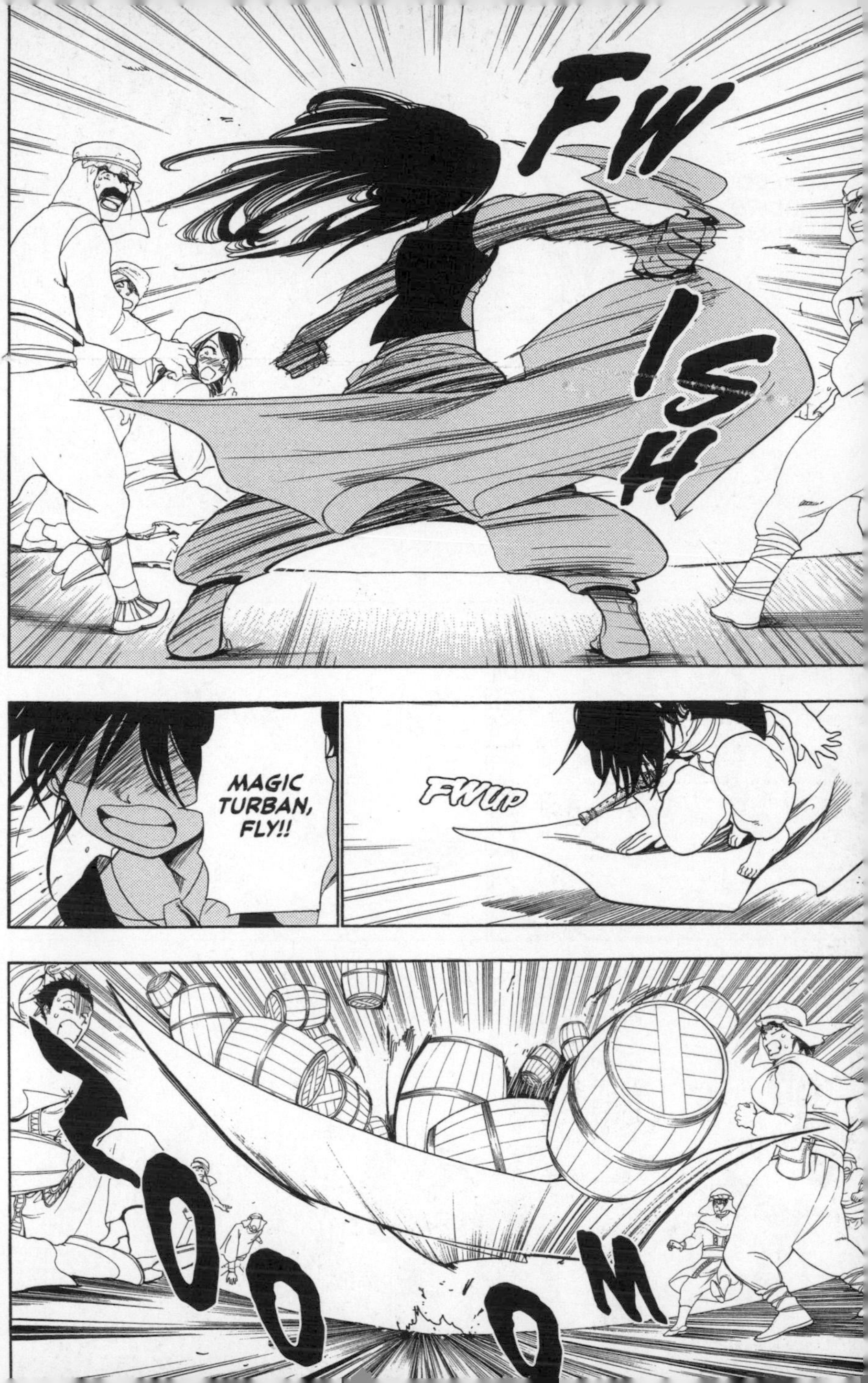
FWISH
FWUP
MAGIC TURBAN, FLY!!
OOOM

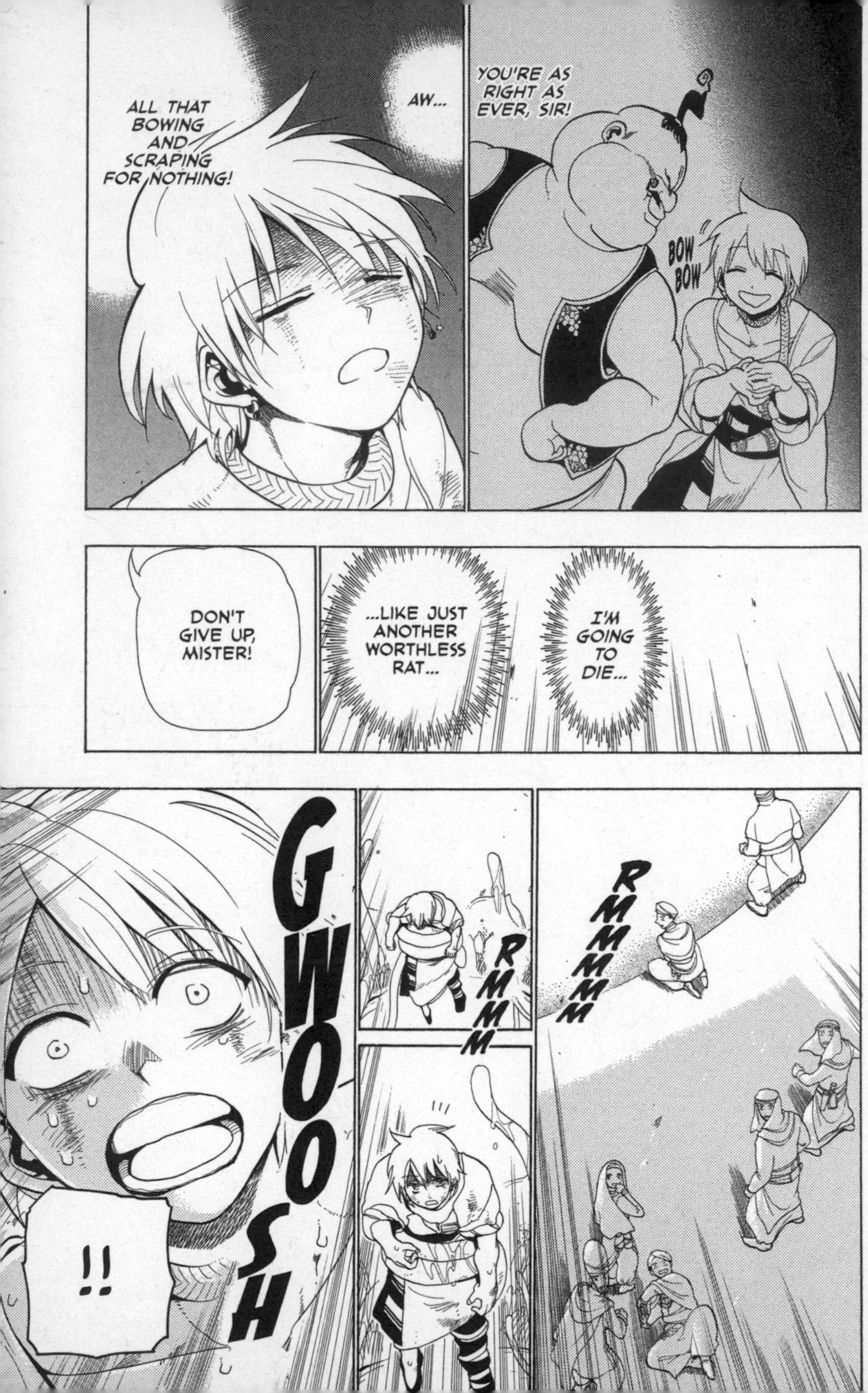
YOU'RE AS RIGHT AS EVER, SIR!
BOW BOW
AW...
ALL THAT BOWING AND SCRAPING FOR NOTHING!
I'M GOING TO DIE...
...LIKE JUST ANOTHER WORTHLESS RAT...
DON'T GIVE UP, MISTER!
RMMMMMM
RMMM
GWOOSH
!!

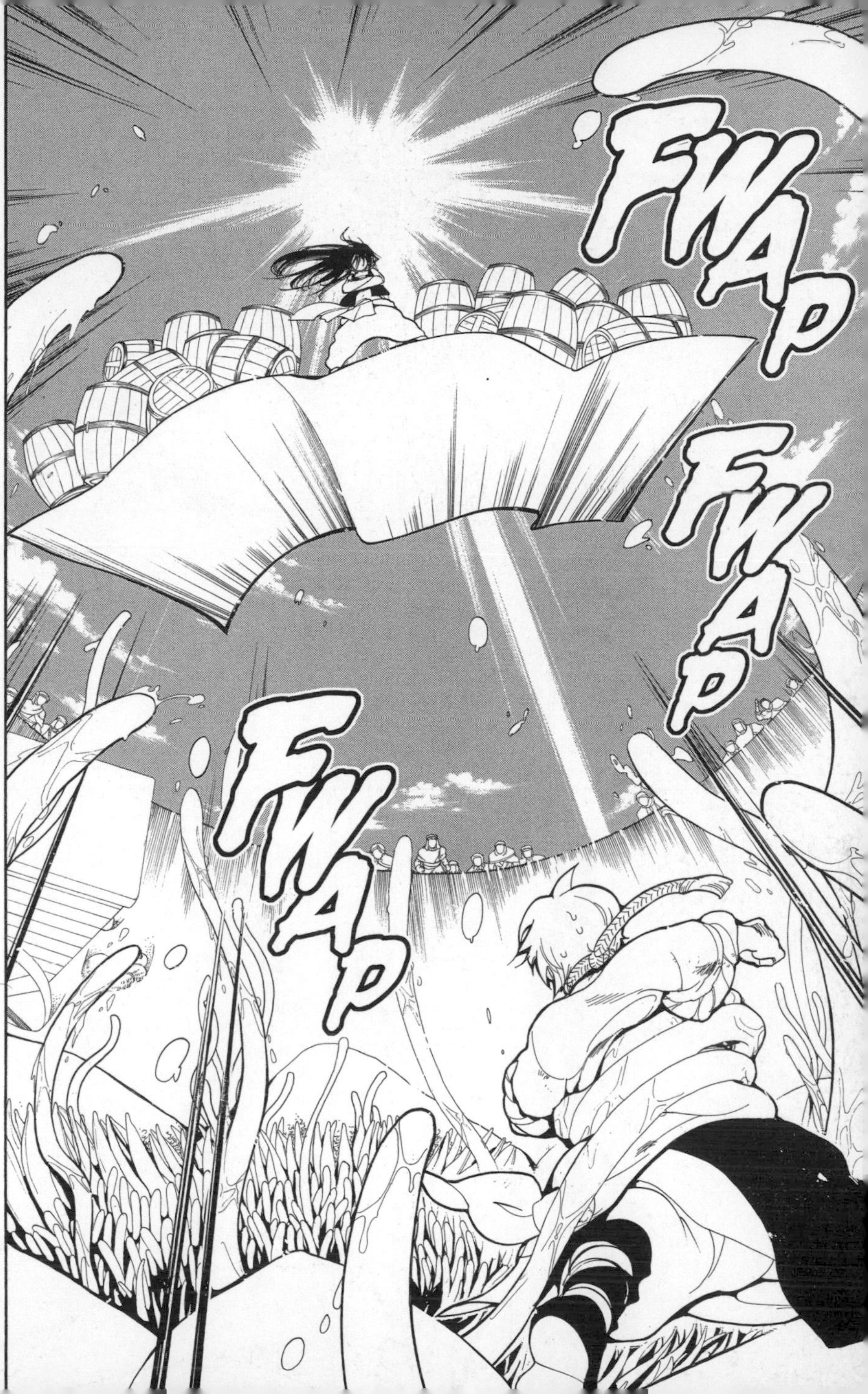
FWAP
FWAP
FWAP

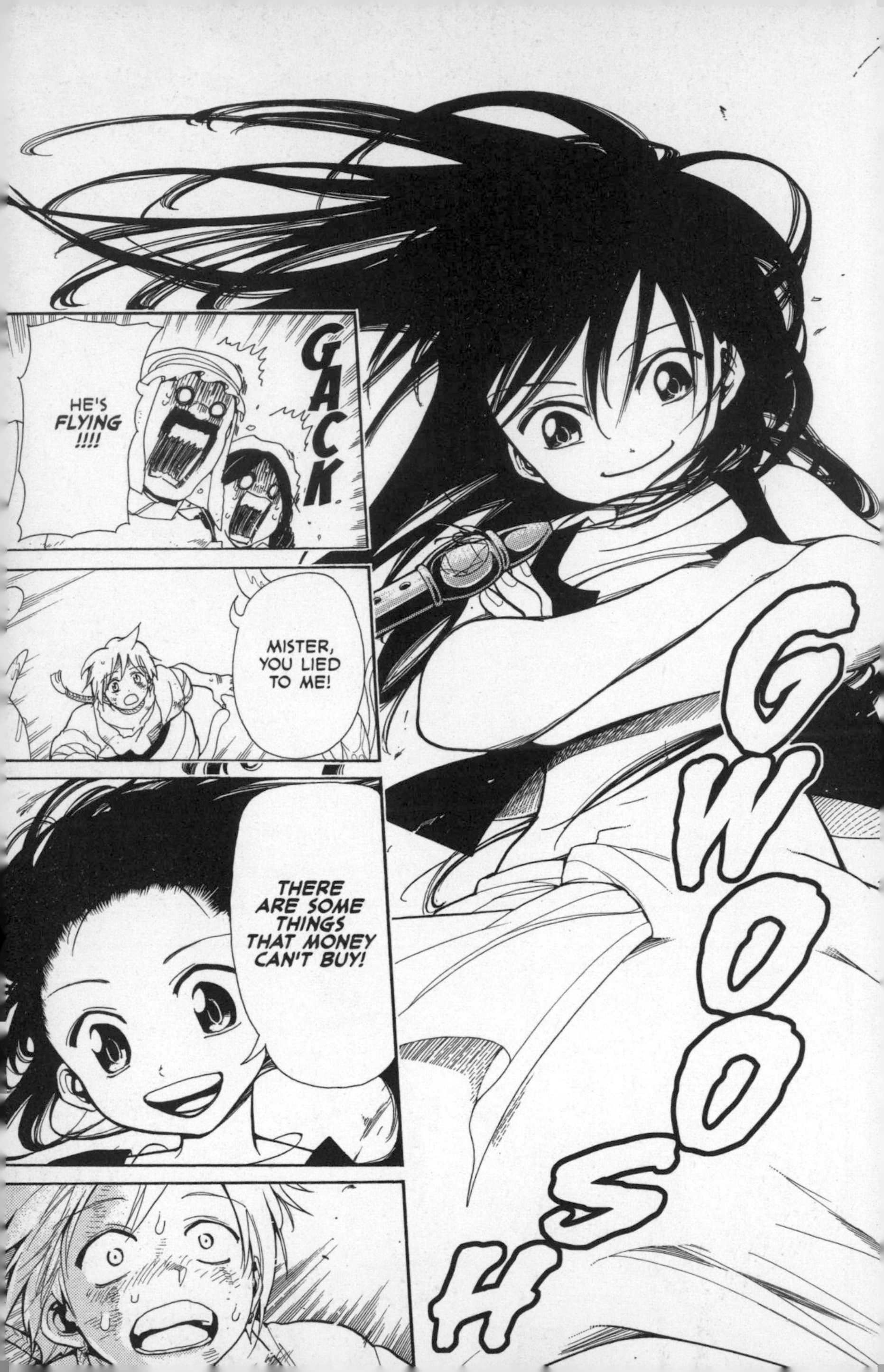
GWOOSH
GACK
HE'S FLYING!!!!
MISTER, YOU LIED TO ME!
THERE ARE SOME THINGS THAT MONEY CAN'T BUY!

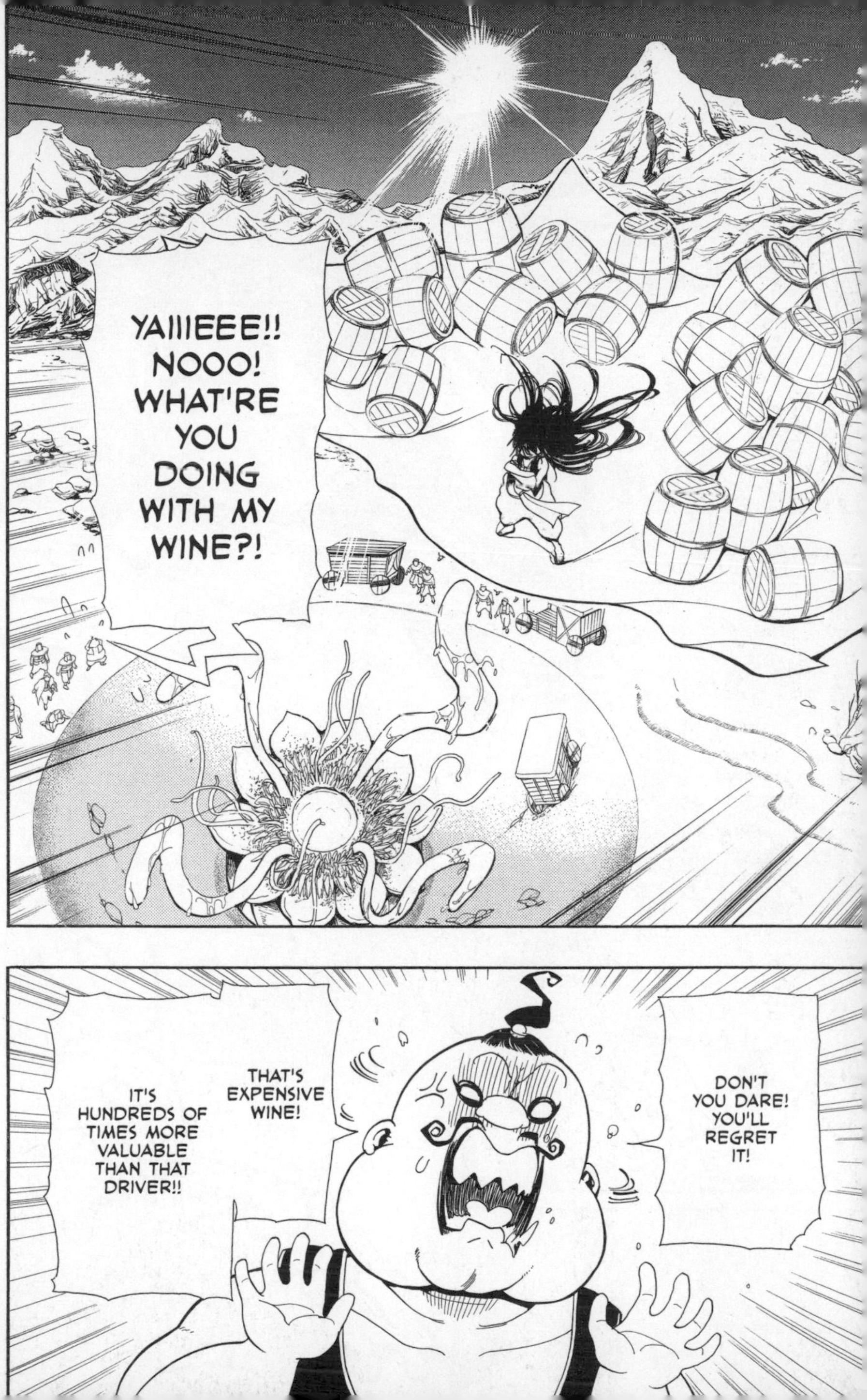
YAIIIEEE!! NOOO! WHAT'RE YOU DOING WITH MY WINE?!
DON'T YOU DARE! YOU'LL REGRET IT!
THAT'S EXPENSIVE WINE!
IT'S HUNDREDS OF TIMES MORE VALUABLE THAN THAT DRIVER!!

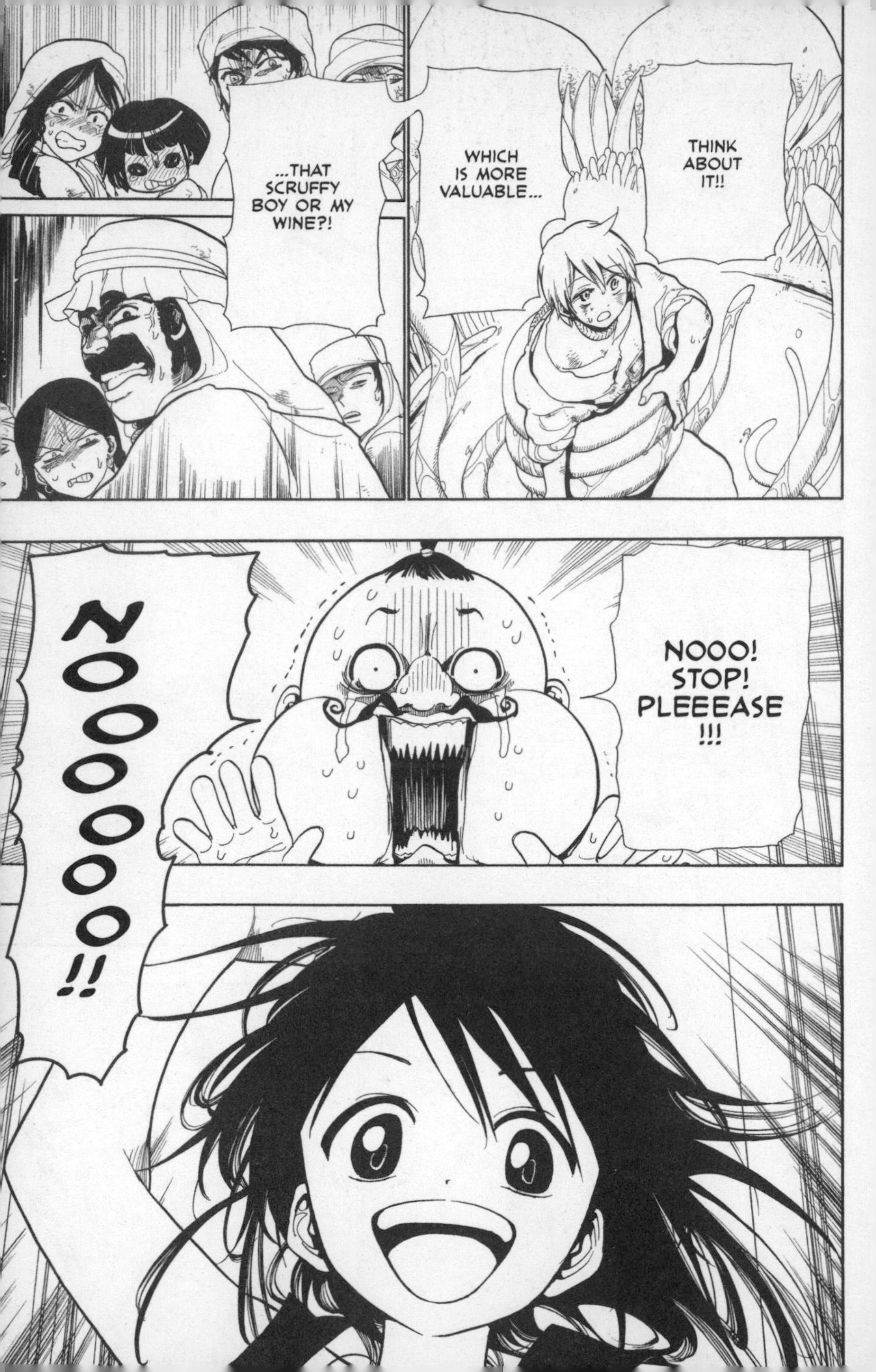
THINK ABOUT IT!!
WHICH IS MORE VALUABLE...
...THAT SCRUFFY BOY OR MY WINE?!
NOOO! STOP! PLEEEASE !!!
NOOOOOO!!

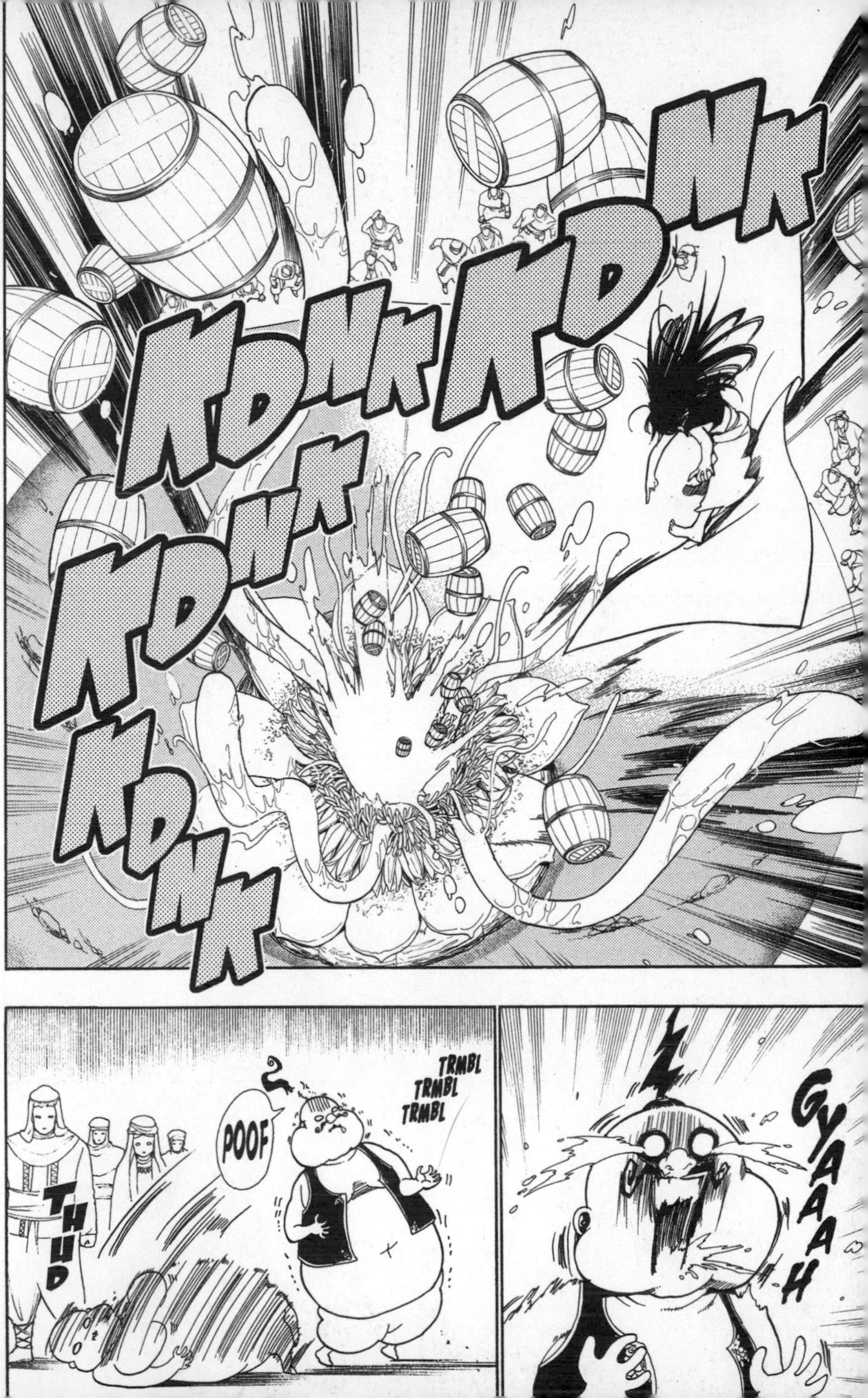
KDONK
KDONK
KDONK
KDONK
GYAAAAH
TRMBL TRMBL TRMBL
POOF
THUD

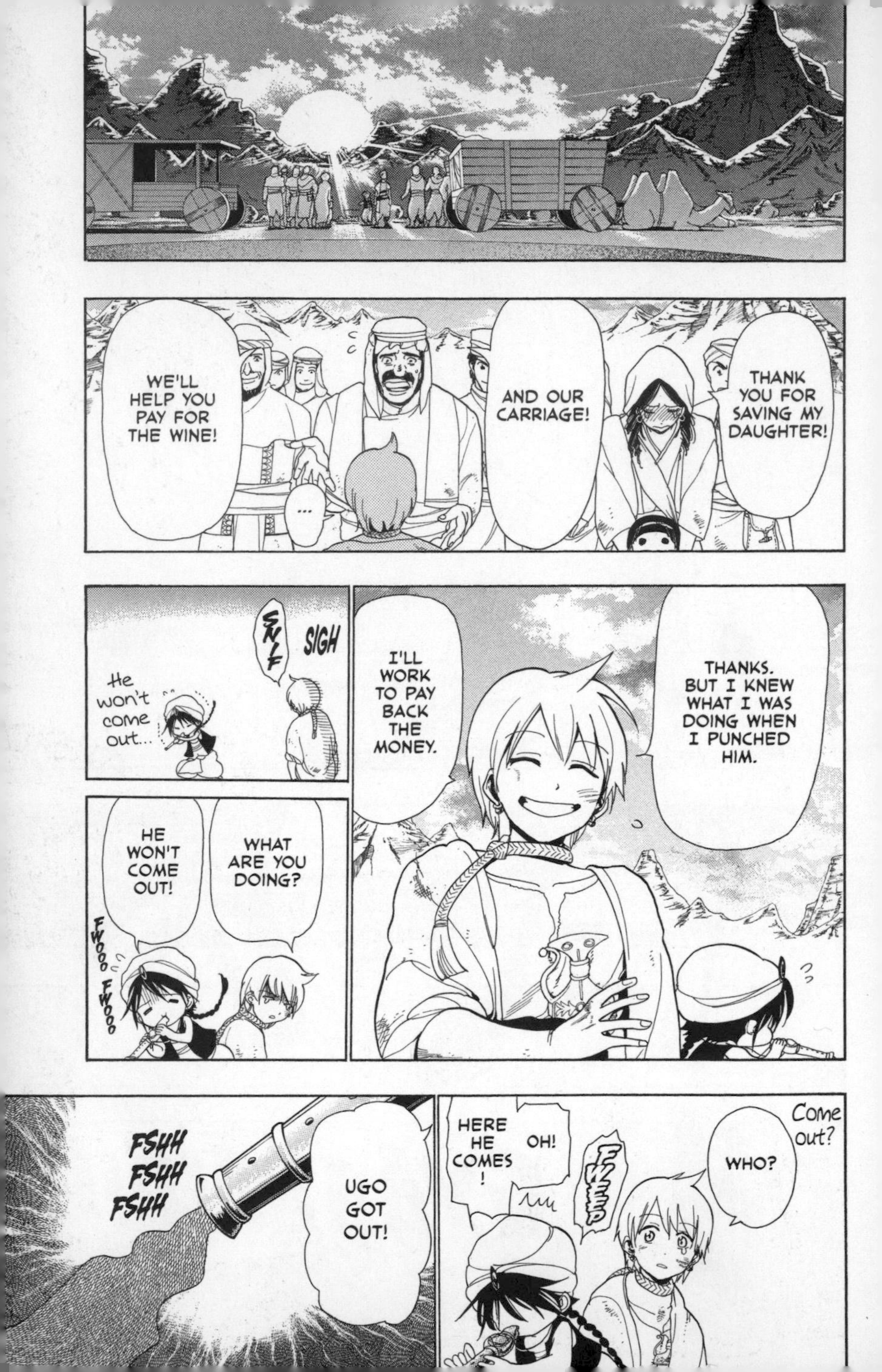
THANK YOU FOR SAVING MY DAUGHTER!
AND OUR CARRIAGE!
WE'LL HELP YOU PAY FOR THE WINE!
...
THANKS. BUT I KNEW WHAT I WAS DOING WHEN I PUNCHED HIM.
I'LL WORK TO PAY BACK THE MONEY.
SIGH
SNIF
He won't come out...
WHAT ARE YOU DOING?
HE WON'T COME OUT!
FWOOO FWOOO
Come out?
WHO?
OH!
HERE HE COMES!
UGO GOT OUT!
FSHH FSHH FSHH

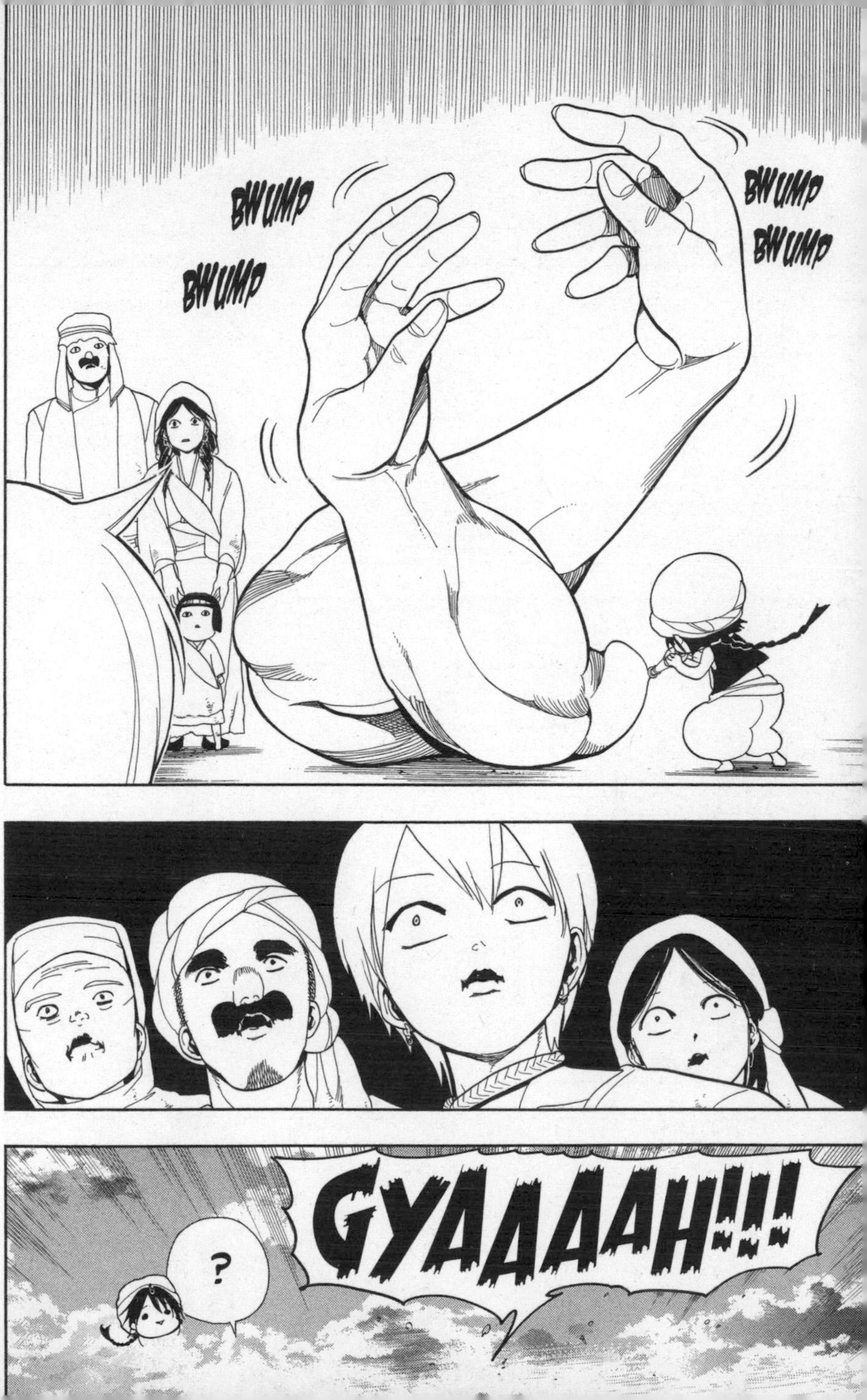
BWUMP
BWUMP
BWUMP
BWUMP
GYAAAH!!!
?

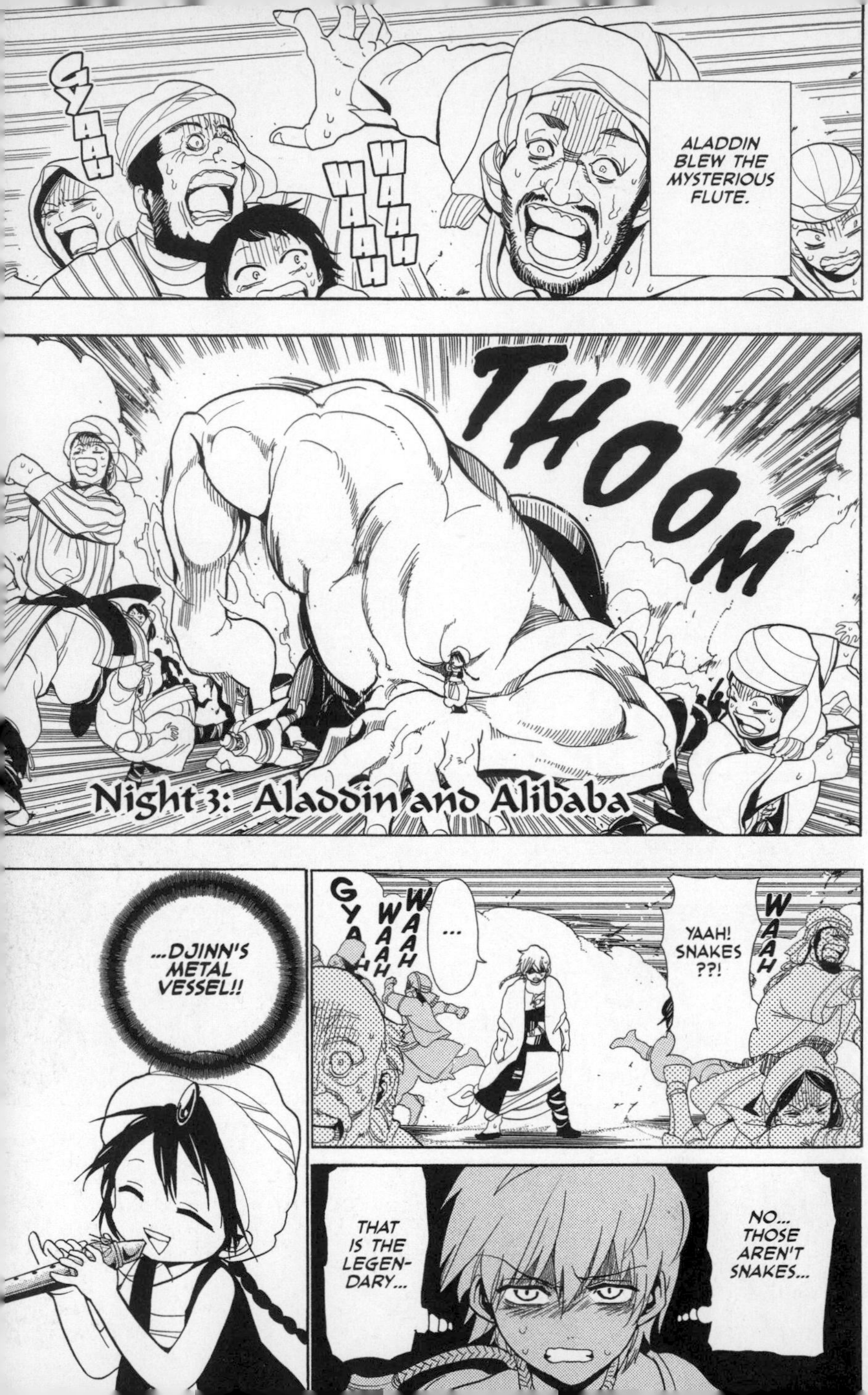
ALADDIN BLEW THE MYSTERIOUS FLUTE.
WAAH
WAAH
GYAAAH
THOOM
Night 3: Aladdin and Alibaba
WAAH
YAAH! SNAKES ??!
...
WAAH
WAAH
GYAAH
NO... THOSE AREN'T SNAKES...
THAT IS THE LEGEN-DARY...
...DJINN'S METAL VESSEL!!

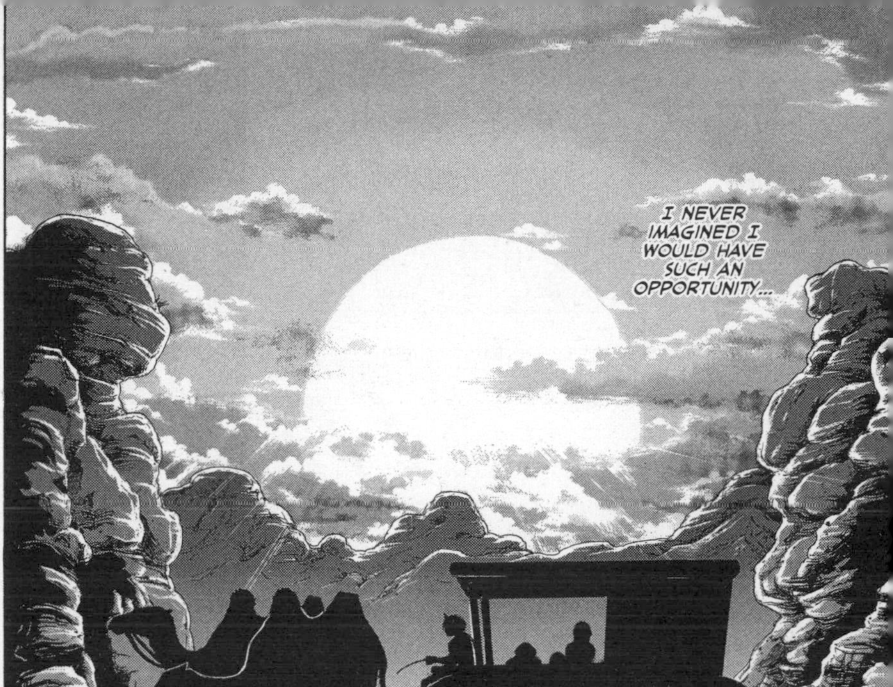
I NEVER IMAGINED I WOULD HAVE SUCH AN OPPORTUNITY...
Night 3: Aladdin and Alibaba

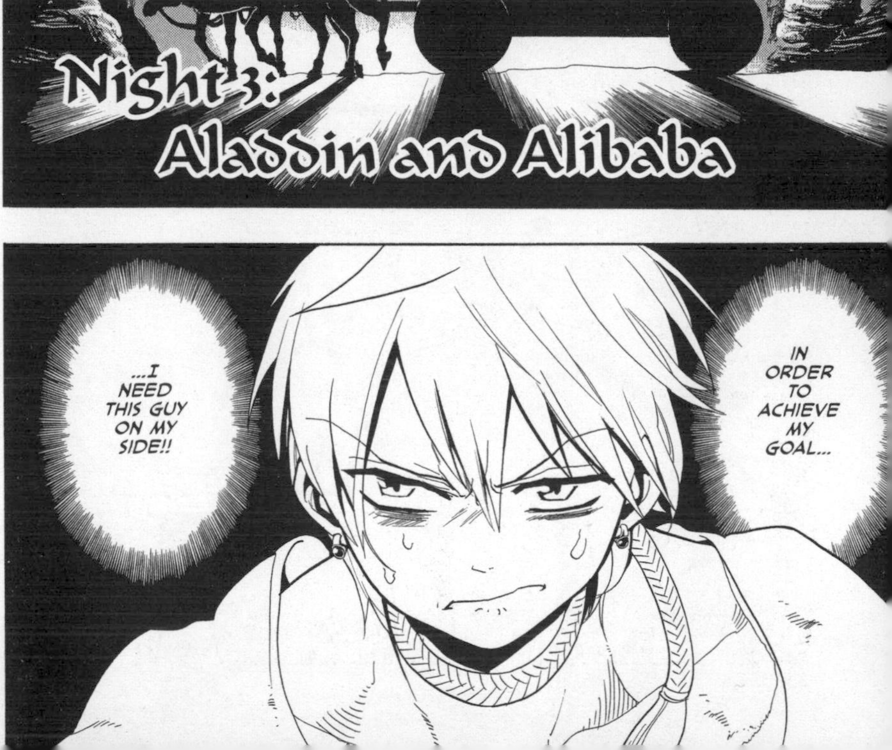
IN ORDER TO ACHIEVE MY GOAL...
...I NEED THIS GUY ON MY SIDE!!

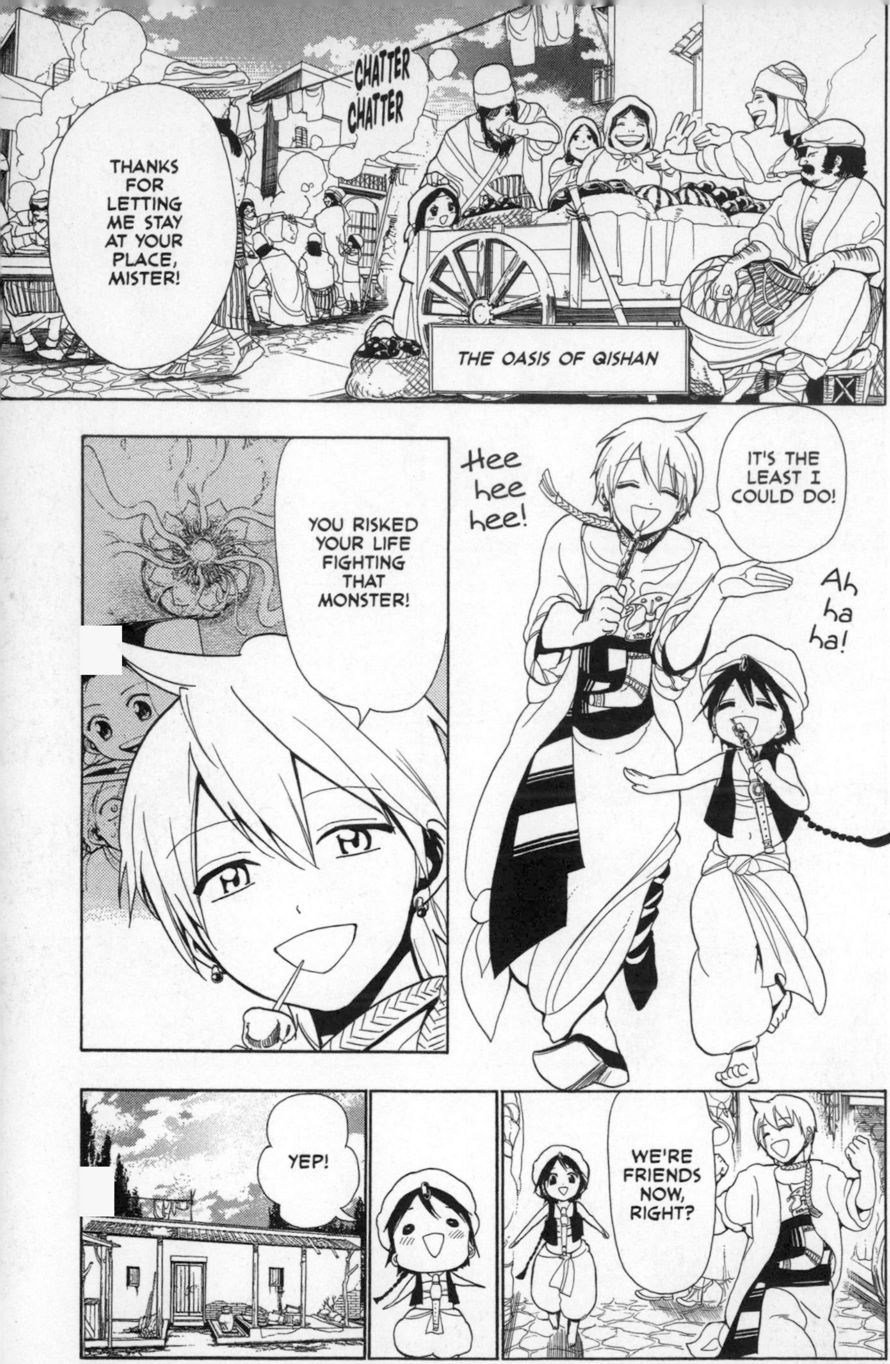
CHATTER CHATTER
THANKS FOR LETTING ME STAY AT YOUR PLACE, MISTER!
THE OASIS OF QISHAN
Hee hee hee!
IT'S THE LEAST I COULD DO!
Ah ha ha!
YOU RISKED YOUR LIFE FIGHTING THAT MONSTER!
WE'RE FRIENDS NOW, RIGHT?
YEP!

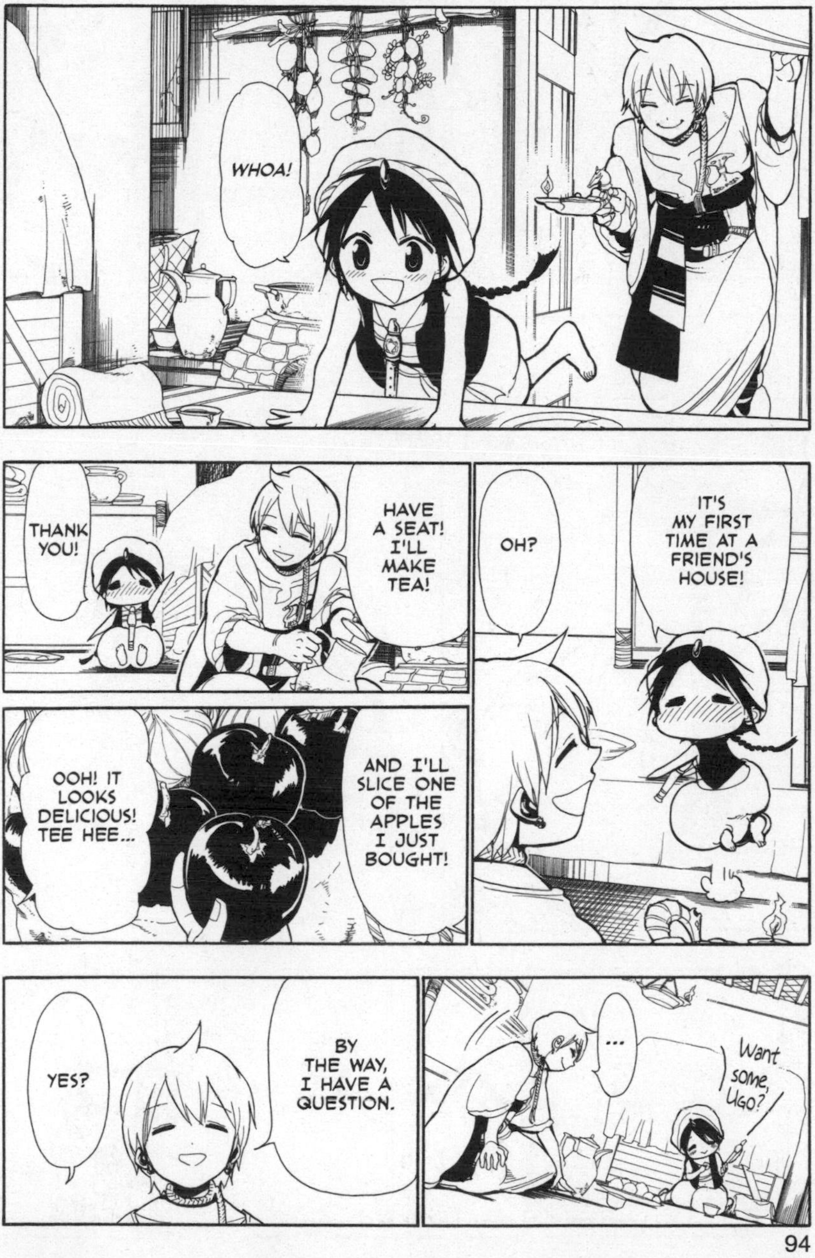
WHOA!
IT'S MY FIRST TIME AT A FRIEND'S HOUSE!
OH?
HAVE A SEAT! I'LL MAKE TEA!
THANK YOU!
AND I'LL SLICE ONE OF THE APPLES I JUST BOUGHT!
OOH! IT LOOKS DELICIOUS! TEE HEE...
Want some, Ugo?
...
BY THE WAY, I HAVE A QUESTION.
YES?

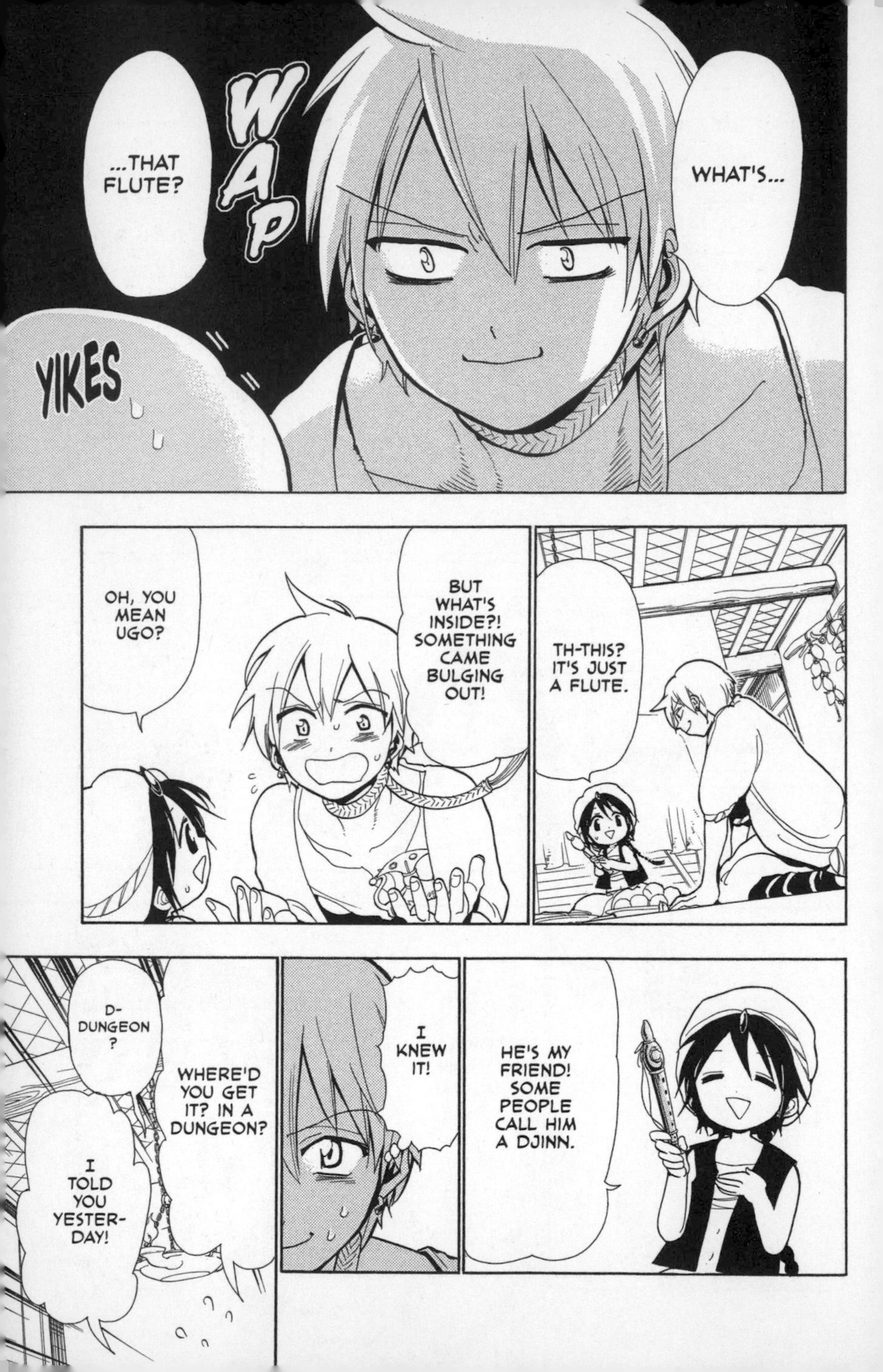
WHAT'S...
WAP
...THAT FLUTE?
YIKES
TH-THIS? IT'S JUST A FLUTE.
BUT WHAT'S INSIDE?! SOMETHING CAME BULGING OUT!
OH, YOU MEAN UGO?
HE'S MY FRIEND! SOME PEOPLE CALL HIM A DJINN.
I KNEW IT!
WHERE'D YOU GET IT? IN A DUNGEON?
D-DUNGEON?
I TOLD YOU YESTER-DAY!

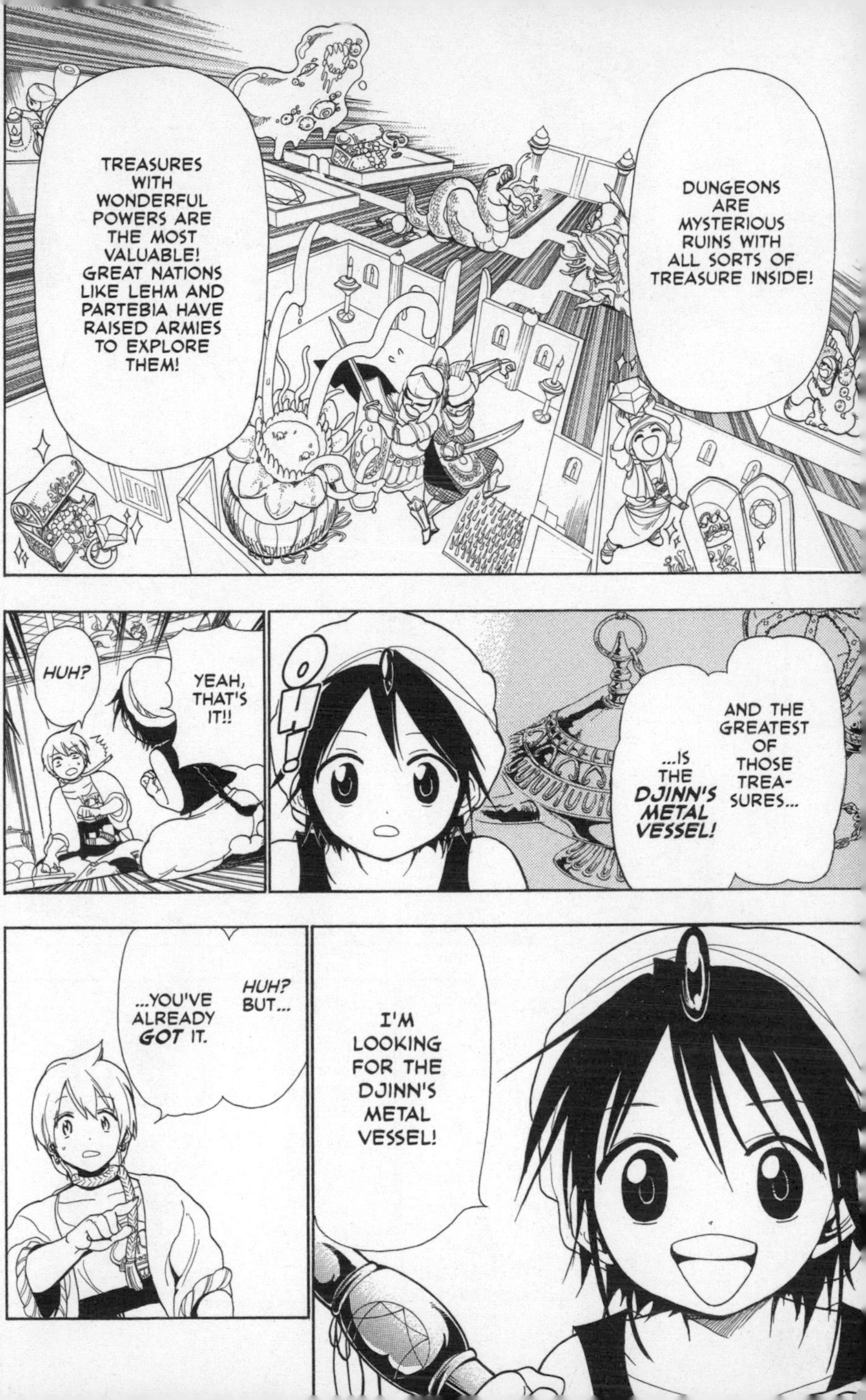

DUNGEONS ARE MYSTERIOUS RUINS WITH ALL SORTS OF TREASURE INSIDE!
TREASURES WITH WONDERFUL POWERS ARE THE MOST VALUABLE! GREAT NATIONS LIKE LEHM AND PARTEBIA HAVE RAISED ARMIES TO EXPLORE THEM!
AND THE GREATEST OF THOSE TREA-SURES...
...IS THE *DJINN'S METAL VESSEL!*
OH!
YEAH, THAT'S IT!!
HUH?
I'M LOOKING FOR THE DJINN'S METAL VESSEL!
HUH? BUT...
...YOU'VE ALREADY ***GOT*** IT.

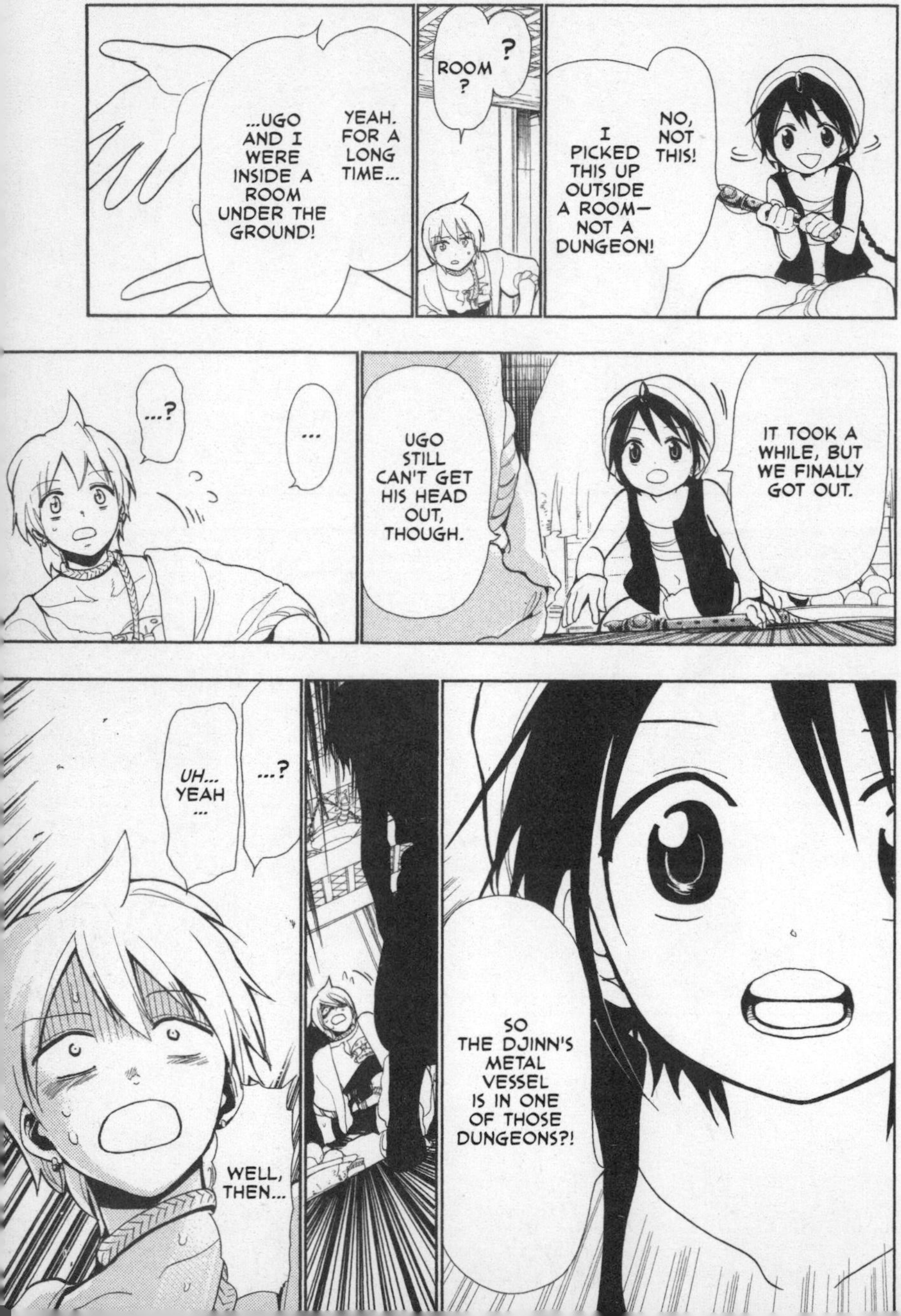
NO, NOT THIS!
I PICKED THIS UP OUTSIDE A ROOM— NOT A DUNGEON!
ROOM ?
?
YEAH. FOR A LONG TIME...
...UGO AND I WERE INSIDE A ROOM UNDER THE GROUND!
IT TOOK A WHILE, BUT WE FINALLY GOT OUT.
UGO STILL CAN'T GET HIS HEAD OUT, THOUGH.
...
...?
SO THE DJINN'S METAL VESSEL IS IN ONE OF THOSE DUNGEONS?!
...?
UH... YEAH...
WELL, THEN...

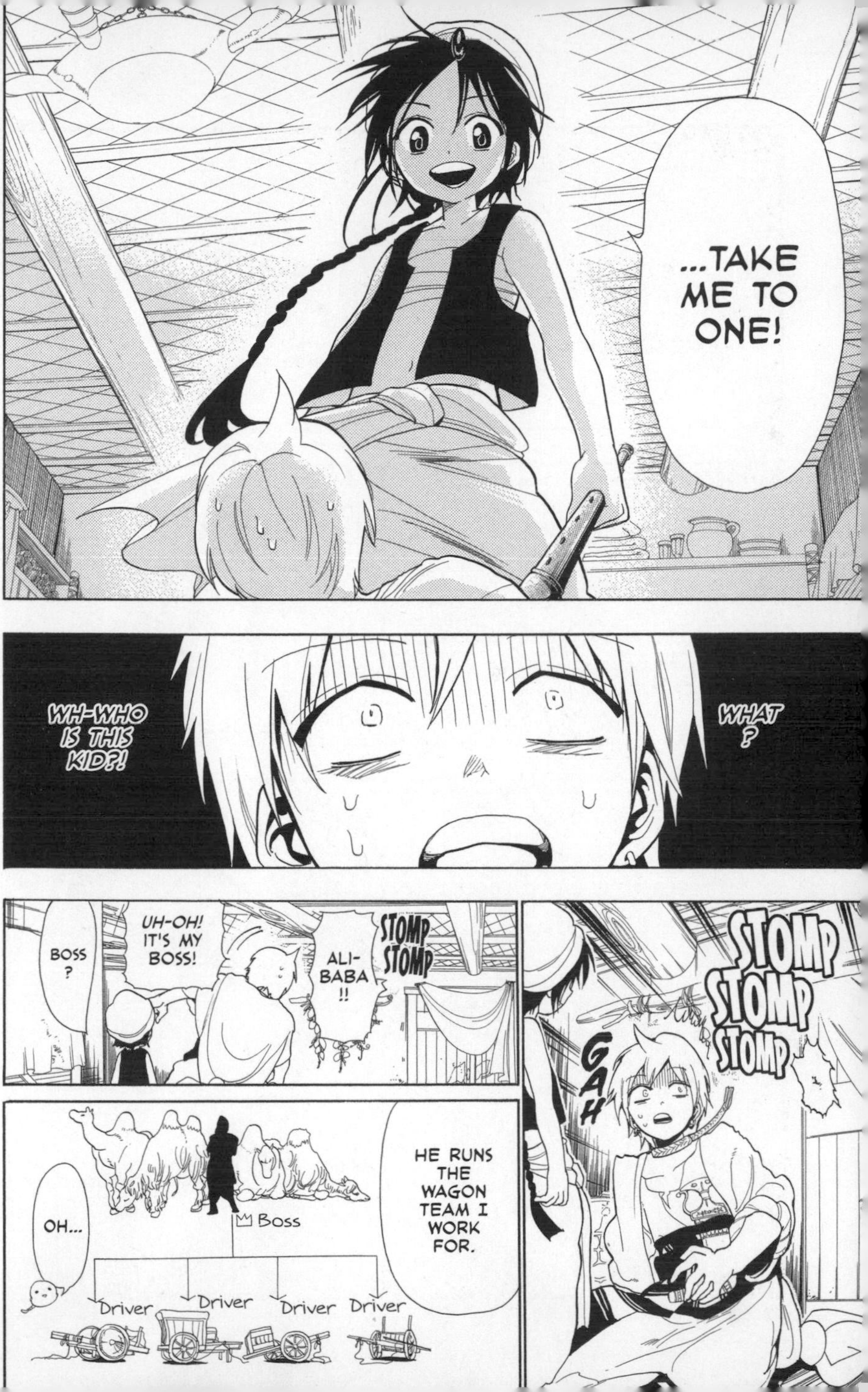
...TAKE ME TO ONE!
WHAT?
WH-WHO IS THIS KID?!
STOMP STOMP STOMP
GAH
STOMP STOMP
ALI-BABA!!
UH-OH! IT'S MY BOSS!
BOSS?
HE RUNS THE WAGON TEAM I WORK FOR.
OH...
Boss
Driver
Driver
Driver
Driver

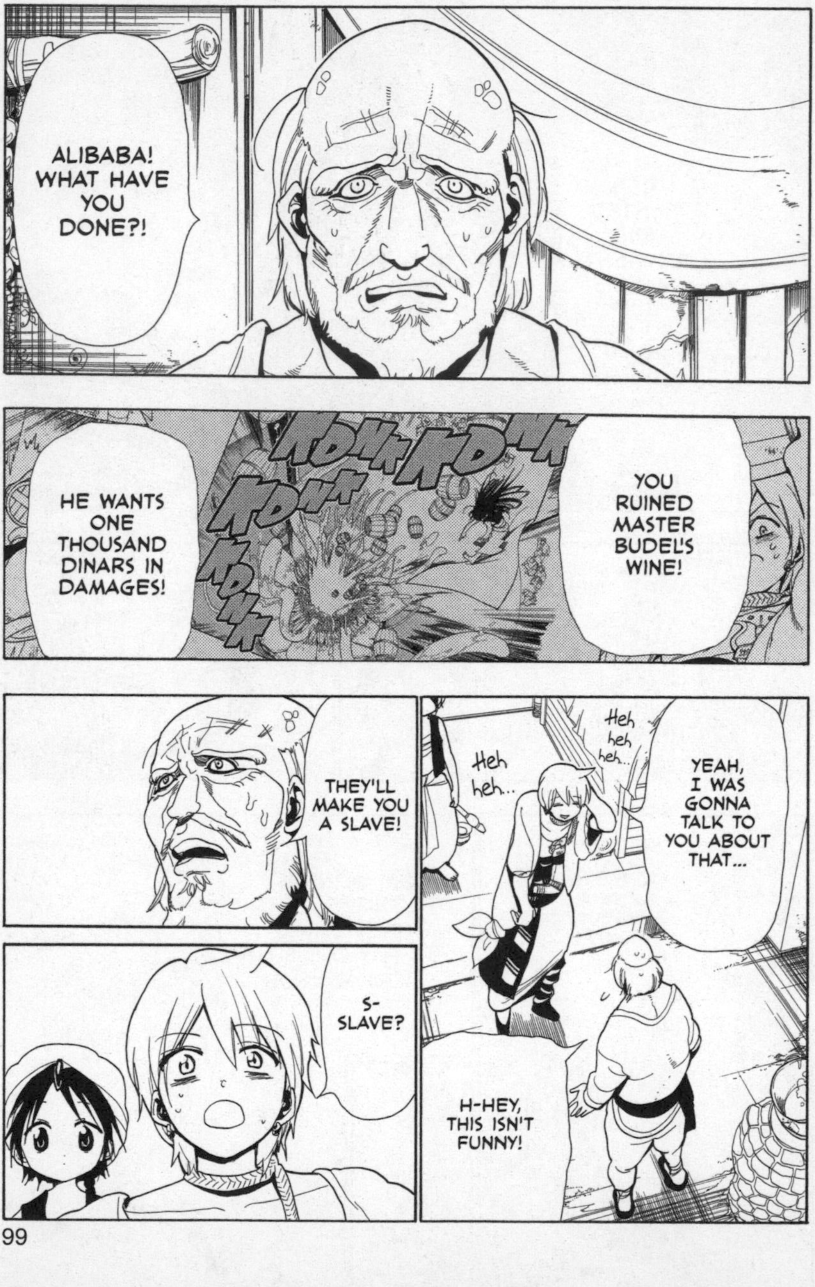
ALIBABA! WHAT HAVE YOU DONE?!
YOU RUINED MASTER BUDEL'S WINE!
KDONK
HE WANTS ONE THOUSAND DINARS IN DAMAGES!
Heh heh heh...
YEAH, I WAS GONNA TALK TO YOU ABOUT THAT...
Heh heh...
H-HEY, THIS ISN'T FUNNY!
THEY'LL MAKE YOU A SLAVE!
S-SLAVE?

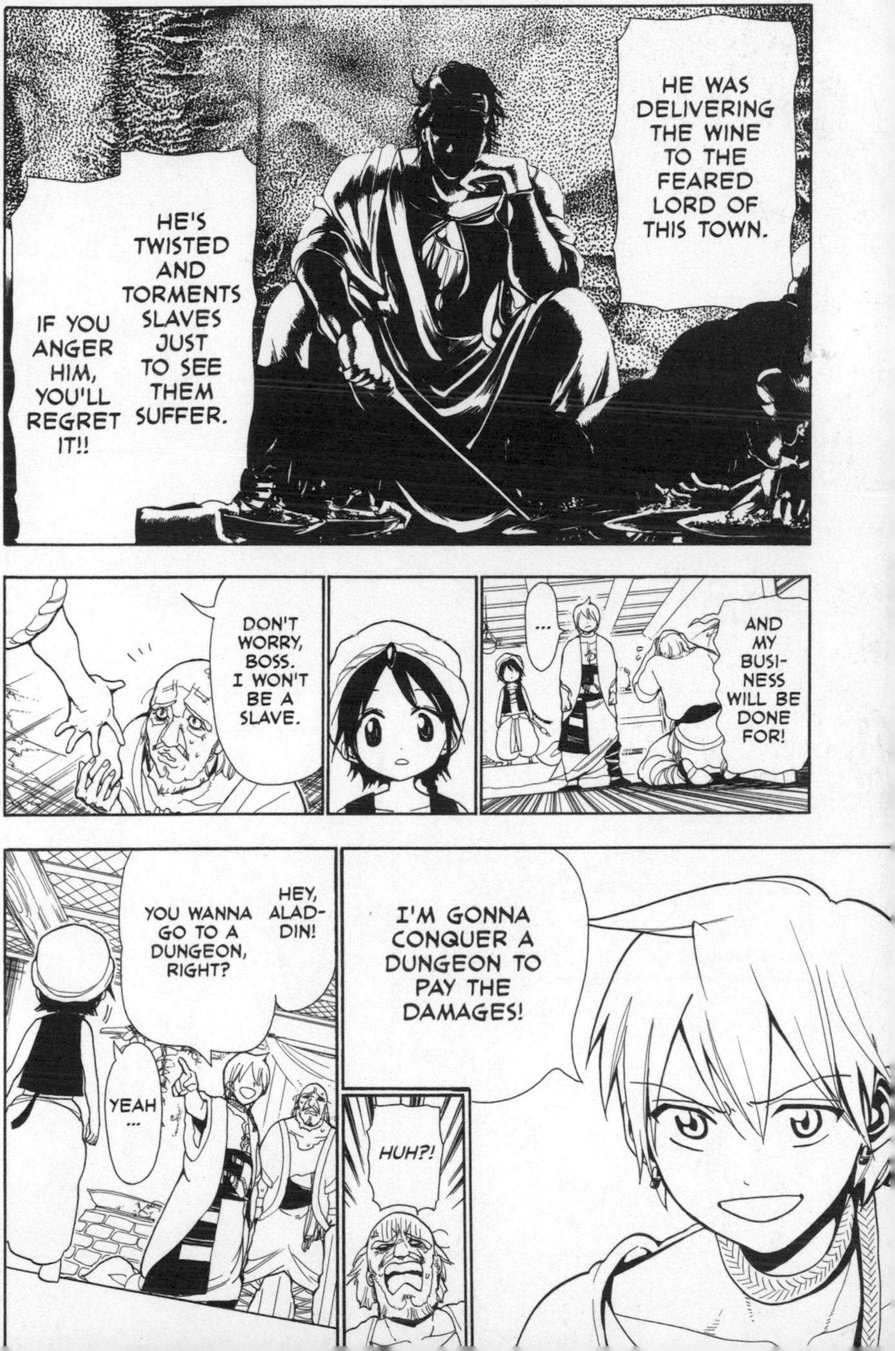
HE WAS DELIVERING THE WINE TO THE FEARED LORD OF THIS TOWN.
HE'S TWISTED AND TORMENTS SLAVES JUST TO SEE THEM SUFFER.
IF YOU ANGER HIM, YOU'LL REGRET IT!!
AND MY BUSINESS WILL BE DONE FOR!
...
DON'T WORRY, BOSS. I WON'T BE A SLAVE.
I'M GONNA CONQUER A DUNGEON TO PAY THE DAMAGES!
HUH?!
HEY, ALAD-DIN!
YOU WANNA GO TO A DUNGEON, RIGHT?
YEAH ...

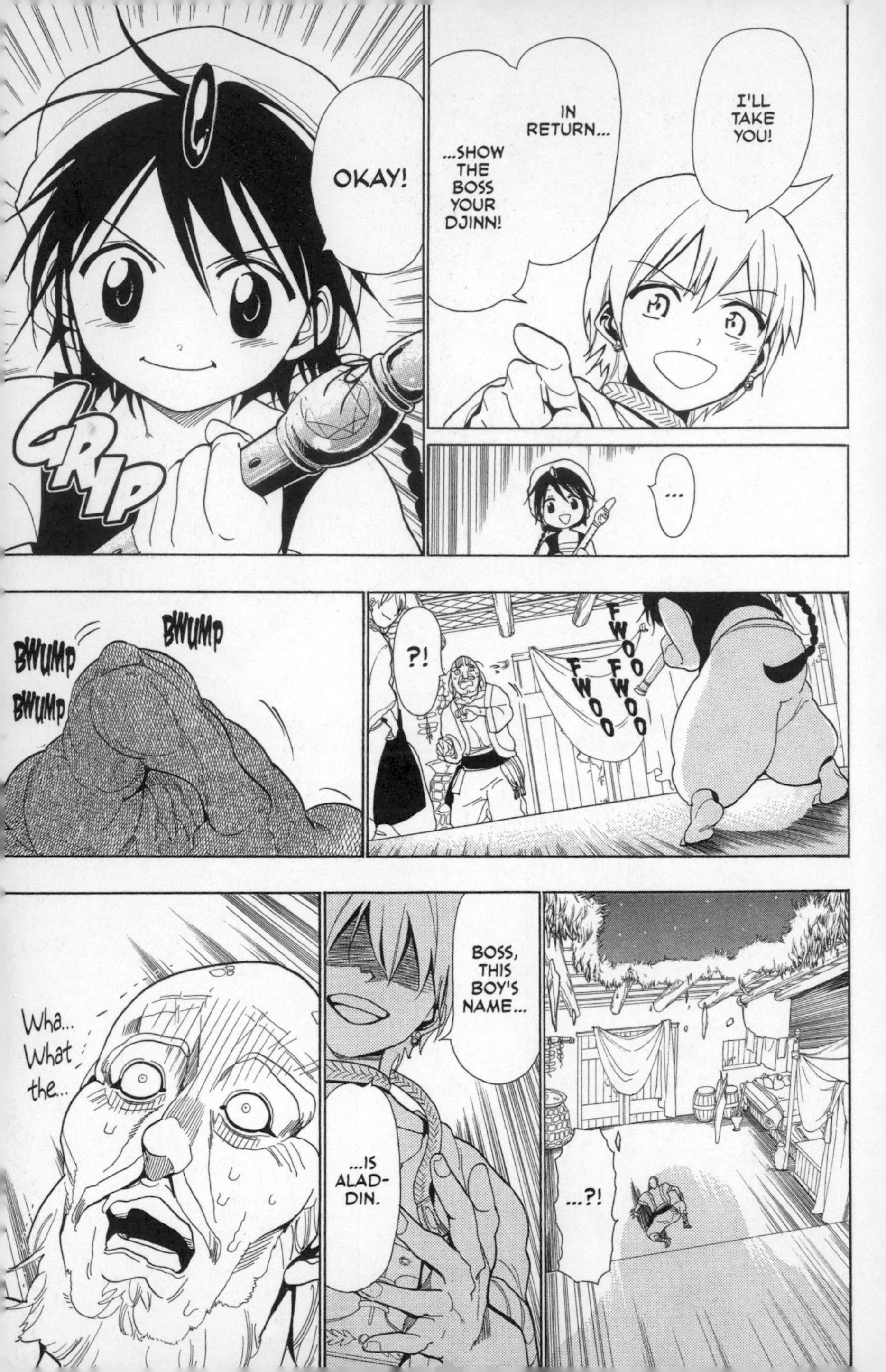
I'LL TAKE YOU!
IN RETURN...
...SHOW THE BOSS YOUR DJINN!
...
OKAY!
GRIP
?!
FWOO FWOO FWOO FWOO
BWUMP BWUMP BWUMP
...?!
BOSS, THIS BOY'S NAME...
...IS ALAD-DIN.
Wha... What the...

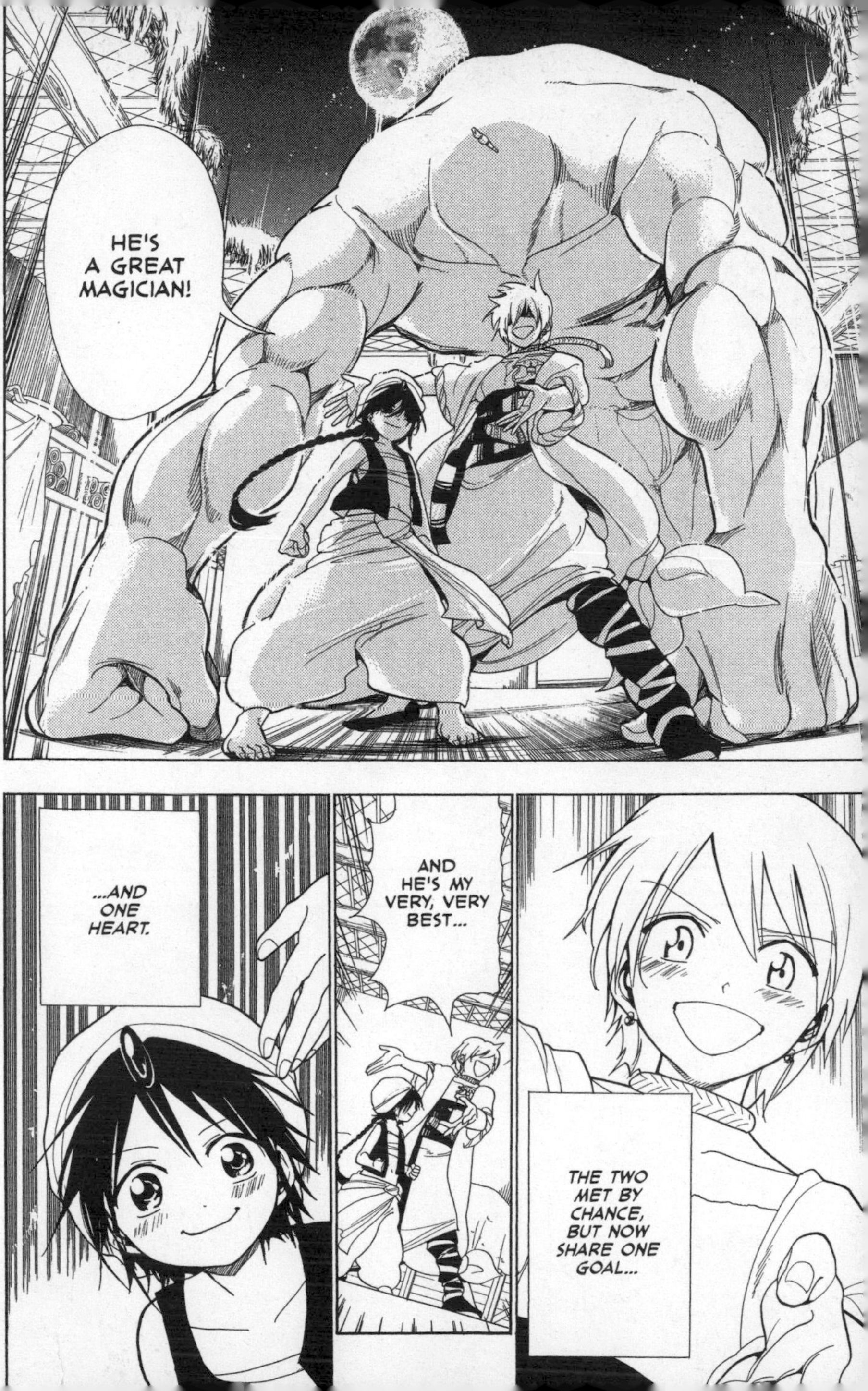
HE'S A GREAT MAGICIAN!
THE TWO MET BY CHANCE, BUT NOW SHARE ONE GOAL...
AND HE'S MY VERY, VERY BEST...
...AND ONE HEART.

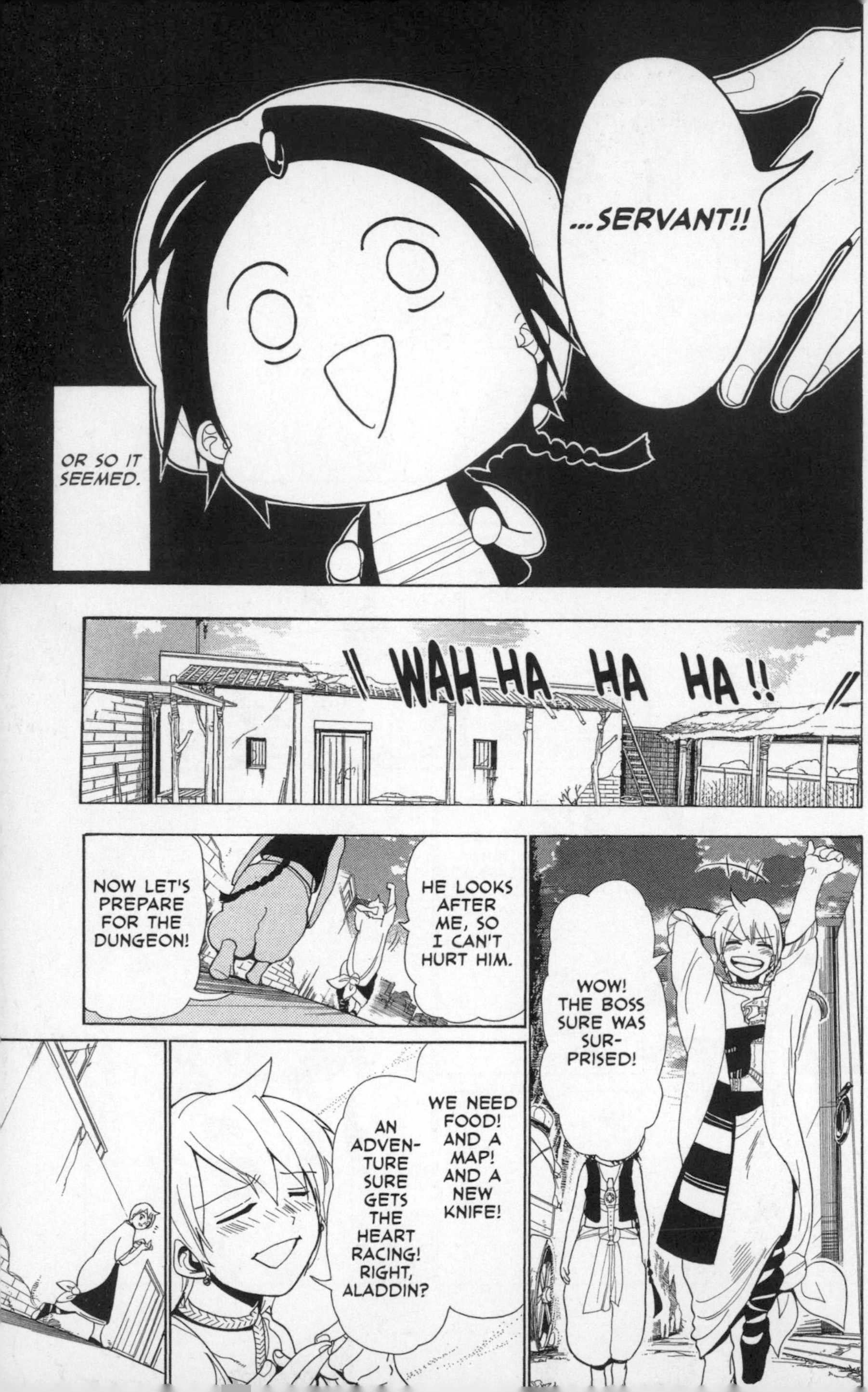
...SERVANT!!
OR SO IT SEEMED.
WAH HA HA HA!!
WOW! THE BOSS SURE WAS SUR- PRISED!
HE LOOKS AFTER ME, SO I CAN'T HURT HIM.
NOW LET'S PREPARE FOR THE DUNGEON!
WE NEED FOOD! AND A MAP! AND A NEW KNIFE!
AN ADVEN- TURE SURE GETS THE HEART RACING! RIGHT, ALADDIN?

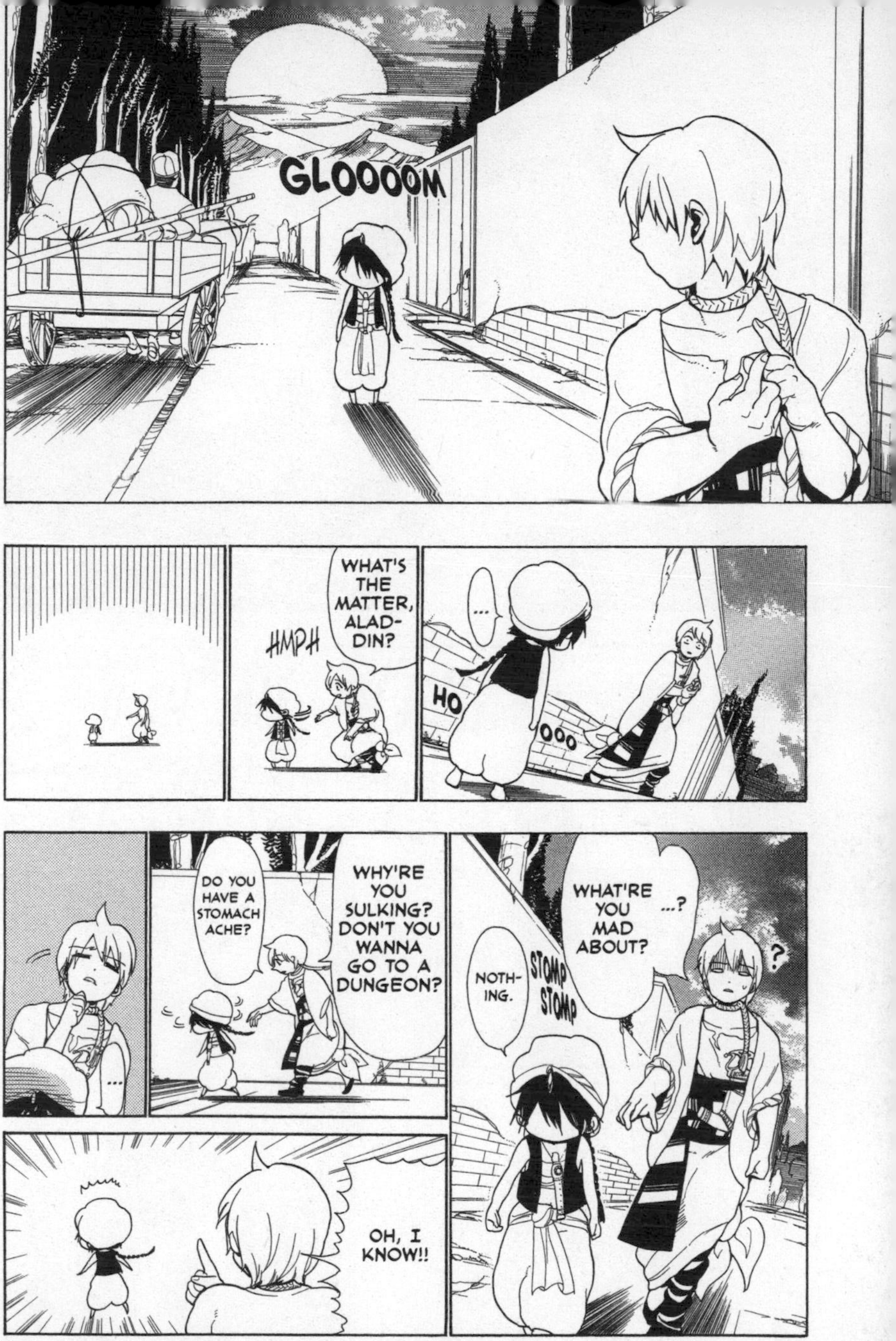
GLOOOOM
...
HO
OOO
WHAT'S THE MATTER, ALAD-DIN?
HMPH
WHAT'RE YOU MAD ABOUT?
...?
?
NOTH-ING.
STOMP STOMP
WHY'RE YOU SULKING? DON'T YOU WANNA GO TO A DUNGEON?
DO YOU HAVE A STOMACH ACHE?
...
OH, I KNOW!!

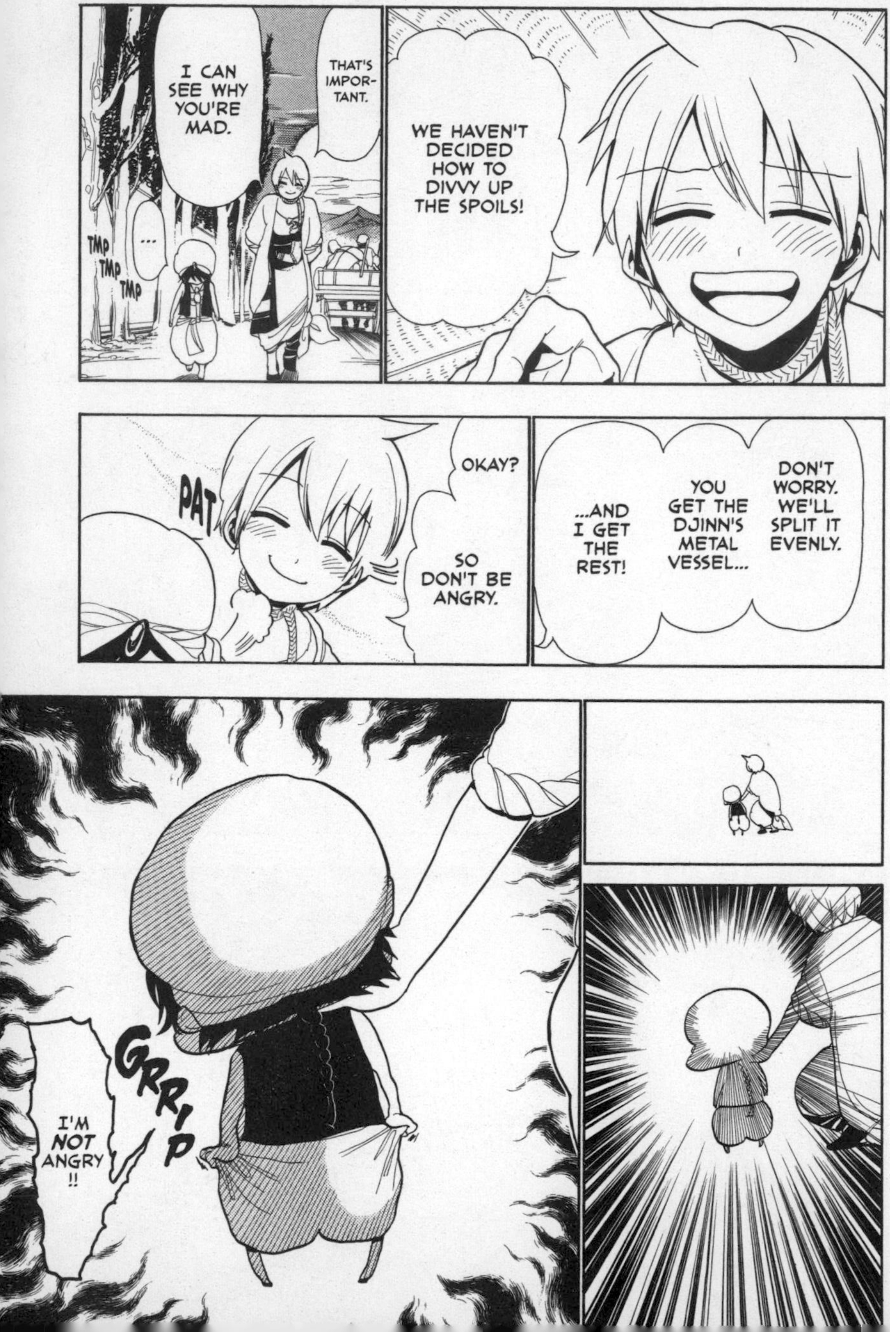
WE HAVEN'T DECIDED HOW TO DIVVY UP THE SPOILS!
THAT'S IMPOR-TANT.
I CAN SEE WHY YOU'RE MAD.
...
TMP TMP TMP
DON'T WORRY. WE'LL SPLIT IT EVENLY.
YOU GET THE DJINN'S METAL VESSEL...
...AND I GET THE REST!
OKAY?
SO DON'T BE ANGRY.
PAT
GRRIP
I'M NOT ANGRY!!

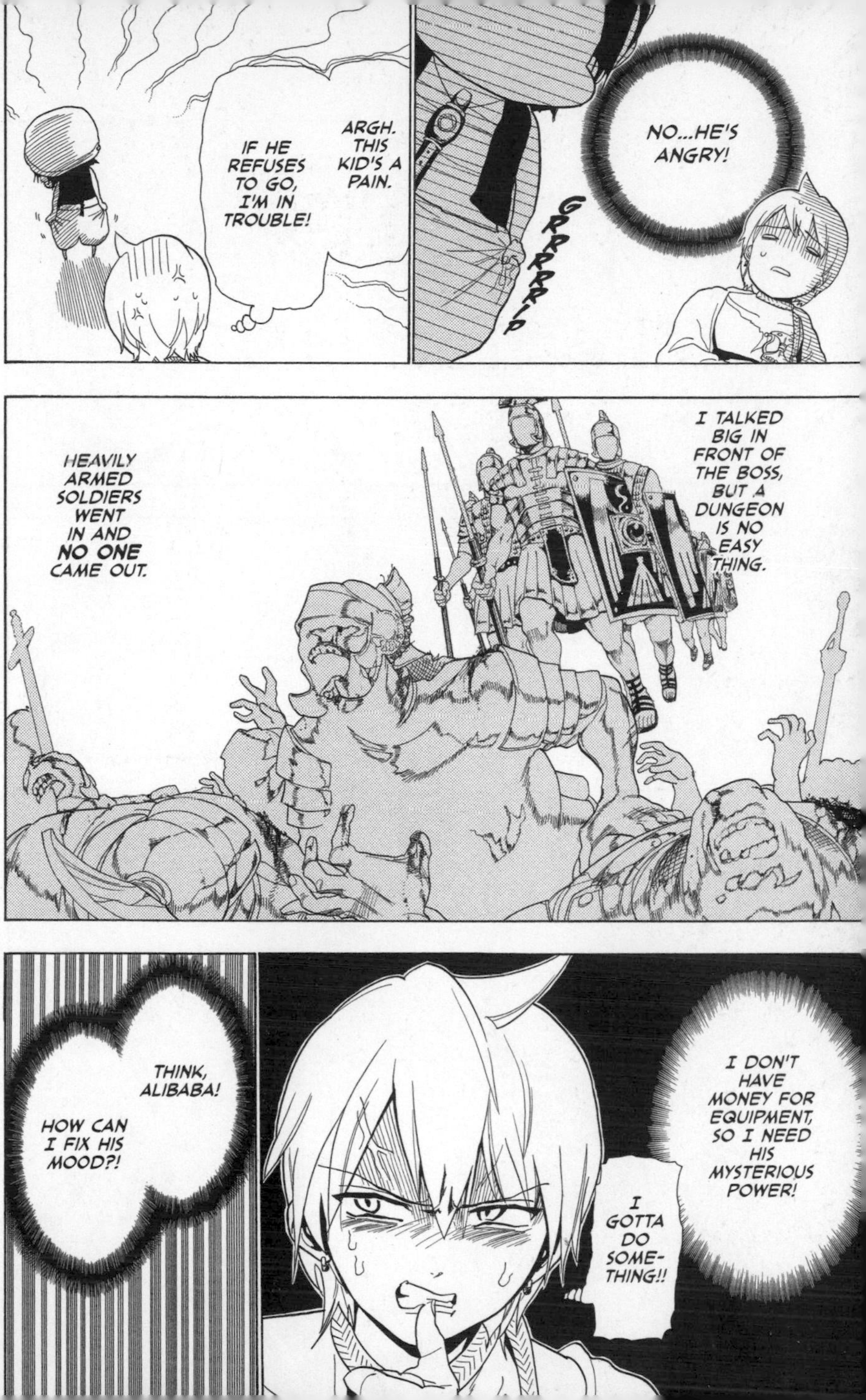
NO...HE'S ANGRY!
GRRRRRIP
ARGH. THIS KID'S A PAIN.
IF HE REFUSES TO GO, I'M IN TROUBLE!
I TALKED BIG IN FRONT OF THE BOSS, BUT A DUNGEON IS NO EASY THING.
HEAVILY ARMED SOLDIERS WENT IN AND **NO ONE** CAME OUT.
I DON'T HAVE MONEY FOR EQUIPMENT, SO I NEED HIS MYSTERIOUS POWER!
I GOTTA DO SOME-THING!!
THINK, ALIBABA!
HOW CAN I FIX HIS MOOD?!

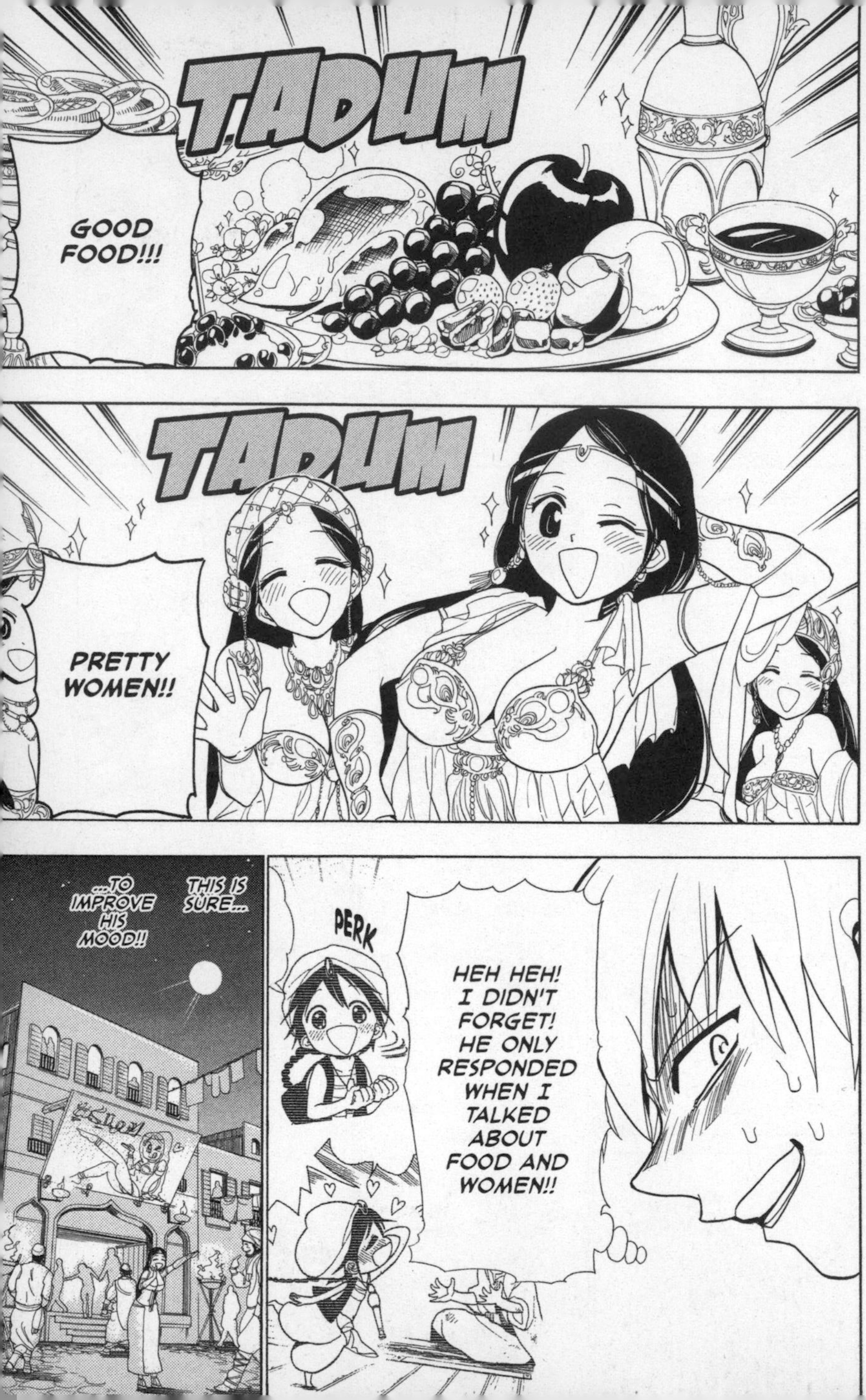
TADUM
GOOD FOOD!!!
TADUM
PRETTY WOMEN!!
HEH HEH! I DIDN'T FORGET! HE ONLY RESPONDED WHEN I TALKED ABOUT FOOD AND WOMEN!!
PERK
THIS IS SURE...
...TO IMPROVE HIS MOOD!!

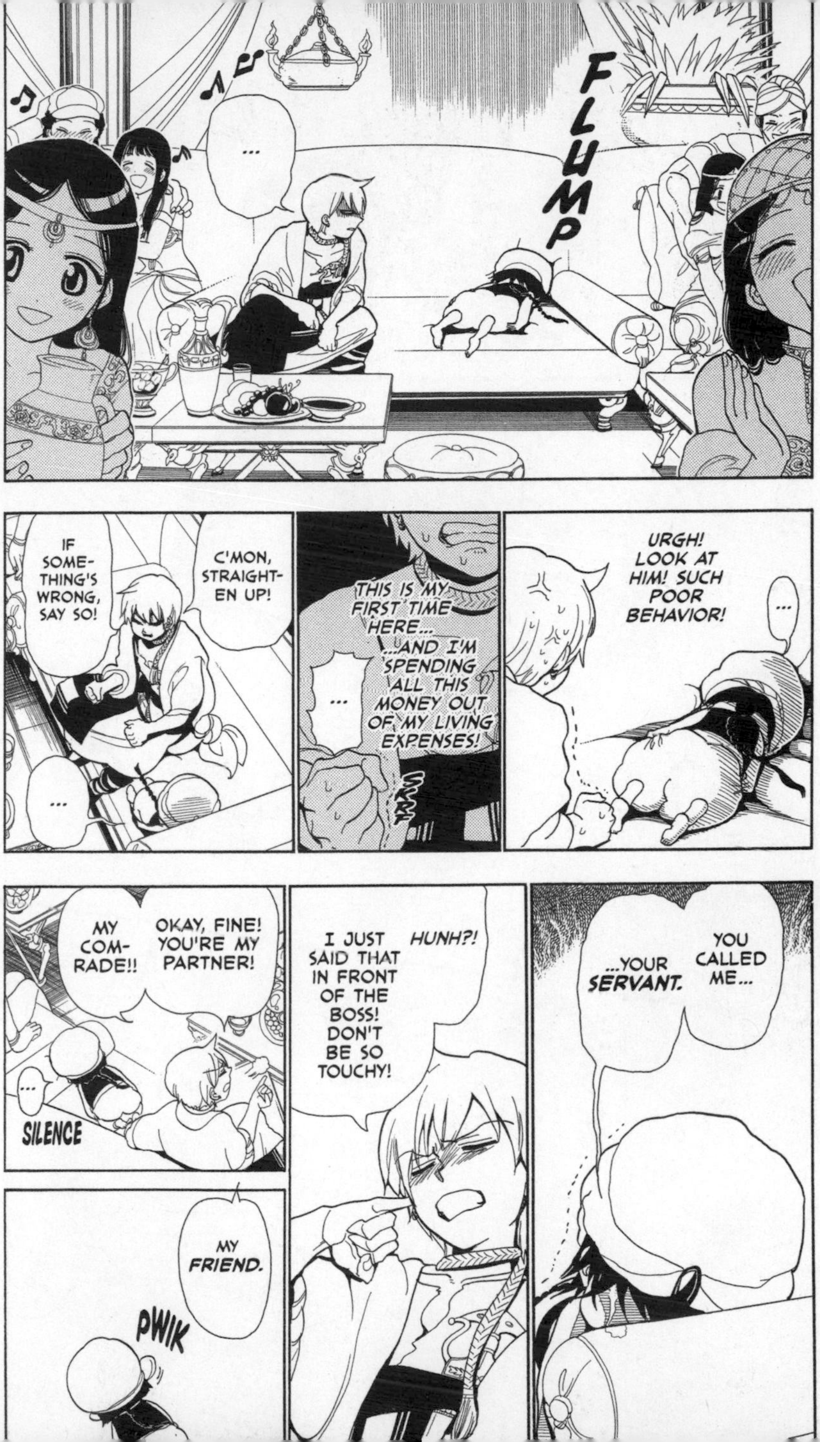
...
FLUMP
URGH! LOOK AT HIM! SUCH POOR BEHAVIOR!
...
THIS IS MY FIRST TIME HERE... ...AND I'M SPENDING ALL THIS MONEY OUT OF MY LIVING EXPENSES!
...
SKRT
C'MON, STRAIGHTEN UP!
IF SOMETHING'S WRONG, SAY SO!
...
YOU CALLED ME...
...YOUR SERVANT.
HUNH?!
I JUST SAID THAT IN FRONT OF THE BOSS! DON'T BE SO TOUCHY!
OKAY, FINE! YOU'RE MY PARTNER!
MY COMRADE!!
...
SILENCE
MY FRIEND.
PWIK

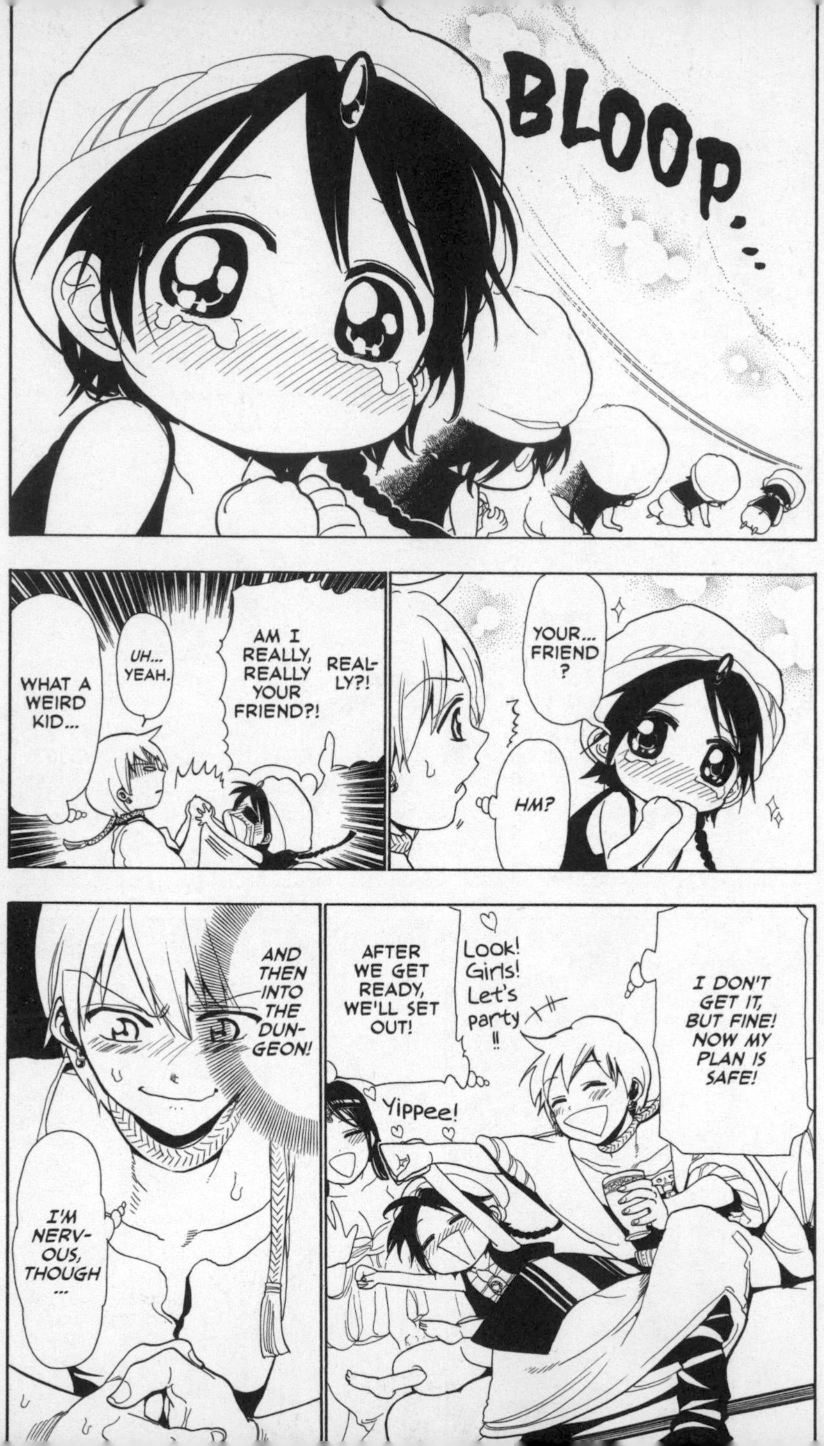
BLOOP...
YOUR... FRIEND?
HM?
AM I REALLY, REALLY YOUR FRIEND?!
REAL-LY?!
UH... YEAH.
WHAT A WEIRD KID...
I DON'T GET IT, BUT FINE! NOW MY PLAN IS SAFE!
Look! Girls! Let's party!!
AFTER WE GET READY, WE'LL SET OUT!
Yippee!
AND THEN INTO THE DUN-GEON!
I'M NERV-OUS, THOUGH...

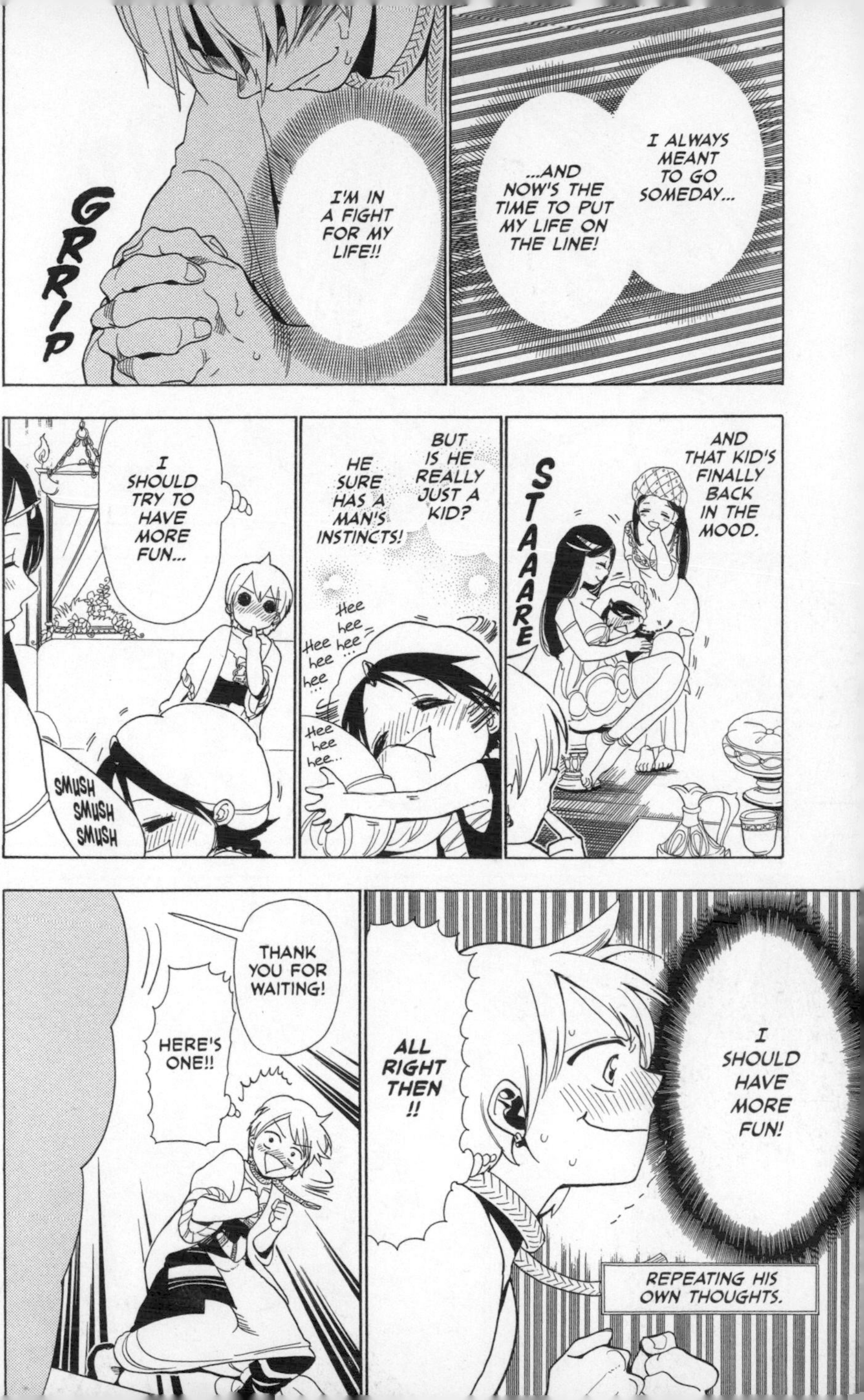

I ALWAYS MEANT TO GO SOMEDAY...
...AND NOW'S THE TIME TO PUT MY LIFE ON THE LINE!
I'M IN A FIGHT FOR MY LIFE!!
GRRIP
AND THAT KID'S FINALLY BACK IN THE MOOD.
STAAAARE
BUT IS HE REALLY JUST A KID?
HE SURE HAS A MAN'S INSTINCTS!
Hee hee hee...
Hee hee hee...
Hee hee hee...
I SHOULD TRY TO HAVE MORE FUN...
SMUSH SMUSH SMUSH
I SHOULD HAVE MORE FUN!
ALL RIGHT THEN!!
REPEATING HIS OWN THOUGHTS.
THANK YOU FOR WAITING!
HERE'S ONE!!

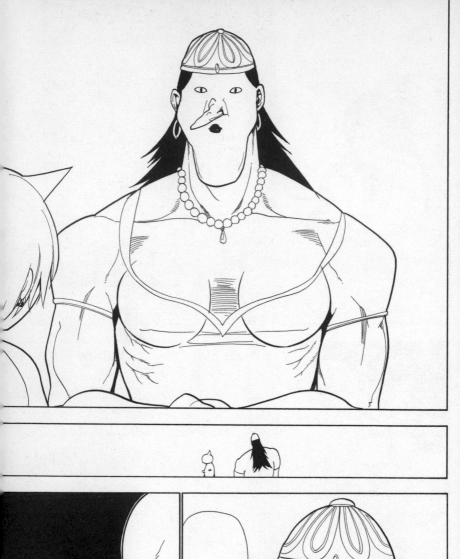

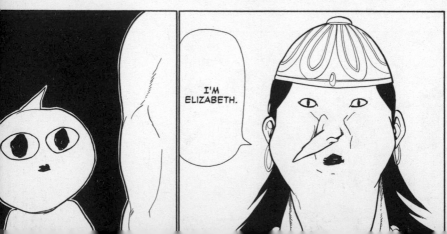

I'M
ELIZABETH.

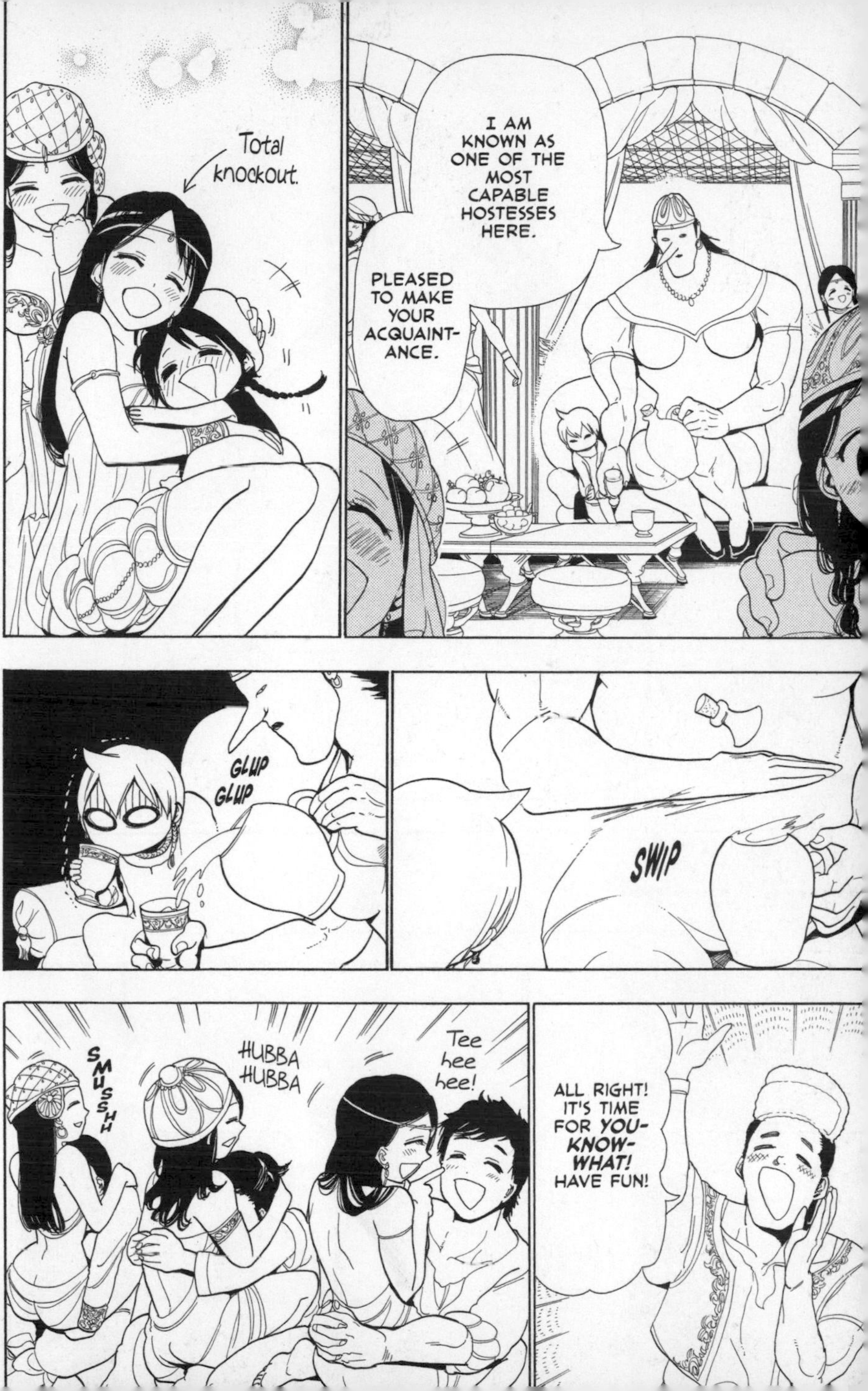
I AM KNOWN AS ONE OF THE MOST CAPABLE HOSTESSES HERE.
PLEASED TO MAKE YOUR ACQUAINT-ANCE.
Total knockout.
SWIP
GLUP GLUP
ALL RIGHT! IT'S TIME FOR YOU-KNOW-WHAT! HAVE FUN!
Tee hee hee!
HUBBA HUBBA
SMUSHH

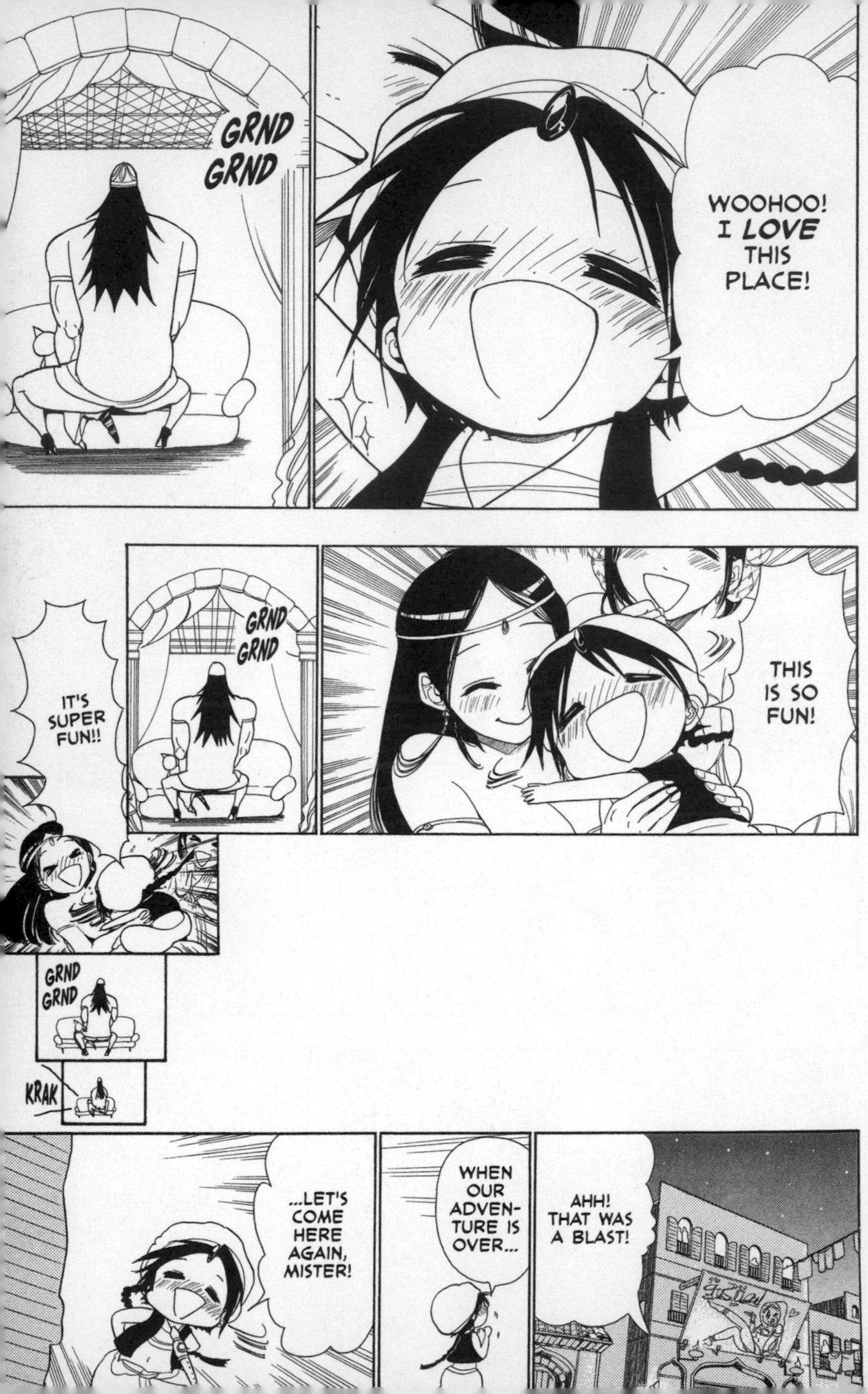
WOOHOO! I LOVE THIS PLACE!
GRND GRND
THIS IS SO FUN!
GRND GRND
IT'S SUPER FUN!!
GRND GRND
KRAK
AHH! THAT WAS A BLAST!
WHEN OUR ADVEN-TURE IS OVER...
...LET'S COME HERE AGAIN, MISTER!

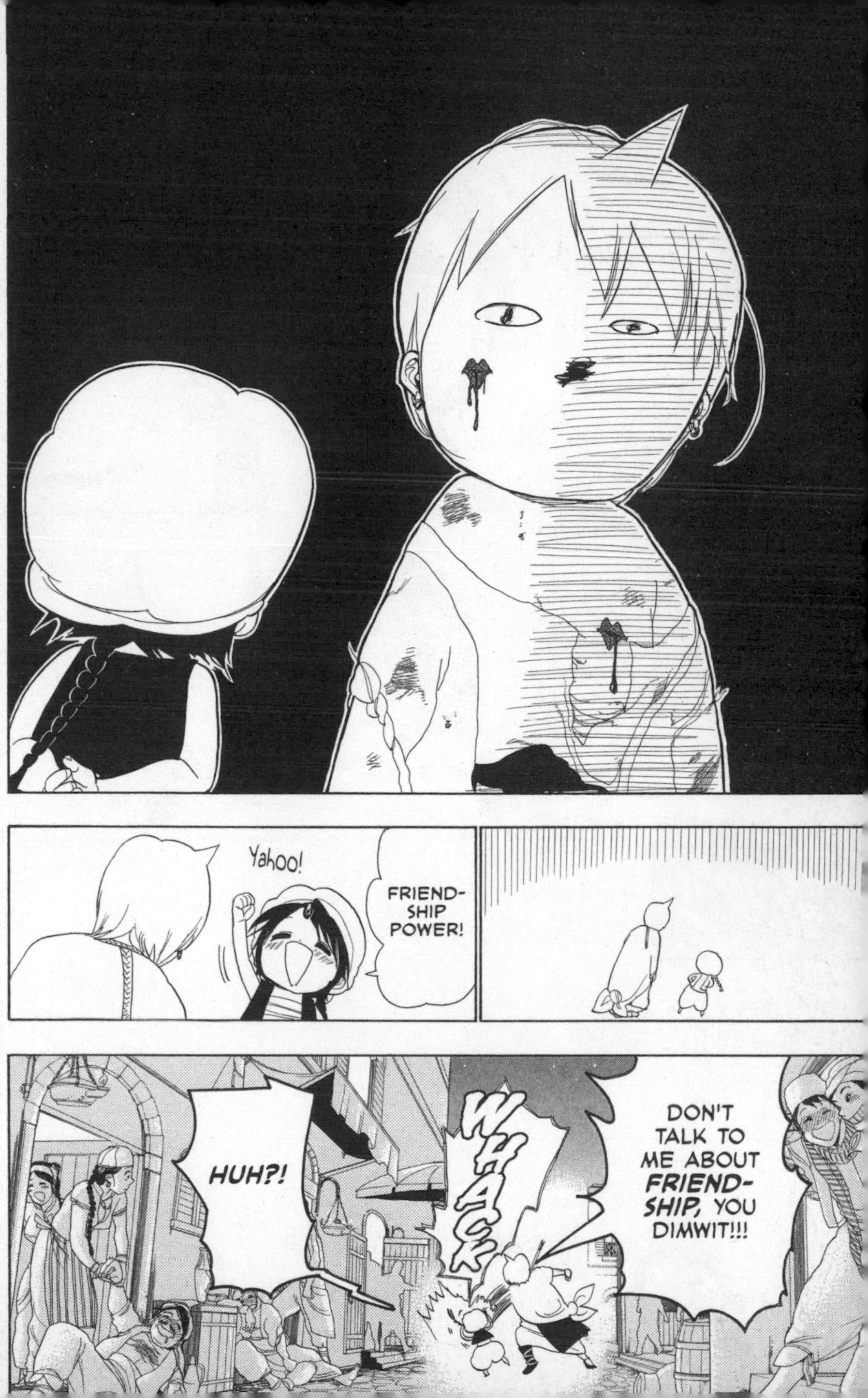
FRIEND-SHIP POWER!
Yahoo!
DON'T TALK TO ME ABOUT FRIEND-SHIP, YOU DIMWIT!!!
WHACK
HUH?!

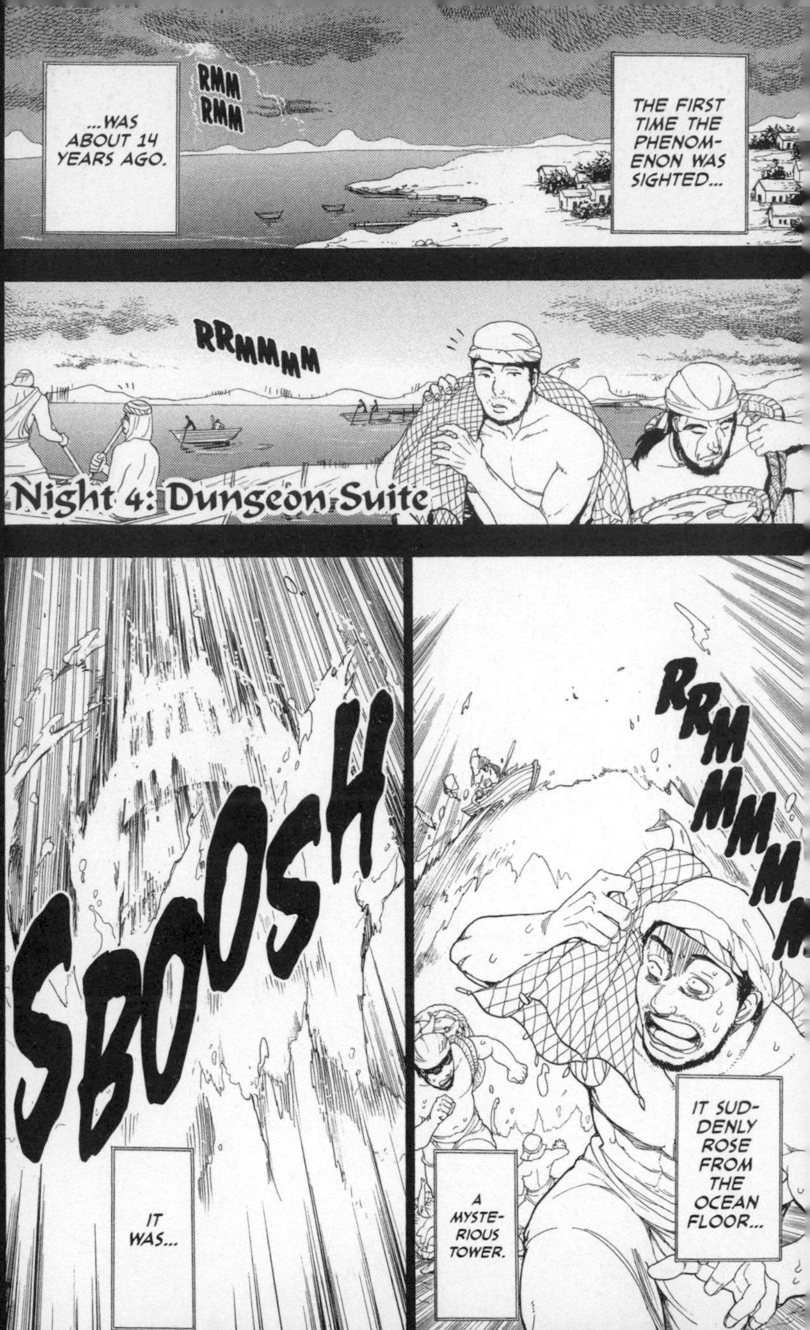
THE FIRST TIME THE PHENOM-ENON WAS SIGHTED...
RMM RMM
...WAS ABOUT 14 YEARS AGO.
RRMMMM
Night 4: Dungeon Suite
RRMMMMM
IT SUD-DENLY ROSE FROM THE OCEAN FLOOR...
A MYSTE-RIOUS TOWER.
SBOOSH
IT WAS...

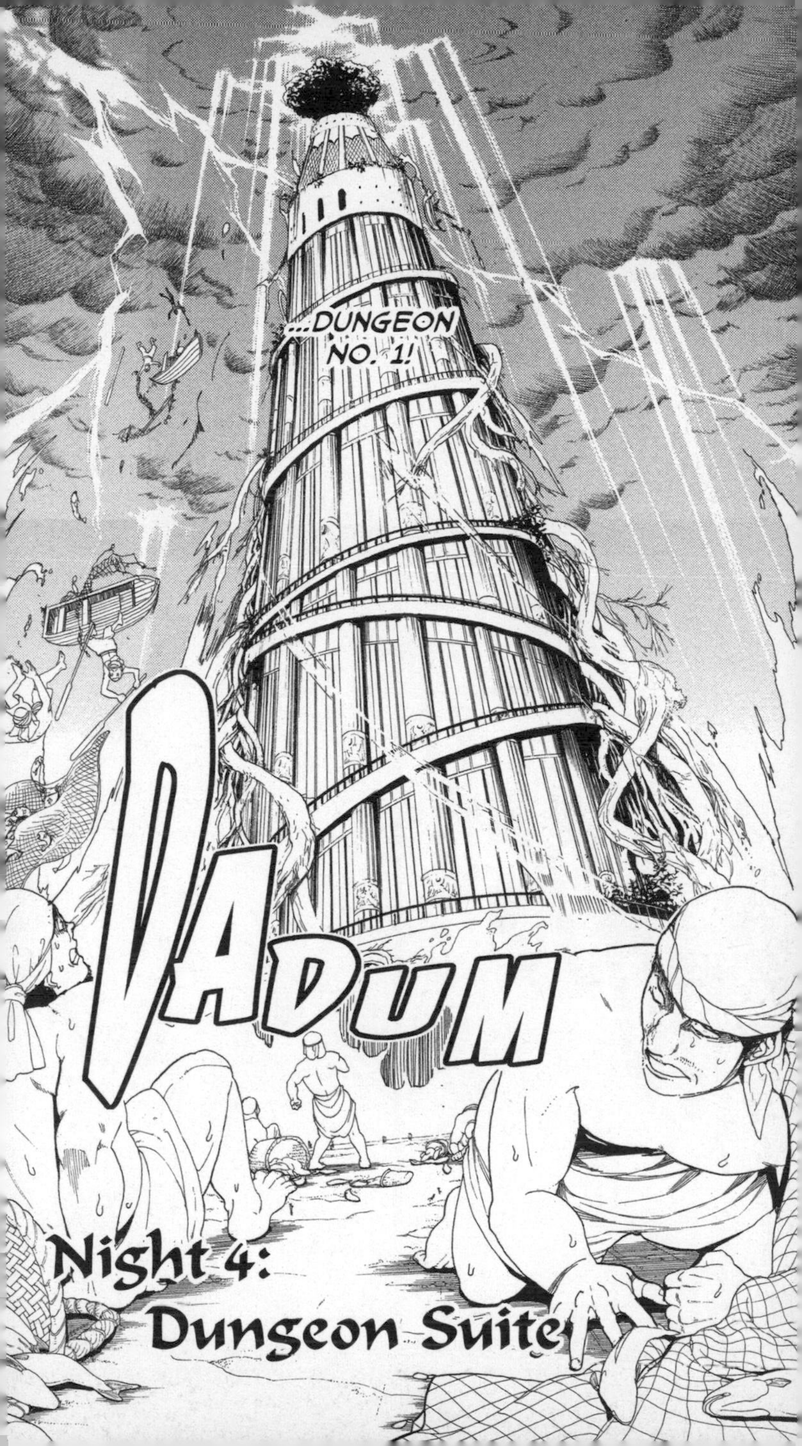
...DUNGEON NO. 1!
VADUM
Night 4:
Dungeon Suite

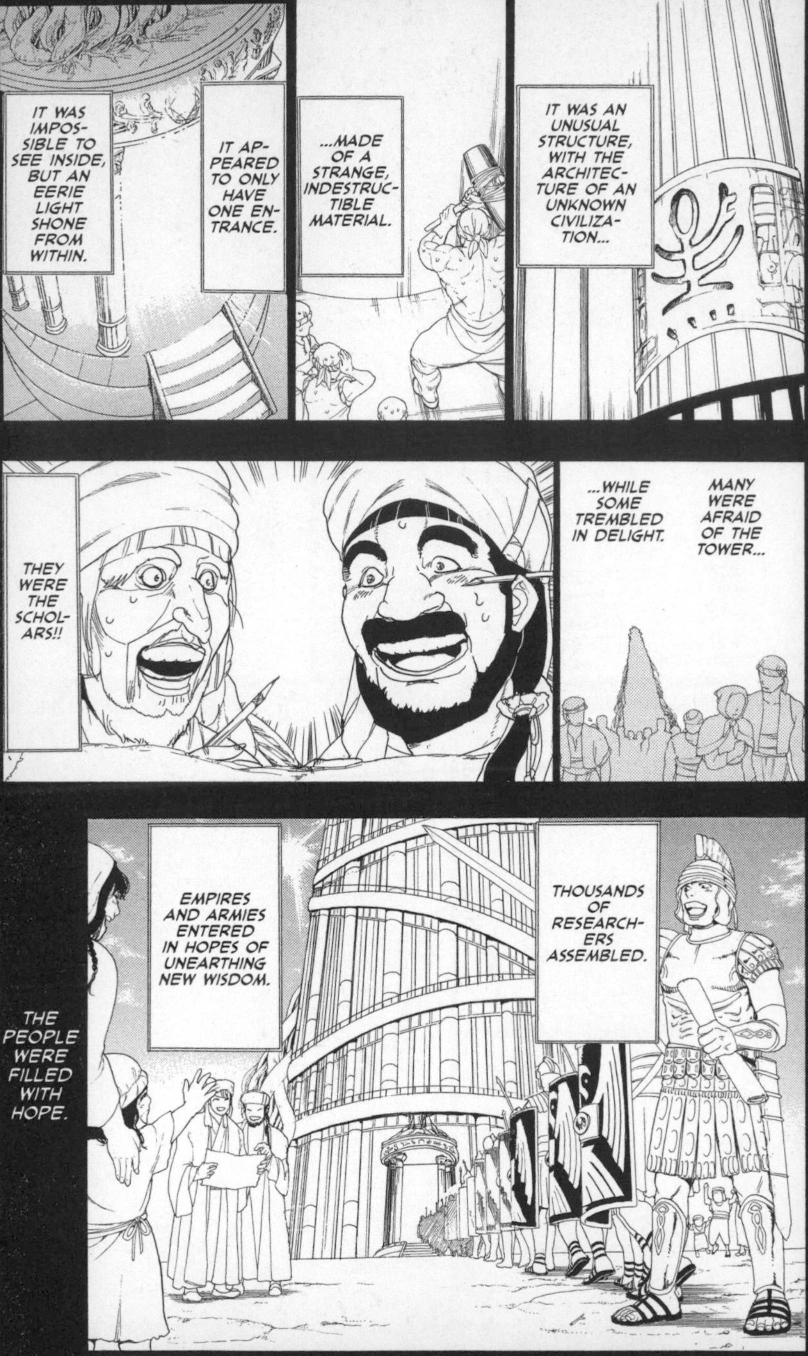
IT WAS AN UNUSUAL STRUCTURE, WITH THE ARCHITECTURE OF AN UNKNOWN CIVILIZATION...
...MADE OF A STRANGE, INDESTRUCTIBLE MATERIAL.
IT APPEARED TO ONLY HAVE ONE ENTRANCE.
IT WAS IMPOSSIBLE TO SEE INSIDE, BUT AN EERIE LIGHT SHONE FROM WITHIN.
MANY WERE AFRAID OF THE TOWER...
...WHILE SOME TREMBLED IN DELIGHT.
THEY WERE THE SCHOLARS!!
THOUSANDS OF RESEARCHERS ASSEMBLED.
EMPIRES AND ARMIES ENTERED IN HOPES OF UNEARTHING NEW WISDOM.
THE PEOPLE WERE FILLED WITH HOPE.

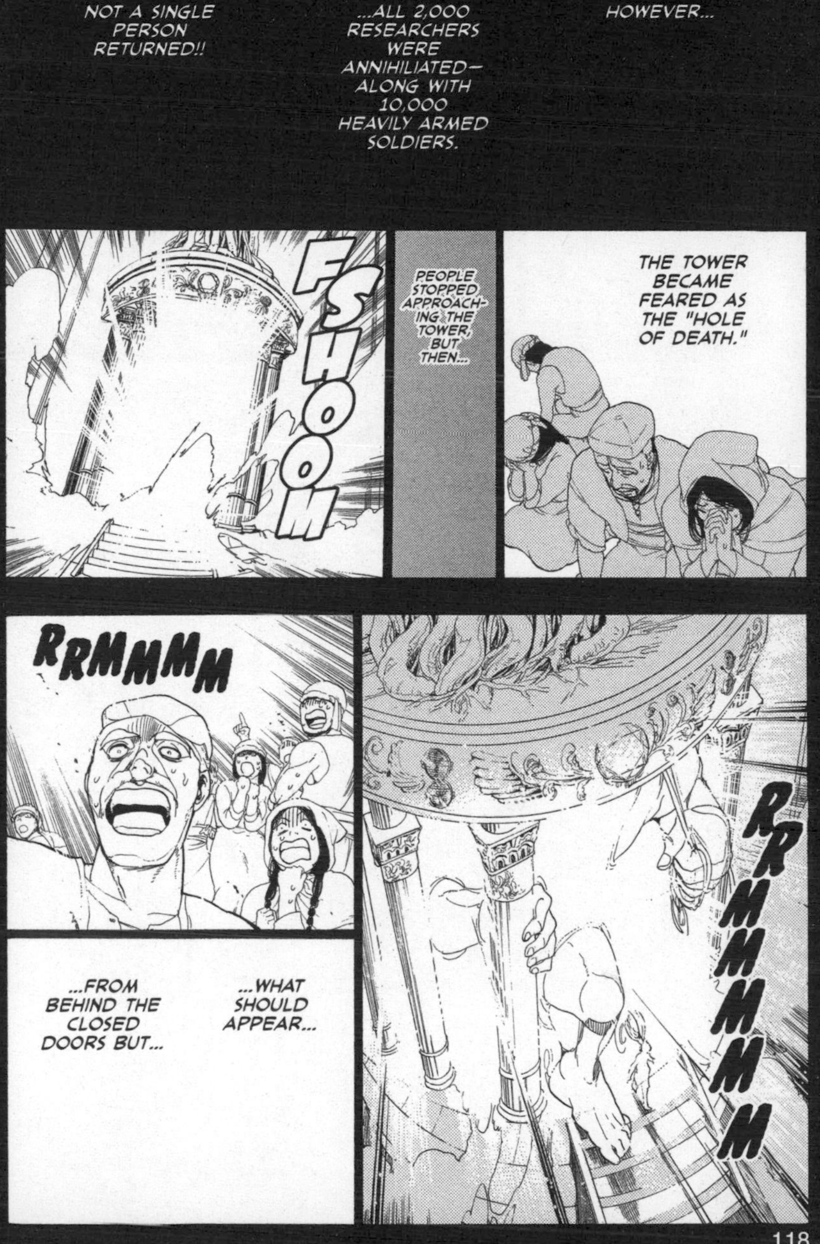
HOWEVER...
...ALL 2,000 RESEARCHERS WERE ANNIHILIATED—ALONG WITH 10,000 HEAVILY ARMED SOLDIERS.
NOT A SINGLE PERSON RETURNED!!
THE TOWER BECAME FEARED AS THE "HOLE OF DEATH."
PEOPLE STOPPED APPROACHING THE TOWER, BUT THEN...
FSHOOOM
RRMMMMMMMM
RRMMMMM
...WHAT SHOULD APPEAR...
...FROM BEHIND THE CLOSED DOORS BUT...

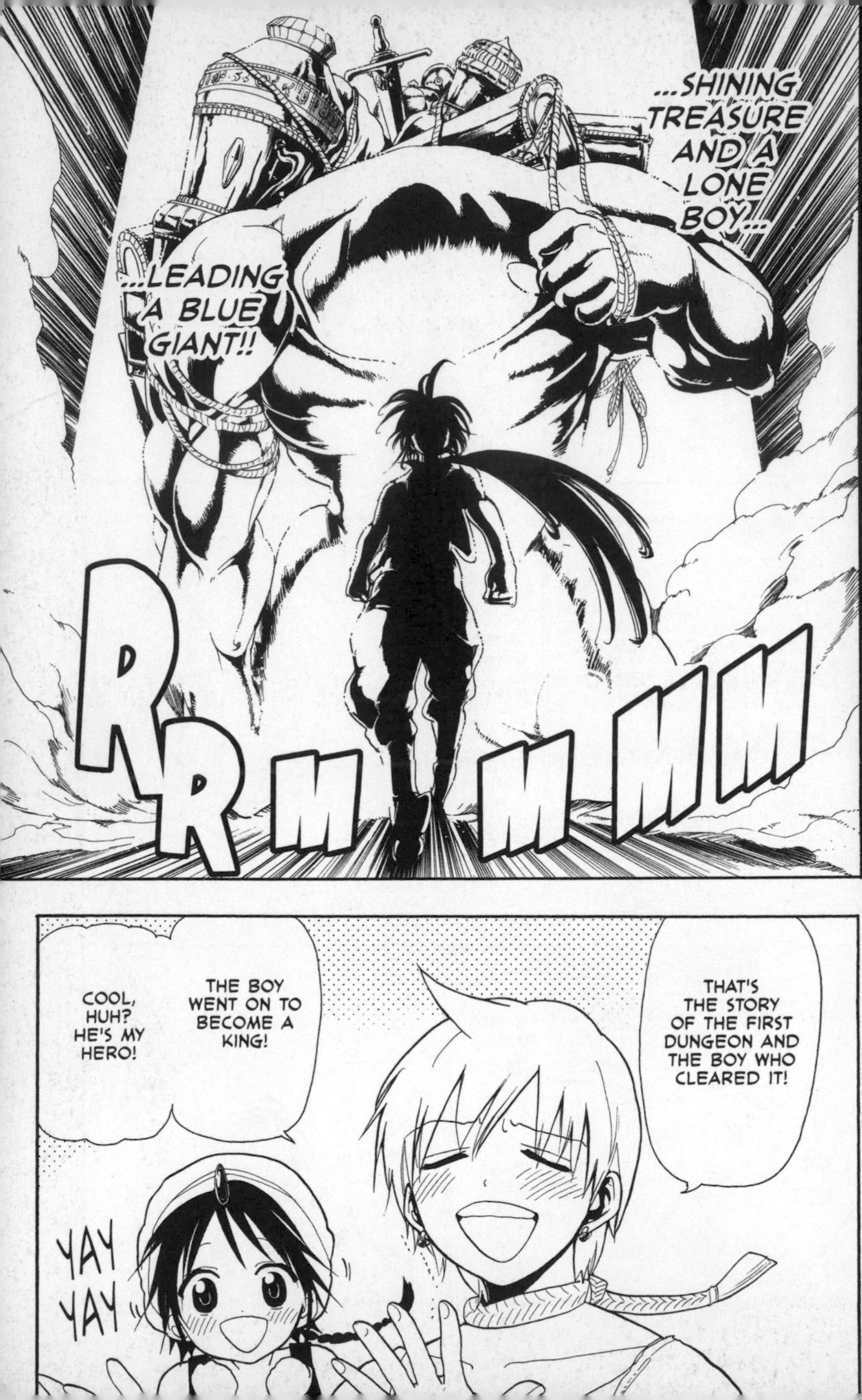
...SHINING TREASURE AND A LONE BOY...
...LEADING A BLUE GIANT!!
RRMMMMMM
THAT'S THE STORY OF THE FIRST DUNGEON AND THE BOY WHO CLEARED IT!
THE BOY WENT ON TO BECOME A KING!
COOL, HUH? HE'S MY HERO!
YAY YAY

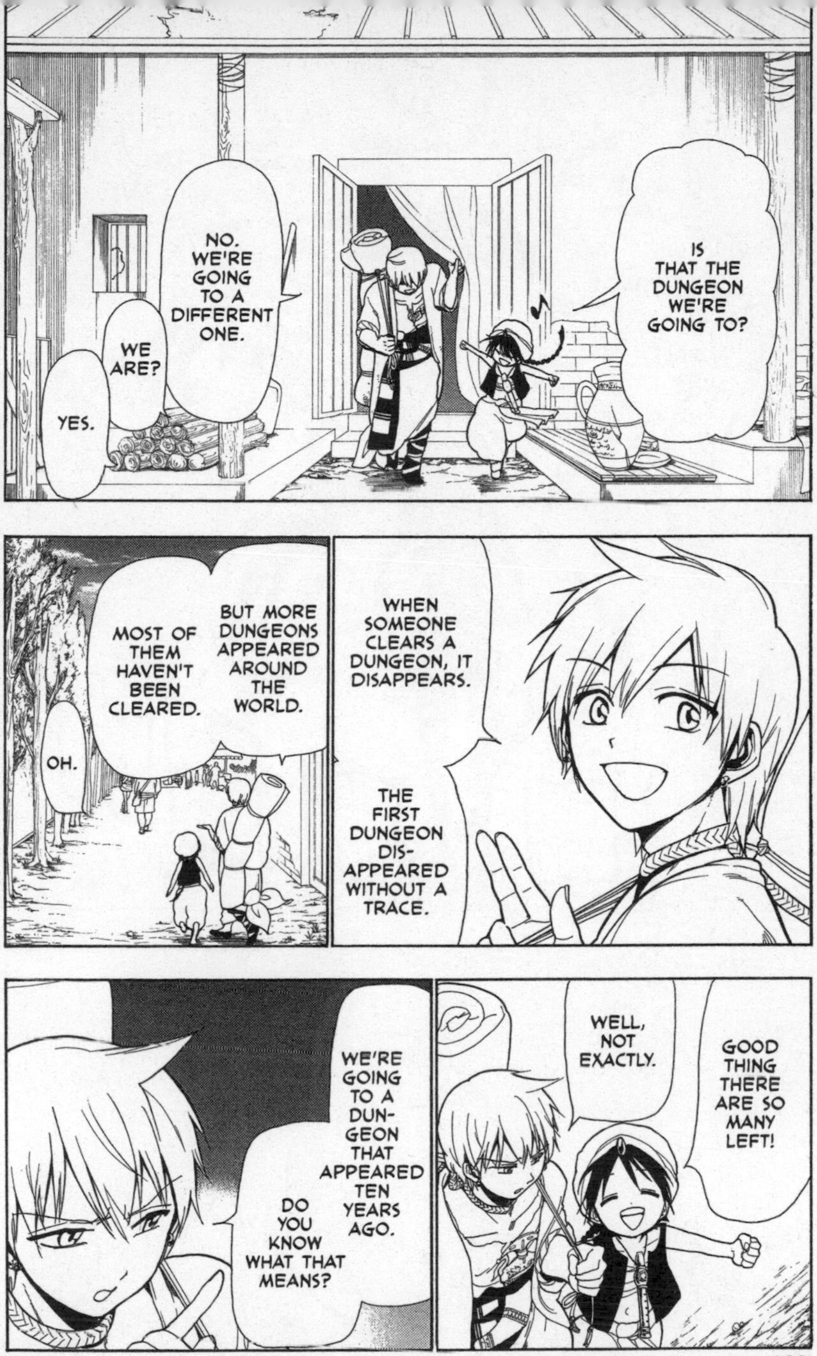
IS THAT THE DUNGEON WE'RE GOING TO?
NO. WE'RE GOING TO A DIFFERENT ONE.
WE ARE?
YES.
WHEN SOMEONE CLEARS A DUNGEON, IT DISAPPEARS.
THE FIRST DUNGEON DIS-APPEARED WITHOUT A TRACE.
BUT MORE DUNGEONS APPEARED AROUND THE WORLD.
MOST OF THEM HAVEN'T BEEN CLEARED.
OH.
GOOD THING THERE ARE SO MANY LEFT!
WELL, NOT EXACTLY.
WE'RE GOING TO A DUN-GEON THAT APPEARED TEN YEARS AGO.
DO YOU KNOW WHAT THAT MEANS?

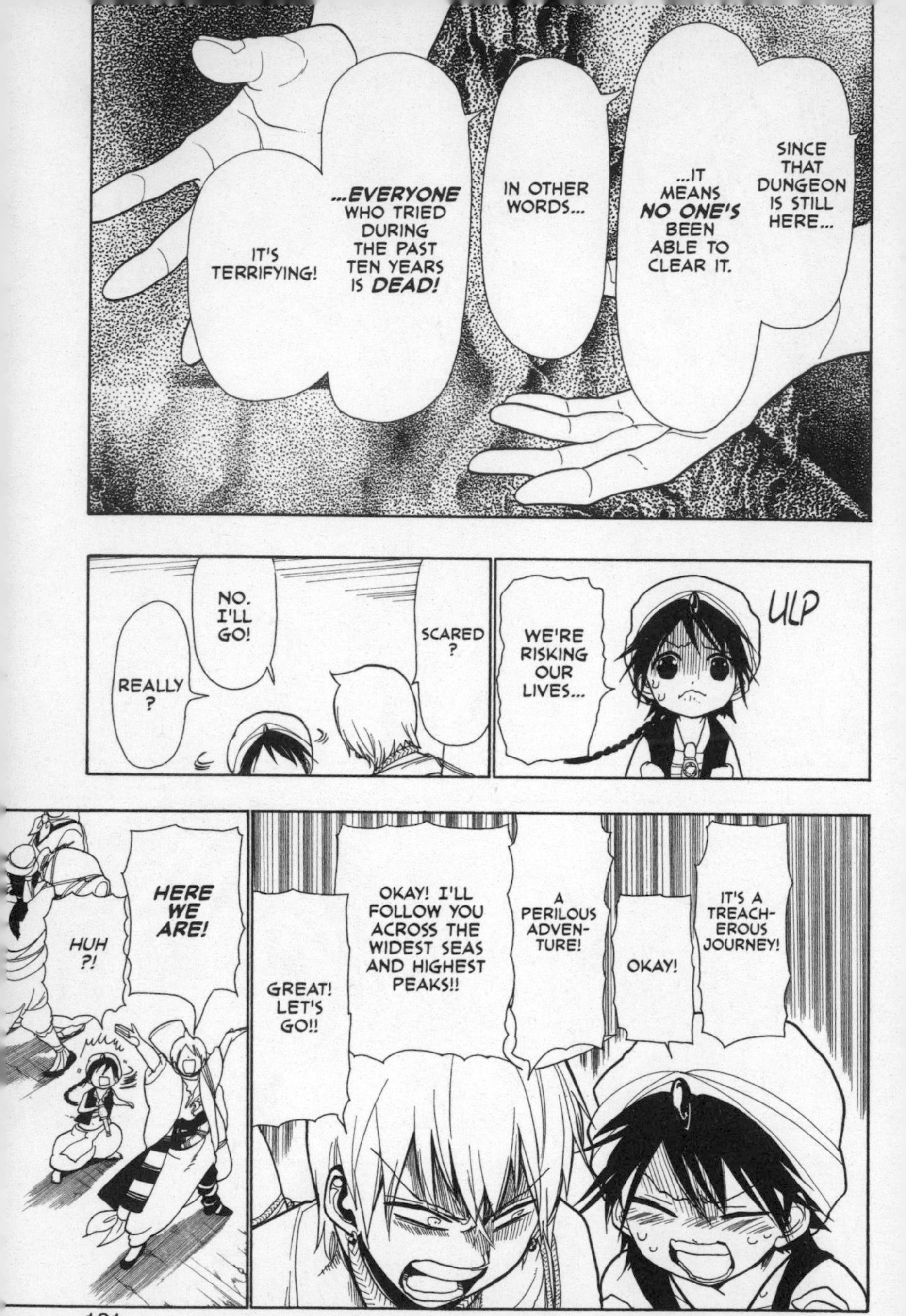
SINCE THAT DUNGEON IS STILL HERE...
...IT MEANS NO ONE'S BEEN ABLE TO CLEAR IT.
IN OTHER WORDS...
...EVERYONE WHO TRIED DURING THE PAST TEN YEARS IS DEAD!
IT'S TERRIFYING!
ULP
WE'RE RISKING OUR LIVES...
SCARED?
NO. I'LL GO!
REALLY?
IT'S A TREACHEROUS JOURNEY!
OKAY!
A PERILOUS ADVENTURE!
OKAY! I'LL FOLLOW YOU ACROSS THE WIDEST SEAS AND HIGHEST PEAKS!!
GREAT! LET'S GO!!
HERE WE ARE!
HUH?!

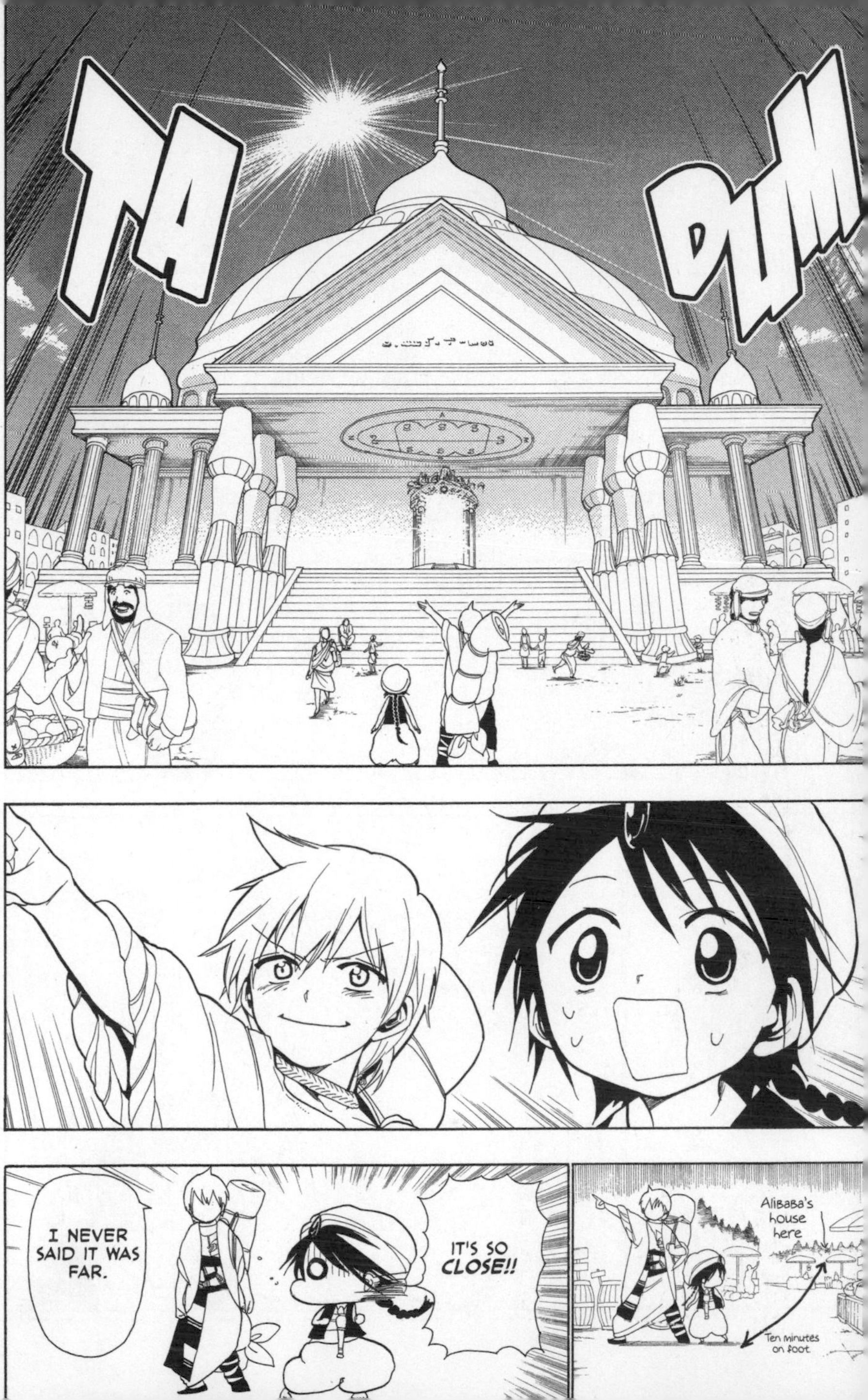
TA
DUM
Alibaba's house here
Ten minutes on foot
IT'S SO CLOSE!!
I NEVER SAID IT WAS FAR.

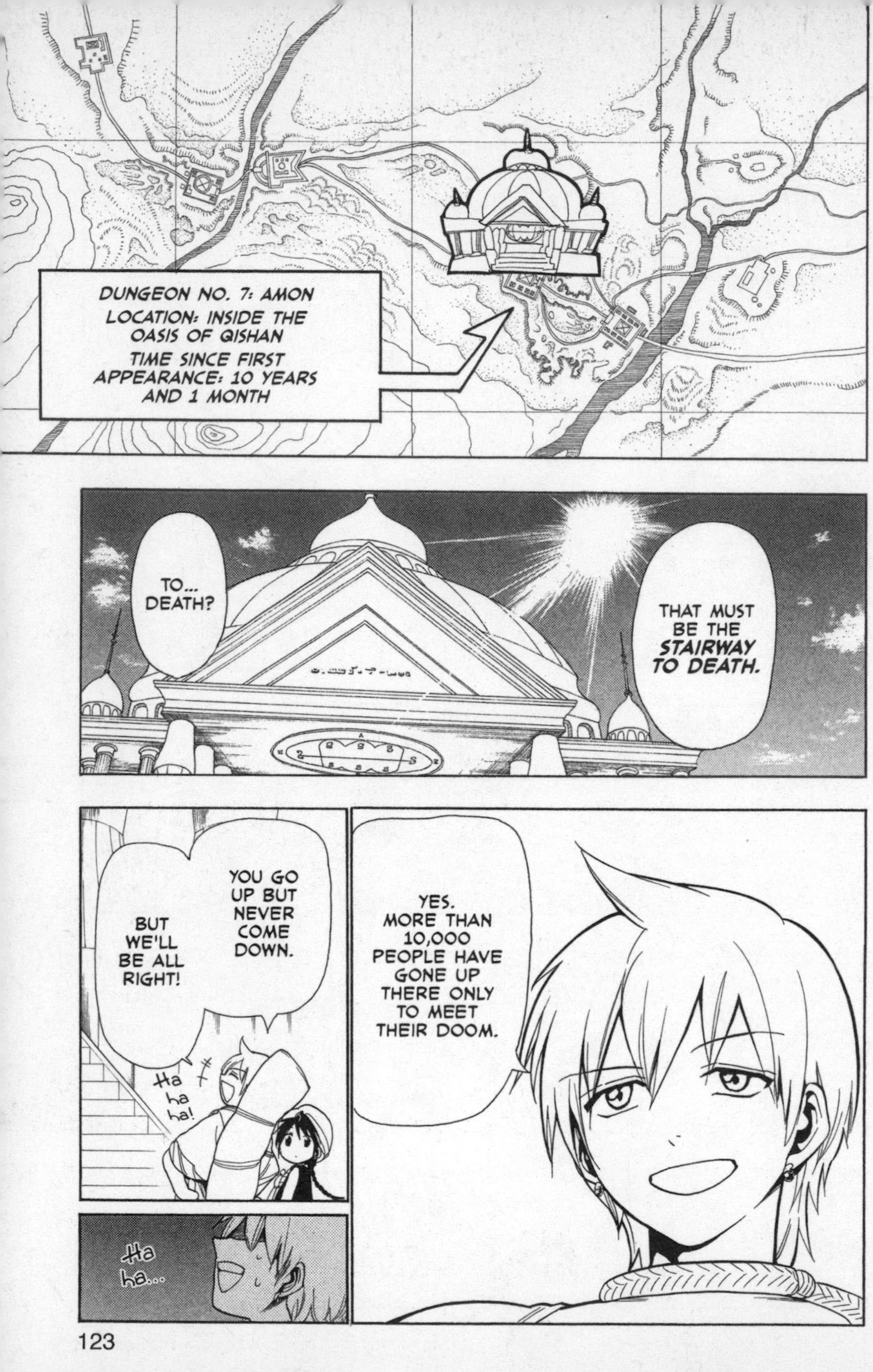
DUNGEON NO. 7: AMON
LOCATION: INSIDE THE OASIS OF QISHAN
TIME SINCE FIRST APPEARANCE: 10 YEARS AND 1 MONTH
THAT MUST BE THE *STAIRWAY TO DEATH.*
TO... DEATH?
YES. MORE THAN 10,000 PEOPLE HAVE GONE UP THERE ONLY TO MEET THEIR DOOM.
YOU GO UP BUT NEVER COME DOWN.
BUT WE'LL BE ALL RIGHT!
Ha ha ha!
Ha ha...

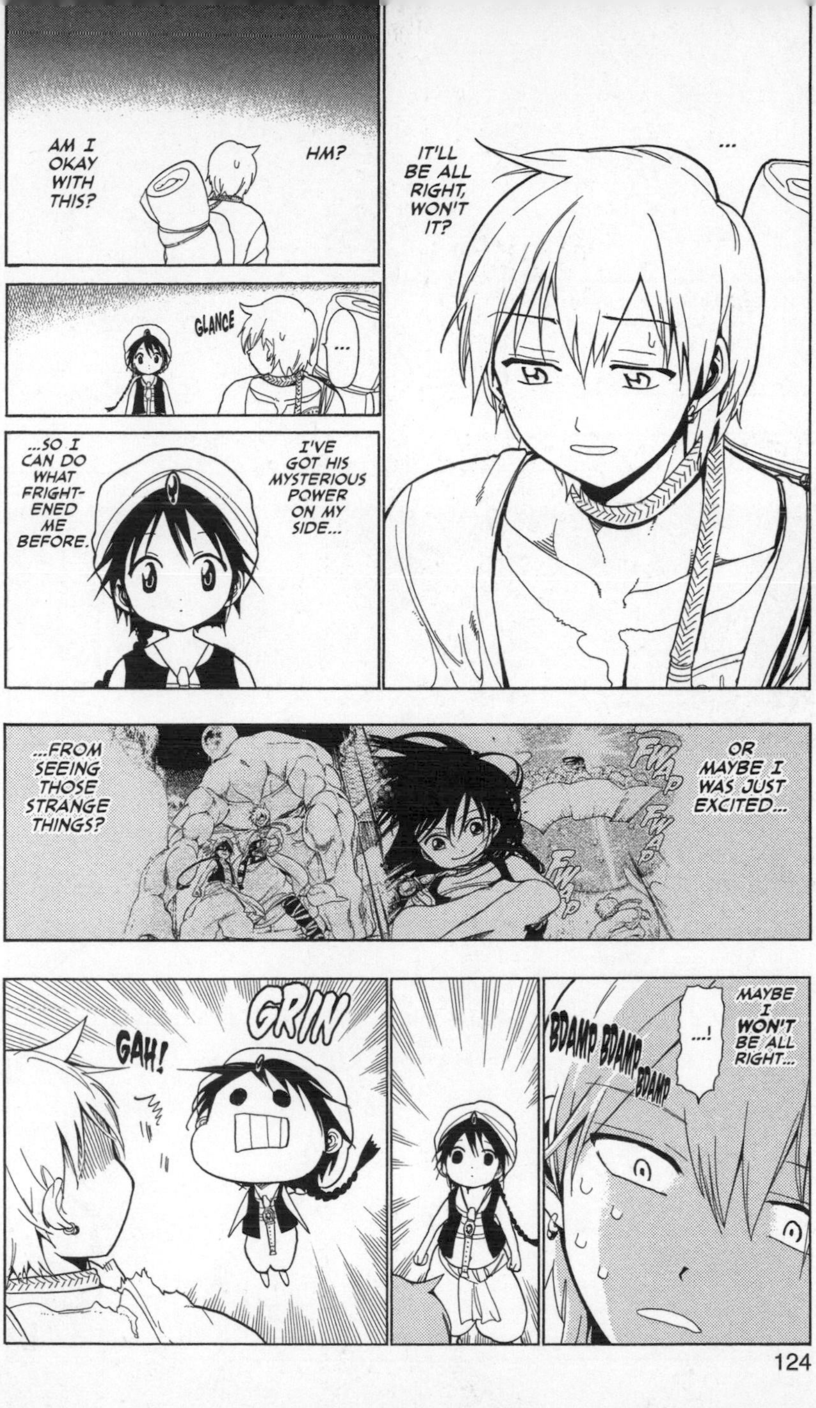
...
IT'LL BE ALL RIGHT, WON'T IT?
HM?
AM I OKAY WITH THIS?
...
GLANCE
I'VE GOT HIS MYSTERIOUS POWER ON MY SIDE...!
...SO I CAN DO WHAT FRIGHT-ENED ME BEFORE.
OR MAYBE I WAS JUST EXCITED...
FWAP FWAP FWAP
...FROM SEEING THOSE STRANGE THINGS?
MAYBE I WON'T BE ALL RIGHT...
...!
BDAMP BDAMP BDAMP
GRIN
GAH!

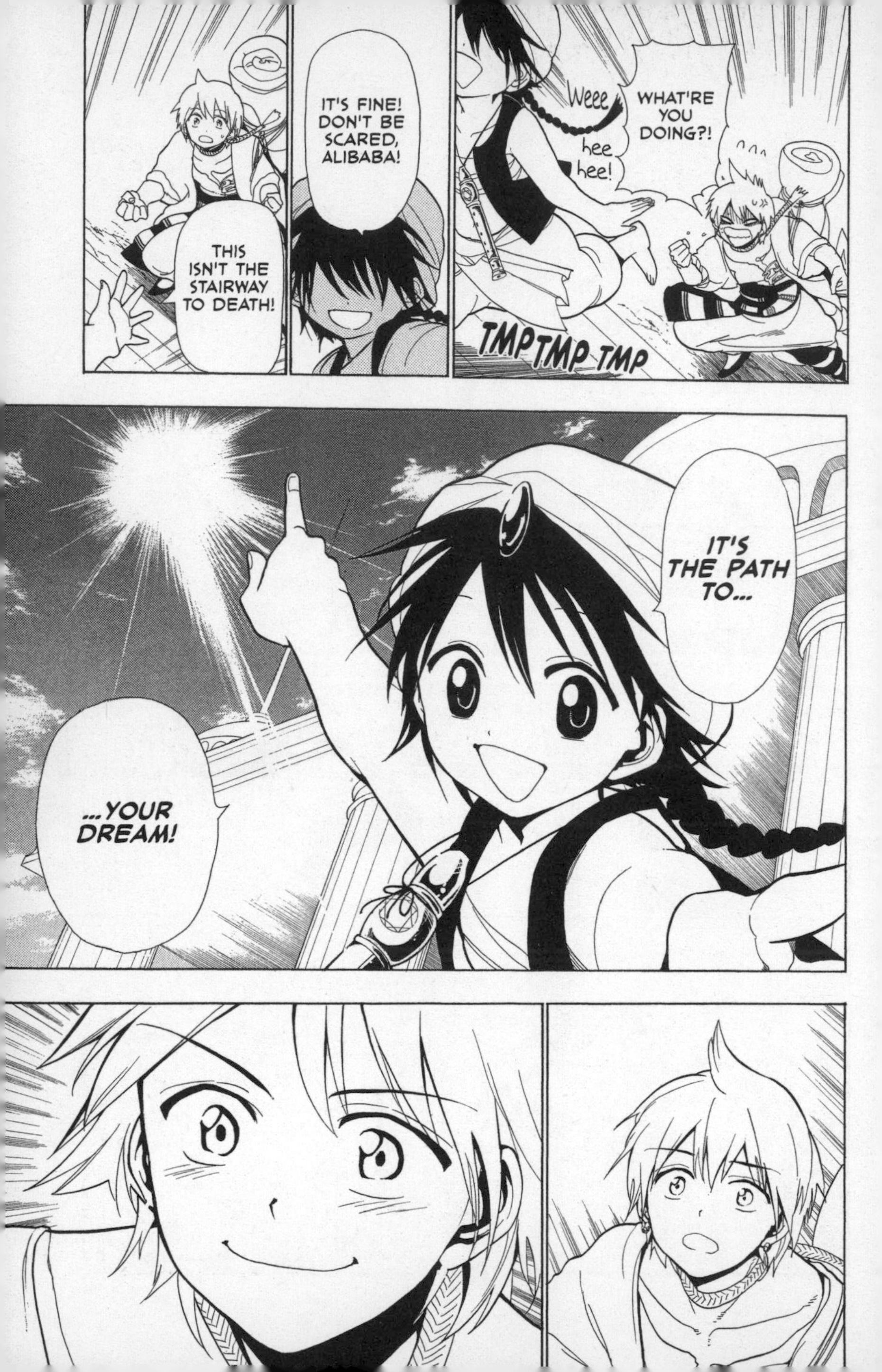
WHAT'RE YOU DOING?!
Weee hee hee!
TMPTMP TMP
IT'S FINE! DON'T BE SCARED, ALIBABA!
THIS ISN'T THE STAIRWAY TO DEATH!
IT'S THE PATH TO...
...YOUR DREAM!

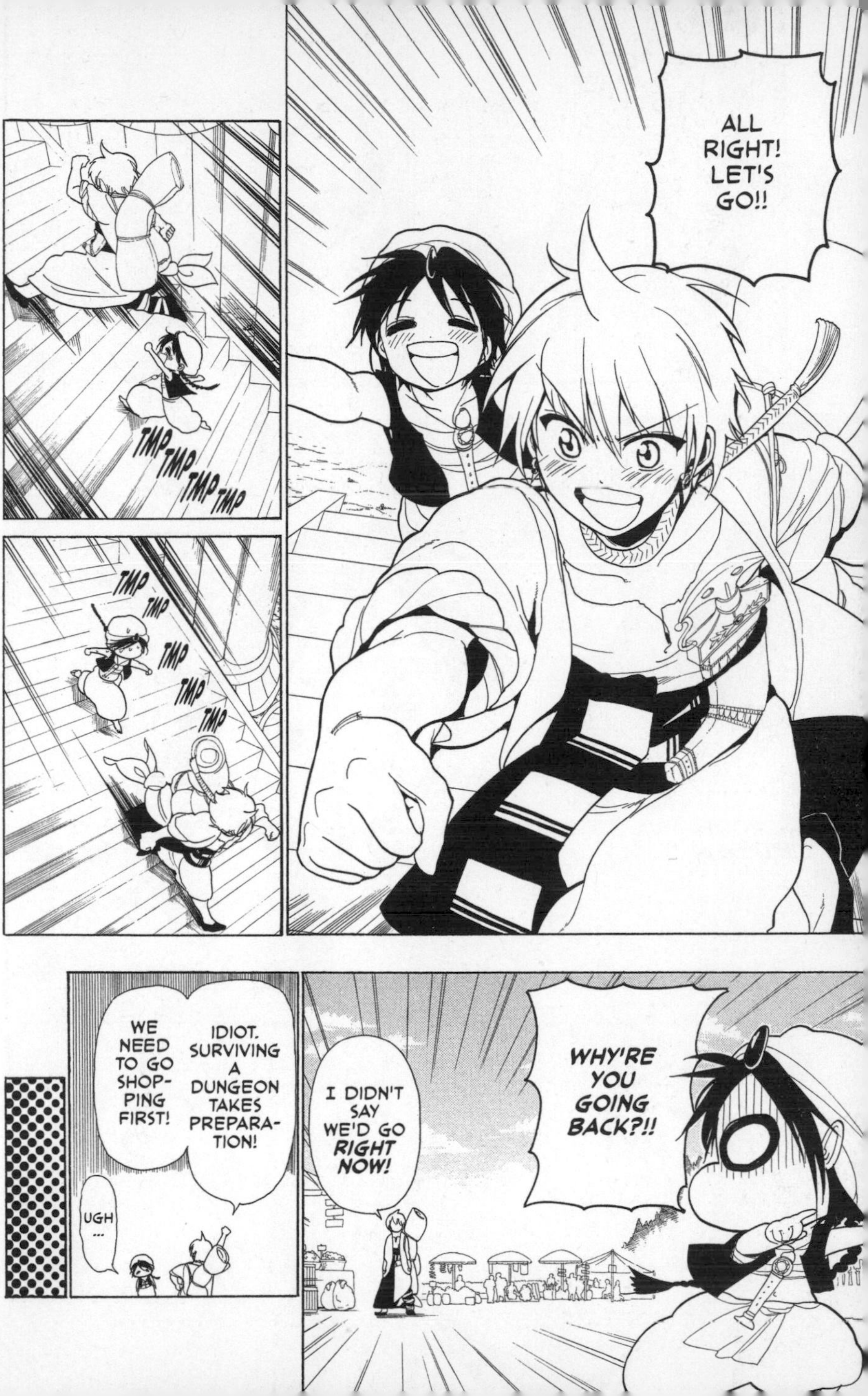
ALL RIGHT! LET'S GO!!
TMP TMP TMP TMP
TMP TMP TMP TMP TMP
WHY'RE YOU GOING BACK?!!
I DIDN'T SAY WE'D GO RIGHT NOW!
IDIOT. SURVIVING A DUNGEON TAKES PREPARA-TION!
WE NEED TO GO SHOP-PING FIRST!
UGH...

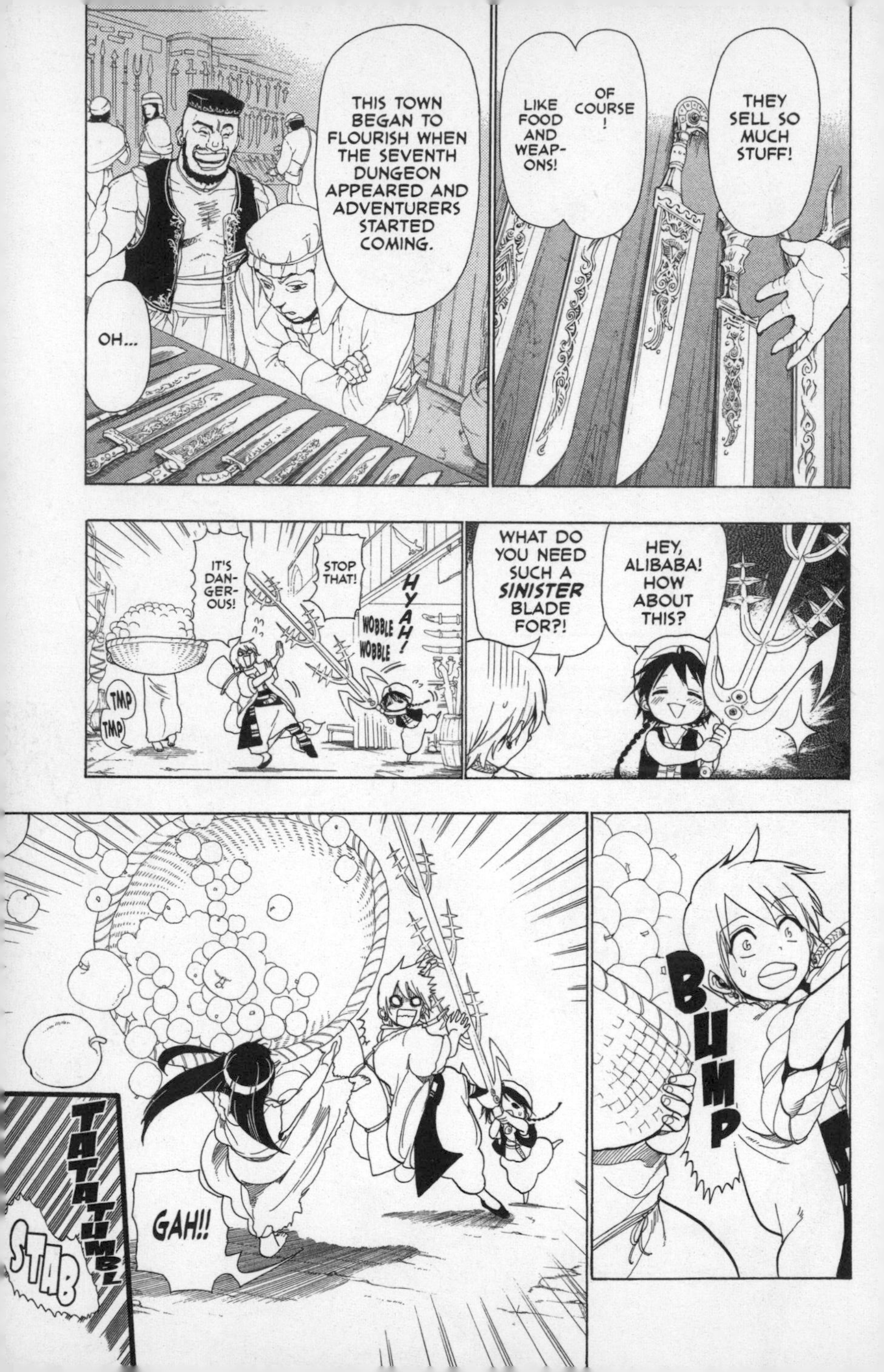
THEY SELL SO MUCH STUFF!
OF COURSE!
LIKE FOOD AND WEAPONS!
THIS TOWN BEGAN TO FLOURISH WHEN THE SEVENTH DUNGEON APPEARED AND ADVENTURERS STARTED COMING.
OH...
HEY, ALIBABA! HOW ABOUT THIS?
WHAT DO YOU NEED SUCH A *SINISTER* BLADE FOR?!
HYAH!
WOBBLE WOBBLE
STOP THAT!
IT'S DANGEROUS!
TMP TMP
BUMP
GAH!!
TATATUMBL
STAB

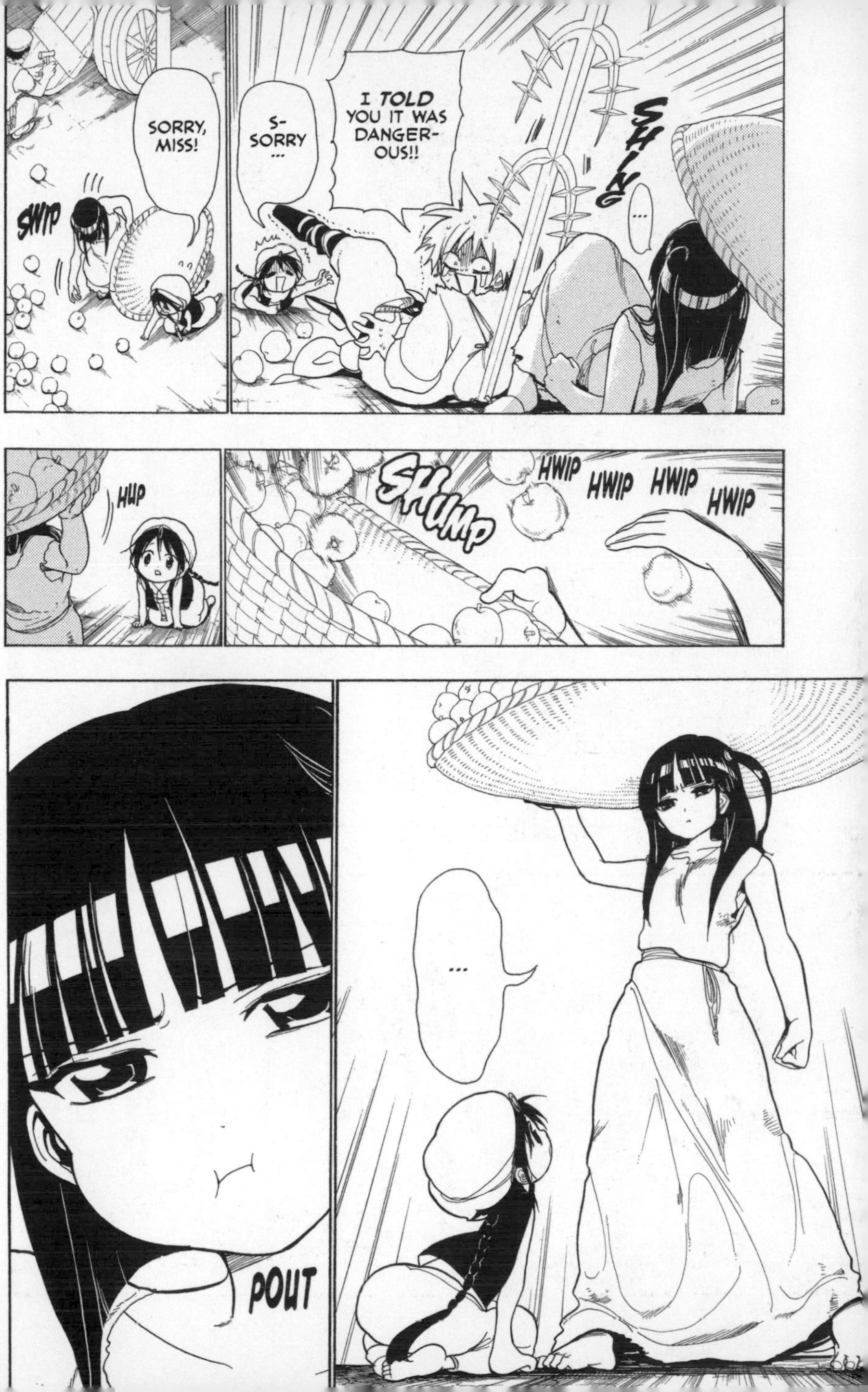
SHING
...
I TOLD YOU IT WAS DANGER-OUS!!
S-SORRY ...
SORRY, MISS!
SWIP
SHUMP
HWIP HWIP HWIP HWIP
HUP
...
POUT

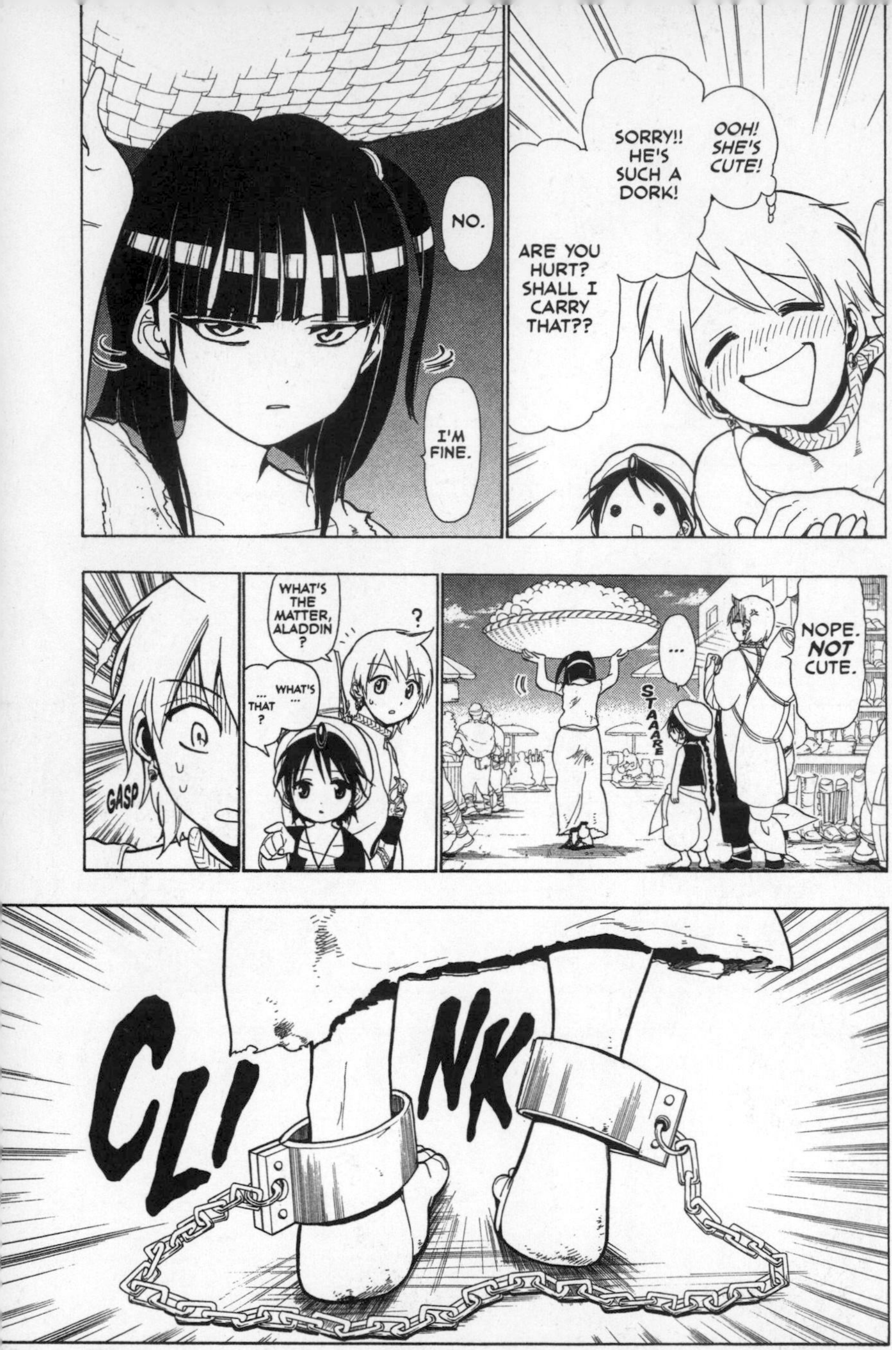
OOH! SHE'S CUTE!
SORRY!! HE'S SUCH A DORK!
ARE YOU HURT? SHALL I CARRY THAT??
NO.
I'M FINE.
NOPE. ***NOT*** CUTE.
...
STAAARE
WHAT'S THE MATTER, ALADDIN?
?
... WHAT'S ... THAT?
GASP
CLINK

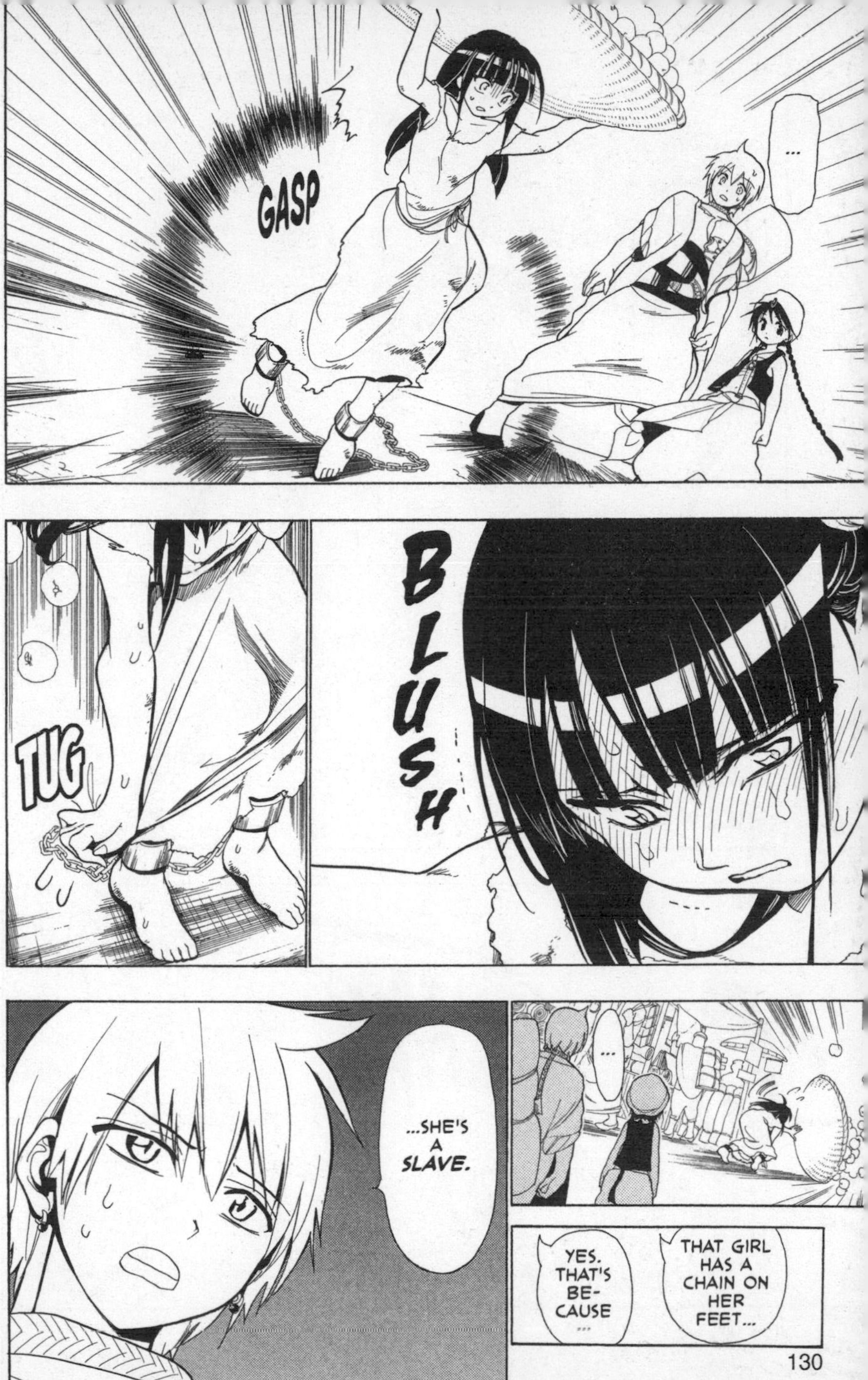
...
GASP
BLUSH
TUG
...
THAT GIRL HAS A CHAIN ON HER FEET...
YES. THAT'S BE-CAUSE ...
...SHE'S A SLAVE.

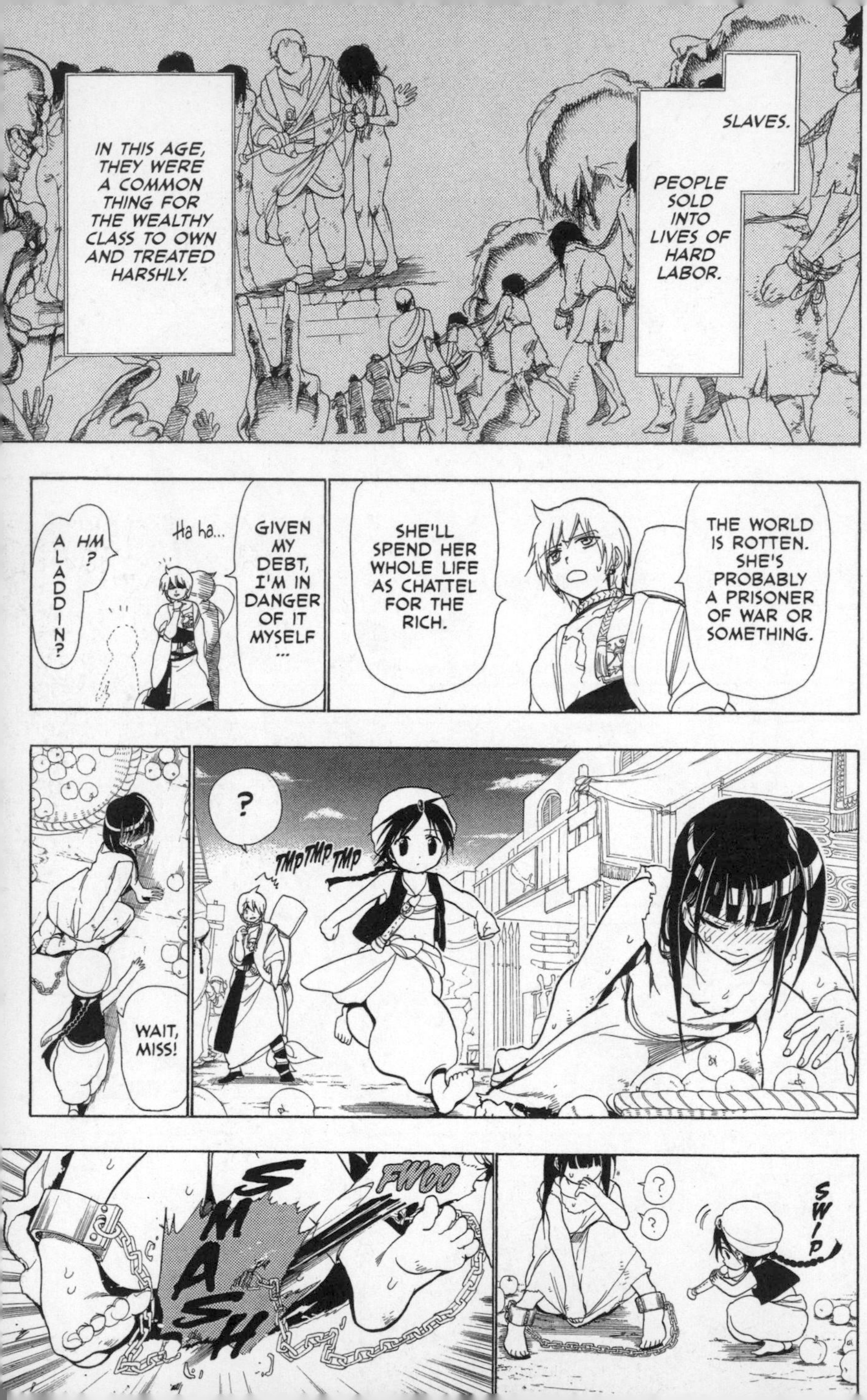
SLAVES.
PEOPLE SOLD INTO LIVES OF HARD LABOR.
IN THIS AGE, THEY WERE A COMMON THING FOR THE WEALTHY CLASS TO OWN AND TREATED HARSHLY.
THE WORLD IS ROTTEN. SHE'S PROBABLY A PRISONER OF WAR OR SOMETHING.
SHE'LL SPEND HER WHOLE LIFE AS CHATTEL FOR THE RICH.
GIVEN MY DEBT, I'M IN DANGER OF IT MYSELF ...
Ha ha...
HM?
ALADDIN?
?
TMPTMP TMP
WAIT, MISS!
SWIP
?
?
FWOO
SMASH

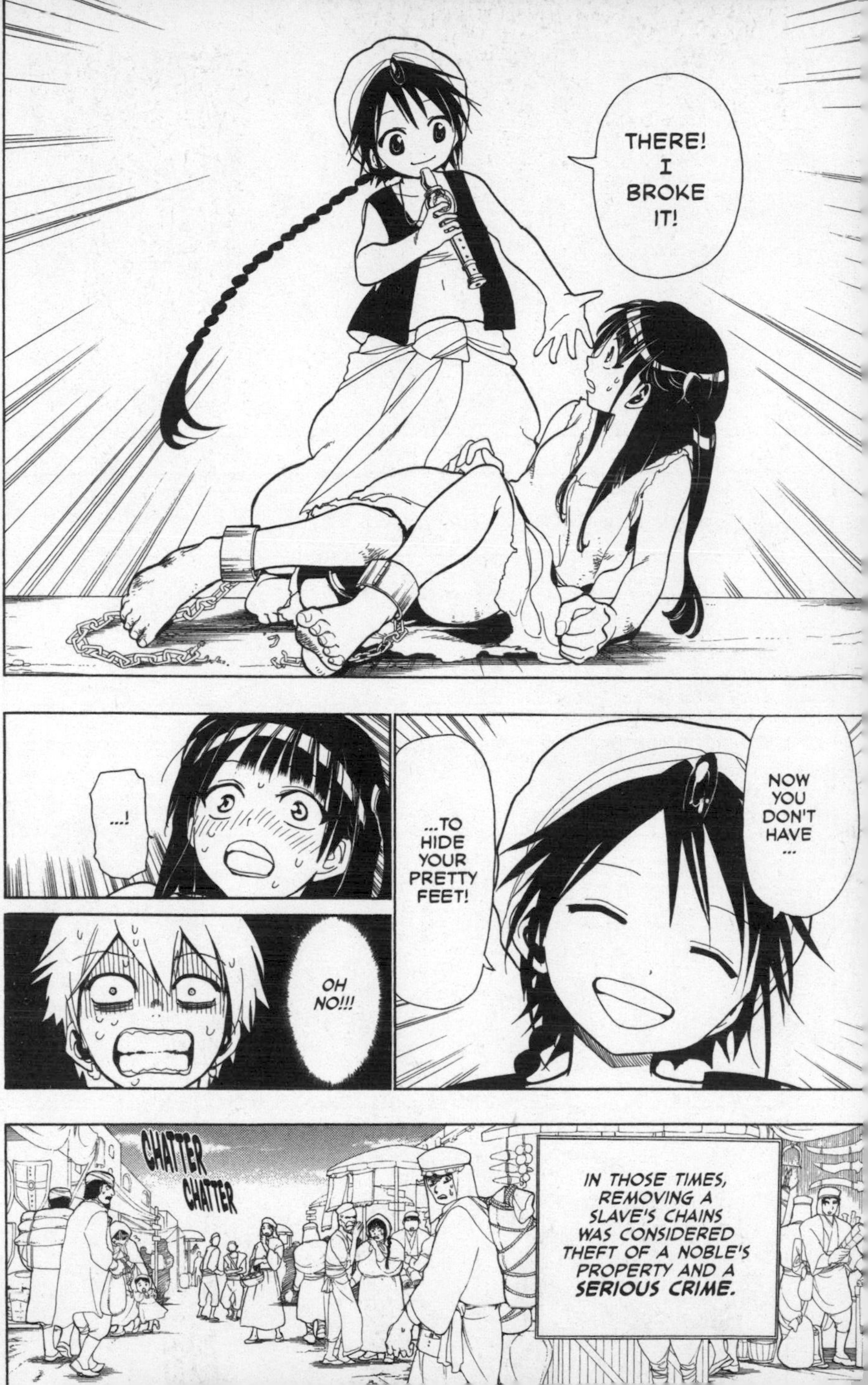
THERE! I BROKE IT!
NOW YOU DON'T HAVE ...
...TO HIDE YOUR PRETTY FEET!
...!
OH NO!!!
IN THOSE TIMES, REMOVING A SLAVE'S CHAINS WAS CONSIDERED THEFT OF A NOBLE'S PROPERTY AND A SERIOUS CRIME.
CHATTER CHATTER

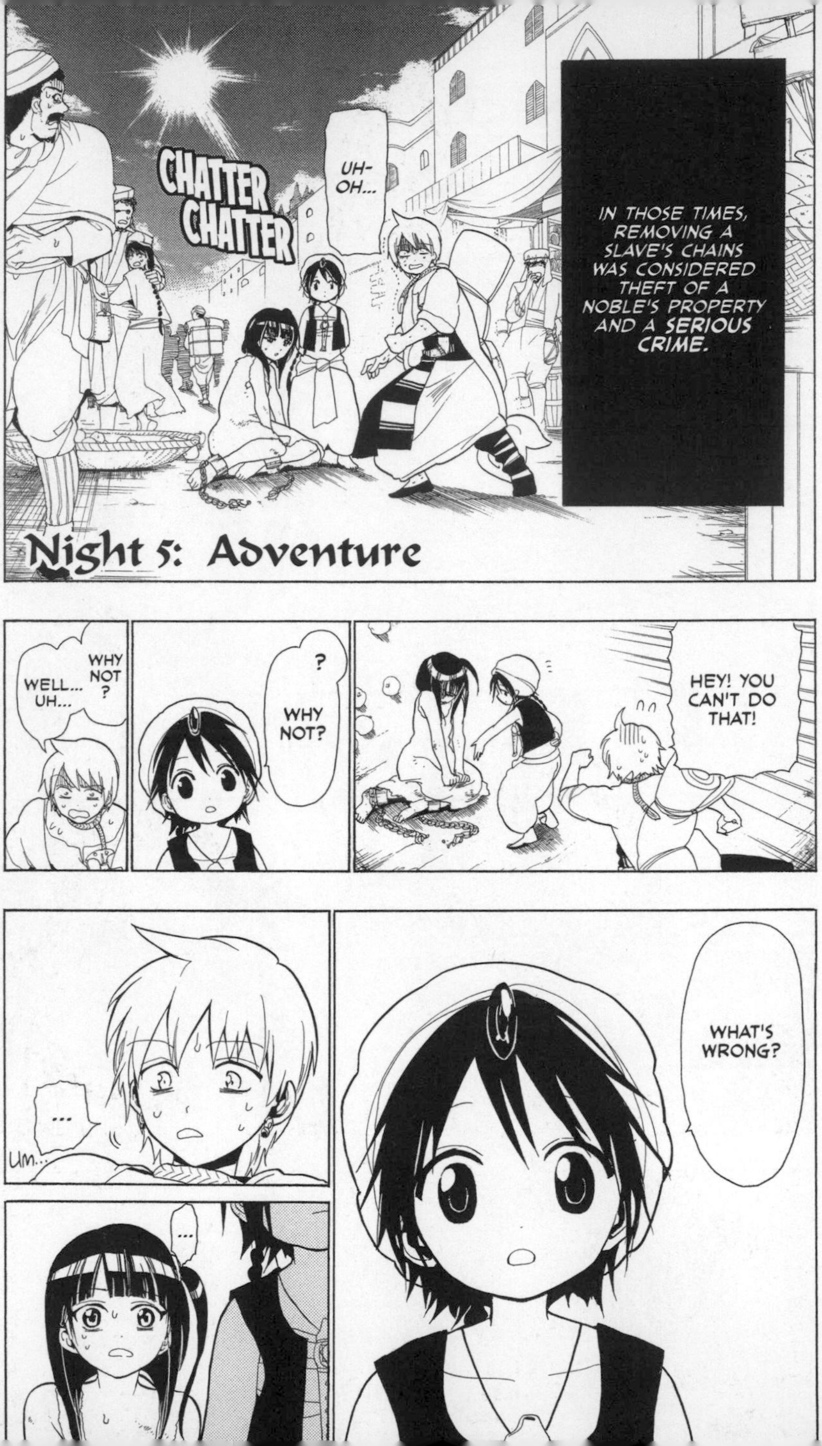
IN THOSE TIMES, REMOVING A SLAVE'S CHAINS WAS CONSIDERED THEFT OF A NOBLE'S PROPERTY AND A SERIOUS CRIME.
UH-OH...
CHATTER CHATTER
Night 5: Adventure
HEY! YOU CAN'T DO THAT!
?
WHY NOT?
WHY NOT ?
WELL... UH...
WHAT'S WRONG?
...
Um...
...

Night 5: Adventure

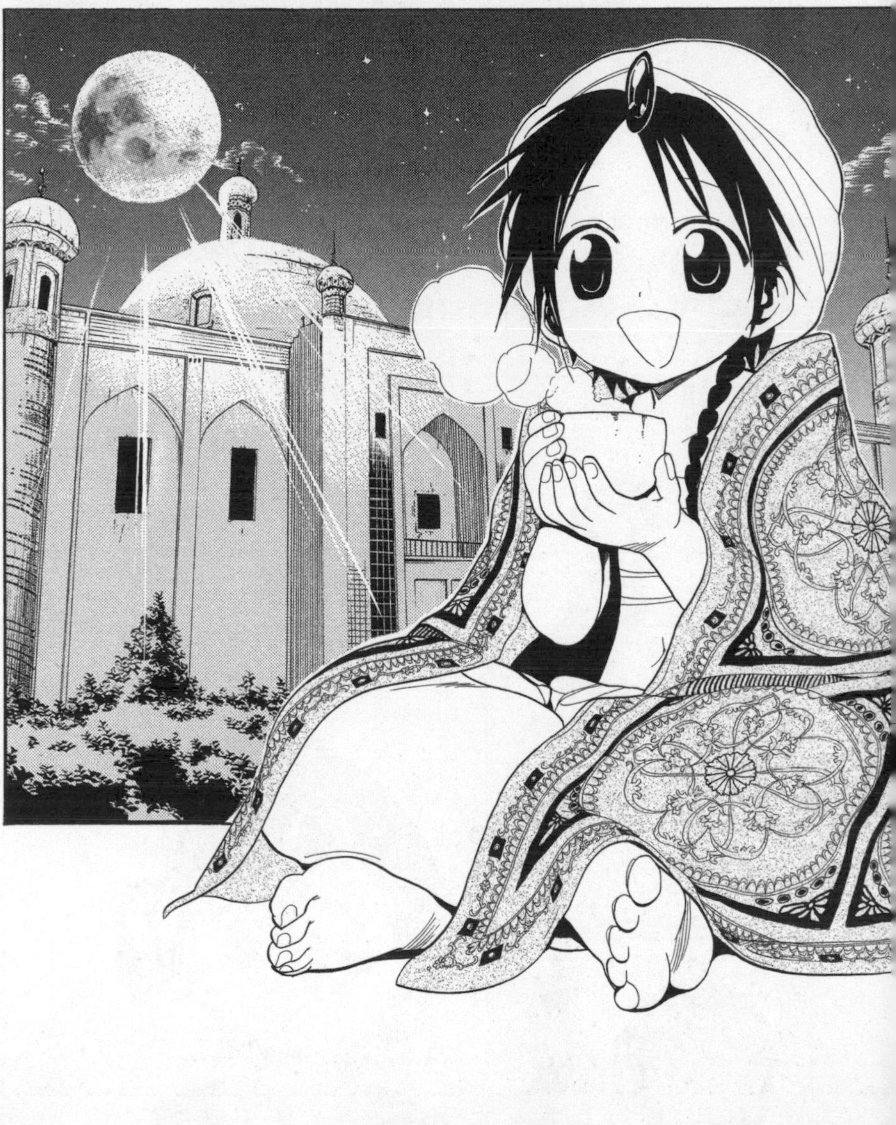

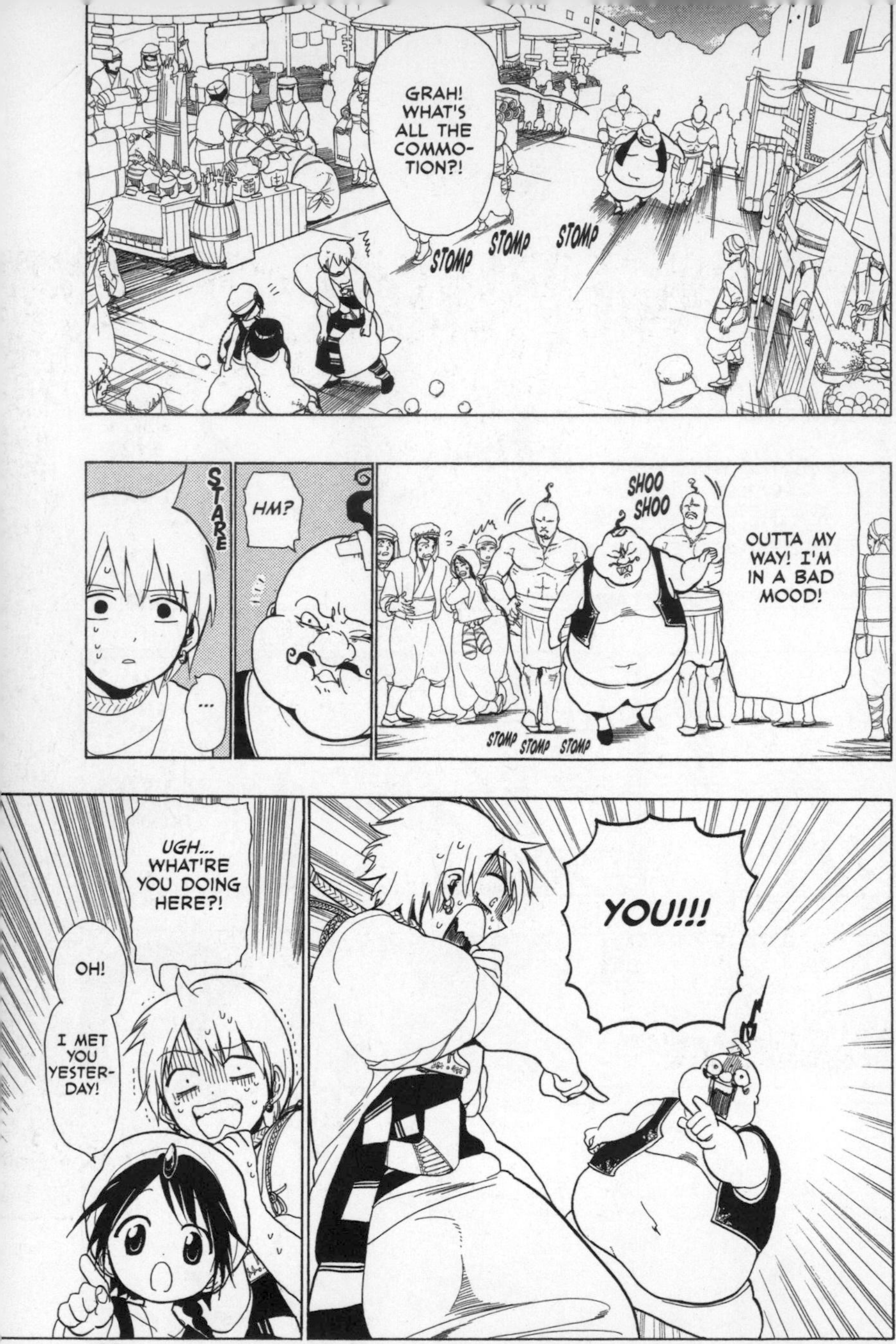
GRAH! WHAT'S ALL THE COMMO-TION?!
STOMP STOMP STOMP
SHOO SHOO
OUTTA MY WAY! I'M IN A BAD MOOD!
STOMP STOMP STOMP
HM?
STARE
...
YOU!!!
UGH... WHAT'RE YOU DOING HERE?!
OH!
I MET YOU YESTER-DAY!

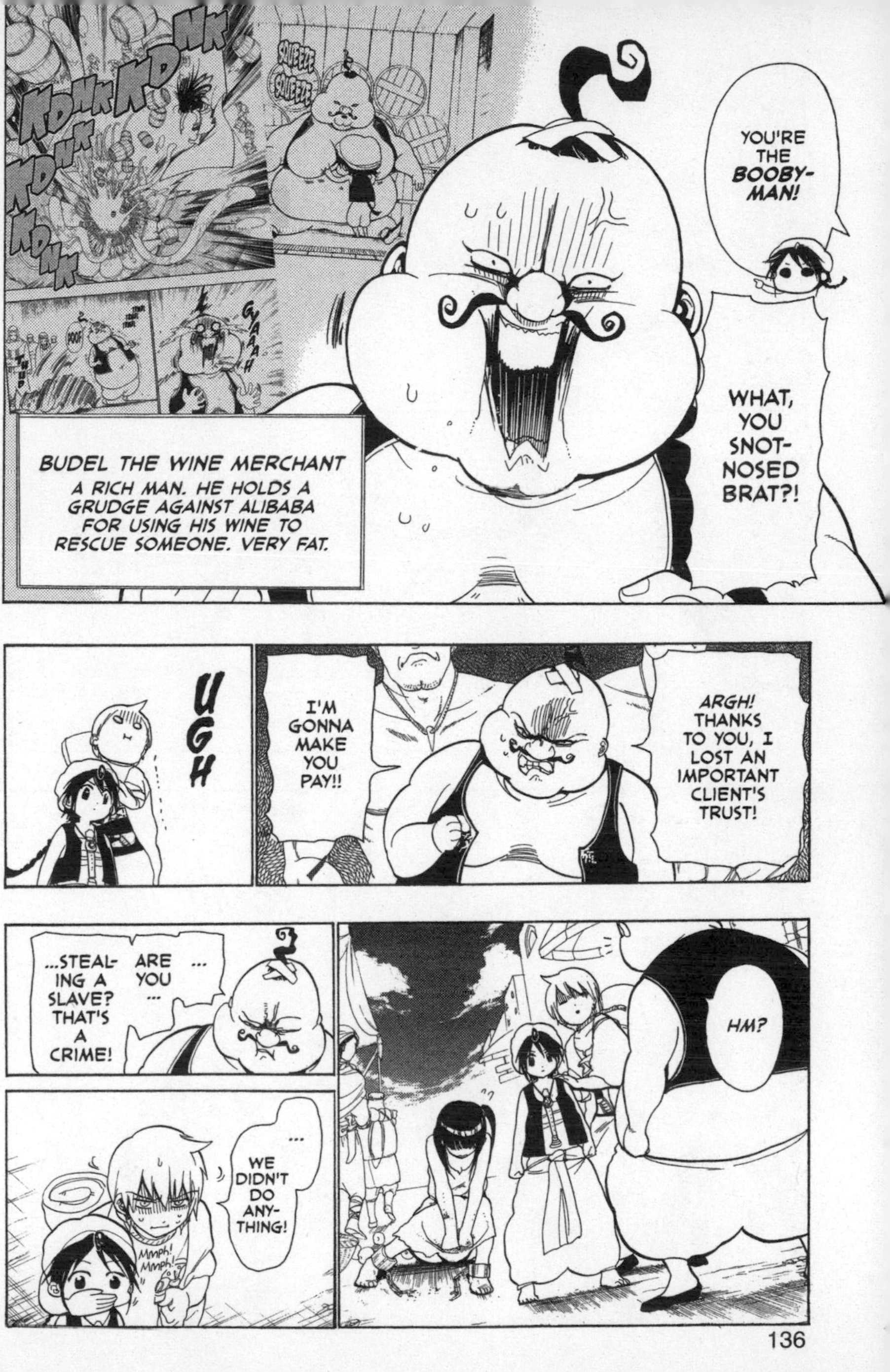
YOU'RE THE BOOBY-MAN!
WHAT, YOU SNOT-NOSED BRAT?!
SQUEEZE SQUEEZE
KDONK KDONK KDONK KDONK
GYAAAH
BUDEL THE WINE MERCHANT
A RICH MAN. HE HOLDS A GRUDGE AGAINST ALIBABA FOR USING HIS WINE TO RESCUE SOMEONE. VERY FAT.
ARGH! THANKS TO YOU, I LOST AN IMPORTANT CLIENT'S TRUST!
I'M GONNA MAKE YOU PAY!!
UGH
HM?
...
ARE YOU ...
...STEALING A SLAVE? THAT'S A CRIME!
... WE DIDN'T DO ANYTHING!
Mmph! Mmph!

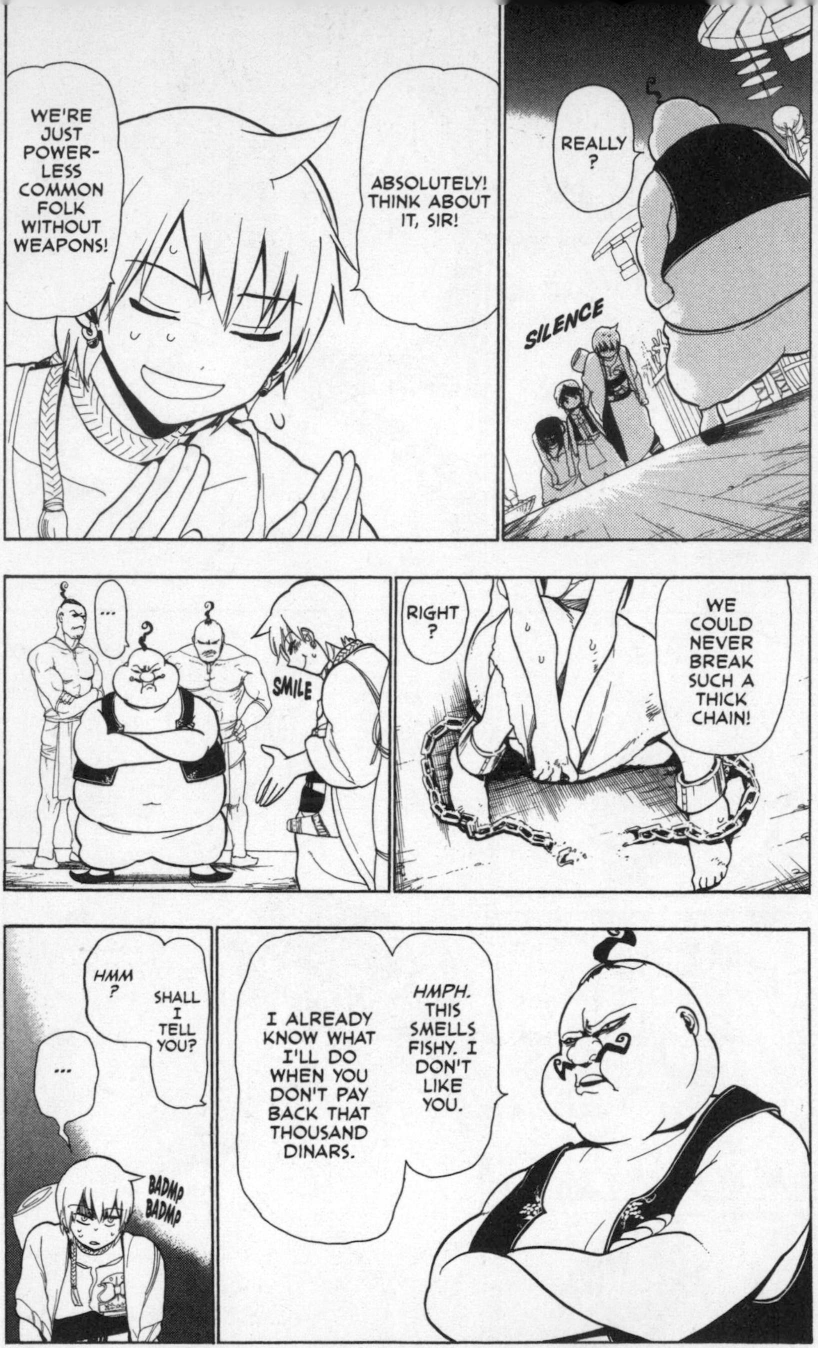
REALLY?
SILENCE
ABSOLUTELY! THINK ABOUT IT, SIR!
WE'RE JUST POWERLESS COMMON FOLK WITHOUT WEAPONS!
WE COULD NEVER BREAK SUCH A THICK CHAIN!
RIGHT?
SMILE
...
HMPH. THIS SMELLS FISHY. I DON'T LIKE YOU.
I ALREADY KNOW WHAT I'LL DO WHEN YOU DON'T PAY BACK THAT THOUSAND DINARS.
HMM?
SHALL I TELL YOU?
...
BADMP BADMP

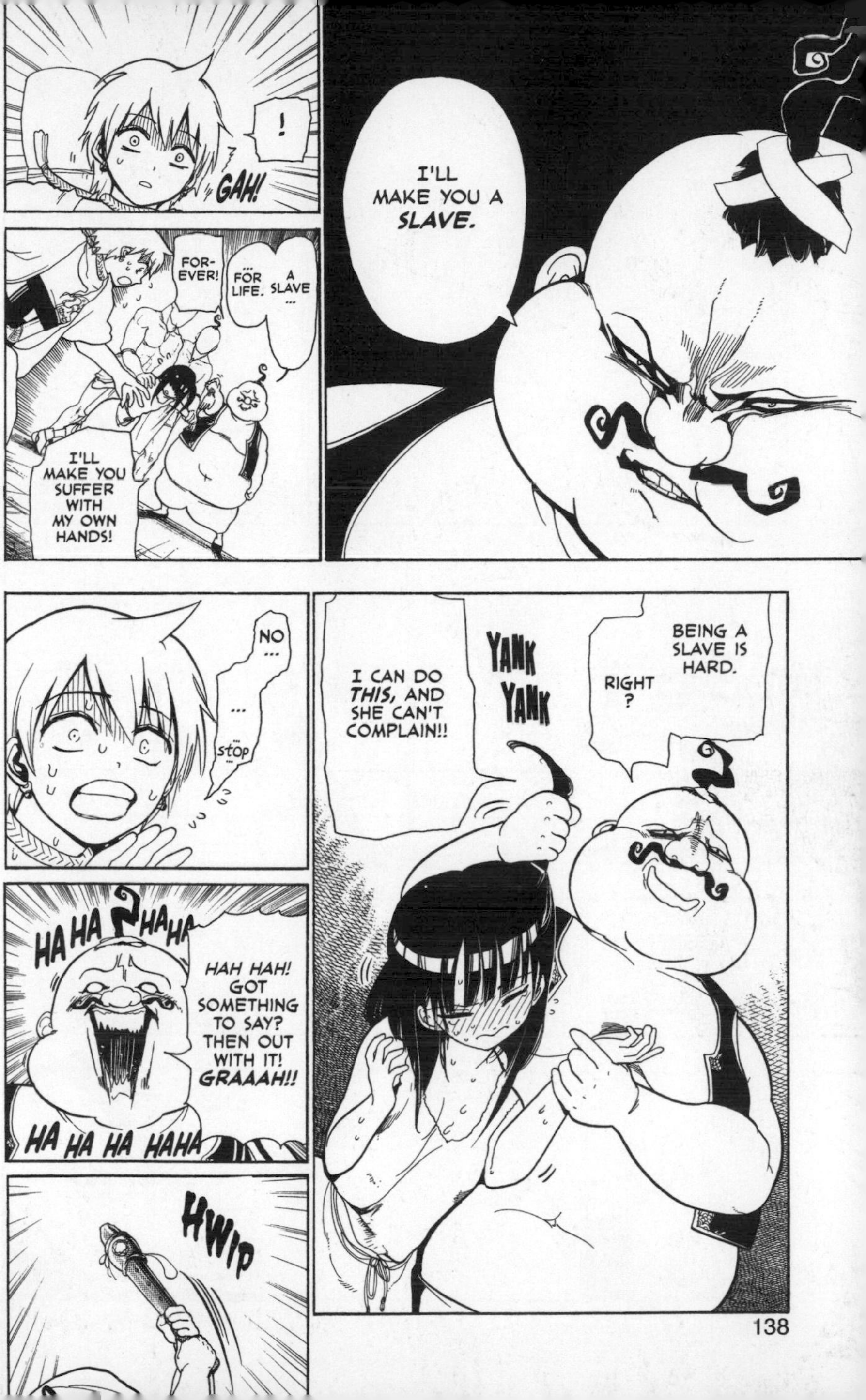
I'LL MAKE YOU A *SLAVE.*
!
GAH!
A SLAVE ...
... FOR LIFE.
FOR-EVER!
I'LL MAKE YOU SUFFER WITH MY OWN HANDS!
BEING A SLAVE IS HARD.
RIGHT ?
YANK YANK
I CAN DO *THIS,* AND SHE CAN'T COMPLAIN!!
NO ...
...
stop ...
HA HA HA HA
HAH HAH! GOT SOMETHING TO SAY? THEN OUT WITH IT! GRAAAH!!
HA HA HA HAHA
HWIP

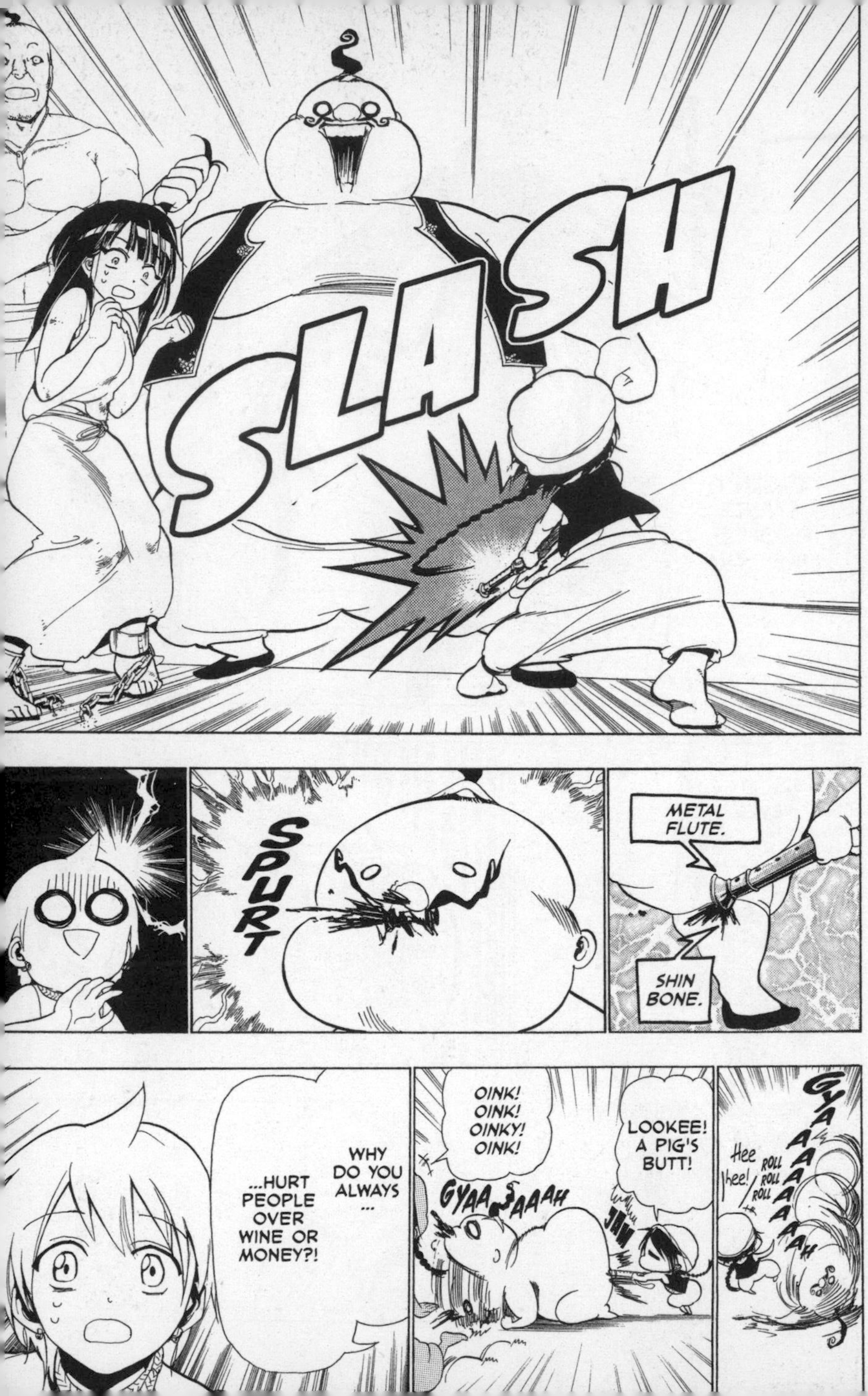
SLASH
METAL FLUTE.
SHIN BONE.
SPURT
GYAAAAAAAAAH
Hee hee!
ROLL ROLL ROLL
LOOKEE! A PIG'S BUTT!
JAM
OINK! OINK! OINKY! OINK!
GYAAAAAAH
WHY DO YOU ALWAYS ...
...HURT PEOPLE OVER WINE OR MONEY?!

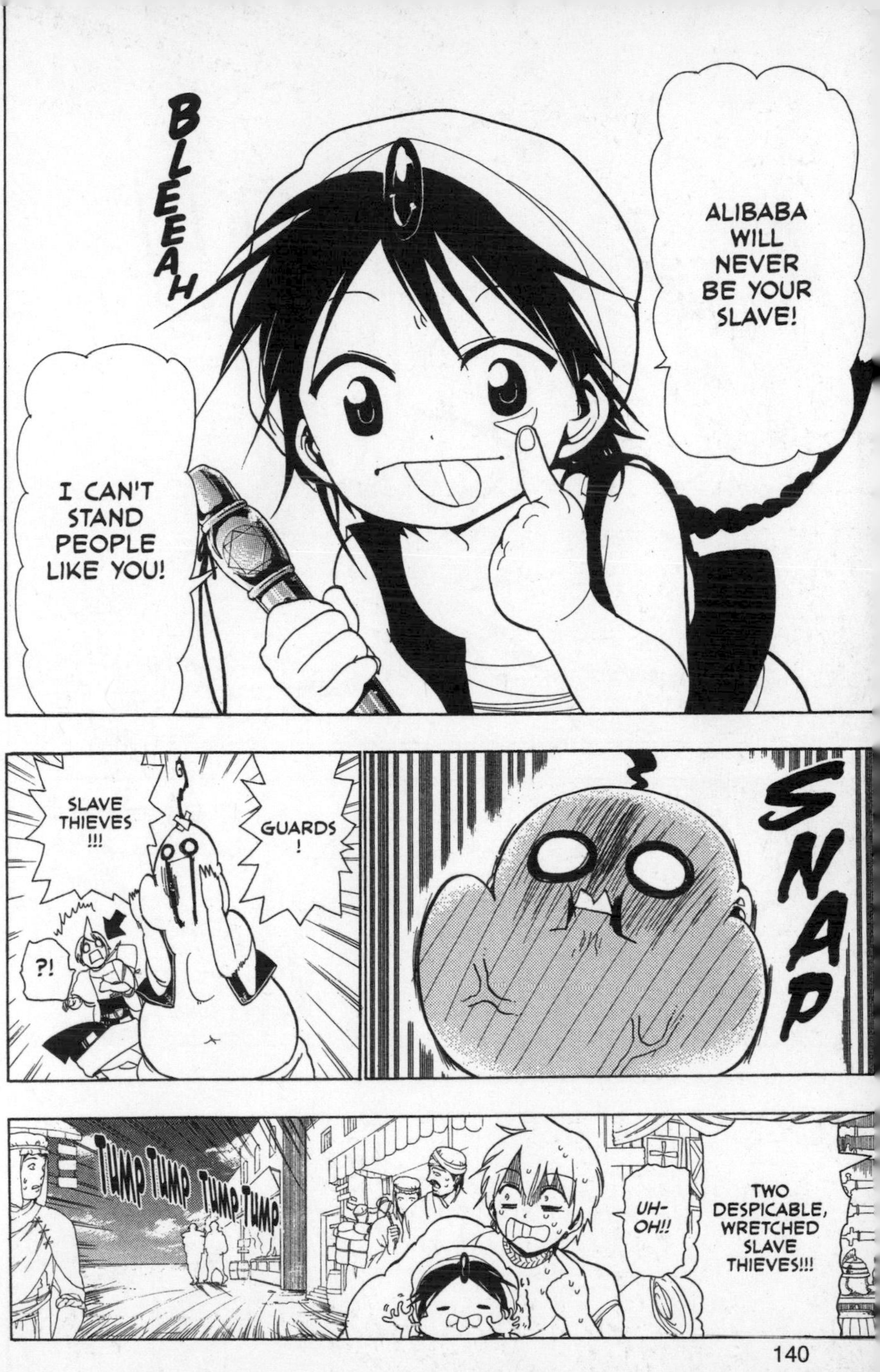
ALIBABA WILL NEVER BE YOUR SLAVE!
BLEEAH
I CAN'T STAND PEOPLE LIKE YOU!
SNAP
GUARDS!
SLAVE THIEVES!!!
?!
TWO DESPICABLE, WRETCHED SLAVE THIEVES!!!
UH-OH!!
TUMP TUMP TUMP TUMP

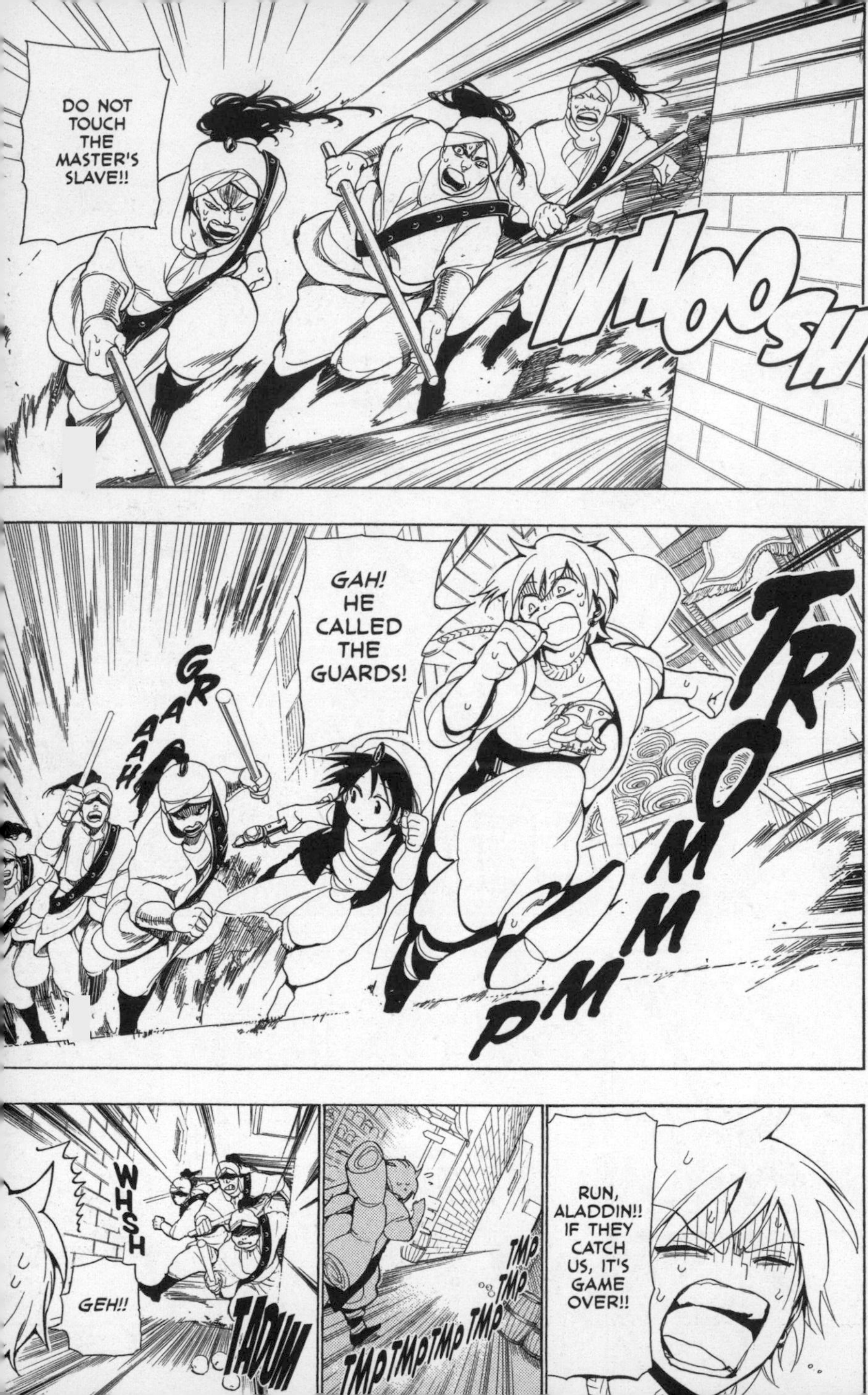
DO NOT TOUCH THE MASTER'S SLAVE!!
WHOOSH
TROMMMMP
GAH! HE CALLED THE GUARDS!
GRAAAH
RUN, ALADDIN!! IF THEY CATCH US, IT'S GAME OVER!!
TMP TMP TMP TMP TMP TMP TMP
WHSH
GEH!!
TADUM

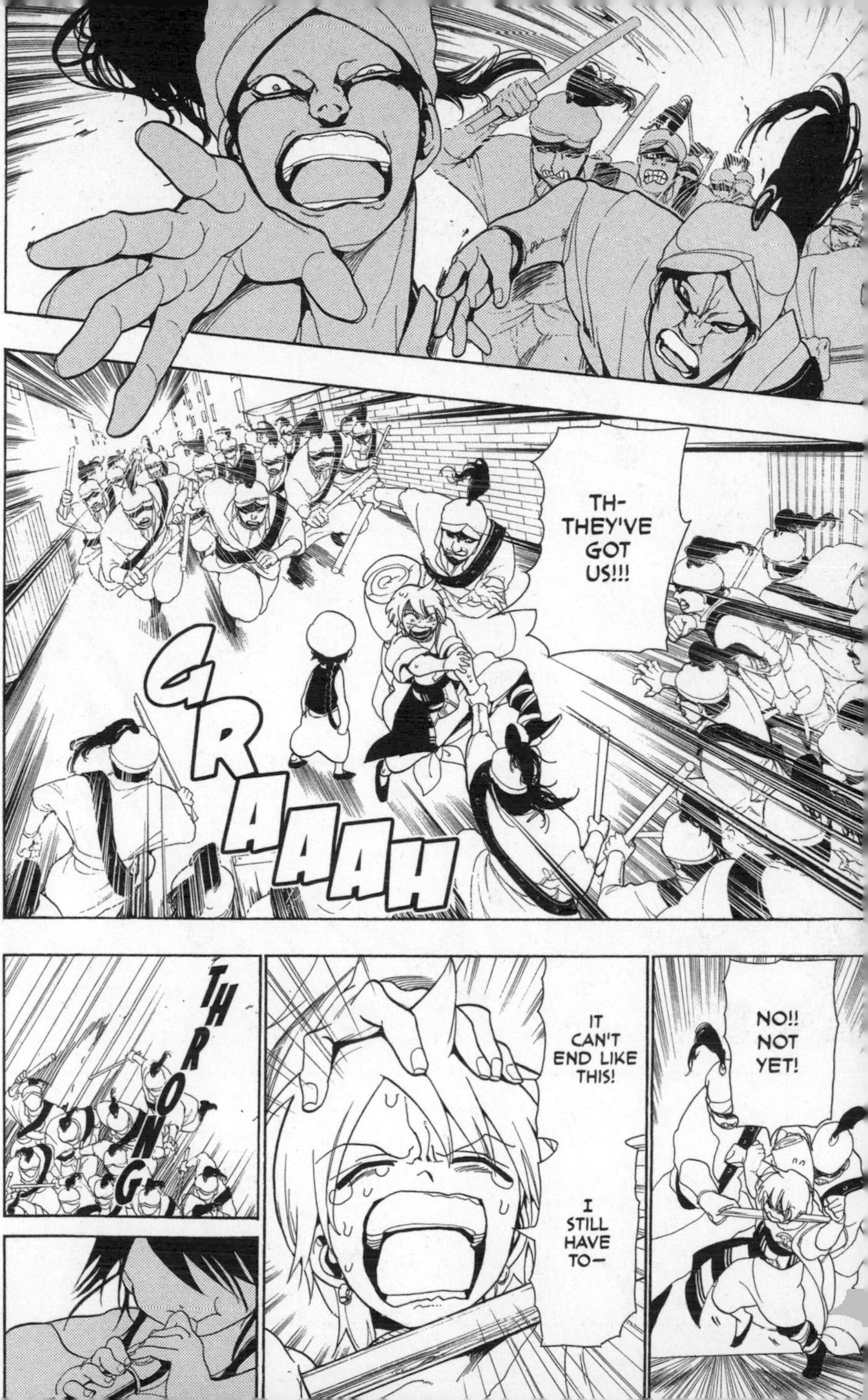
TH- THEY'VE GOT US!!!
GRAAAAH
NO!! NOT YET!
IT CAN'T END LIKE THIS!
I STILL HAVE TO—
THRONG

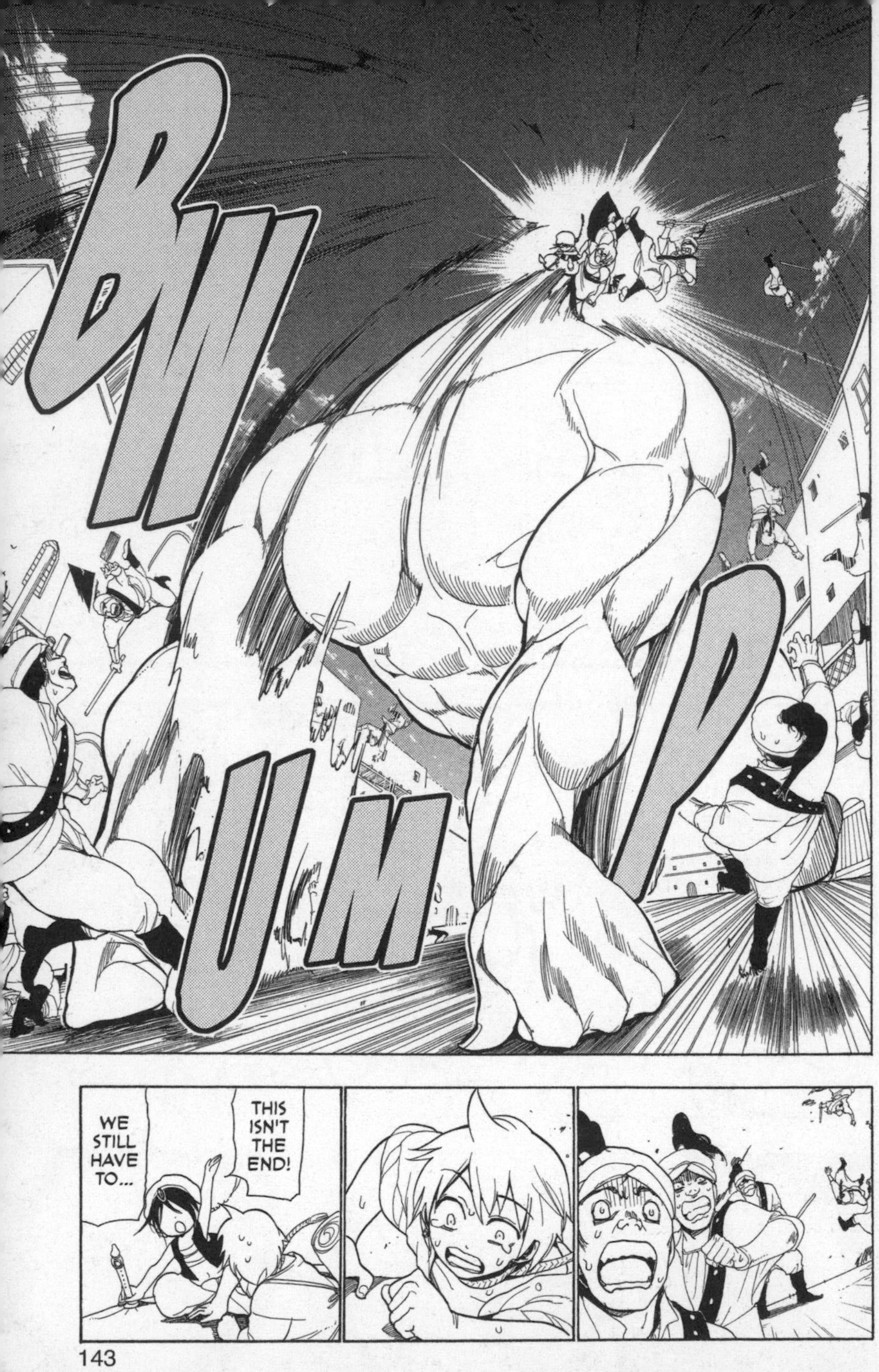
BUMP
THIS ISN'T THE END!
WE STILL HAVE TO...

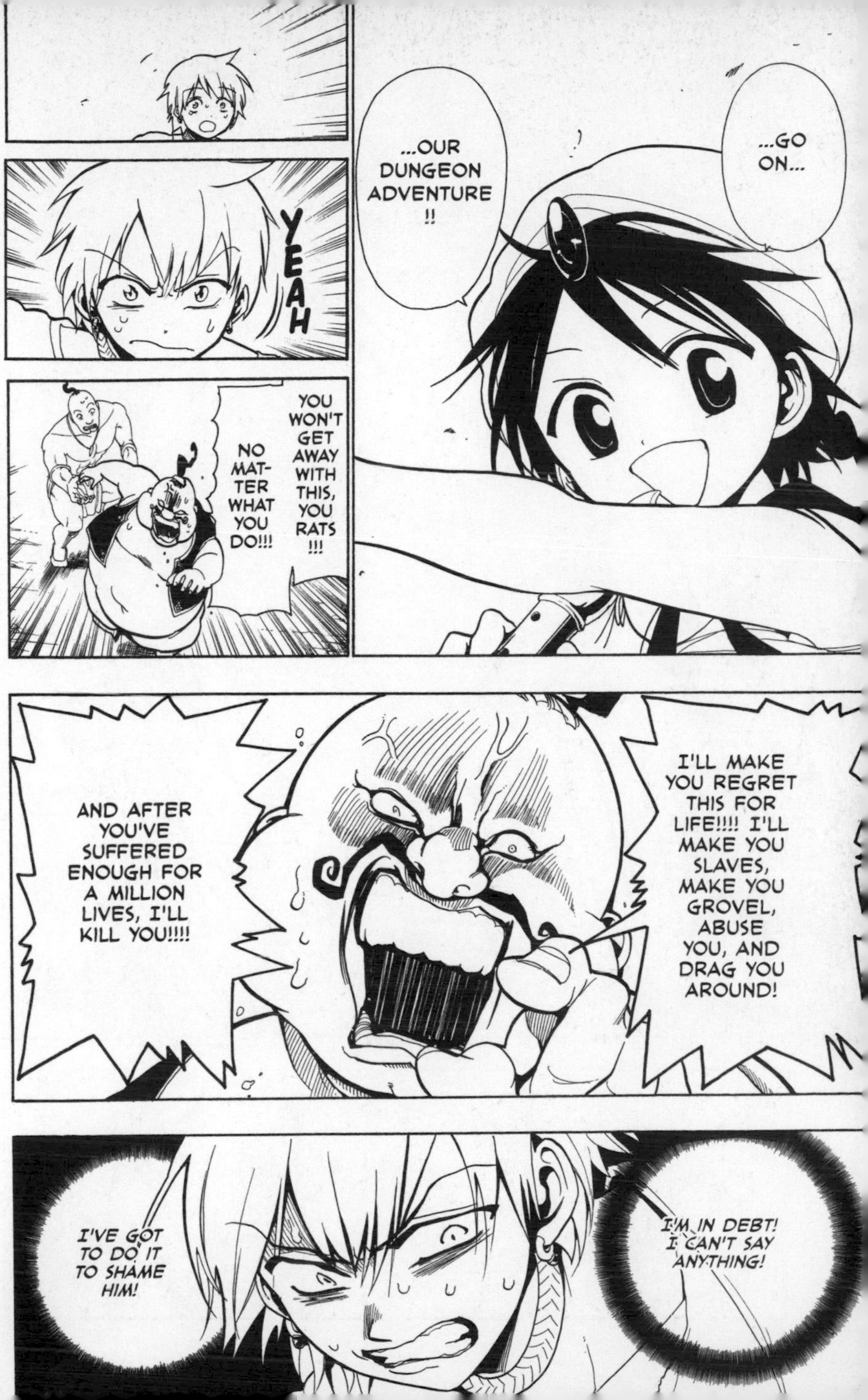
...GO ON...
...OUR DUNGEON ADVENTURE !!
YEAH
YOU WON'T GET AWAY WITH THIS, YOU RATS !!!
NO MATTER WHAT YOU DO!!!
I'LL MAKE YOU REGRET THIS FOR LIFE!!!! I'LL MAKE YOU SLAVES, MAKE YOU GROVEL, ABUSE YOU, AND DRAG YOU AROUND!
AND AFTER YOU'VE SUFFERED ENOUGH FOR A MILLION LIVES, I'LL KILL YOU!!!!
I'M IN DEBT! I CAN'T SAY ANYTHING!
I'VE GOT TO DO IT TO SHAME HIM!

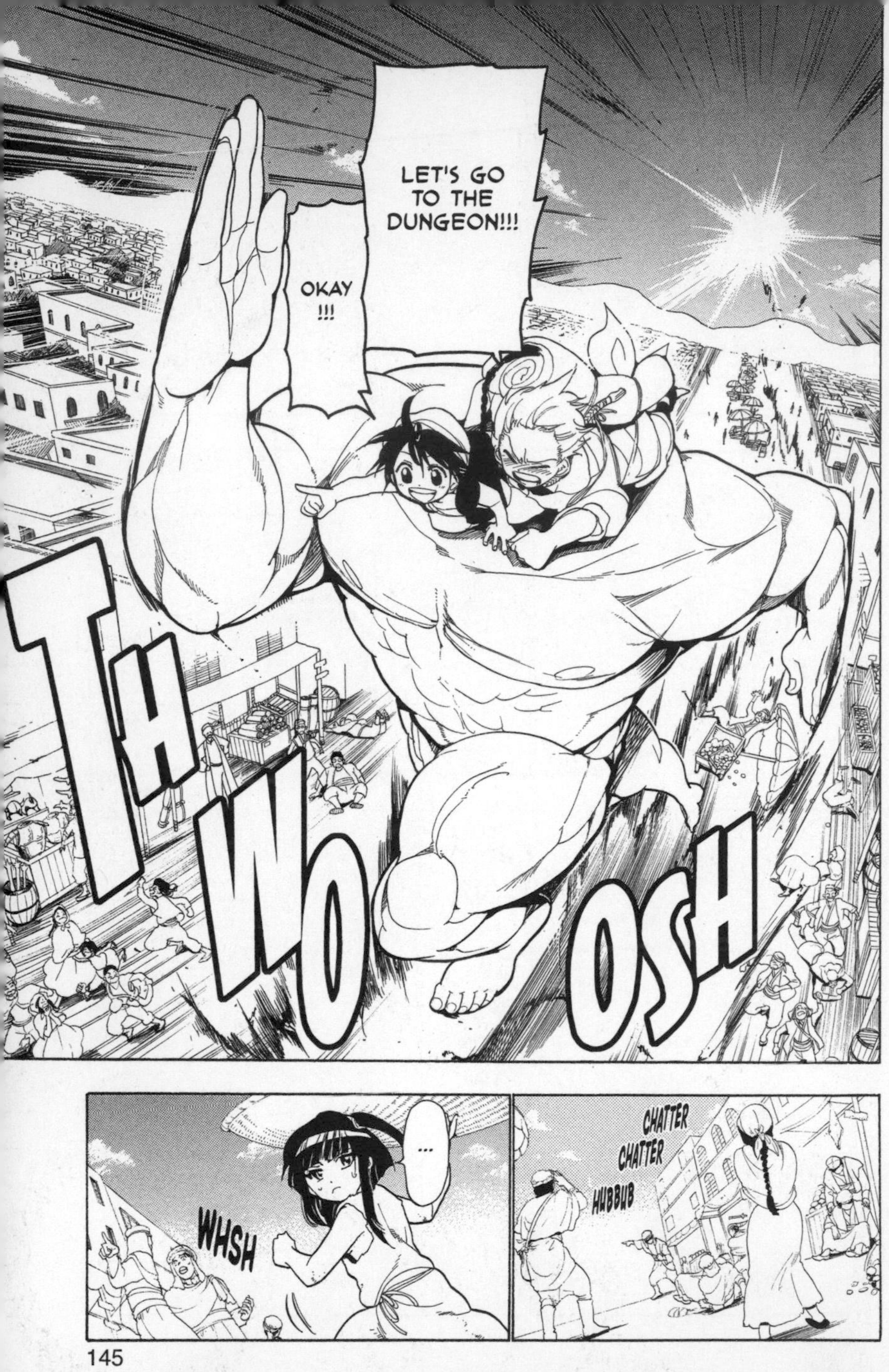
LET'S GO TO THE DUNGEON!!!
OKAY !!!
THWOOSH
CHATTER
CHATTER
HUBBUB
...
WHSH

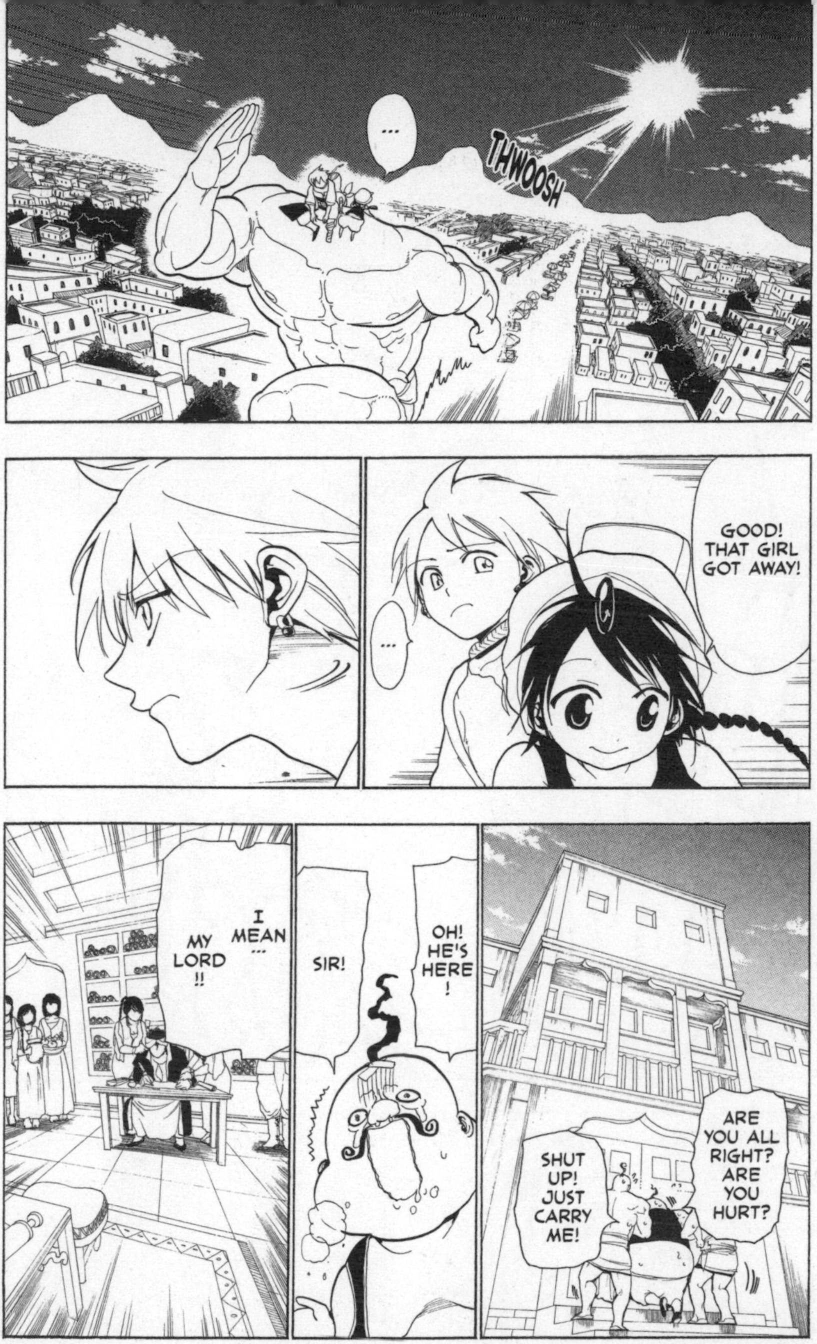
...
THWOOSH
GOOD! THAT GIRL GOT AWAY!
...
ARE YOU ALL RIGHT? ARE YOU HURT?
SHUT UP! JUST CARRY ME!
OH! HE'S HERE!
SIR!
I MEAN ...
MY LORD !!

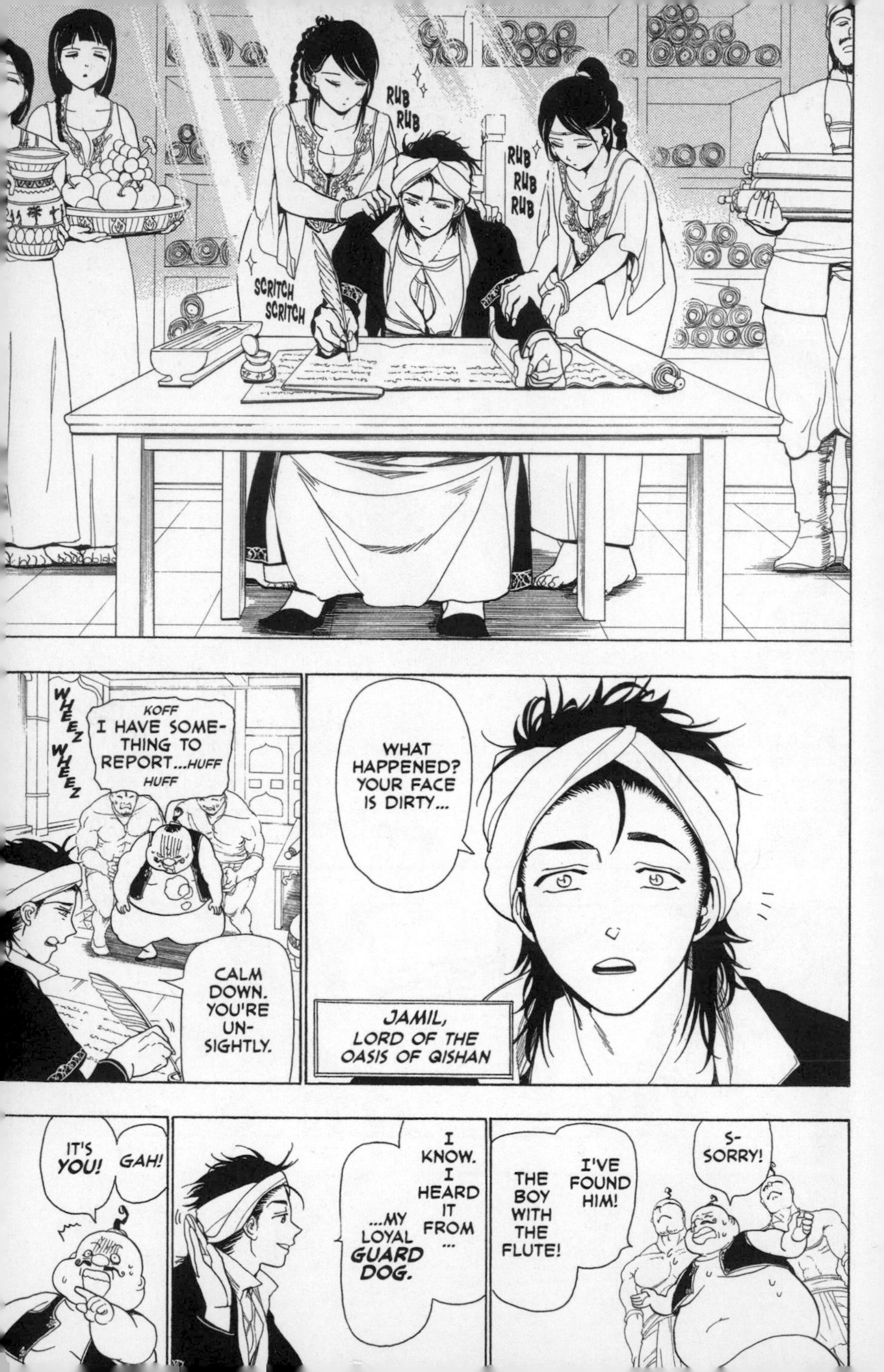
RUB RUB
RUB RUB RUB
SCRITCH SCRITCH
WHAT HAPPENED? YOUR FACE IS DIRTY...
JAMIL, LORD OF THE OASIS OF QISHAN
WHEEZ WHEEZ
KOFF
I HAVE SOMETHING TO REPORT...HUFF HUFF
CALM DOWN. YOU'RE UNSIGHTLY.
S-SORRY!
I'VE FOUND HIM!
THE BOY WITH THE FLUTE!
I KNOW. I HEARD IT FROM ...
...MY LOYAL **GUARD DOG.**
IT'S **YOU!**
GAH!

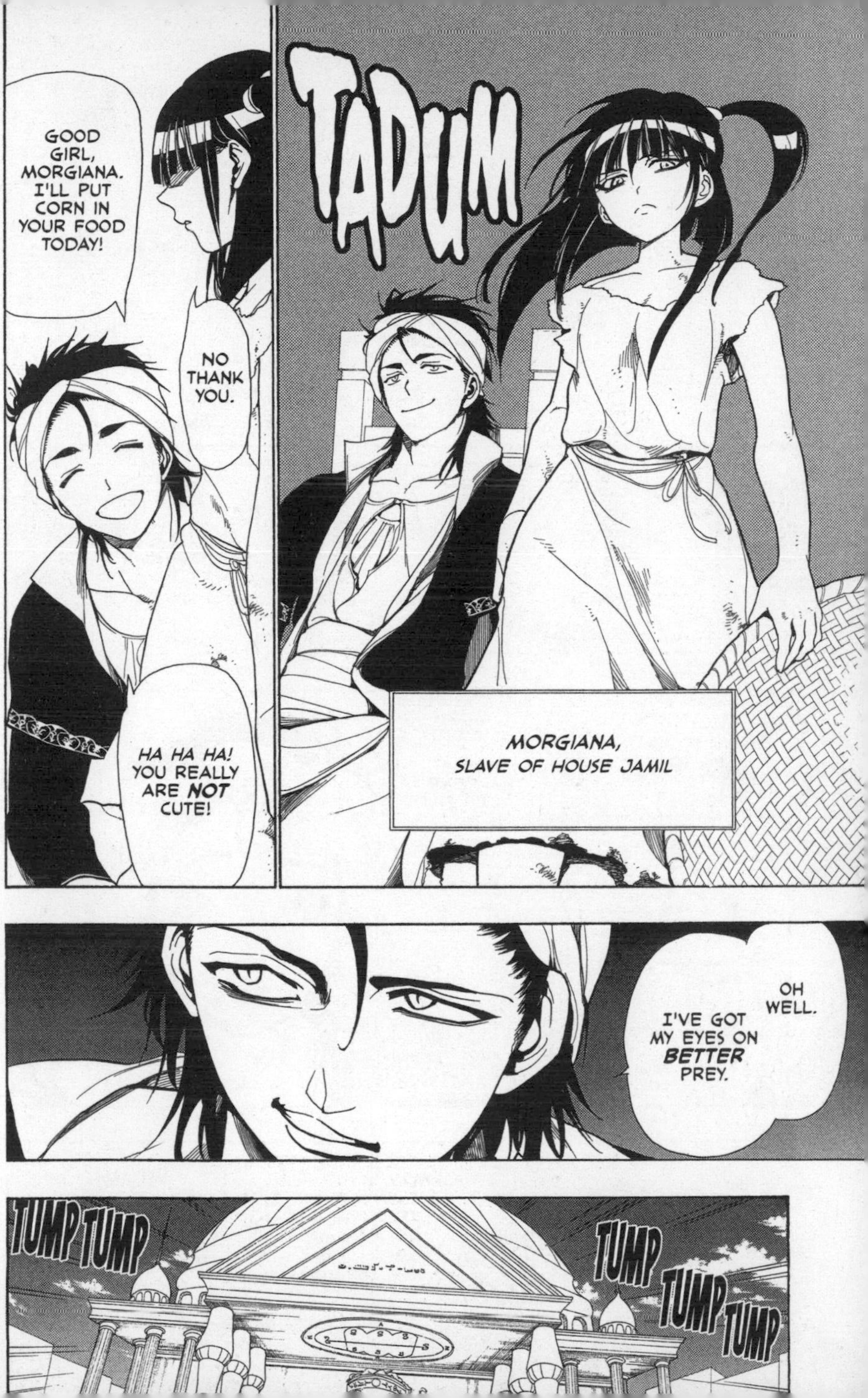
TADUM
MORGIANA, SLAVE OF HOUSE JAMIL
GOOD GIRL, MORGIANA. I'LL PUT CORN IN YOUR FOOD TODAY!
NO THANK YOU.
HA HA HA! YOU REALLY ARE **NOT** CUTE!
OH WELL.
I'VE GOT MY EYES ON **BETTER** PREY.
TUMP TUMP TUMP
TUMP TUMP

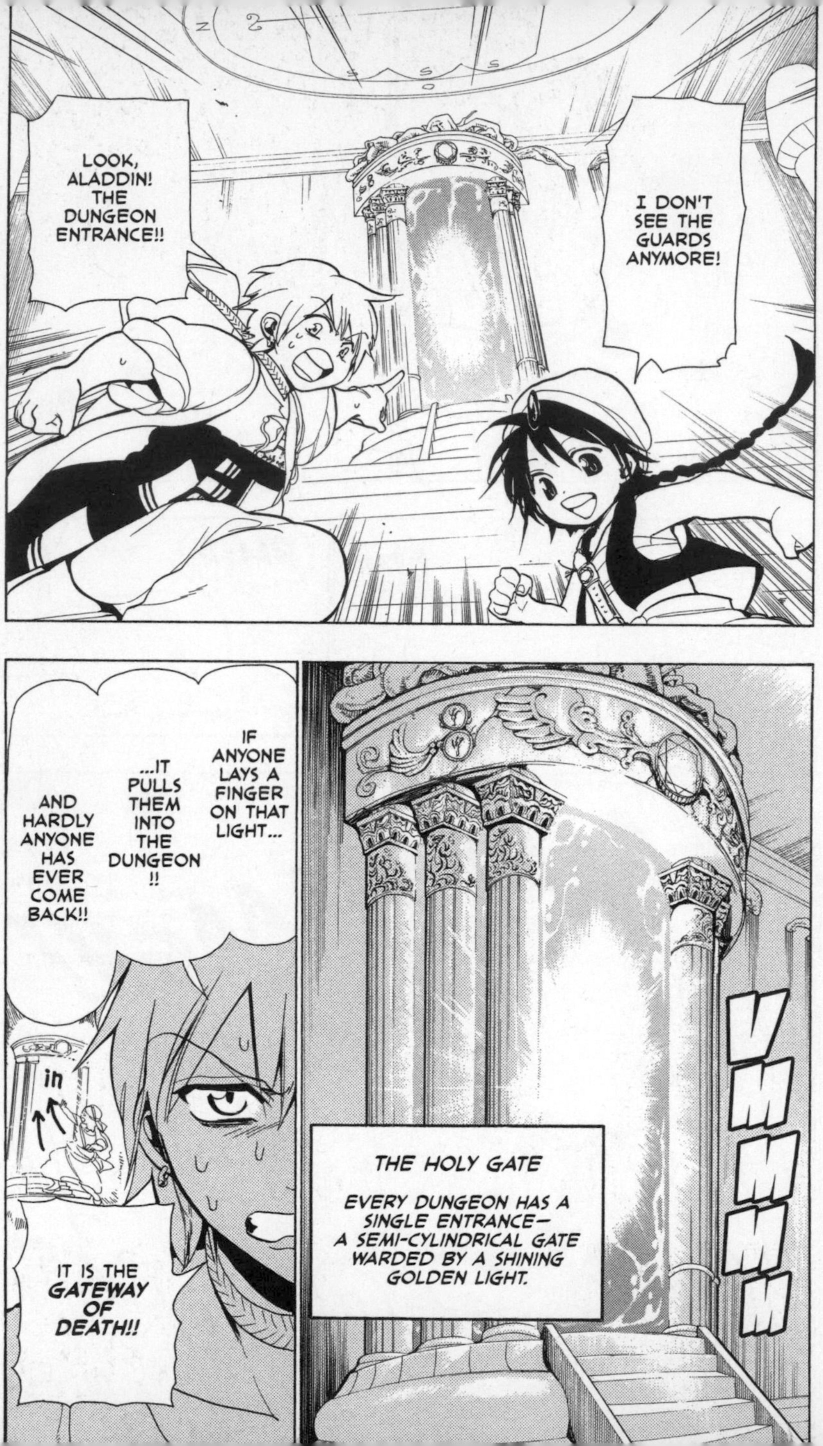
I DON'T SEE THE GUARDS ANYMORE!
LOOK, ALADDIN! THE DUNGEON ENTRANCE!!
THE HOLY GATE
EVERY DUNGEON HAS A SINGLE ENTRANCE— A SEMI-CYLINDRICAL GATE WARDED BY A SHINING GOLDEN LIGHT.
VMMMMM
IF ANYONE LAYS A FINGER ON THAT LIGHT...
...IT PULLS THEM INTO THE DUNGEON!!
AND HARDLY ANYONE HAS EVER COME BACK!!
in
IT IS THE GATEWAY OF DEATH!!

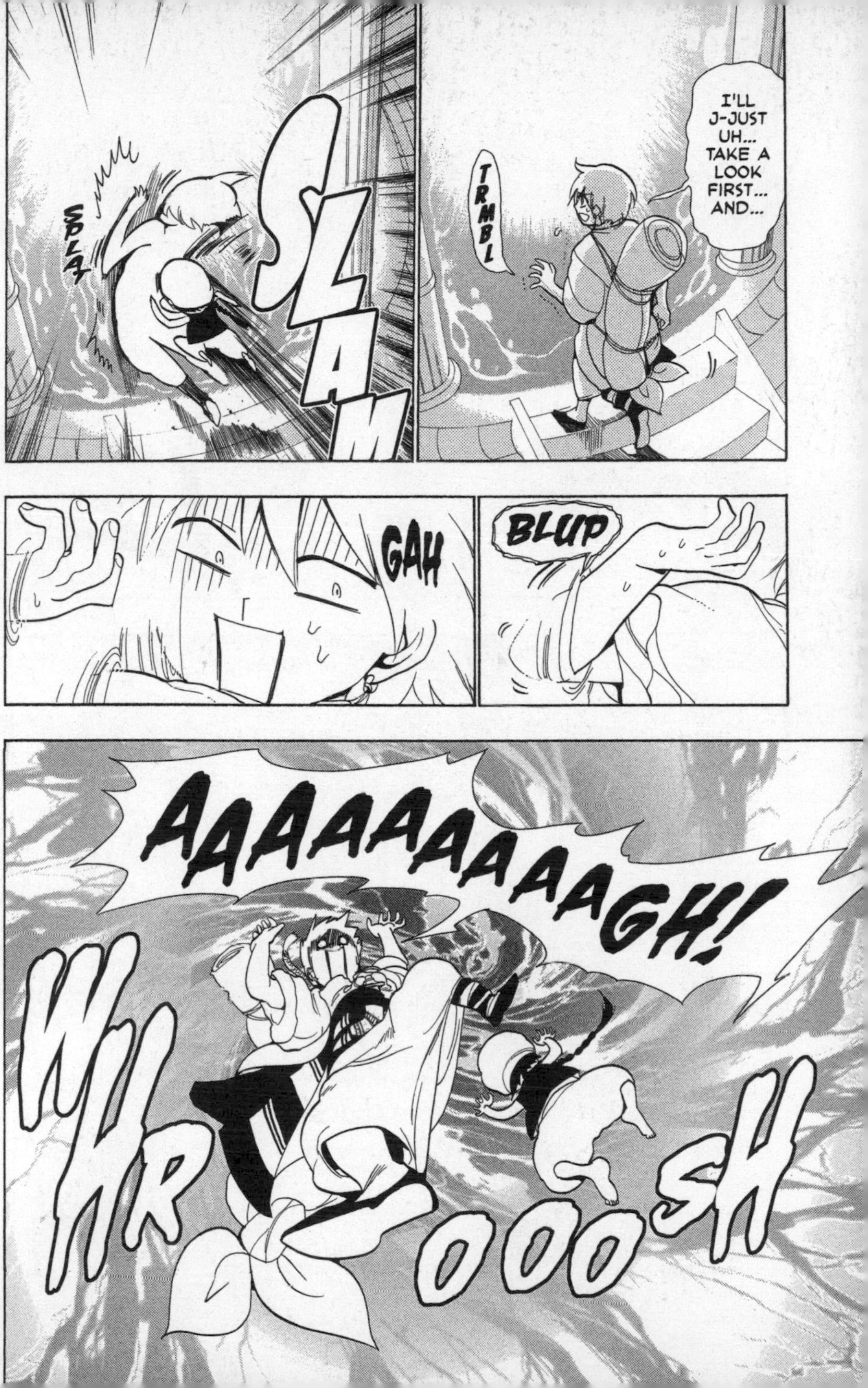
I'LL J-JUST UH... TAKE A LOOK FIRST... AND...
TRMBL
SPLAT
SLAM
BLUP
GAH
AAAAAAAAAAGH!
WHHROOOSH

Night 6: Into the Dungeon

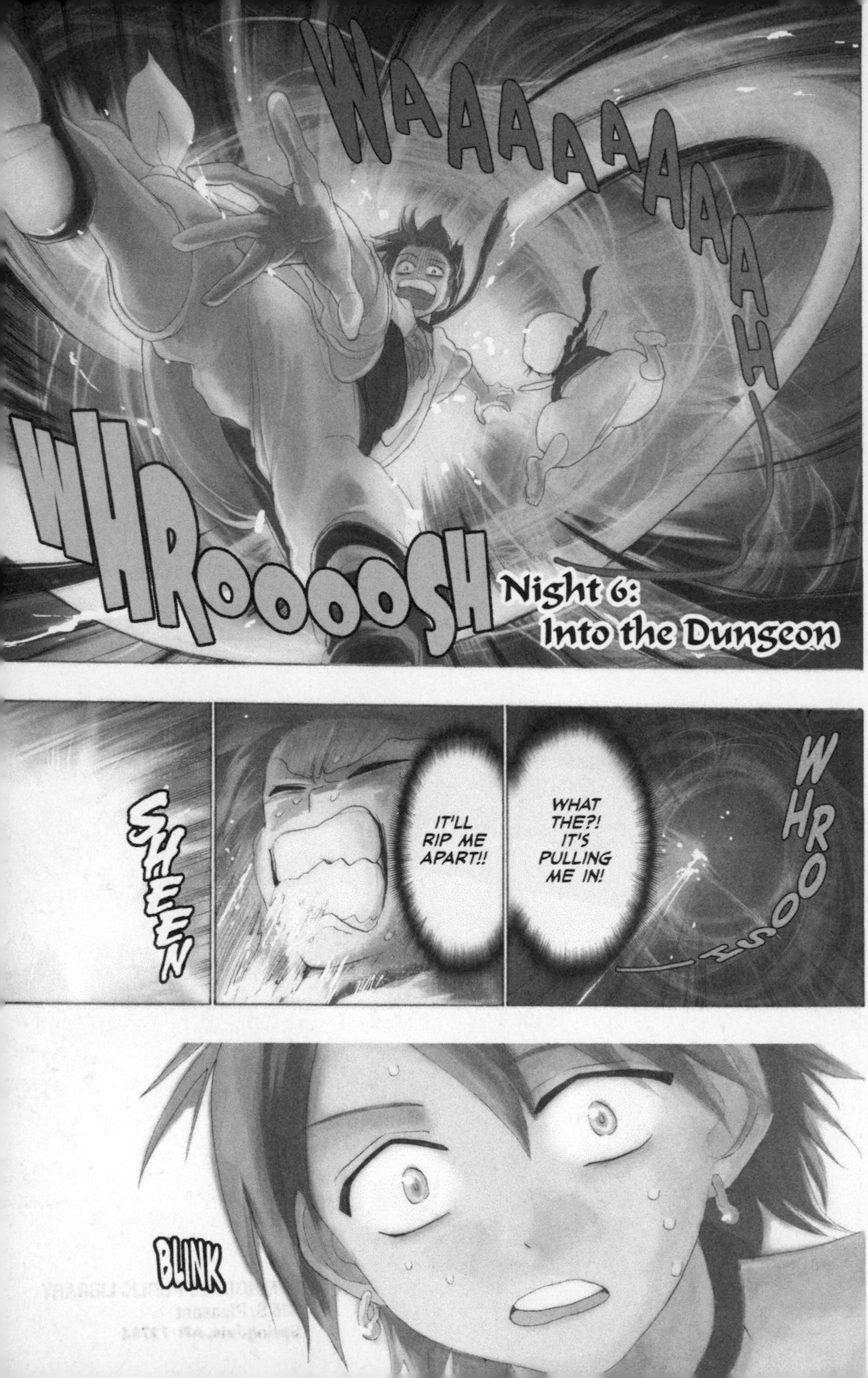
WAAAAAAAAAAH
WHROOOOOSH
Night 6: Into the Dungeon
WHROOSH
WHAT THE?! IT'S PULLING ME IN!
IT'LL RIP ME APART!!
SHEEEN
BLINK

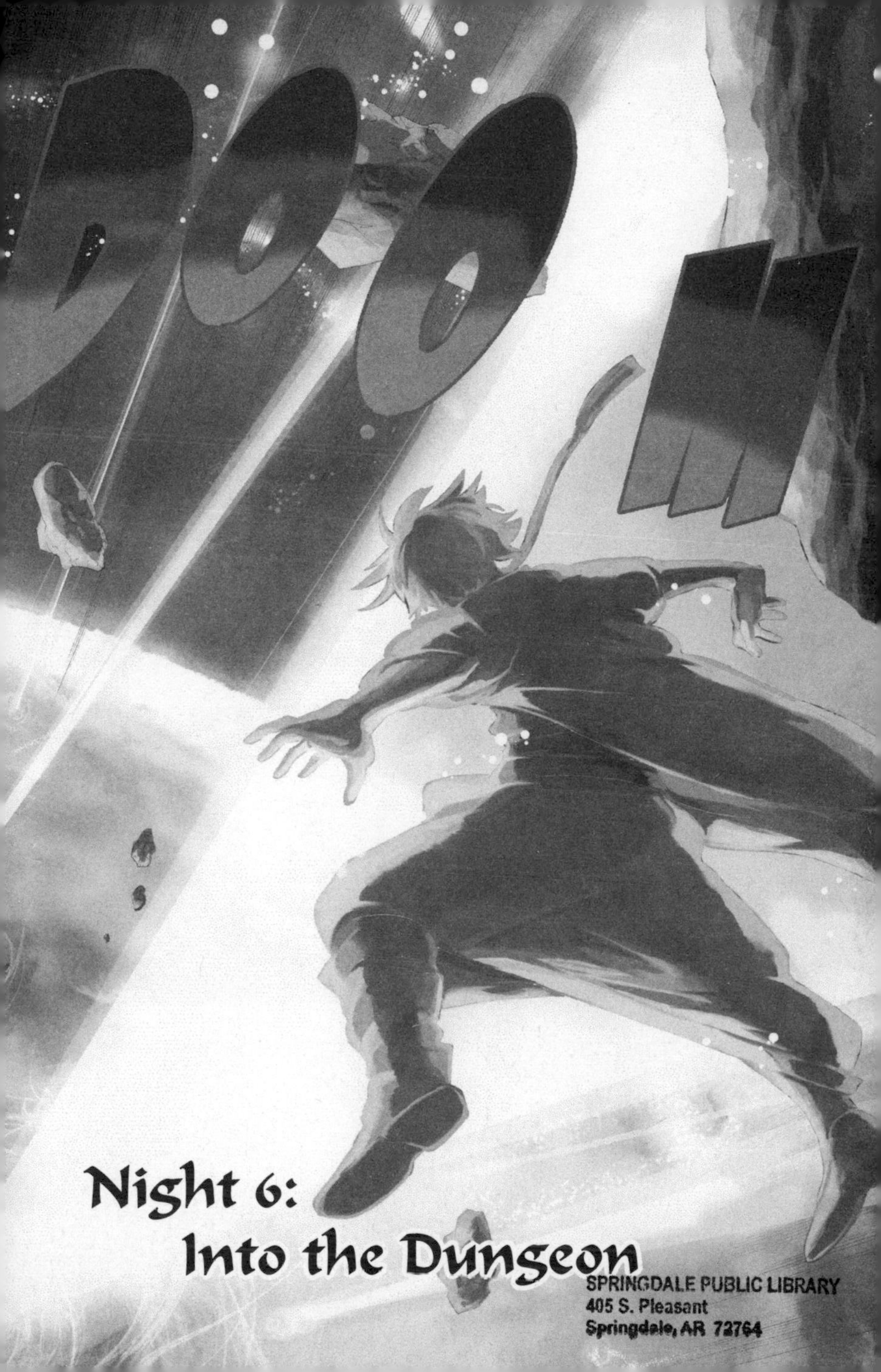
DOOM

Night 6: Into the Dungeon

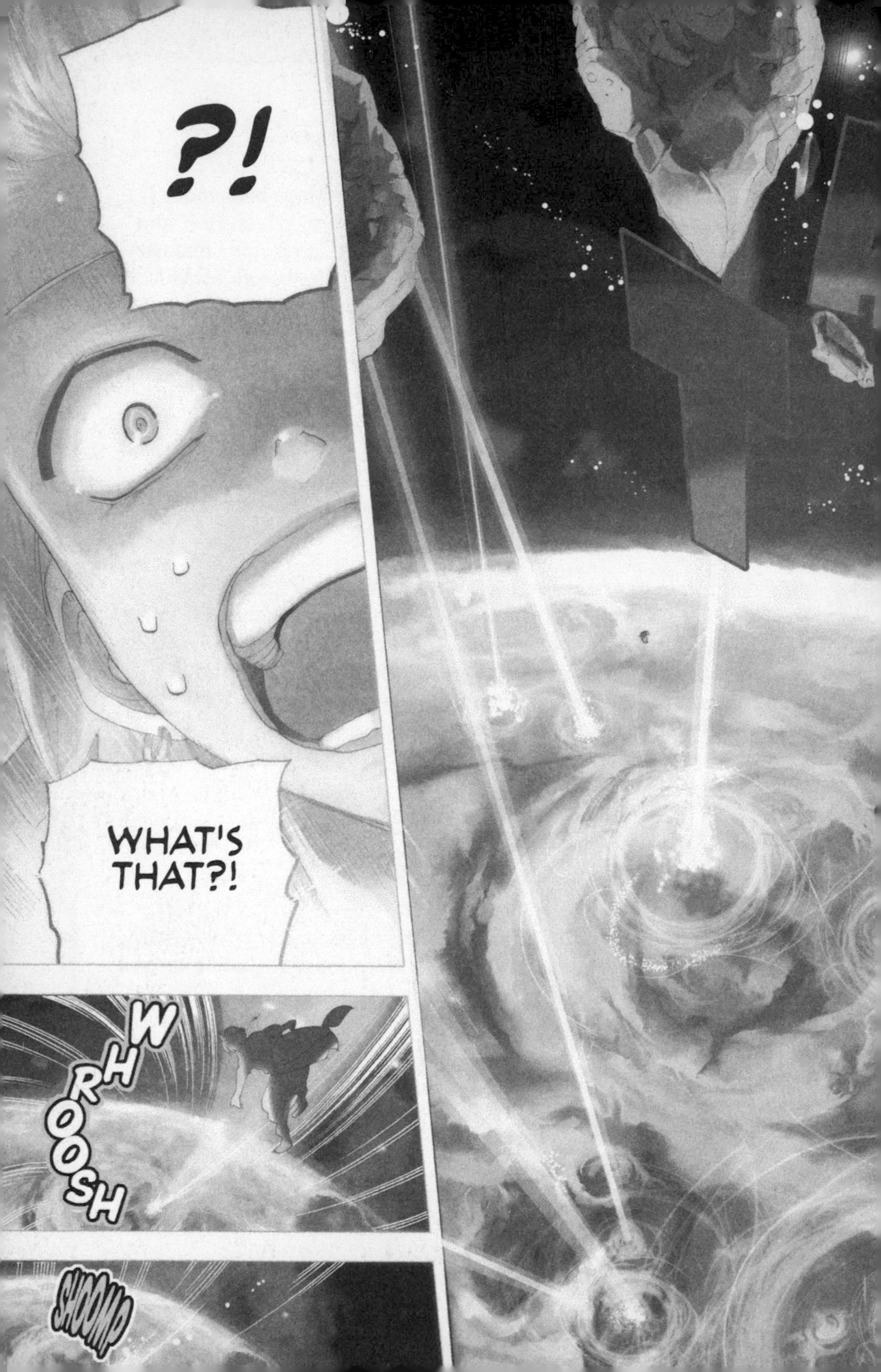
?!
WHAT'S THAT?!
WHHROOOSH
SHOOMP

About Me—Shinobu Ohtaka ②

The reason I kept it secret that I was drawing manga is because I was embarrassed to tell anyone about my dream, which I felt had little chance of coming true. At the time, my submissions had met with absolutely no success. I found a lot of the footwork aside from drawing the actual manga to be a burden (and unmotivating), so my friends and teachers were worried about my future. They didn't know if I had the desire to move forward. I remember that whenever I went to have my hair cut, the hair stylists would always lecture me about the future. I suppose I gave off a certain aura. But I was just getting my hair cut!

I couldn't make my debut during high school, but I won a few small prizes.

I'll never forget how excited I was when I won my first prize. I saw my name and a sample of my work in a magazine and was floored right there in the convenience store! I was so stunned that I missed my bus stop and I was late for school. When I won this prize, a notification arrived at my house, so my family learned for the first time that I was drawing manga.

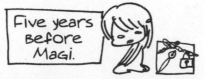

Five years Before Magi.

Later, for about four to five years until my second year of university, I continued to submit manuscripts and visit publishers, but it came to nothing and I couldn't debut.

Around then, for the only time, I gave up drawing manga for a while. I figured I didn't have any talent for it, put away my art materials, and started preparing to look for a job, but the next thing I knew, as if in a daze, I found myself drawing a one-shot. You never know what will happen in life. That one-shot became my debut work.

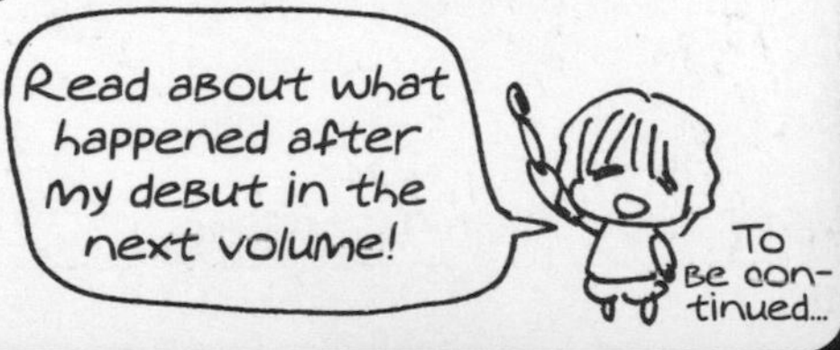

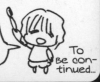

Read about what happened after my debut in the next volume!
To be continued...

Continued in Volume 2

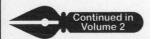

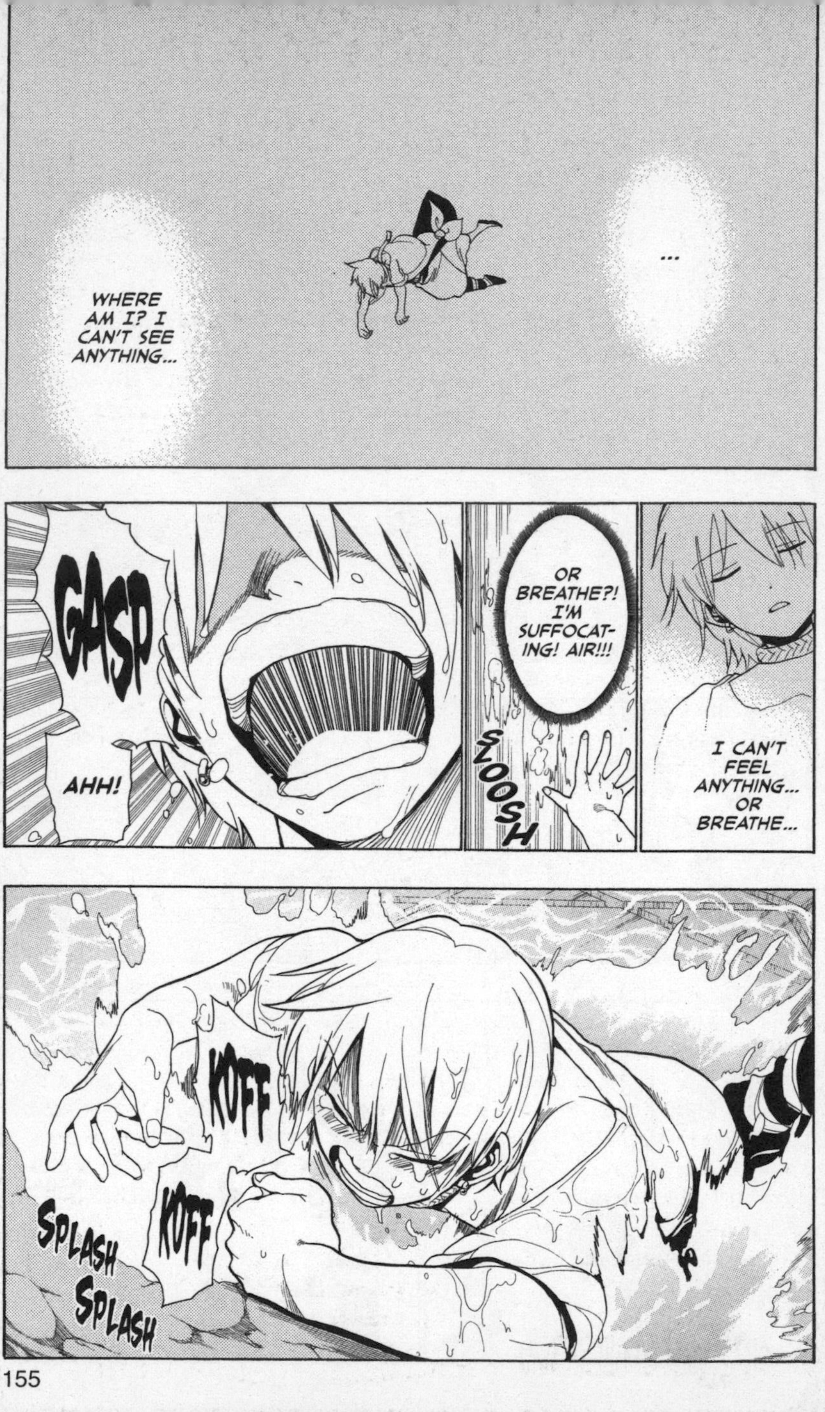
...
WHERE AM I? I CAN'T SEE ANYTHING...
I CAN'T FEEL ANYTHING... OR BREATHE...
OR BREATHE?! I'M SUFFOCATING! AIR!!!
SLOOSH
GASP
AHH!
KOFF
KOFF
SPLASH
SPLASH

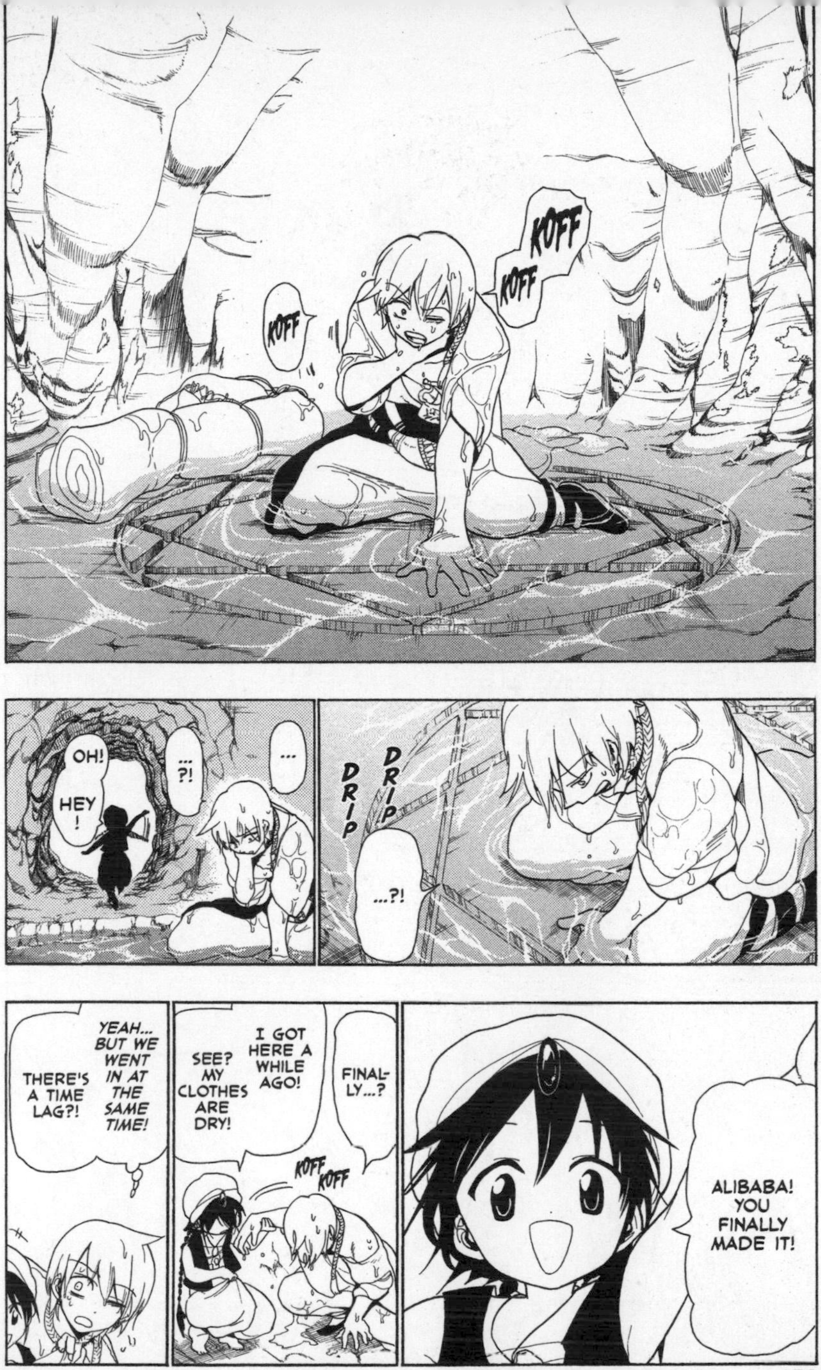
KOFF KOFF
KOFF
DRIP DRIP
...?!
...
...?!
OH! HEY!
ALIBABA! YOU FINALLY MADE IT!
FINAL-LY...?
I GOT HERE A WHILE AGO!
SEE? MY CLOTHES ARE DRY!
KOFF KOFF
YEAH... BUT WE WENT IN AT THE SAME TIME!
THERE'S A TIME LAG?!

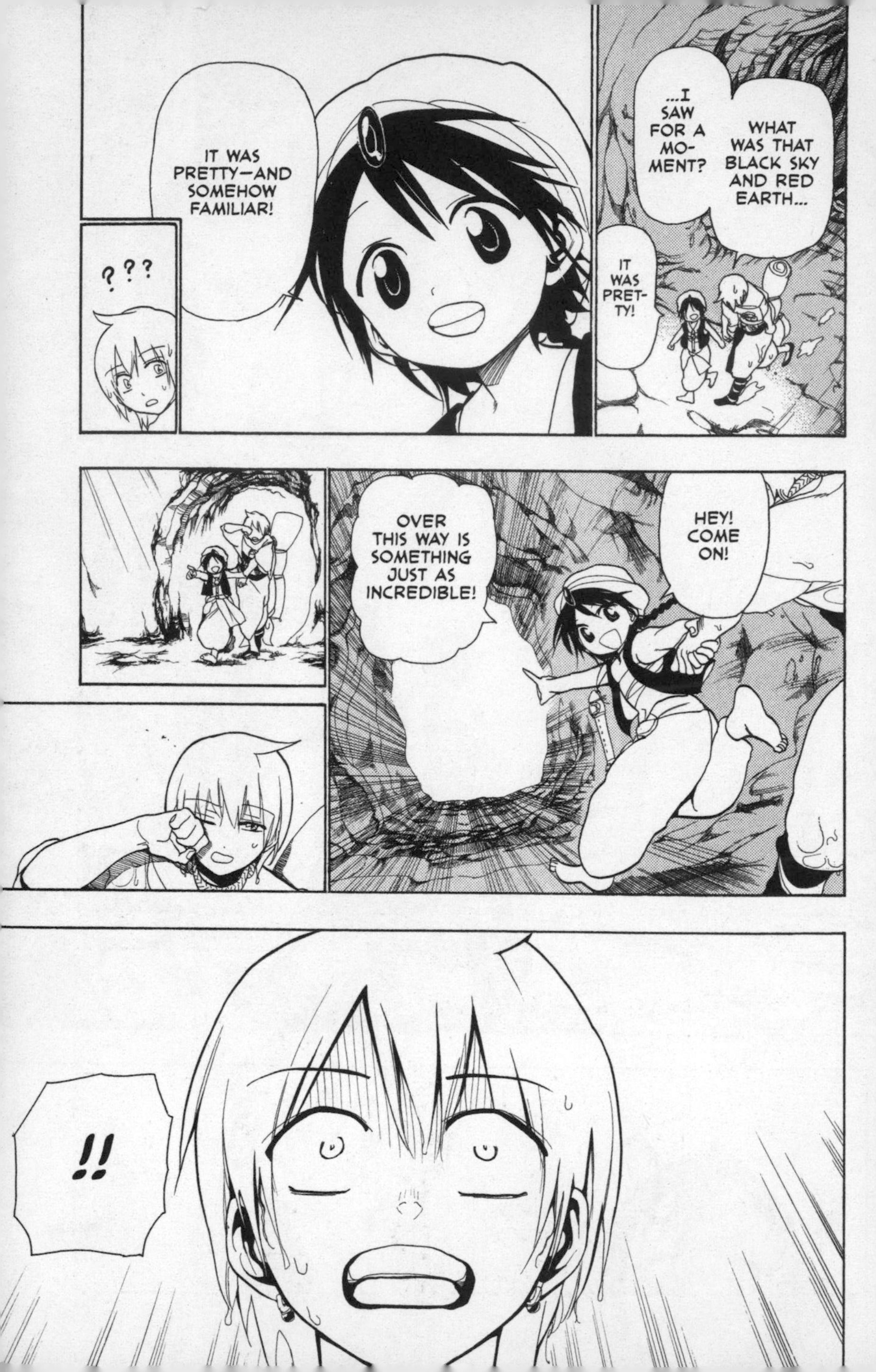
WHAT WAS THAT BLACK SKY AND RED EARTH...
...I SAW FOR A MO-MENT?
IT WAS PRET-TY!
IT WAS PRETTY—AND SOMEHOW FAMILIAR!
???
HEY! COME ON!
OVER THIS WAY IS SOMETHING JUST AS INCREDIBLE!
!!

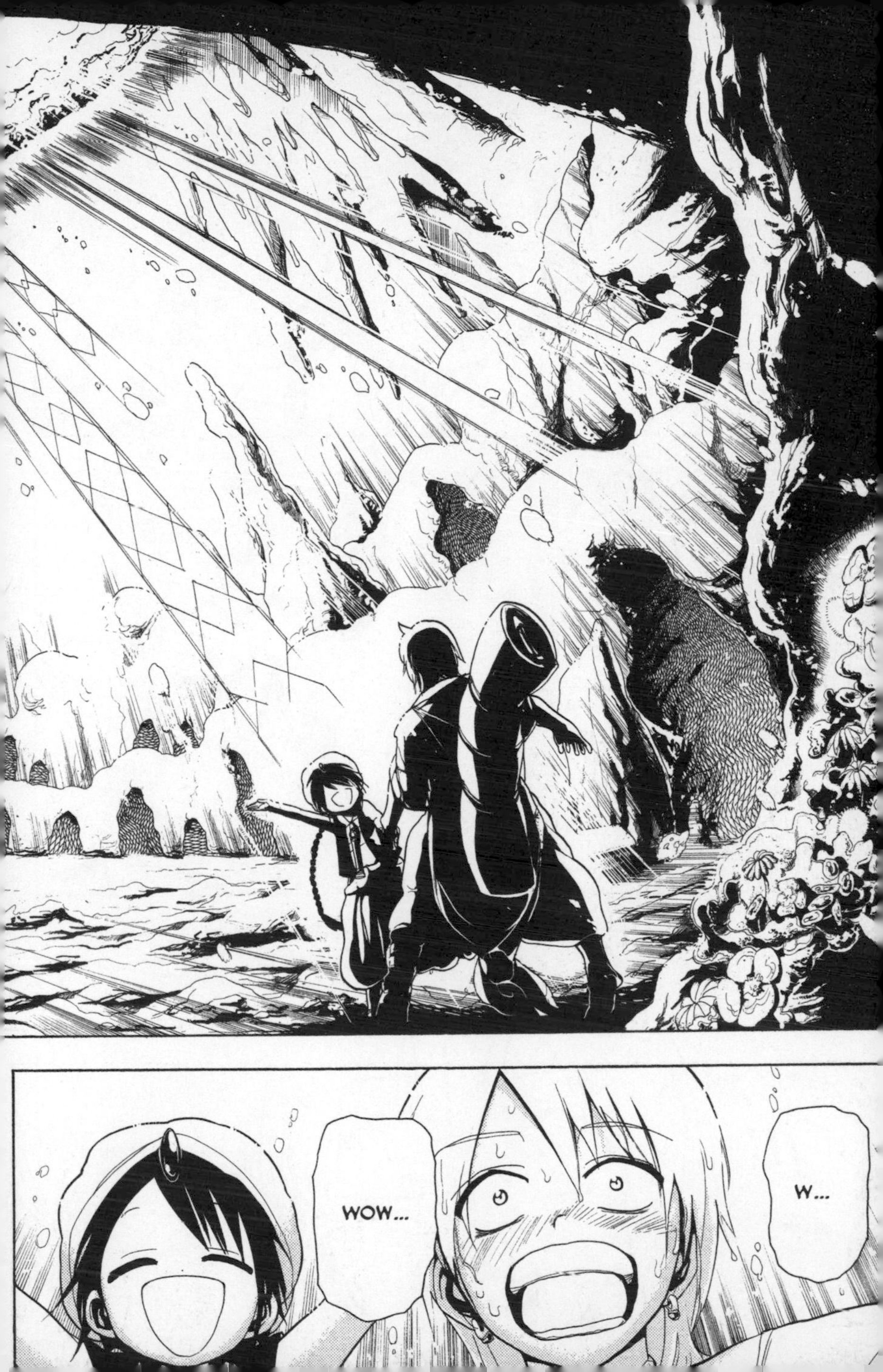

W...
WOW...

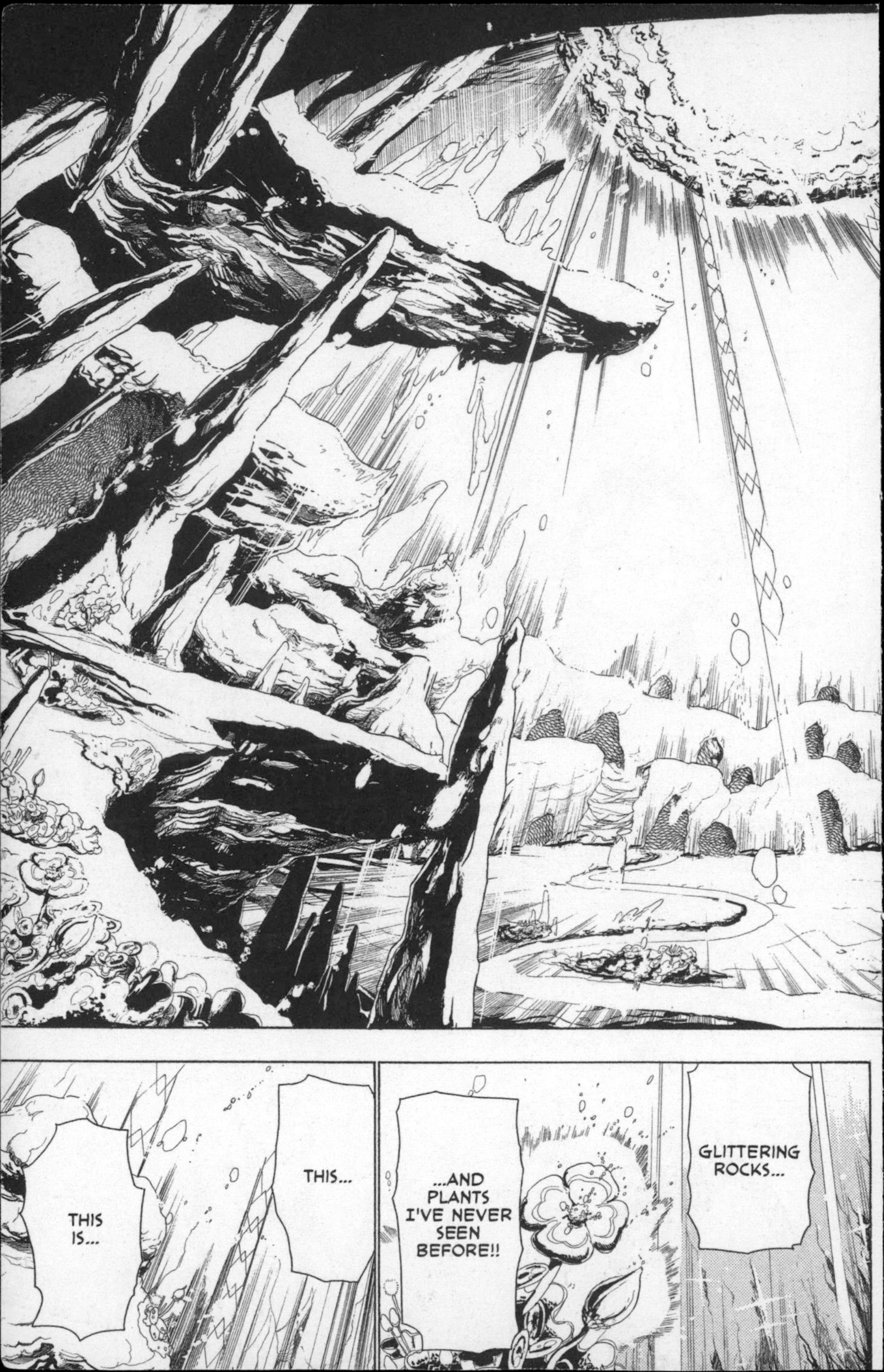
GLITTERING ROCKS...
...AND PLANTS I'VE NEVER SEEN BEFORE!!
THIS...
THIS IS...

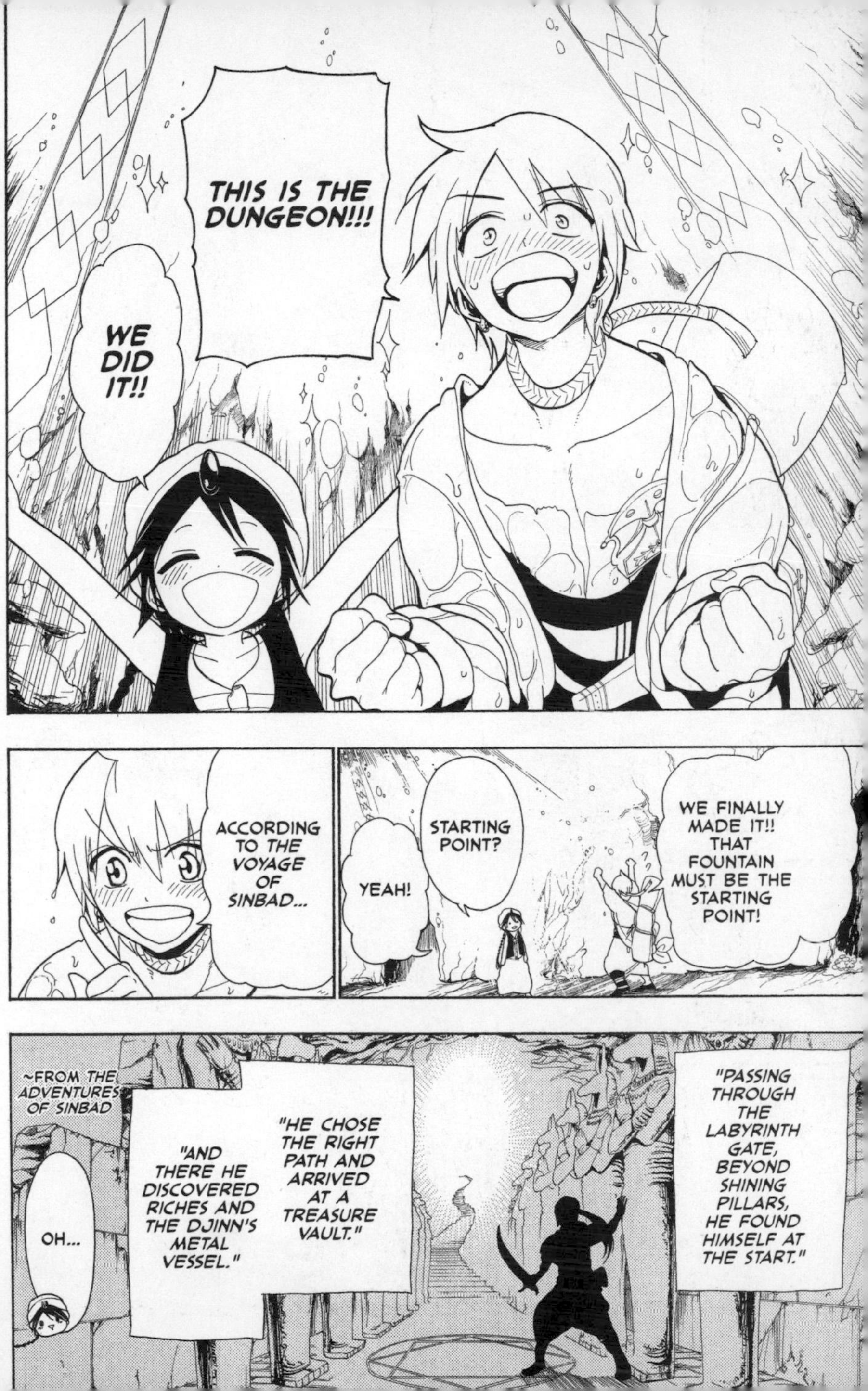
THIS IS THE DUNGEON!!!
WE DID IT!!
WE FINALLY MADE IT!! THAT FOUNTAIN MUST BE THE STARTING POINT!
STARTING POINT?
YEAH!
ACCORDING TO THE VOYAGE OF SINBAD...
"PASSING THROUGH THE LABYRINTH GATE, BEYOND SHINING PILLARS, HE FOUND HIMSELF AT THE START."
"HE CHOSE THE RIGHT PATH AND ARRIVED AT A TREASURE VAULT."
"AND THERE HE DISCOVERED RICHES AND THE DJINN'S METAL VESSEL."
~FROM THE ADVENTURES OF SINBAD
OH...

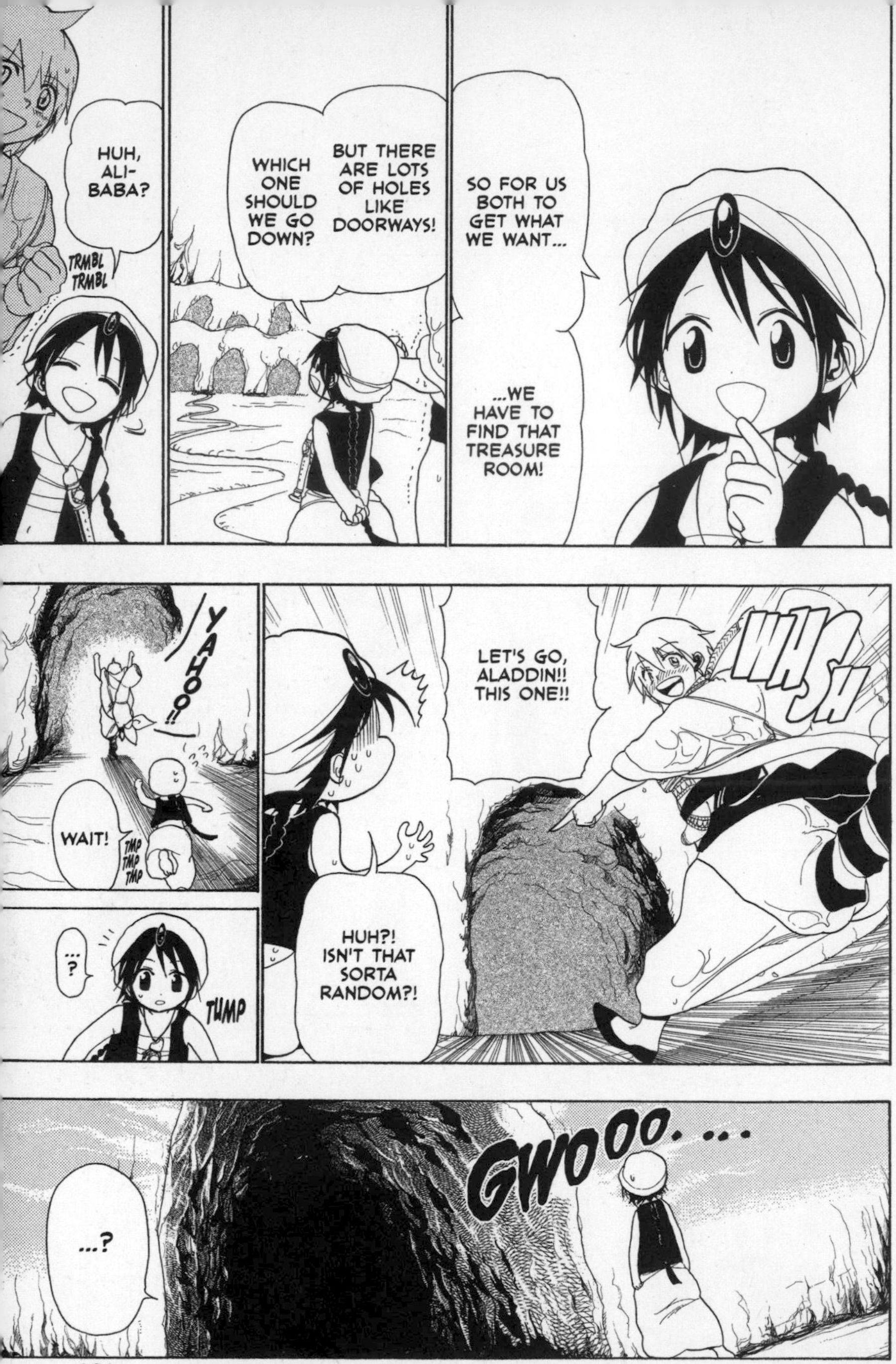
SO FOR US BOTH TO GET WHAT WE WANT...
...WE HAVE TO FIND THAT TREASURE ROOM!
BUT THERE ARE LOTS OF HOLES LIKE DOORWAYS!
WHICH ONE SHOULD WE GO DOWN?
HUH, ALI-BABA?
TRMBL TRMBL
WHSH
LET'S GO, ALADDIN!! THIS ONE!!
HUH?! ISN'T THAT SORTA RANDOM?!
YAHOO!!
WAIT!
TMP TMP TMP
...?
TUMP
GWOOO. ...
...?

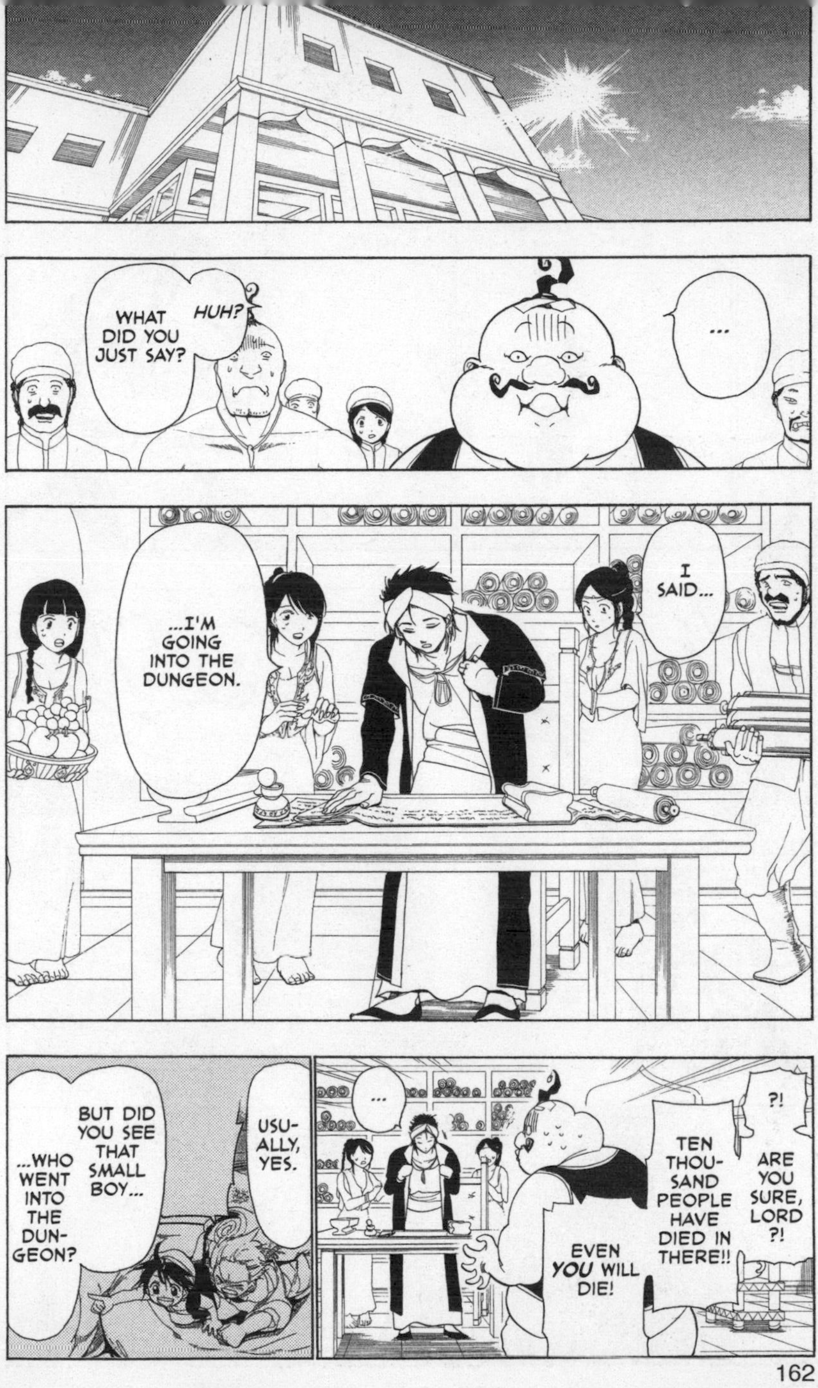
...
HUH?
WHAT DID YOU JUST SAY?
I SAID...
...I'M GOING INTO THE DUNGEON.
?!
ARE YOU SURE, LORD?!
TEN THOUSAND PEOPLE HAVE DIED IN THERE!!
EVEN *YOU* WILL DIE!
...
USUALLY, YES.
BUT DID YOU SEE THAT SMALL BOY...
...WHO WENT INTO THE DUNGEON?

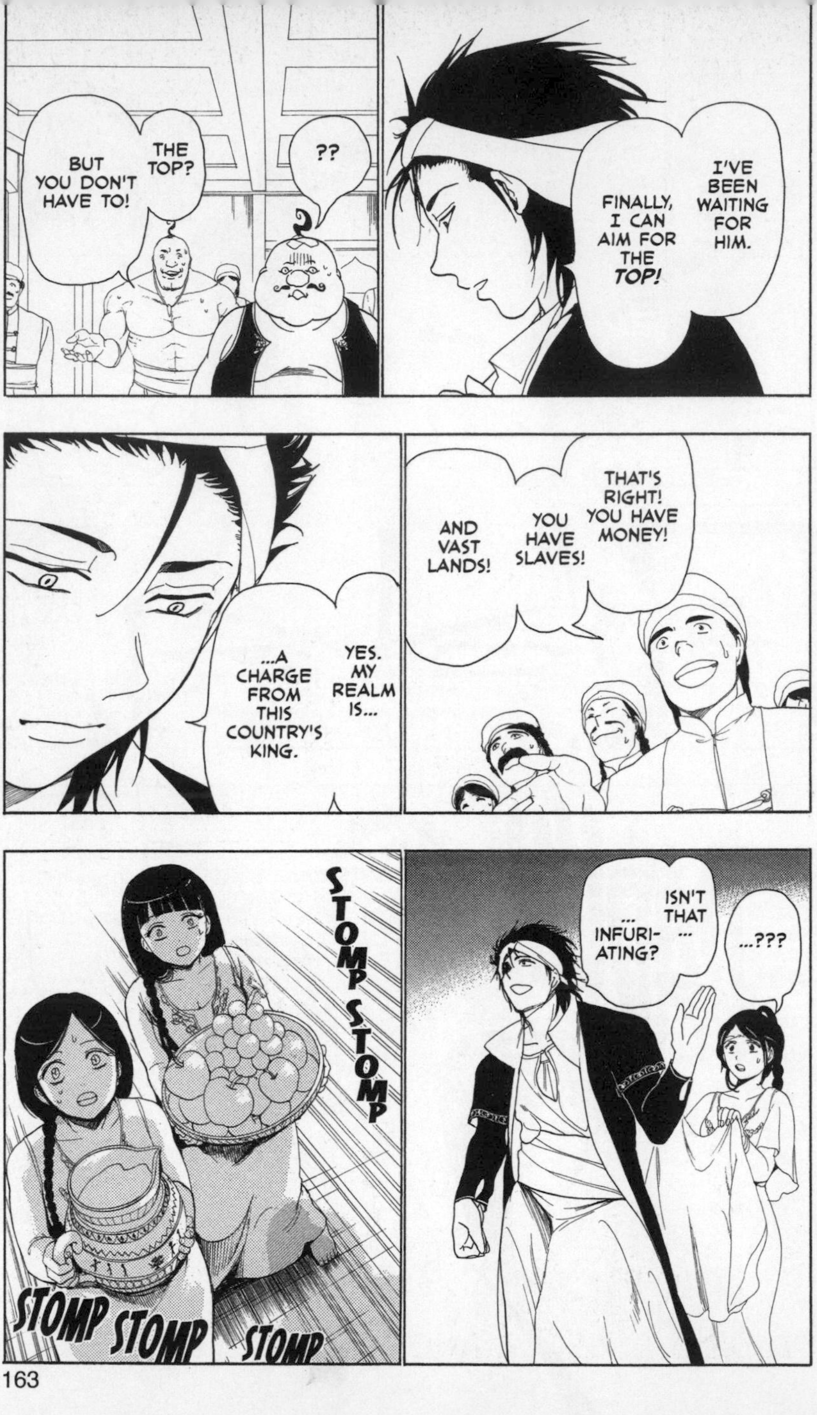
I'VE BEEN WAITING FOR HIM.
FINALLY, I CAN AIM FOR THE *TOP!*
??
THE TOP?
BUT YOU DON'T HAVE TO!
THAT'S RIGHT! YOU HAVE MONEY!
YOU HAVE SLAVES!
AND VAST LANDS!
YES. MY REALM IS...
...A CHARGE FROM THIS COUNTRY'S KING.
ISN'T THAT ...
... INFURIATING?
...???
STOMP STOMP
STOMP STOMP STOMP

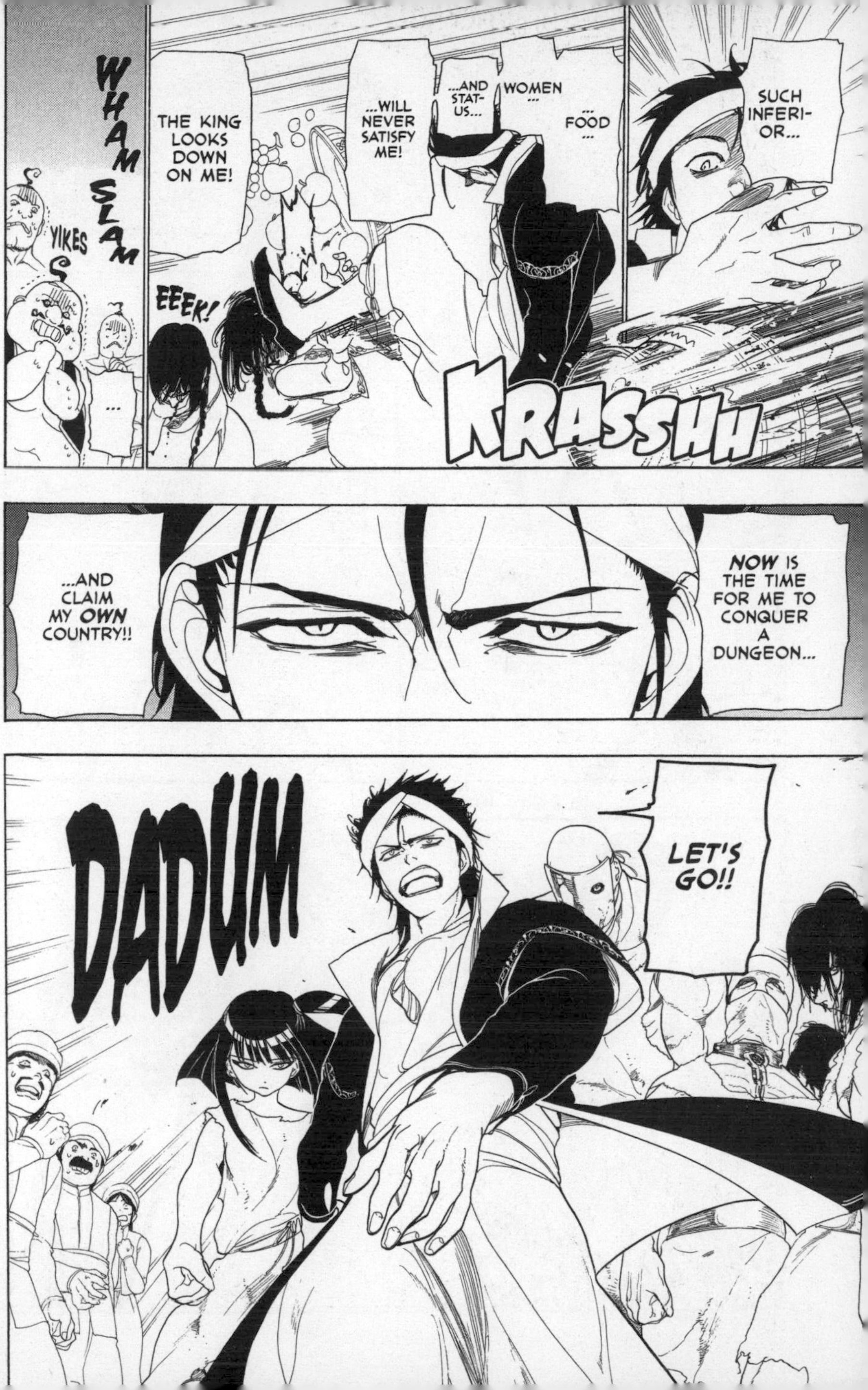
SUCH INFERIOR...
... FOOD ...
WOMEN ...
...AND STATUS...
...WILL NEVER SATISFY ME!
THE KING LOOKS DOWN ON ME!
KRASSHH
EEEK!
WHAM SLAM
YIKES
...
NOW IS THE TIME FOR ME TO CONQUER A DUNGEON...
...AND CLAIM MY OWN COUNTRY!!
LET'S GO!!
DADUM

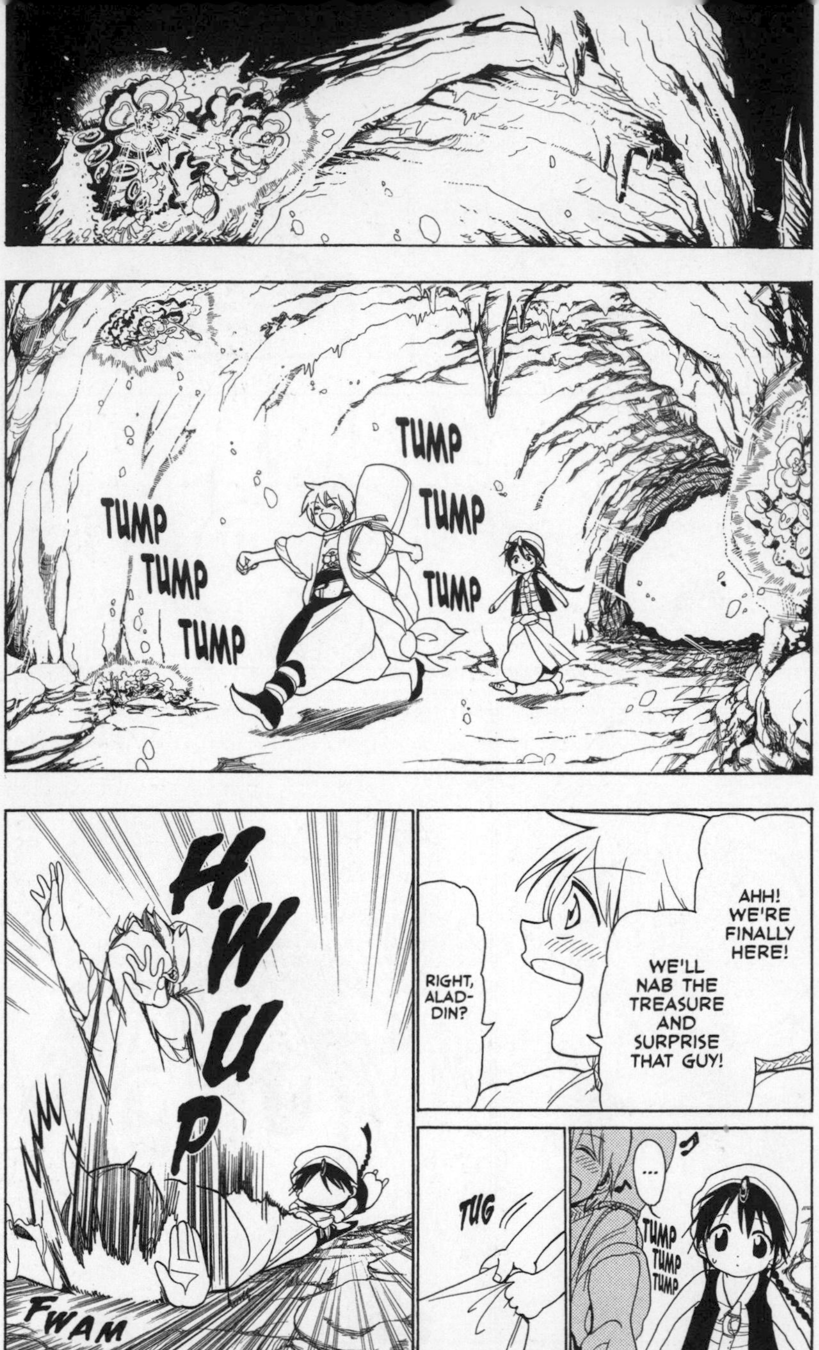
TUMP
TUMP
TUMP
TUMP
TUMP
TUMP
AHH! WE'RE FINALLY HERE!
WE'LL NAB THE TREASURE AND SURPRISE THAT GUY!
RIGHT, ALAD-DIN?
...
TUMP TUMP TUMP
TUG
HWUP
FWAM

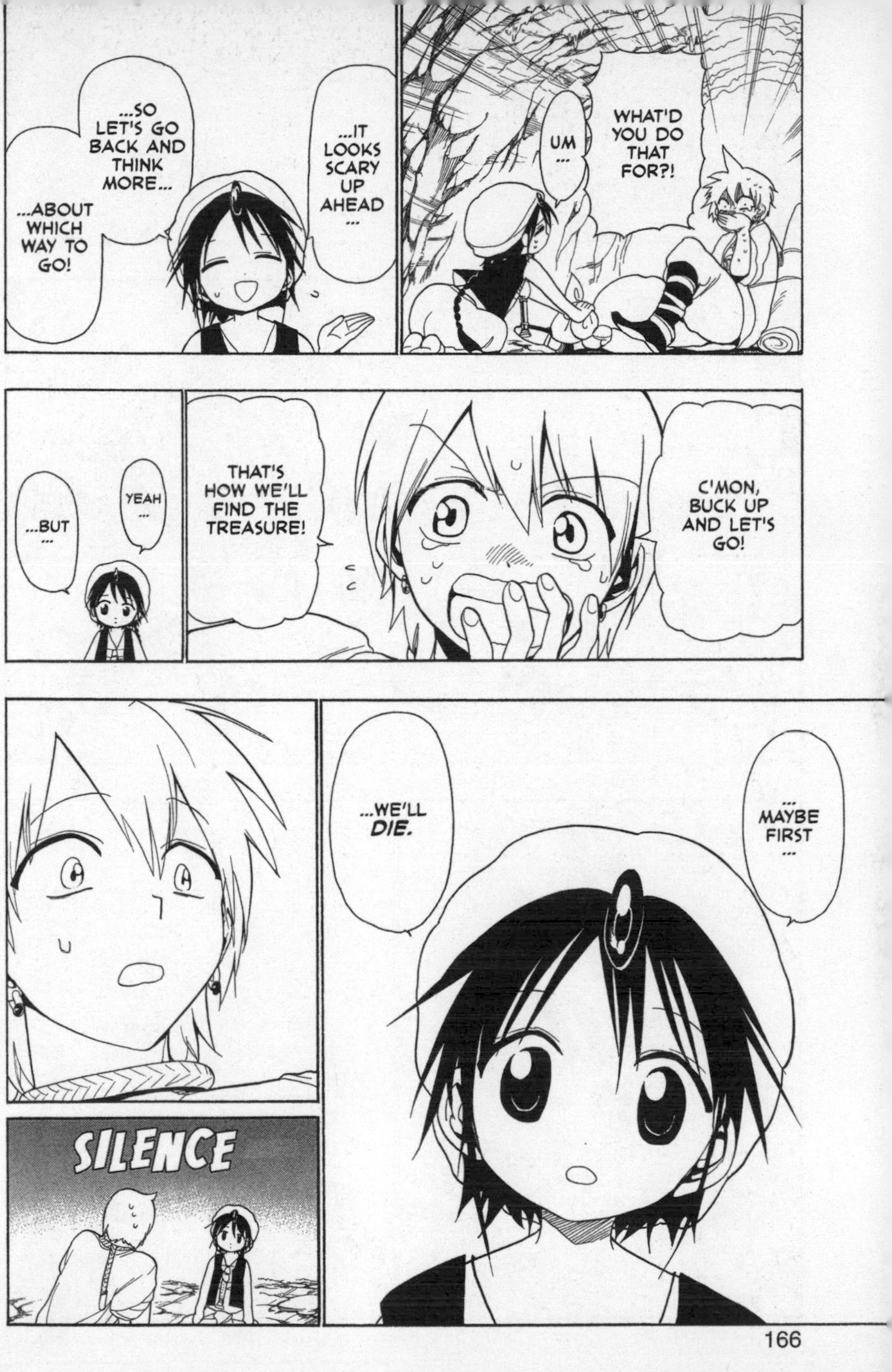
WHAT'D YOU DO THAT FOR?!
UM...
...IT LOOKS SCARY UP AHEAD...
...SO LET'S GO BACK AND THINK MORE...
...ABOUT WHICH WAY TO GO!
C'MON, BUCK UP AND LET'S GO!
THAT'S HOW WE'LL FIND THE TREASURE!
YEAH...
...BUT...
...MAYBE FIRST...
...WE'LL *DIE.*
SILENCE

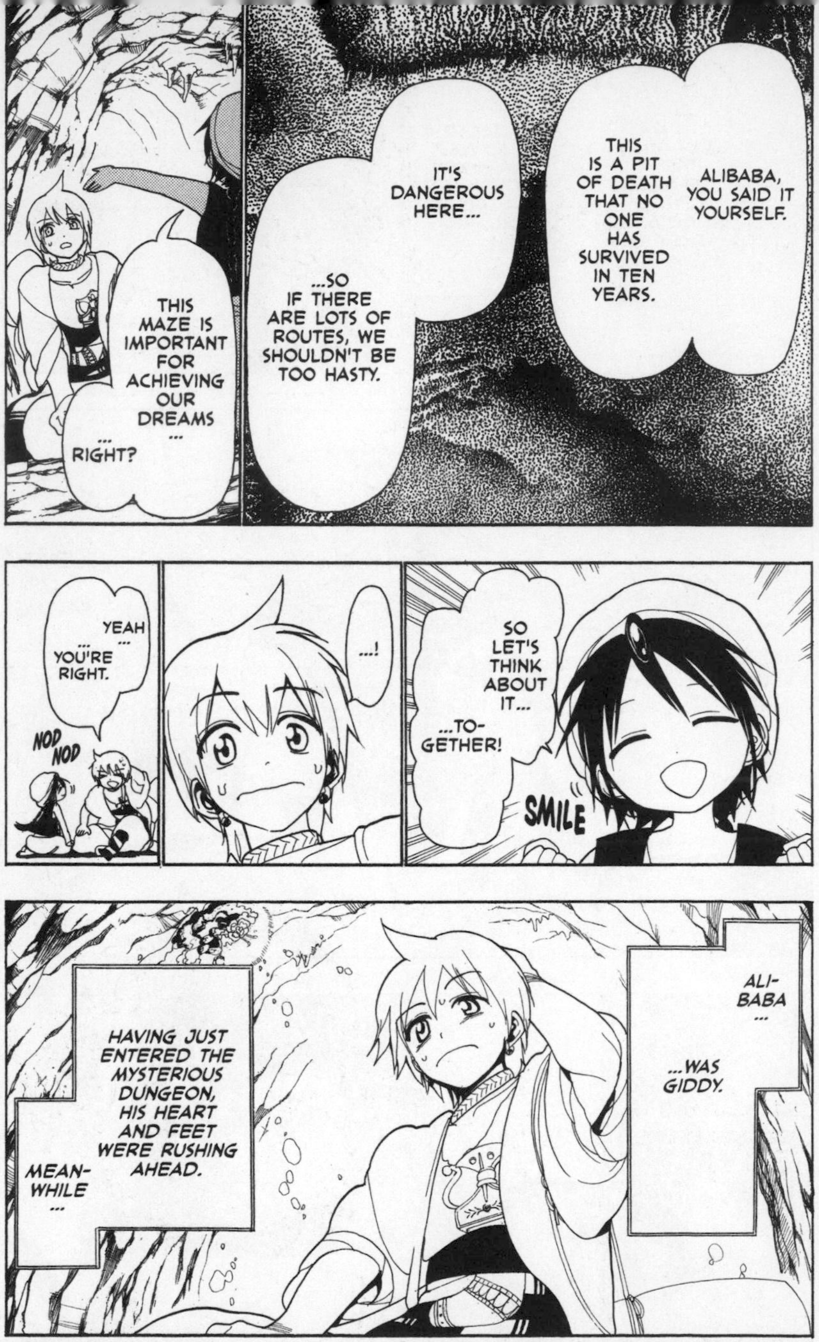
ALIBABA, YOU SAID IT YOURSELF.
THIS IS A PIT OF DEATH THAT NO ONE HAS SURVIVED IN TEN YEARS.
IT'S DANGEROUS HERE...
...SO IF THERE ARE LOTS OF ROUTES, WE SHOULDN'T BE TOO HASTY.
THIS MAZE IS IMPORTANT FOR ACHIEVING OUR DREAMS ...
... RIGHT?
SO LET'S THINK ABOUT IT...
...TO-GETHER!
SMILE
...!
YEAH ... YOU'RE RIGHT.
NOD NOD
ALI-BABA ...
...WAS GIDDY.
HAVING JUST ENTERED THE MYSTERIOUS DUNGEON, HIS HEART AND FEET WERE RUSHING AHEAD.
MEAN-WHILE ...

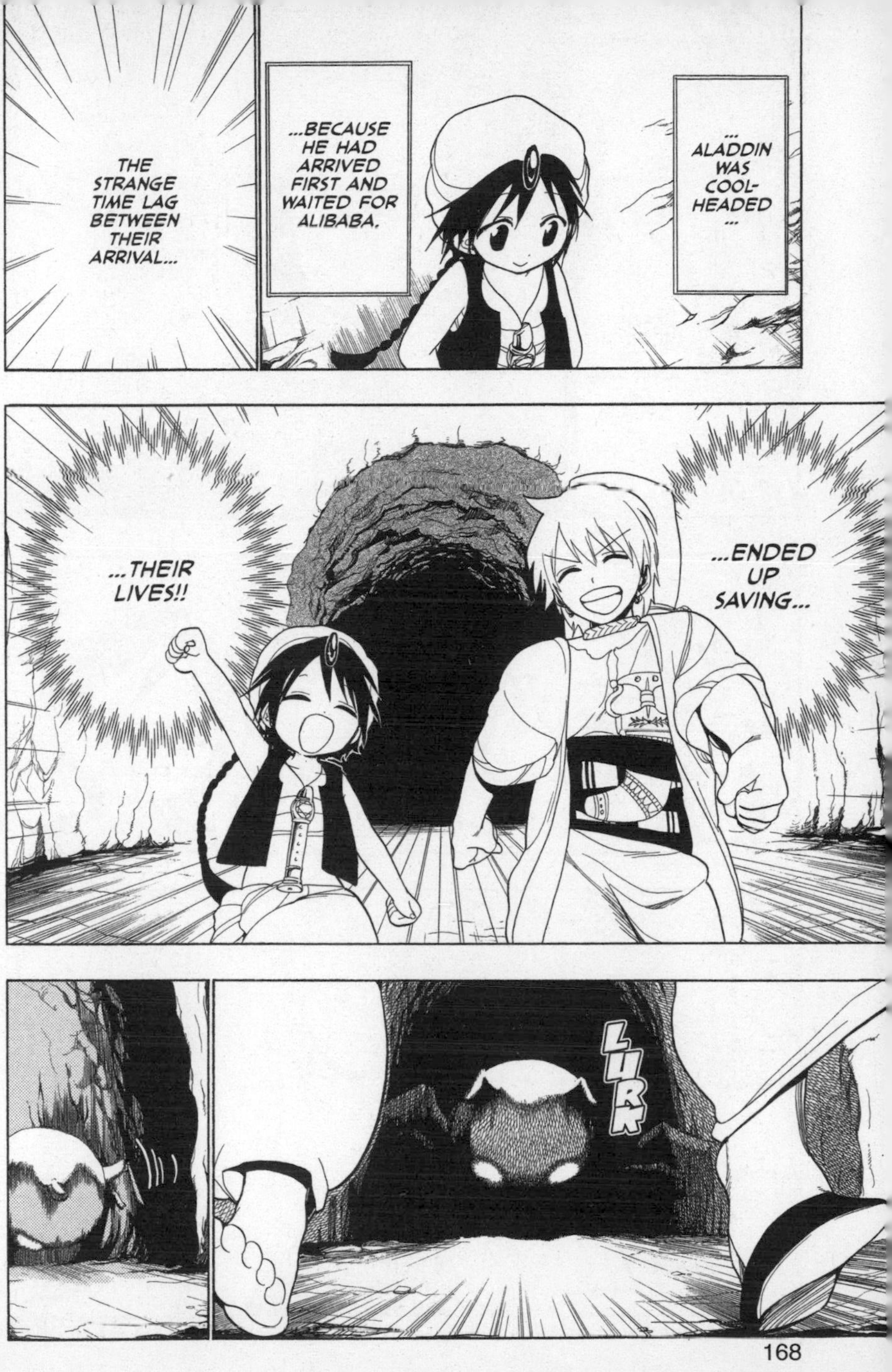
...
ALADDIN
WAS
COOL-
HEADED
...
...BECAUSE HE HAD ARRIVED FIRST AND WAITED FOR ALIBABA.
THE STRANGE TIME LAG BETWEEN THEIR ARRIVAL...
...ENDED UP SAVING...
...THEIR LIVES!!
LURK

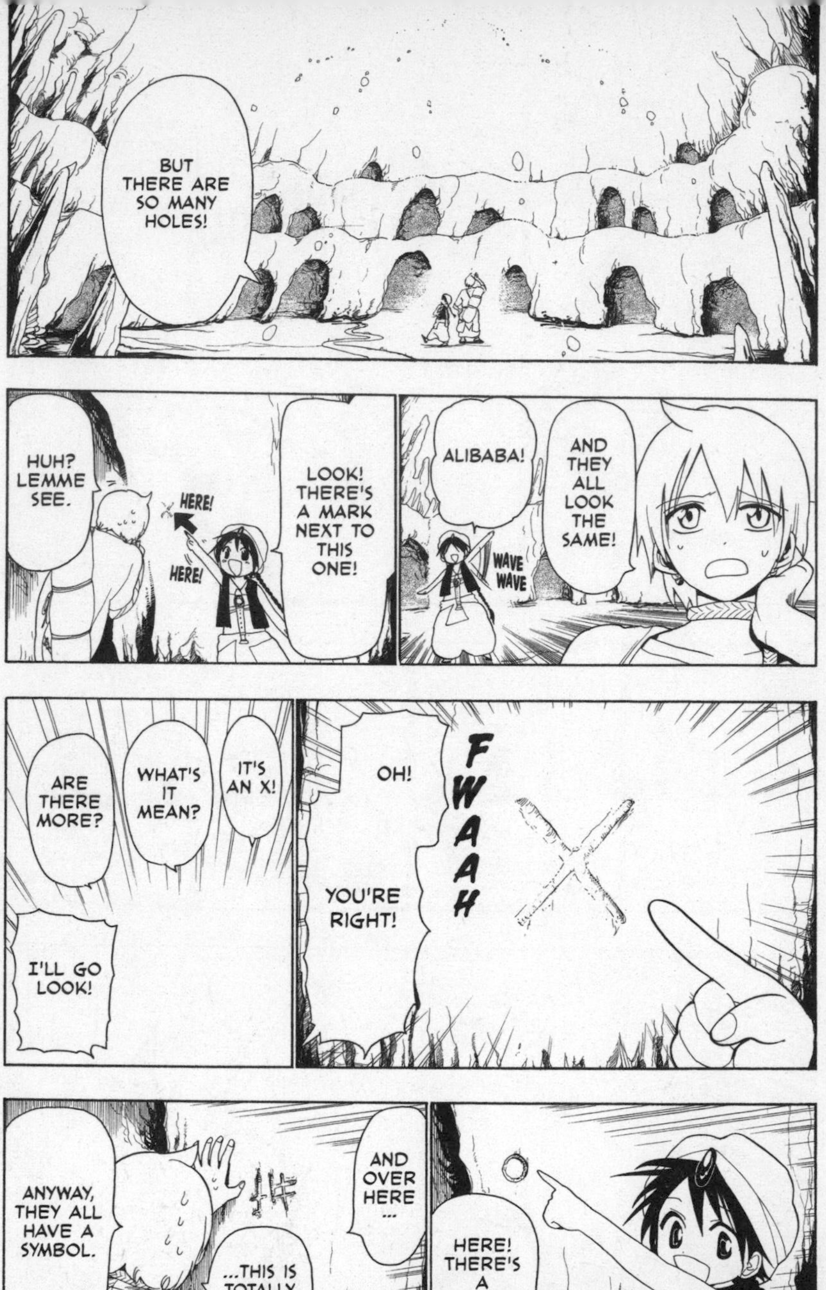
BUT THERE ARE SO MANY HOLES!
AND THEY ALL LOOK THE SAME!
ALIBABA!
WAVE WAVE
LOOK! THERE'S A MARK NEXT TO THIS ONE!
HERE!
HERE!
HUH? LEMME SEE.
OH!
FWAAH
YOU'RE RIGHT!
IT'S AN X!
WHAT'S IT MEAN?
ARE THERE MORE?
I'LL GO LOOK!
HERE! THERE'S A CIRCLE!
AND OVER HERE ...
ANYWAY, THEY ALL HAVE A SYMBOL.
...THIS IS TOTALLY WEIRD!

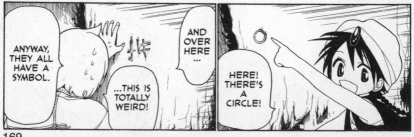

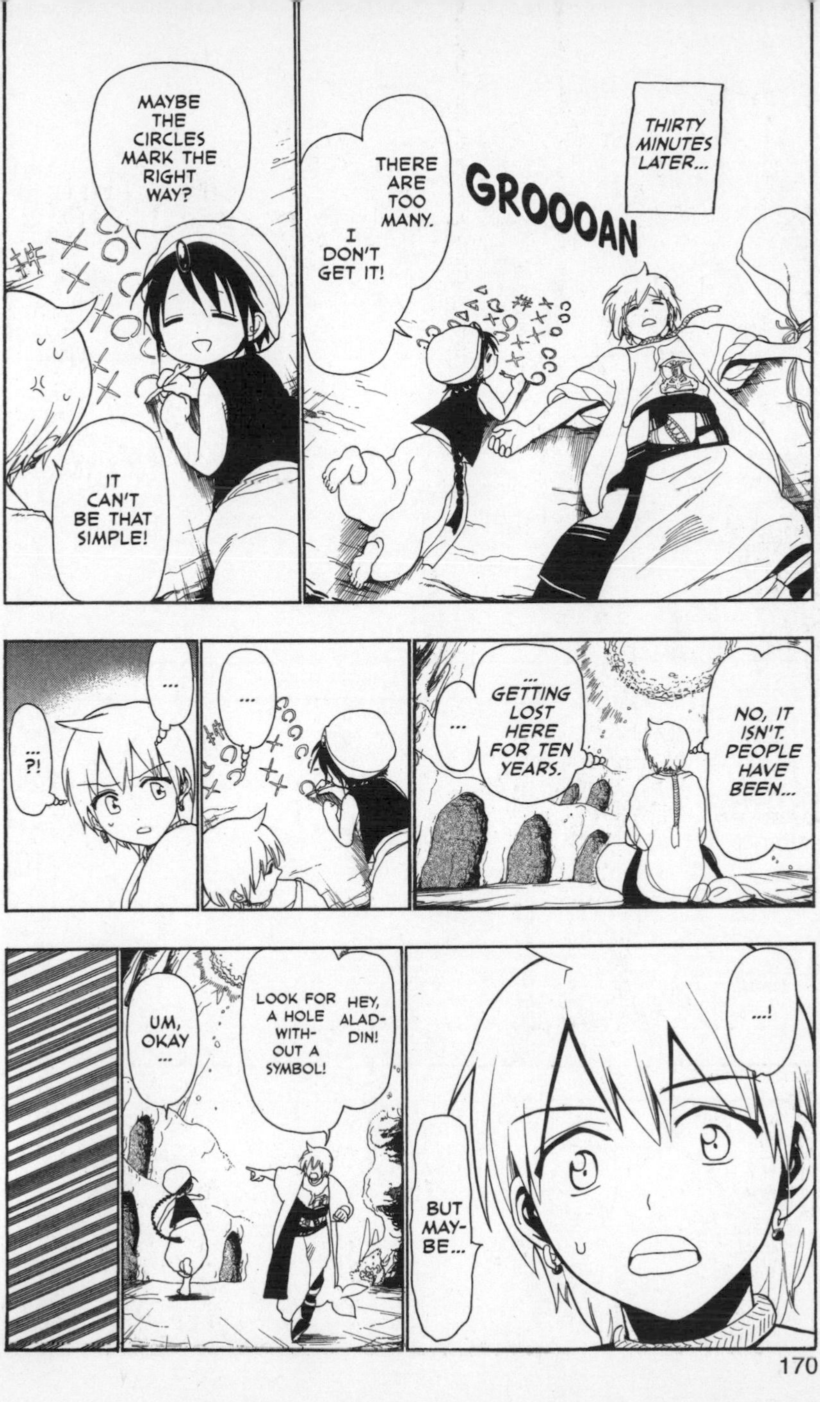
THIRTY MINUTES LATER...
GROOOAN
THERE ARE TOO MANY.
I DON'T GET IT!
MAYBE THE CIRCLES MARK THE RIGHT WAY?
IT CAN'T BE THAT SIMPLE!
NO, IT ISN'T. PEOPLE HAVE BEEN...
... GETTING LOST HERE FOR TEN YEARS.
...
...
...
...?!
...!
BUT MAY-BE...
HEY, ALAD-DIN!
LOOK FOR A HOLE WITH-OUT A SYMBOL!
UM, OKAY ...

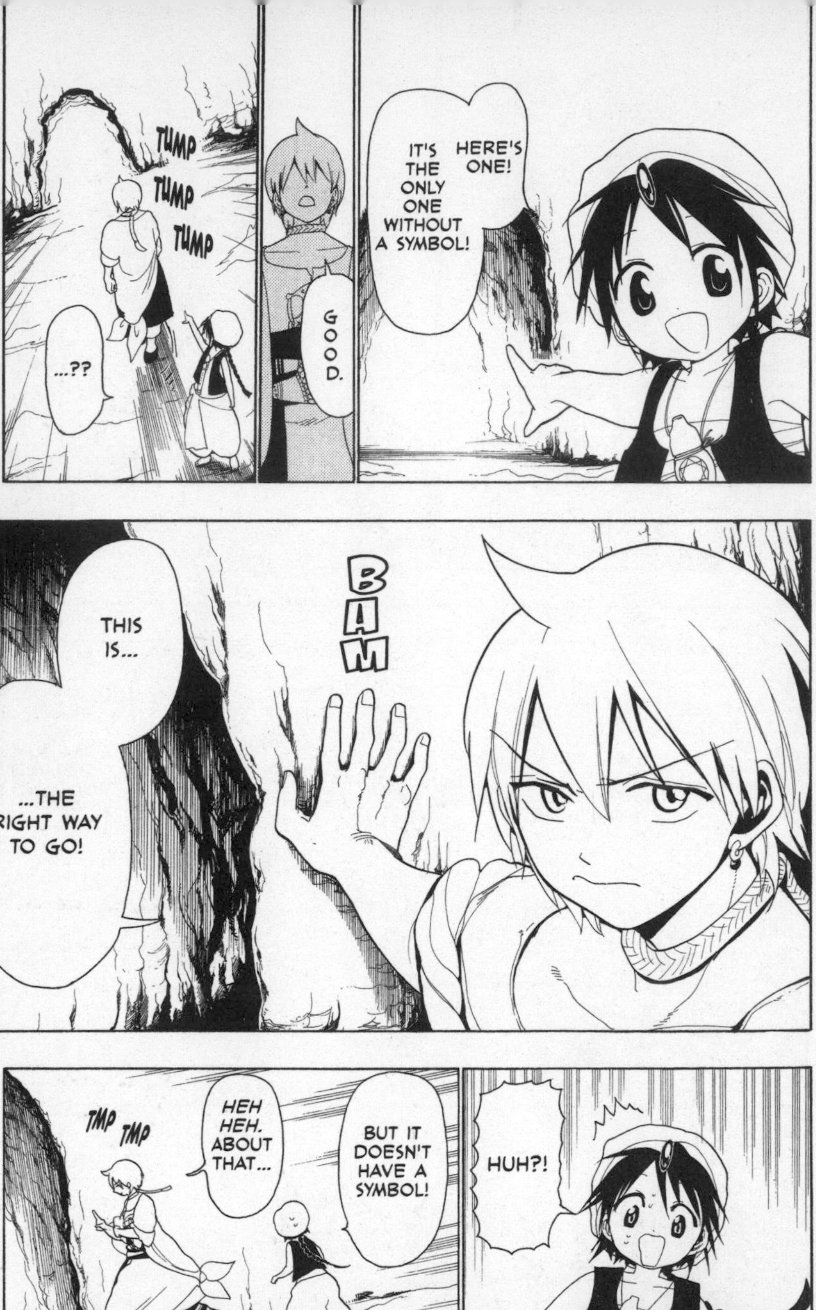
HERE'S ONE!
IT'S THE ONLY ONE WITHOUT A SYMBOL!
GOOD.
TUMP
TUMP
TUMP
...??
BAM
THIS IS...
...THE RIGHT WAY TO GO!
HUH?!
BUT IT DOESN'T HAVE A SYMBOL!
HEH HEH. ABOUT THAT...
TMP TMP

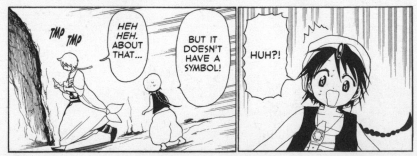

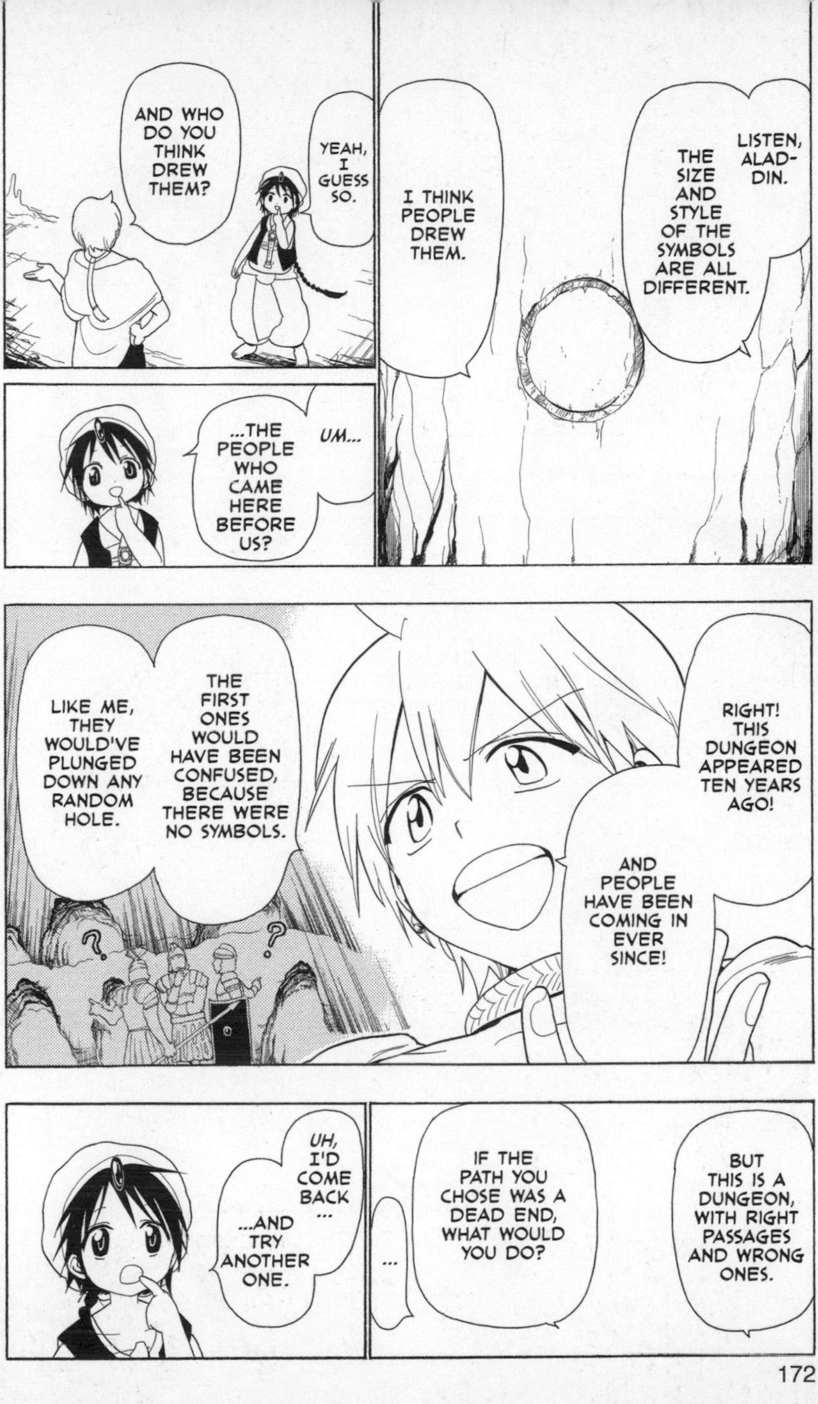
LISTEN, ALADDIN.
THE SIZE AND STYLE OF THE SYMBOLS ARE ALL DIFFERENT.
I THINK PEOPLE DREW THEM.
YEAH, I GUESS SO.
AND WHO DO YOU THINK DREW THEM?
UM...
...THE PEOPLE WHO CAME HERE BEFORE US?
RIGHT! THIS DUNGEON APPEARED TEN YEARS AGO!
AND PEOPLE HAVE BEEN COMING IN EVER SINCE!
THE FIRST ONES WOULD HAVE BEEN CONFUSED, BECAUSE THERE WERE NO SYMBOLS.
LIKE ME, THEY WOULD'VE PLUNGED DOWN ANY RANDOM HOLE.
BUT THIS IS A DUNGEON, WITH RIGHT PASSAGES AND WRONG ONES.
IF THE PATH YOU CHOSE WAS A DEAD END, WHAT WOULD YOU DO?
...
UH, I'D COME BACK...
...AND TRY ANOTHER ONE.

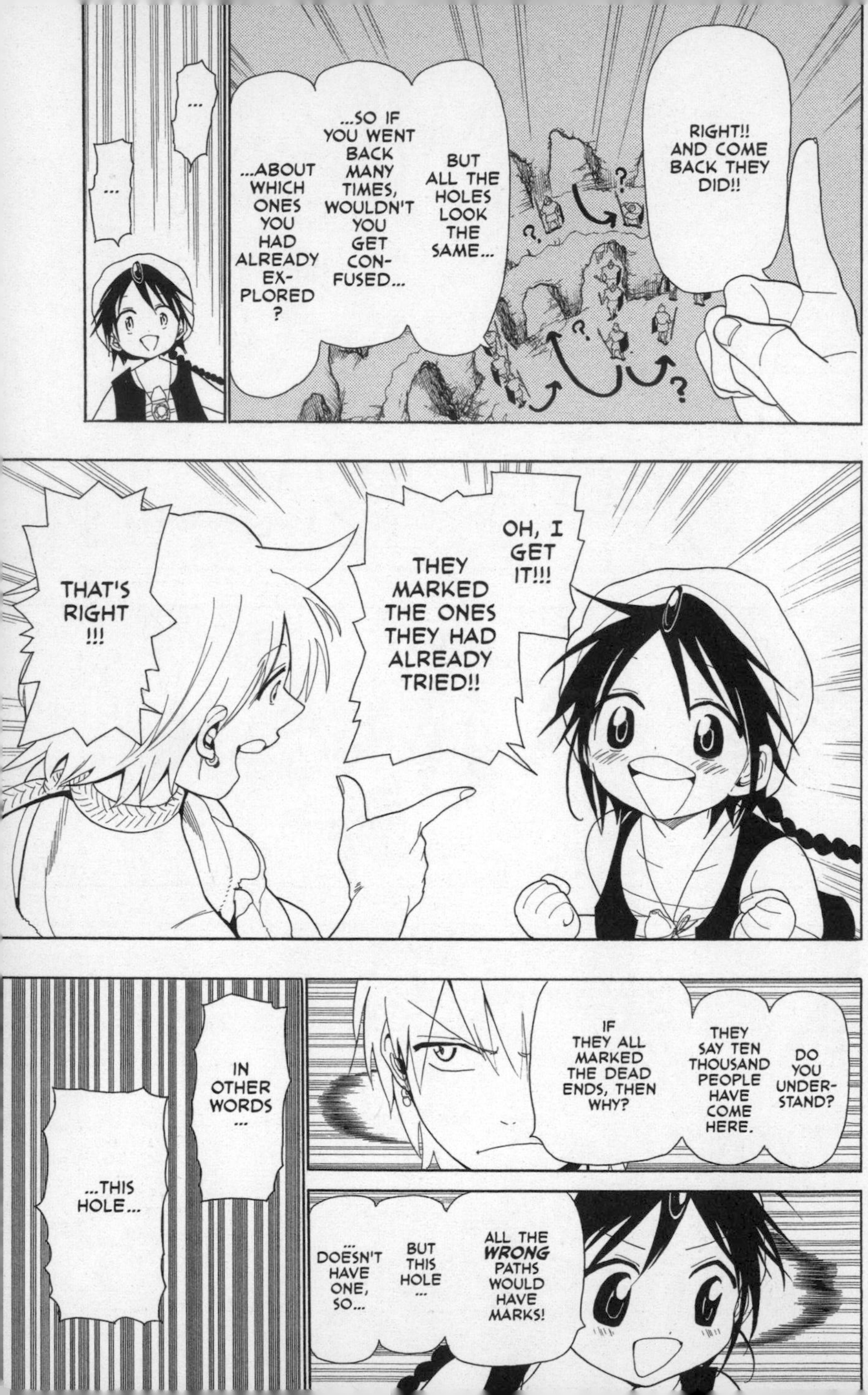
RIGHT!! AND COME BACK THEY DID!!
BUT ALL THE HOLES LOOK THE SAME...
...SO IF YOU WENT BACK MANY TIMES, WOULDN'T YOU GET CON-FUSED...
...ABOUT WHICH ONES YOU HAD ALREADY EX-PLORED?
...
...
OH, I GET IT!!!
THEY MARKED THE ONES THEY HAD ALREADY TRIED!!
THAT'S RIGHT!!!
DO YOU UNDER-STAND?
THEY SAY TEN THOUSAND PEOPLE HAVE COME HERE.
IF THEY ALL MARKED THE DEAD ENDS, THEN WHY?
ALL THE *WRONG* PATHS WOULD HAVE MARKS!
BUT THIS HOLE...
...DOESN'T HAVE ONE, SO...
IN OTHER WORDS...
...THIS HOLE...

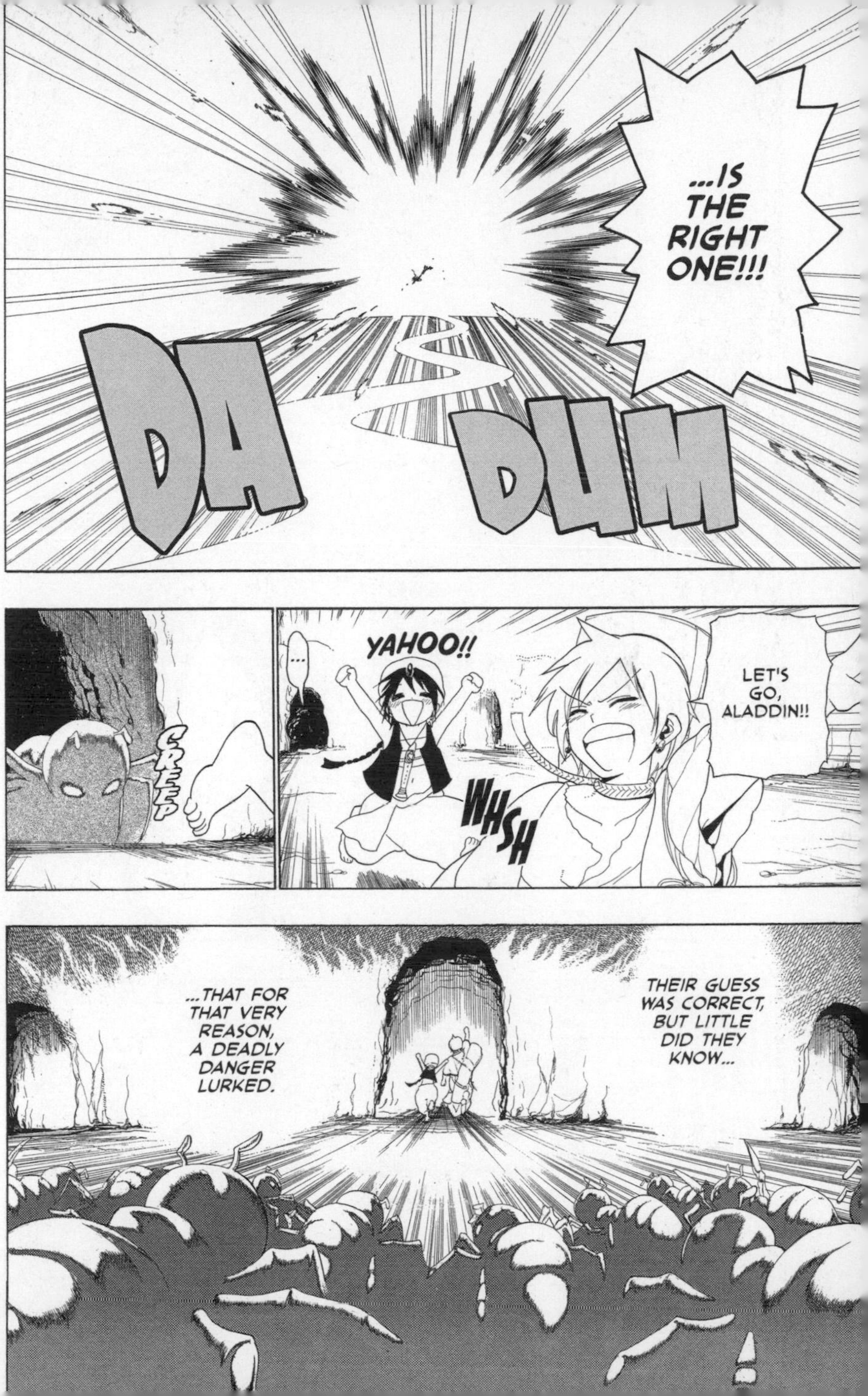
...IS THE RIGHT ONE!!!
DA
DUM
LET'S GO, ALADDIN!!
YAHOO!!
...
WHSH
CREEP
THEIR GUESS WAS CORRECT, BUT LITTLE DID THEY KNOW...
...THAT FOR THAT VERY REASON, A DEADLY DANGER LURKED.

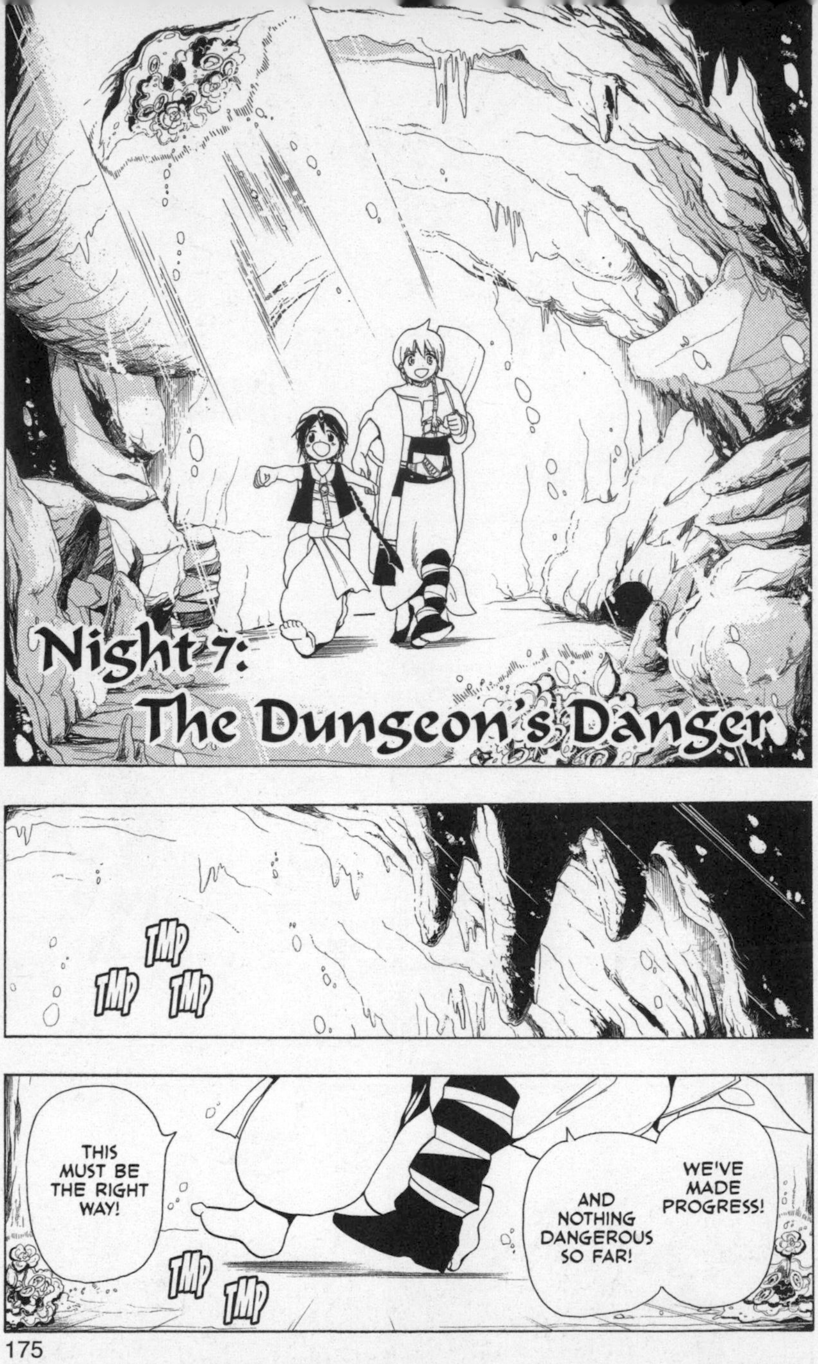
Night 7:
The Dungeon's Danger
TMP
TMP TMP
WE'VE MADE PROGRESS!
AND NOTHING DANGEROUS SO FAR!
THIS MUST BE THE RIGHT WAY!
TMP
TMP

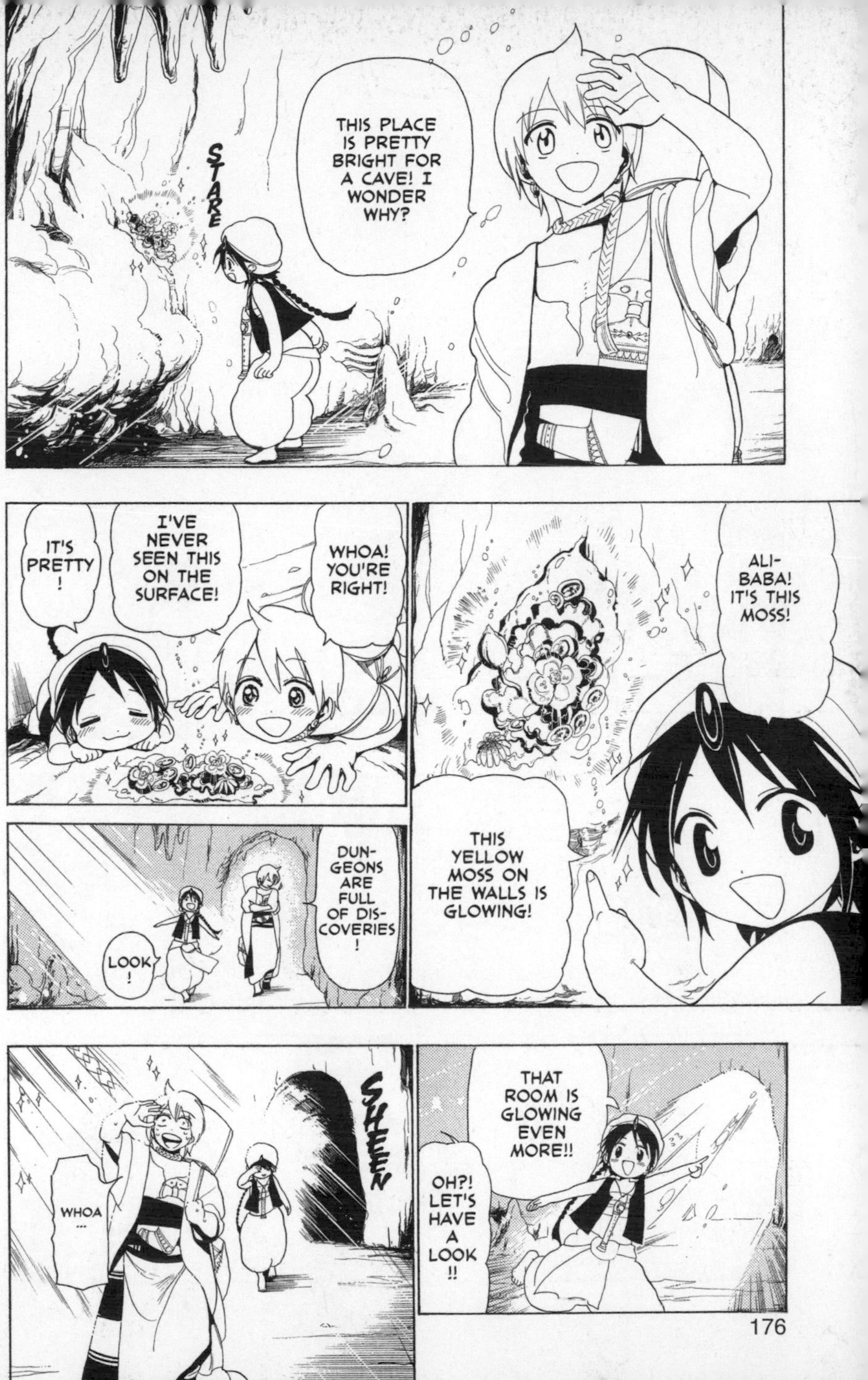
THIS PLACE IS PRETTY BRIGHT FOR A CAVE! I WONDER WHY?
STARE
ALI-BABA! IT'S THIS MOSS!
THIS YELLOW MOSS ON THE WALLS IS GLOWING!
WHOA! YOU'RE RIGHT!
I'VE NEVER SEEN THIS ON THE SURFACE!
IT'S PRETTY!
DUNGEONS ARE FULL OF DISCOVERIES!
LOOK!
THAT ROOM IS GLOWING EVEN MORE!!
OH?! LET'S HAVE A LOOK!!
SHEEN
WHOA...

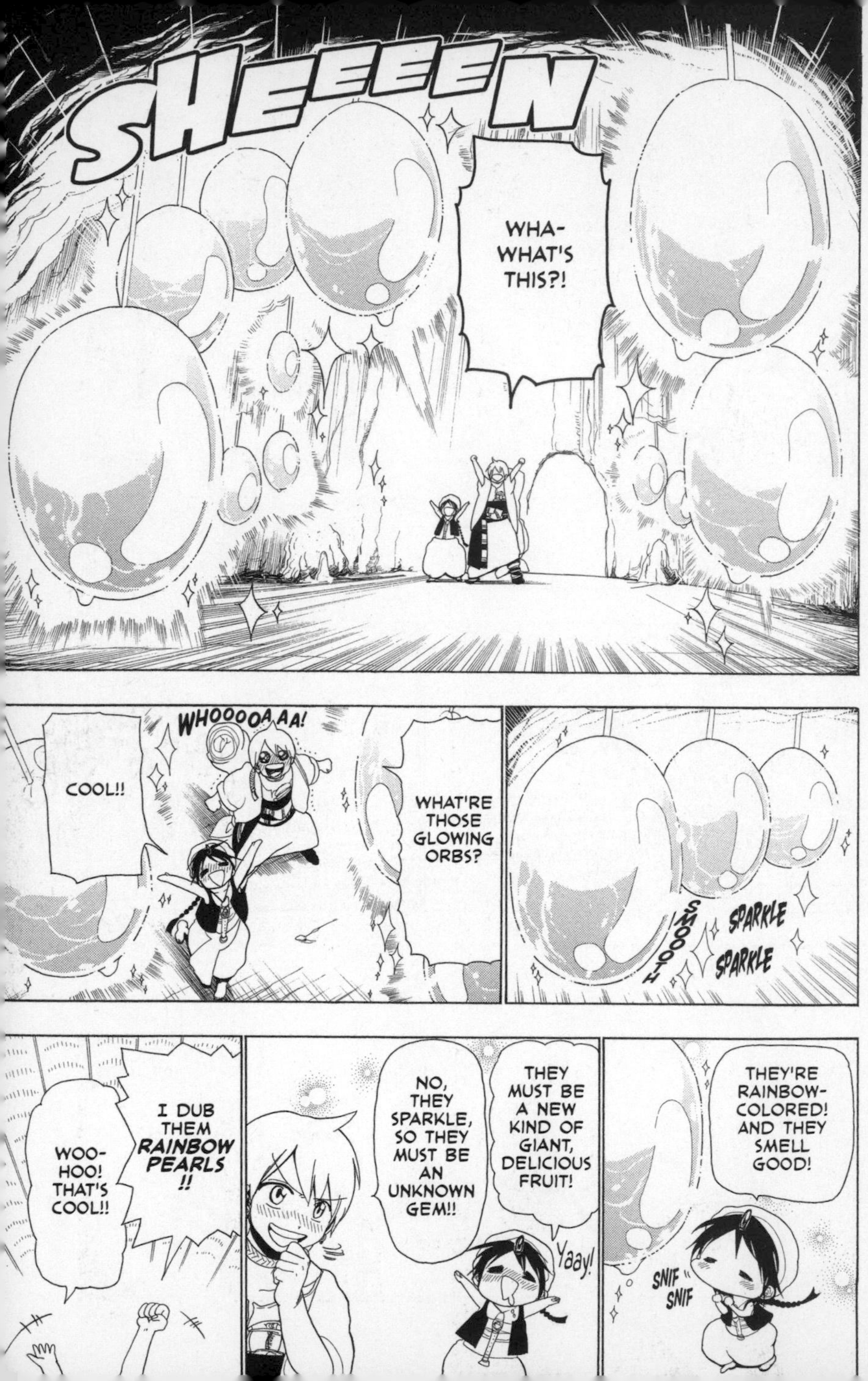
SHEEEEN
WHA- WHAT'S THIS?!
SMOOOTH
SPARKLE
SPARKLE
WHAT'RE THOSE GLOWING ORBS?
WHOOOOAAA!
COOL!!
THEY'RE RAINBOW-COLORED! AND THEY SMELL GOOD!
SNIF
SNIF
THEY MUST BE A NEW KIND OF GIANT, DELICIOUS FRUIT!
NO, THEY SPARKLE, SO THEY MUST BE AN UNKNOWN GEM!!
Yaay!
I DUB THEM RAINBOW PEARLS!!
WOO-HOO! THAT'S COOL!!

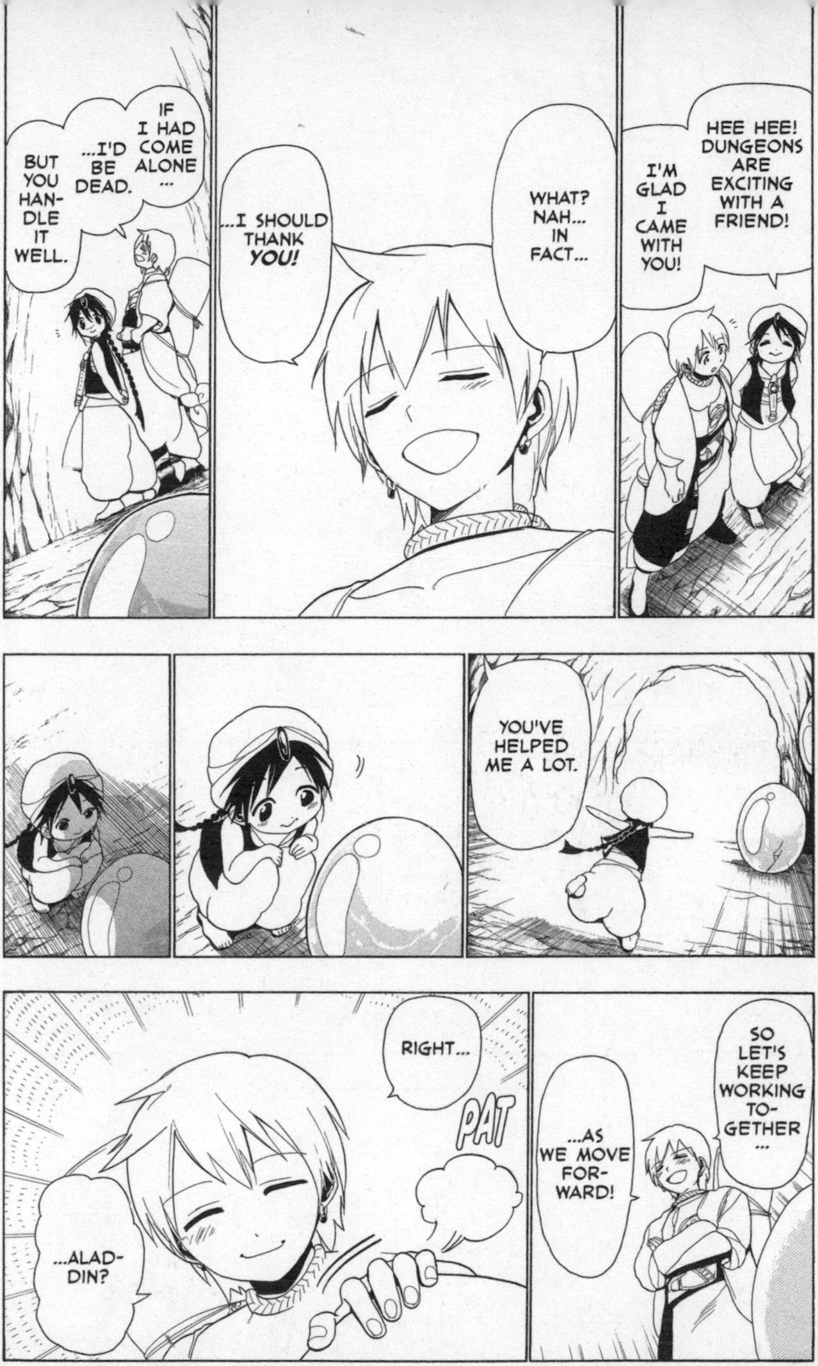
HEE HEE! DUNGEONS ARE EXCITING WITH A FRIEND!
I'M GLAD I CAME WITH YOU!
WHAT? NAH... IN FACT...
...I SHOULD THANK *YOU!*
IF I HAD COME ALONE...
...I'D BE DEAD.
BUT YOU HAND-DLE IT WELL.
YOU'VE HELPED ME A LOT.
SO LET'S KEEP WORKING TO-GETHER...
...AS WE MOVE FOR-WARD!
RIGHT...
PAT
...ALAD-DIN?

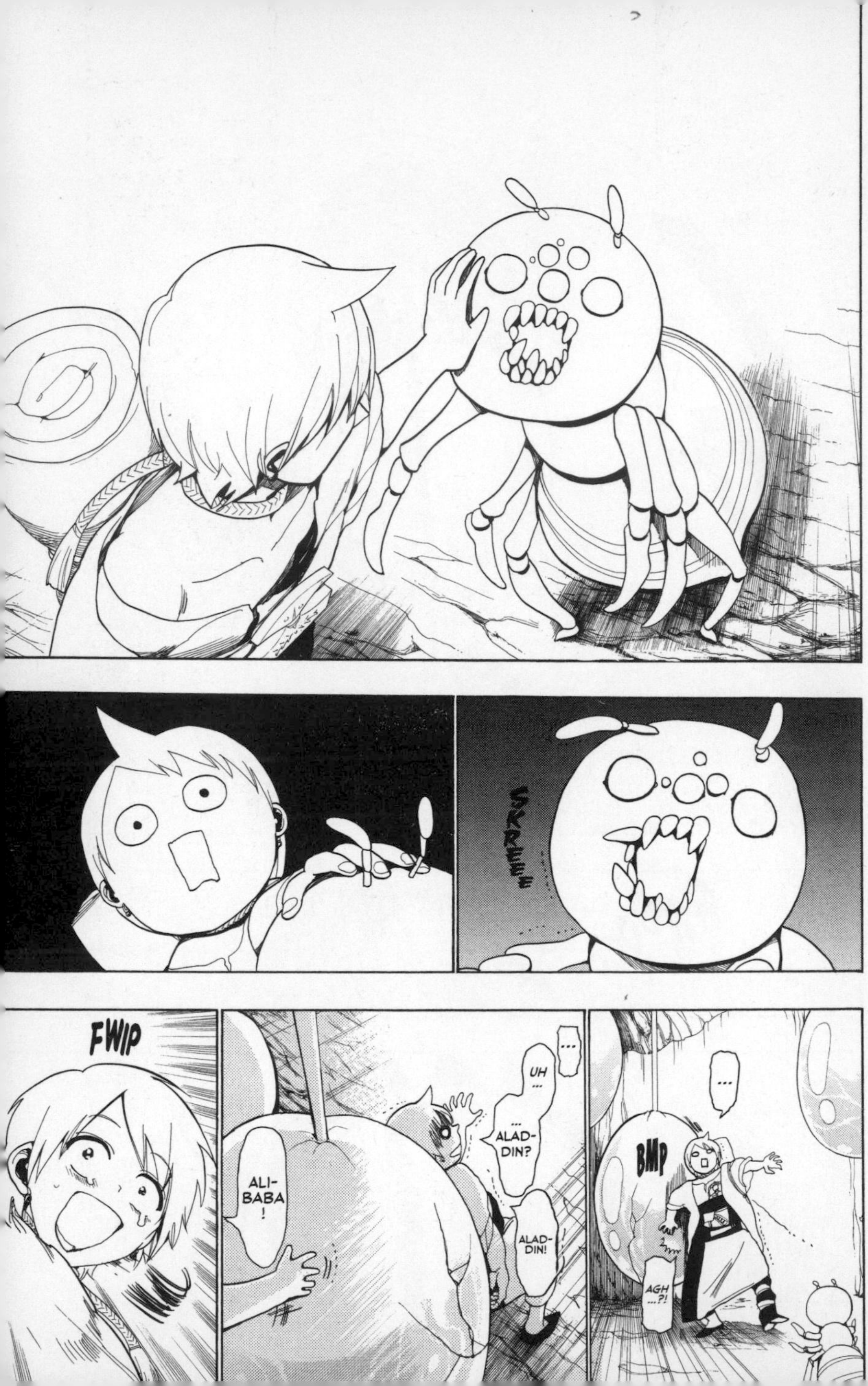
SKREEE
...
BMP
AGH ...?!
...
UH ...
... ALAD-DIN?
ALAD-DIN!
ALI-BABA!
FWIP

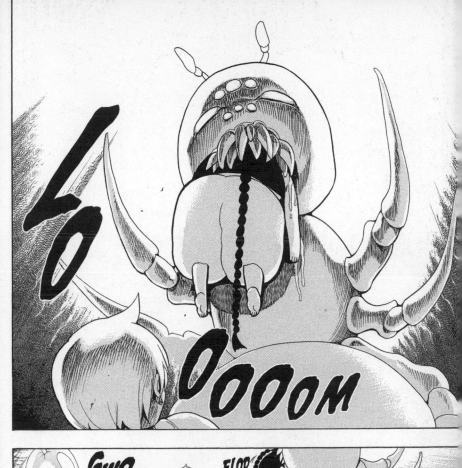

SO OOOOM

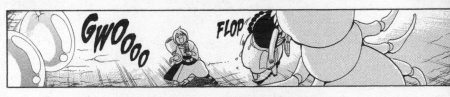

GWOOOoo

FLOP

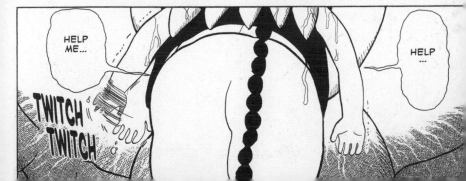

HELP
ME...

HELP
...

TWITCH
TWITCH

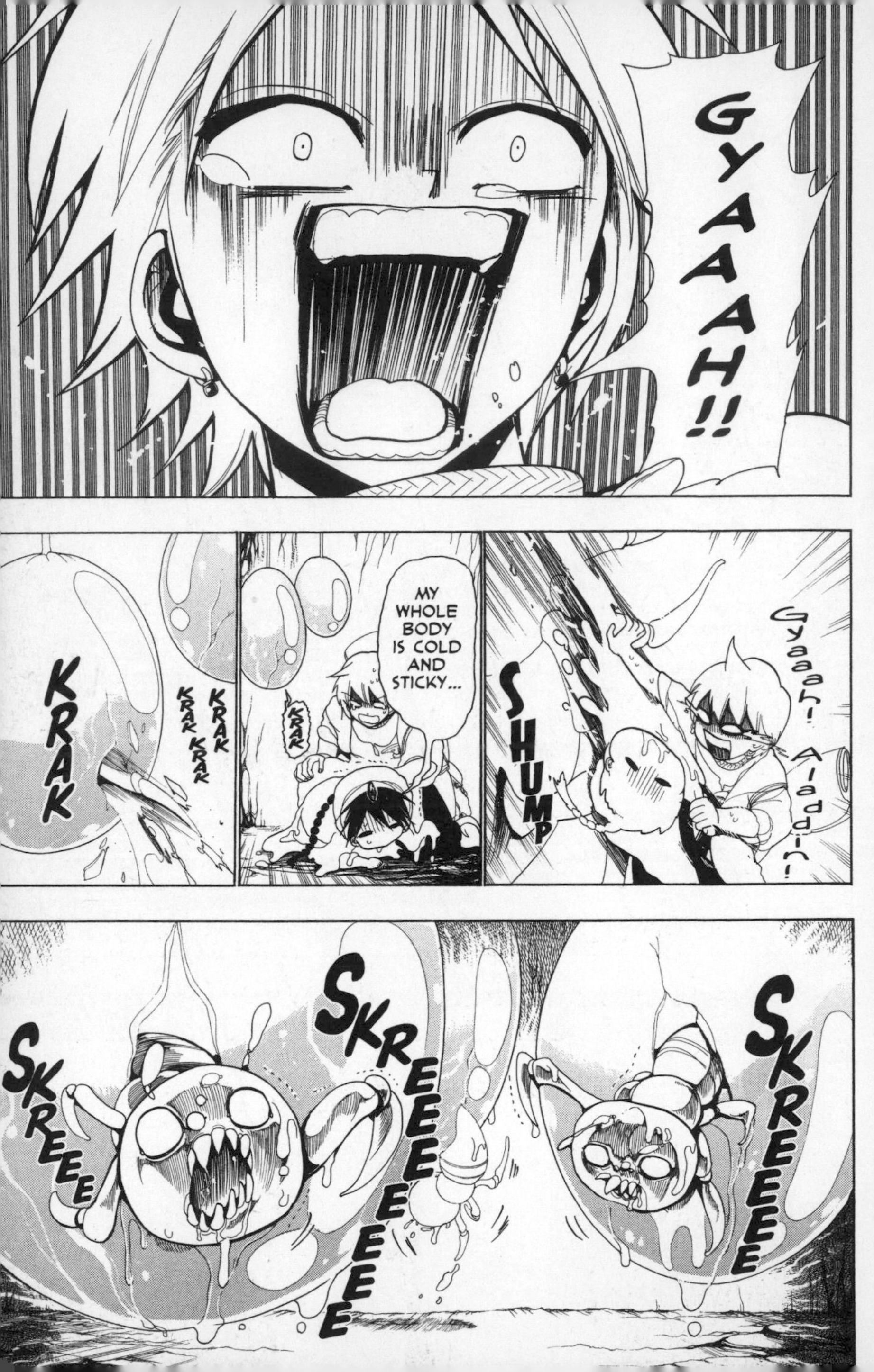
GYAAAH!!
Gyaaah! Aladdin!
SHUMP
MY WHOLE BODY IS COLD AND STICKY...
KRAK
KRAK KRAK KRAK
KRAK
SKREEEEEEE
SKREEEEEEEEEEE
SKREEEE

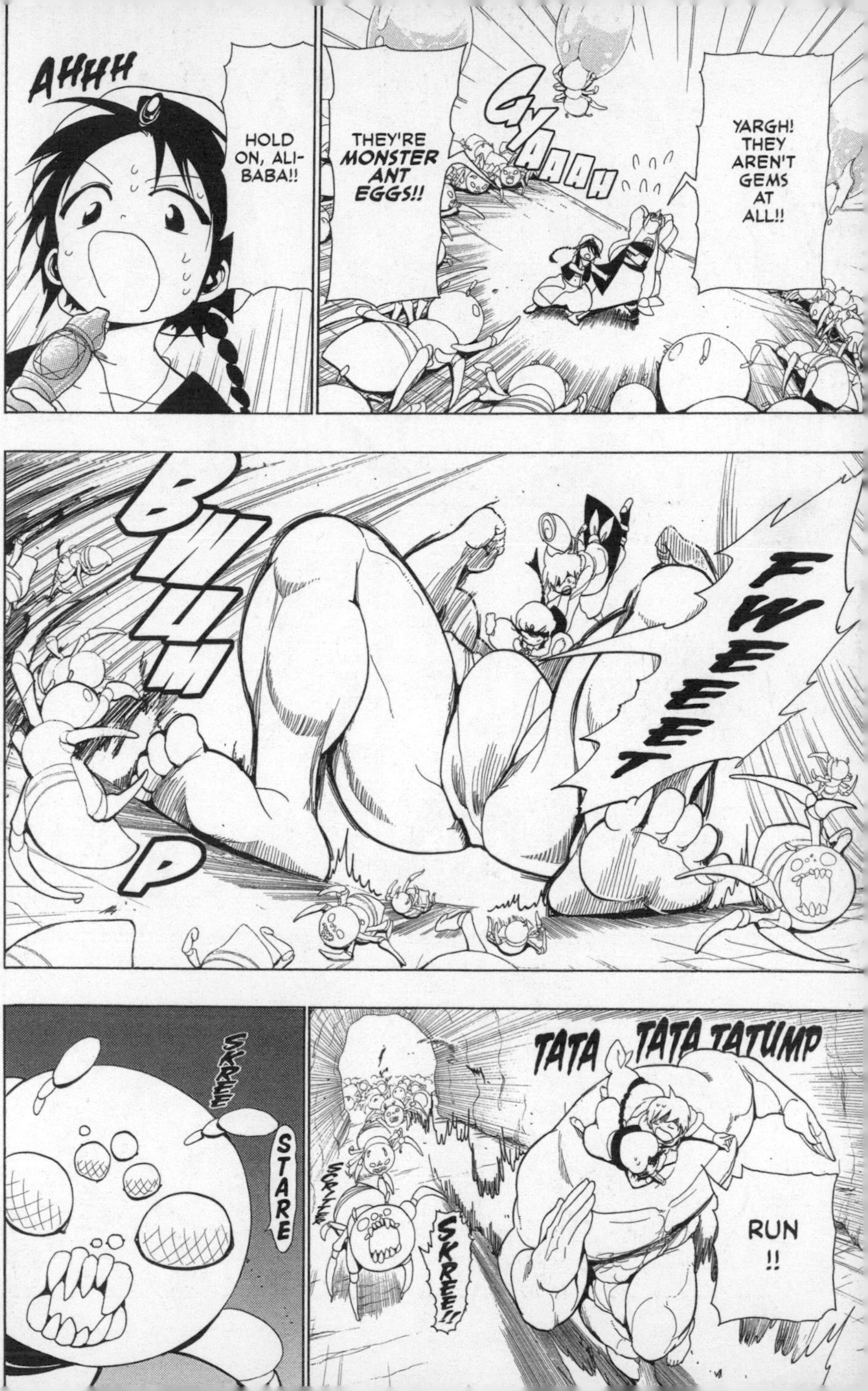

YARGH! THEY AREN'T GEMS AT ALL!!
GYAAAAH
THEY'RE MONSTER ANT EGGS!!
AHHH
HOLD ON, ALI-BABA!!
FWEEEET
BWUMP
TATA TATA TATUMP
RUN!!
SKREE!!
SCRITTER
SKREE
STARE

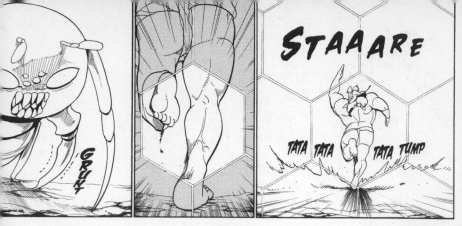

STAAARE
TATA TATA TATA TUMP
GRUNT
BWUP
BWUP BWUP
GOOD! THEY CAN'T KEEP UP!
TMP TMP TMP
PHEW... LET'S GIVE IT A REST THEN...
HUH?

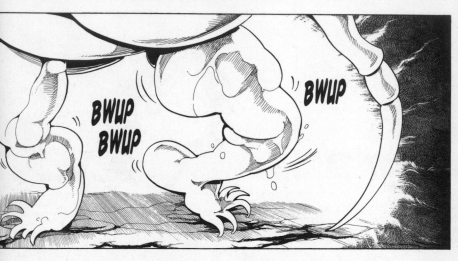

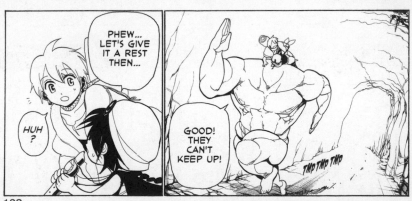

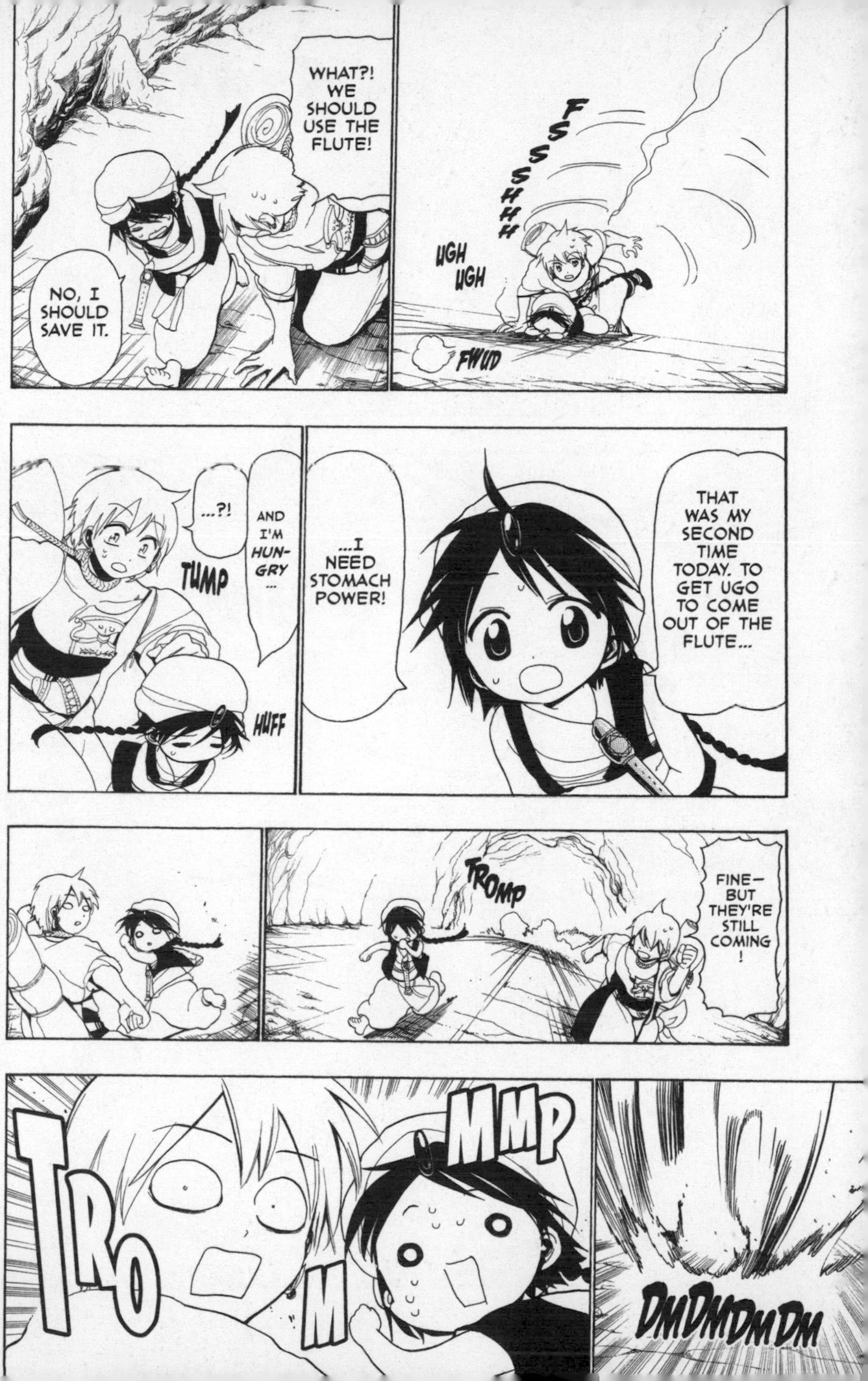
FSSSHHH
UGH
UGH
FWUD
WHAT?! WE SHOULD USE THE FLUTE!
NO, I SHOULD SAVE IT.
THAT WAS MY SECOND TIME TODAY. TO GET UGO TO COME OUT OF THE FLUTE...
...I NEED STOMACH POWER!
AND I'M HUN-GRY ...
...?!
TUMP
HUFF
FINE— BUT THEY'RE STILL COMING!
TROMP
DMDMDMDMDM
MMP
TROMM

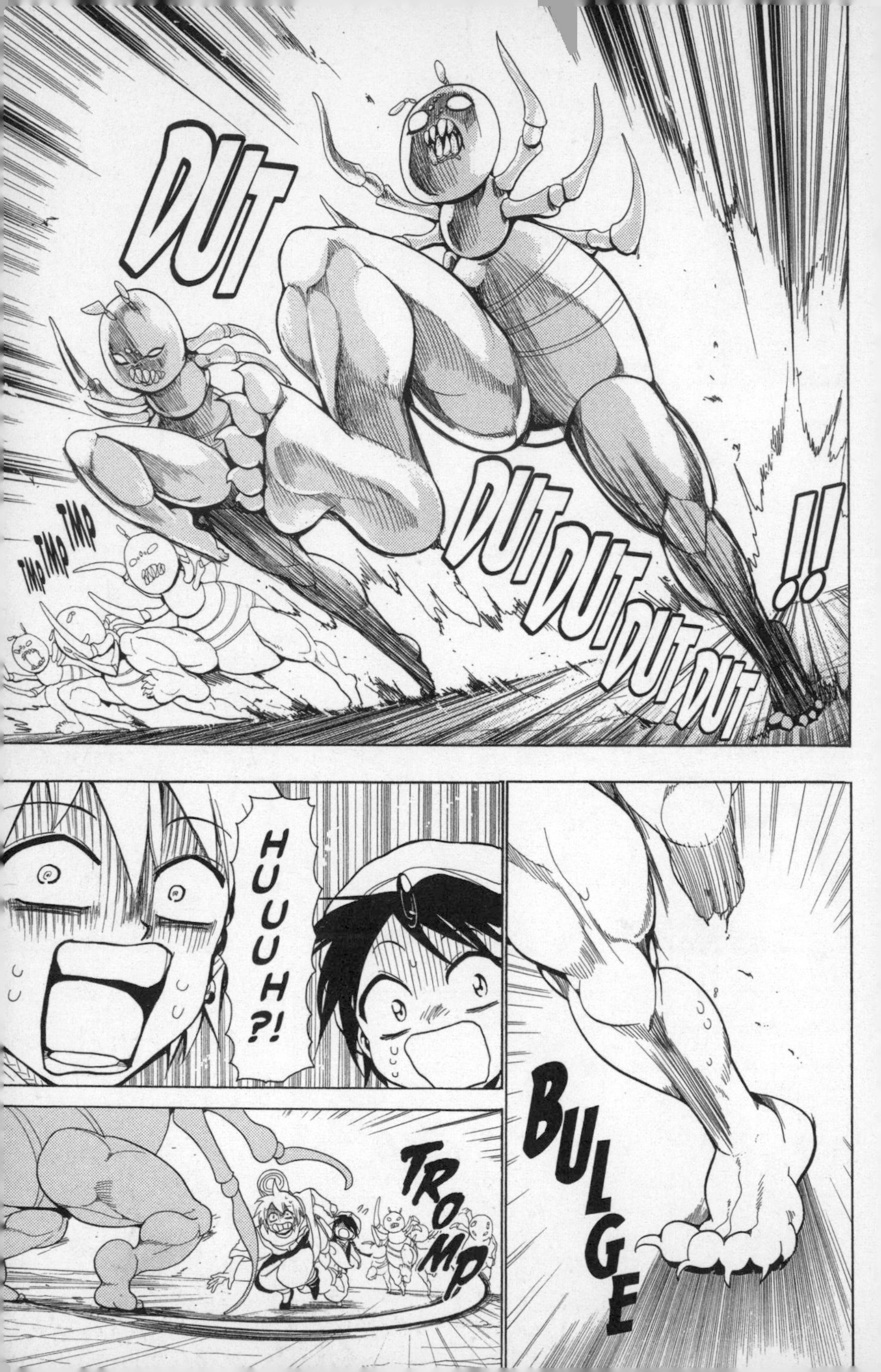
DUIT
DUIT DUIT DUIT DUIT!!
TMP TMP TMP
BULGE
HUUUH?!
TROMP

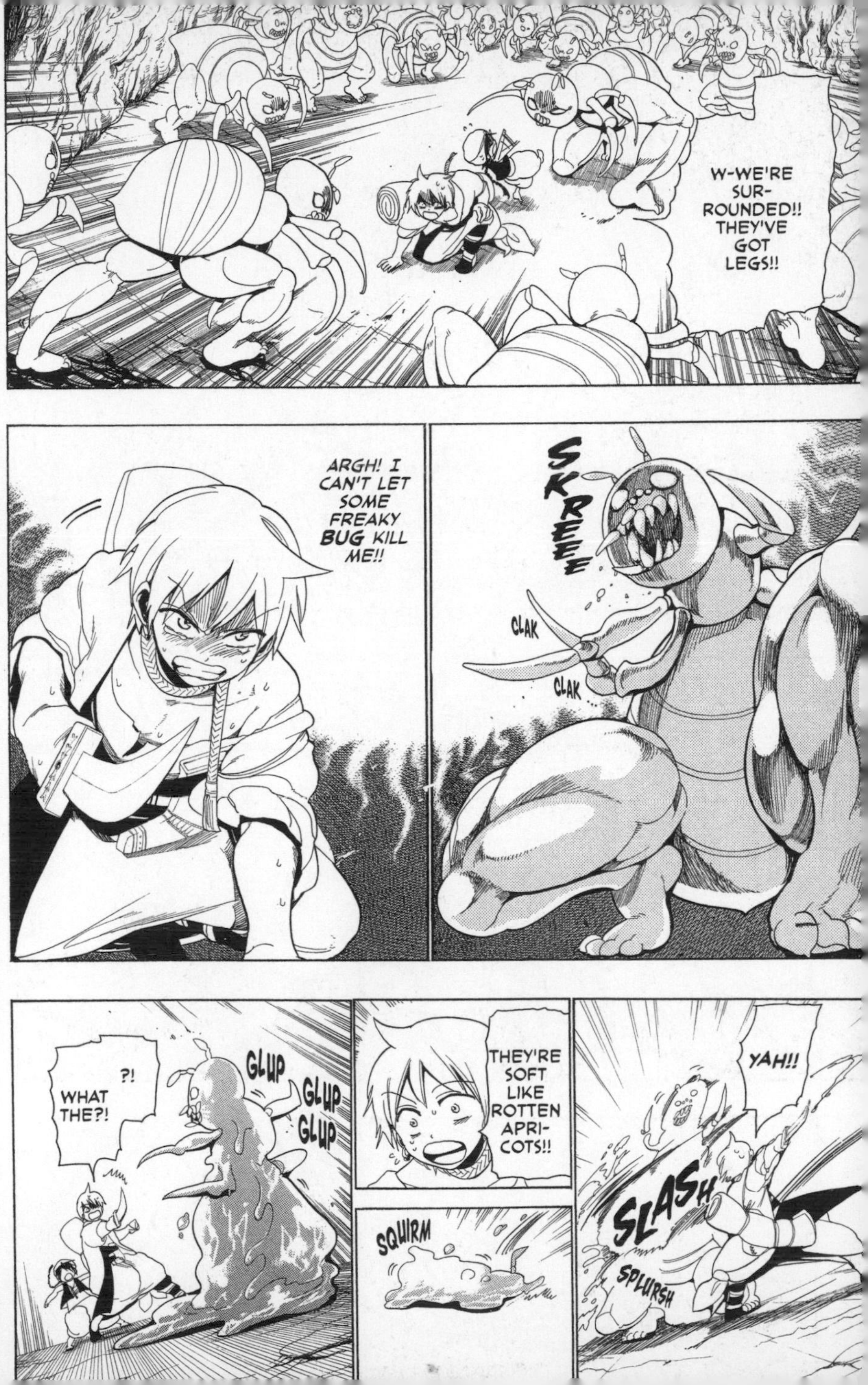
W-WE'RE SUR-ROUNDED!! THEY'VE GOT LEGS!!
SKREEE
CLAK
CLAK
ARGH! I CAN'T LET SOME FREAKY BUG KILL ME!!
YAH!!
SLASH
SPLURSH
THEY'RE SOFT LIKE ROTTEN APRI-COTS!!
SQUIRM
GLUP
GLUP
GLUP
?!
WHAT THE?!

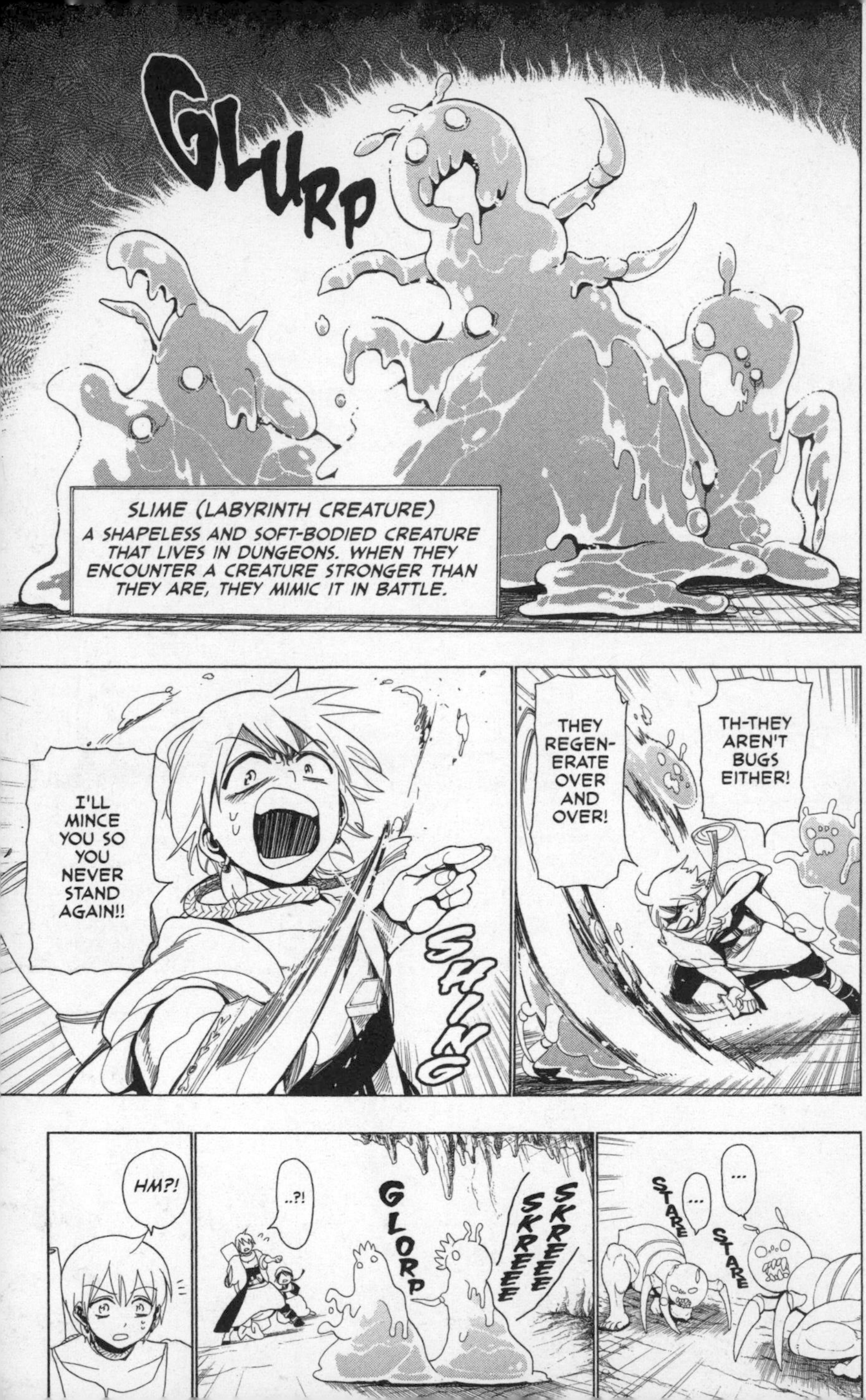
GLURP
SLIME (LABYRINTH CREATURE)
A SHAPELESS AND SOFT-BODIED CREATURE THAT LIVES IN DUNGEONS. WHEN THEY ENCOUNTER A CREATURE STRONGER THAN THEY ARE, THEY MIMIC IT IN BATTLE.
TH-THEY AREN'T BUGS EITHER!
THEY REGENERATE OVER AND OVER!
I'LL MINCE YOU SO YOU NEVER STAND AGAIN!!
SHING
...
...
STARE
STARE
SKREEEE
SKREEEE
GLORP
..?!
HM?!

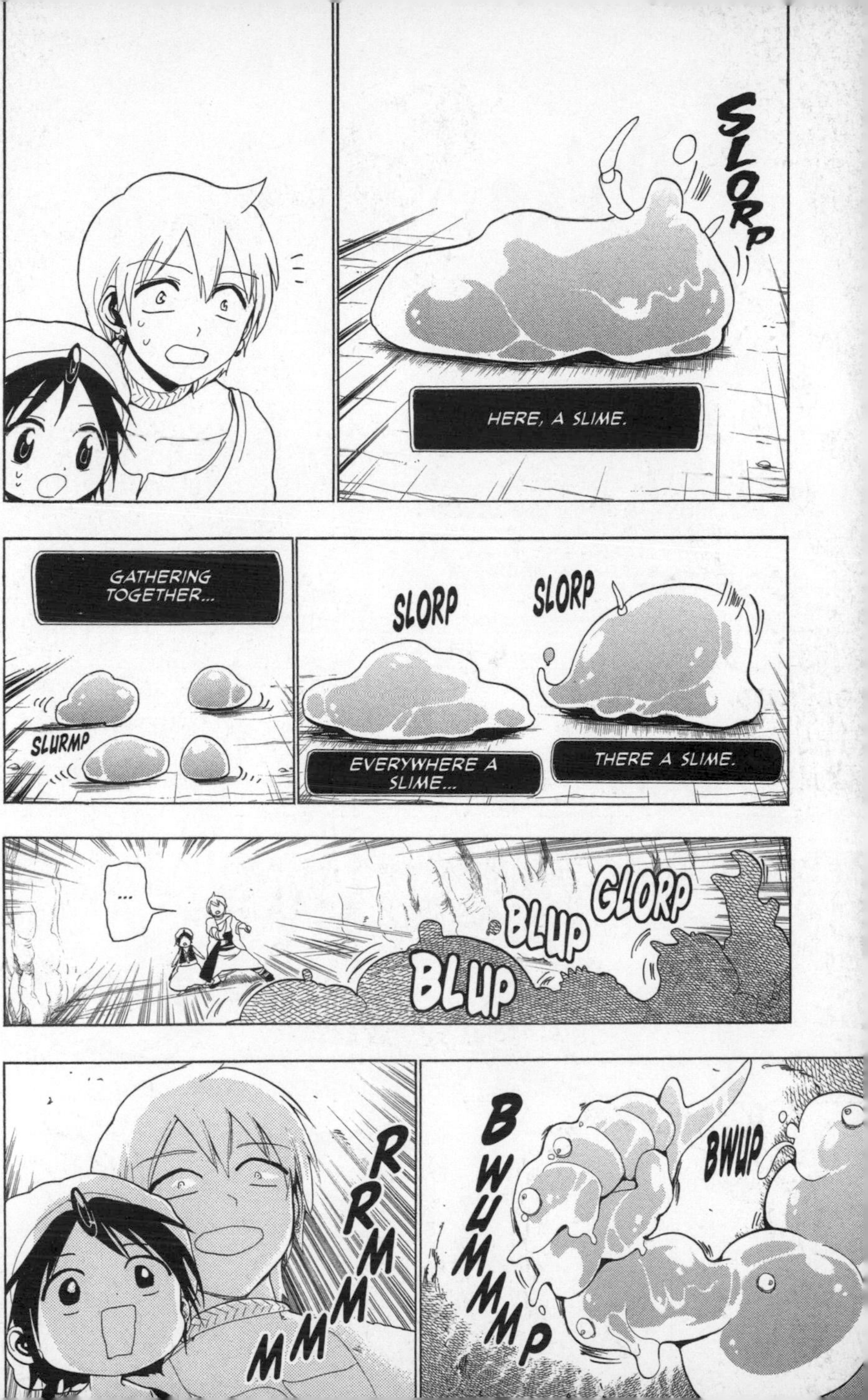
SLORP
HERE, A SLIME.
SLORP
THERE A SLIME.
SLORP
EVERYWHERE A SLIME...
GATHERING TOGETHER...
SLURMP
GLORP
BLUP
BLUP
...
BWUP
BWUMMMP
RRMMMM

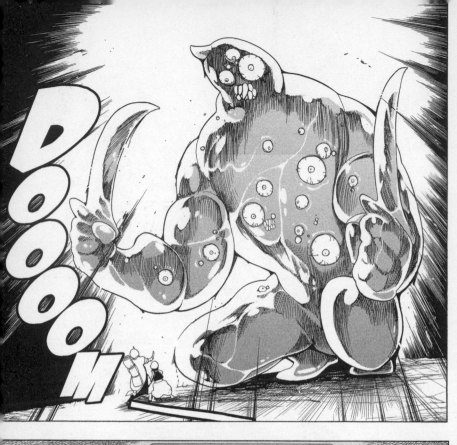

DOOOOM

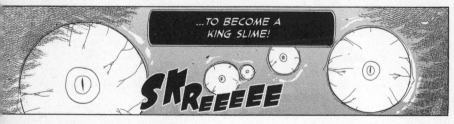

...TO BECOME A
KING SLIME!

SKREEEEE

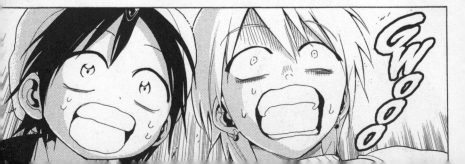

GWOOOO

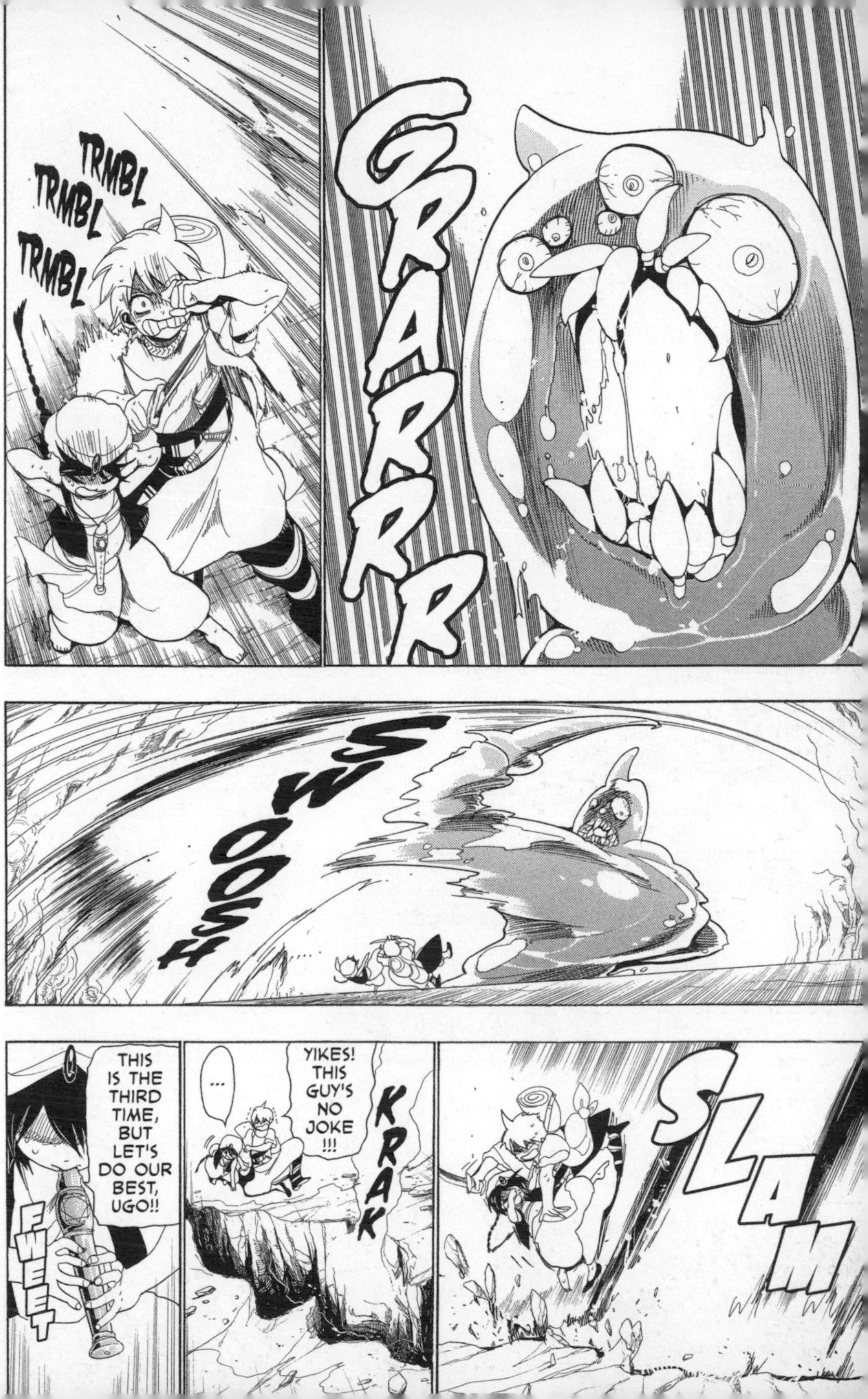
GRARRRR
TRMBL
TRMBL
TRMBL
SWOOSH
.....
SLAM
YIKES! THIS GUY'S NO JOKE!!!
...
KRAK
THIS IS THE THIRD TIME, BUT LET'S DO OUR BEST, UGO!!
FWEET

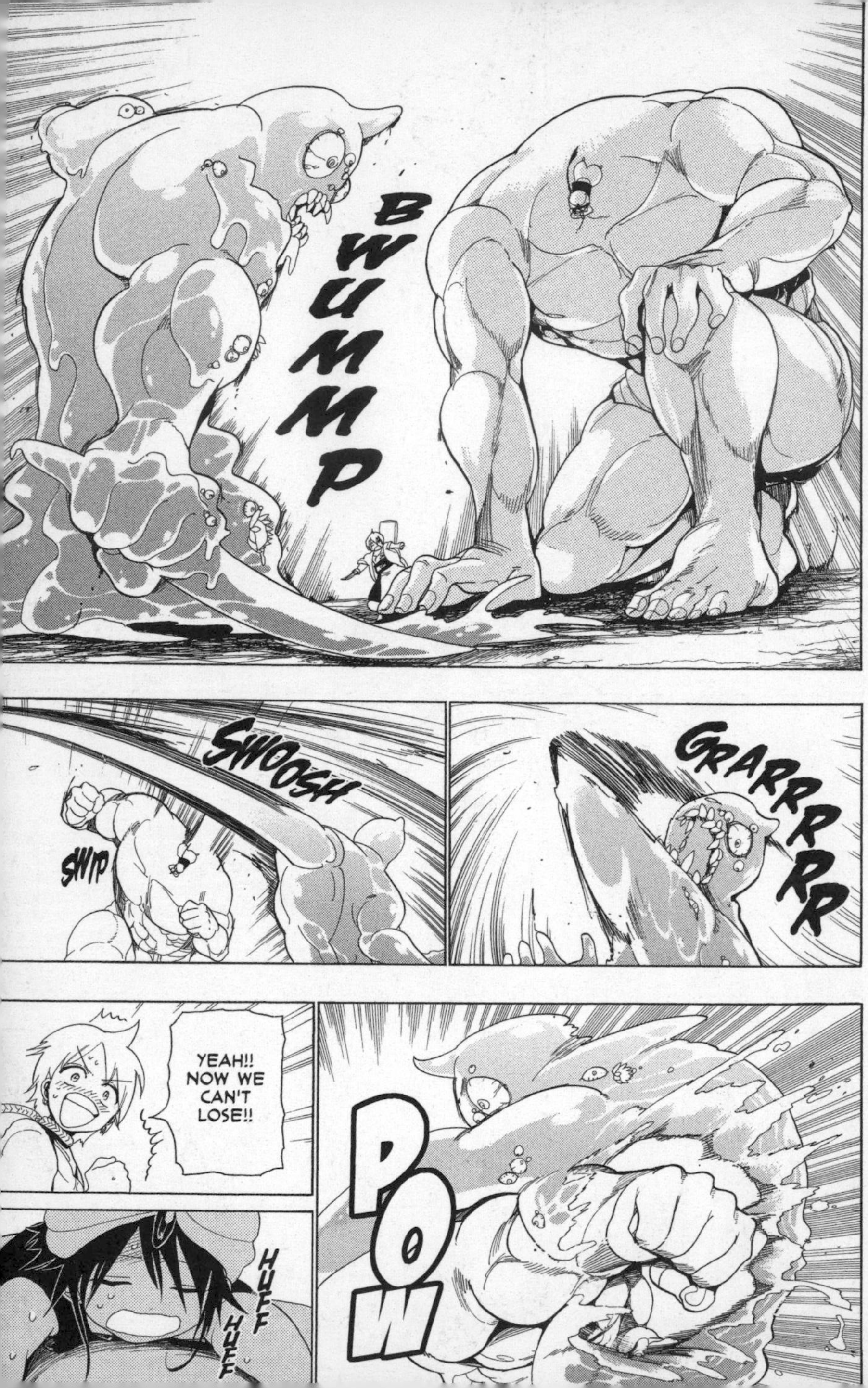
BWUMMP
GRARRRRR
SWOOSH
SWIP
POW
YEAH!! NOW WE CAN'T LOSE!!
HUFF
HUFF

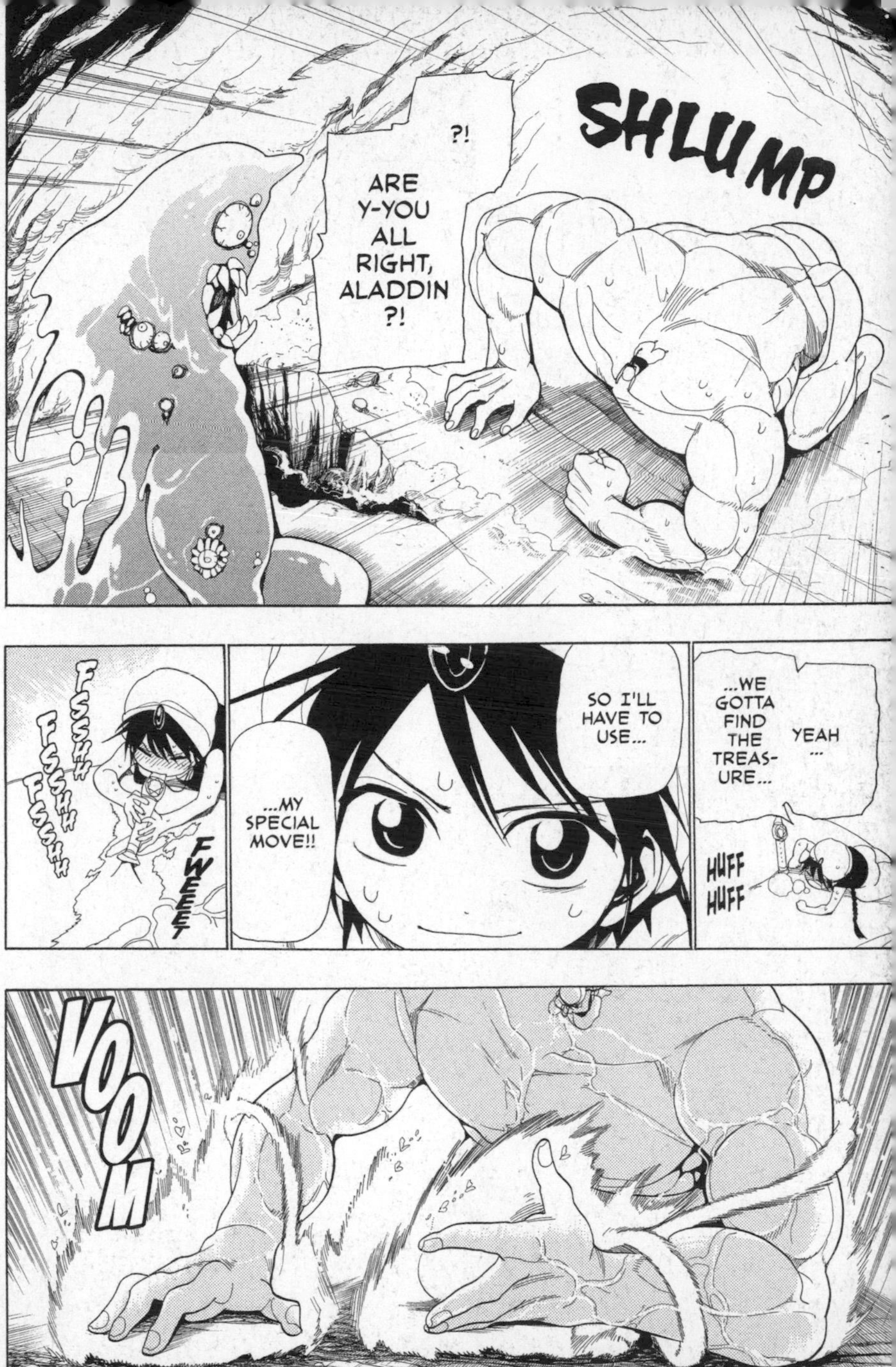
SHLUMP
?!
ARE Y-YOU ALL RIGHT, ALADDIN ?!
YEAH ...
...WE GOTTA FIND THE TREASURE...
HUFF HUFF
SO I'LL HAVE TO USE...
...MY SPECIAL MOVE!!
FSSHH FSSHH FSSHH FSSHH
FWEEET
VOOM

Magi, Volume 1 -END-

MAGI
The labyrinth of magic
1

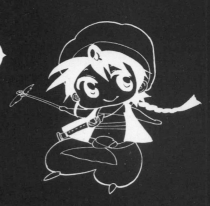

Staff

■ Story & Art
Shinobu Ohtaka

■ Regular Assistants

Matsubara

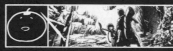

Miho Isshiki

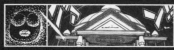

■ Editor
Kazuaki Ishibashi

■ Sales & Promotion
Akira Ozeki
Shinichirou Todaka

■ Designers
Yasuo Shimura + Bay Bridge Studio

■ Special Thanks
Mutsumi Ogasawara

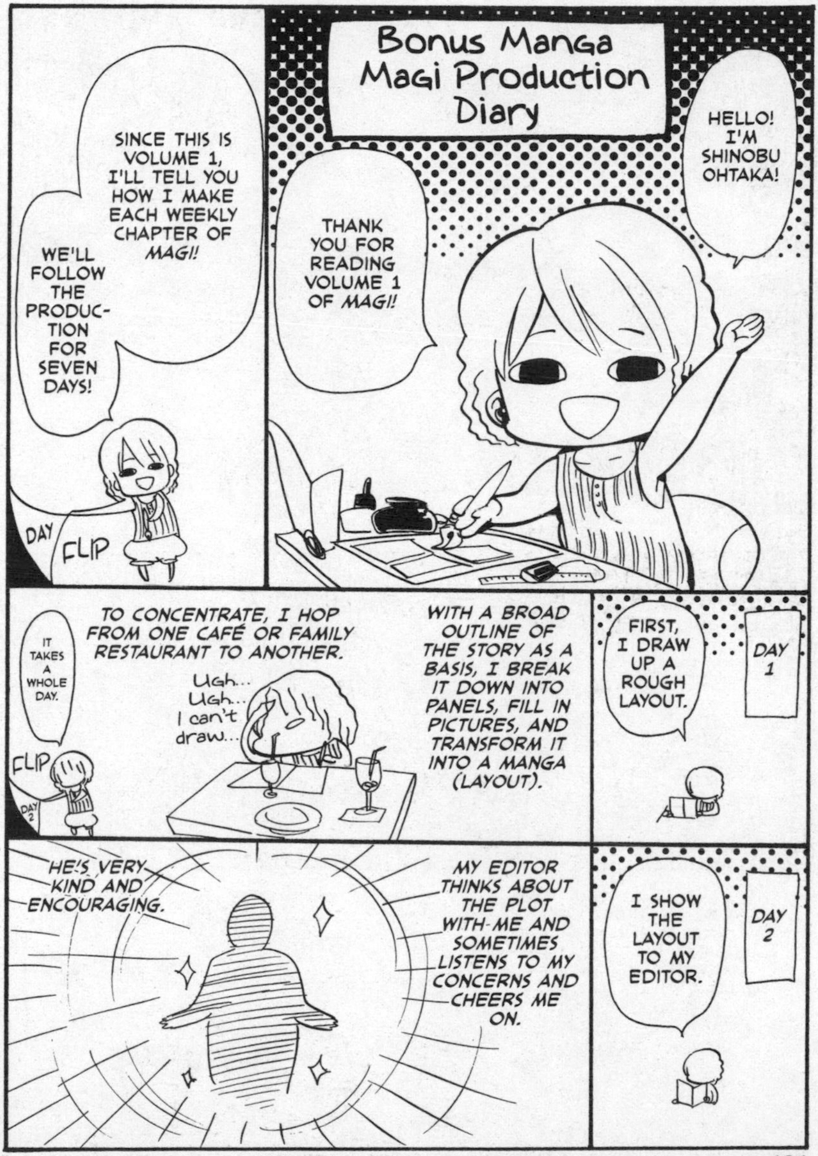
Bonus Manga Magi Production Diary
HELLO! I'M SHINOBU OHTAKA!
THANK YOU FOR READING VOLUME 1 OF MAGI!
SINCE THIS IS VOLUME 1, I'LL TELL YOU HOW I MAKE EACH WEEKLY CHAPTER OF MAGI!
WE'LL FOLLOW THE PRODUCTION FOR SEVEN DAYS!
DAY
FLIP
DAY 1
FIRST, I DRAW UP A ROUGH LAYOUT.
WITH A BROAD OUTLINE OF THE STORY AS A BASIS, I BREAK IT DOWN INTO PANELS, FILL IN PICTURES, AND TRANSFORM IT INTO A MANGA (LAYOUT).
TO CONCENTRATE, I HOP FROM ONE CAFÉ OR FAMILY RESTAURANT TO ANOTHER.
Ugh... Ugh... I can't draw...
IT TAKES A WHOLE DAY.
FLIP
DAY 2
DAY 2
I SHOW THE LAYOUT TO MY EDITOR.
MY EDITOR THINKS ABOUT THE PLOT WITH ME AND SOMETIMES LISTENS TO MY CONCERNS AND CHEERS ME ON.
HE'S VERY KIND AND ENCOURAGING.

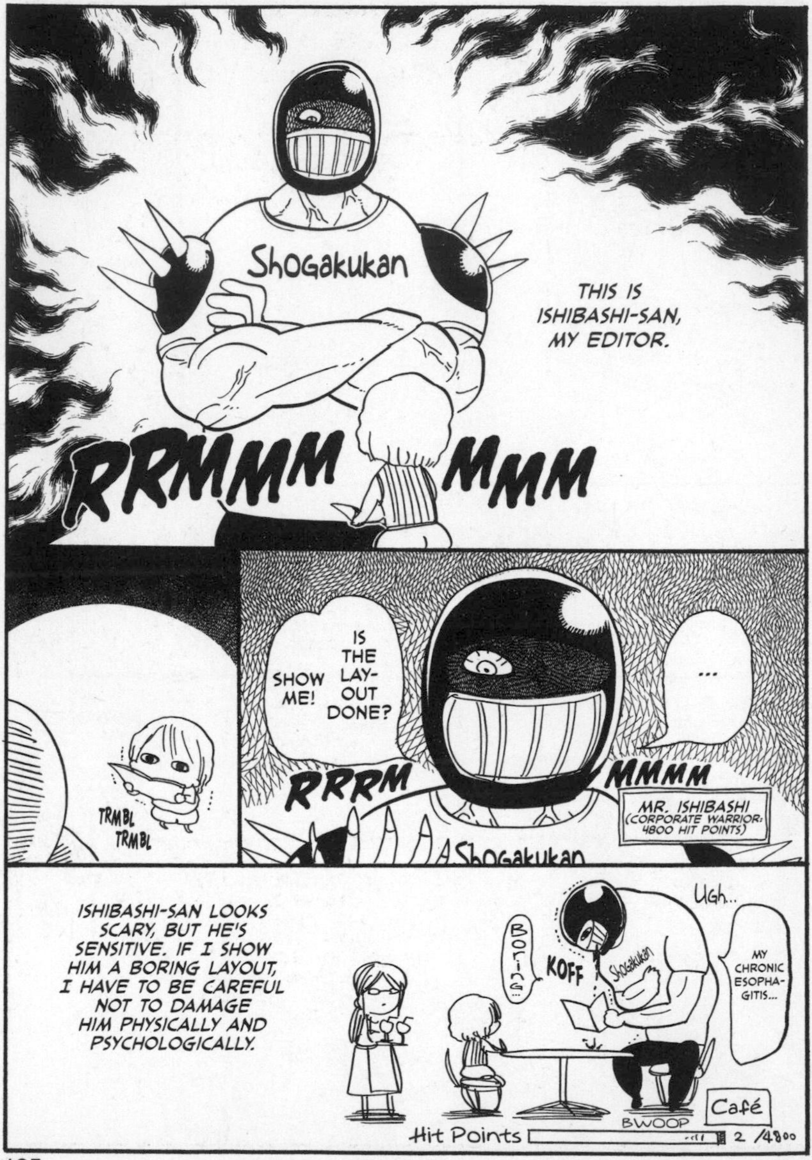
Shogakukan
THIS IS ISHIBASHI-SAN, MY EDITOR.
RRMMM MMM
...
IS THE LAY-OUT DONE?
SHOW ME!
RRRM MMMM
MR. ISHIBASHI (CORPORATE WARRIOR: 4800 HIT POINTS)
Shogakukan
TRMBL TRMBL
Ugh...
MY CHRONIC ESOPHA-GITIS...
Shogakukan
KOFF
Boring...
ISHIBASHI-SAN LOOKS SCARY, BUT HE'S SENSITIVE. IF I SHOW HIM A BORING LAYOUT, I HAVE TO BE CAREFUL NOT TO DAMAGE HIM PHYSICALLY AND PSYCHOLOGICALLY.
Café
BWOOP
Hit Points 2 /4800

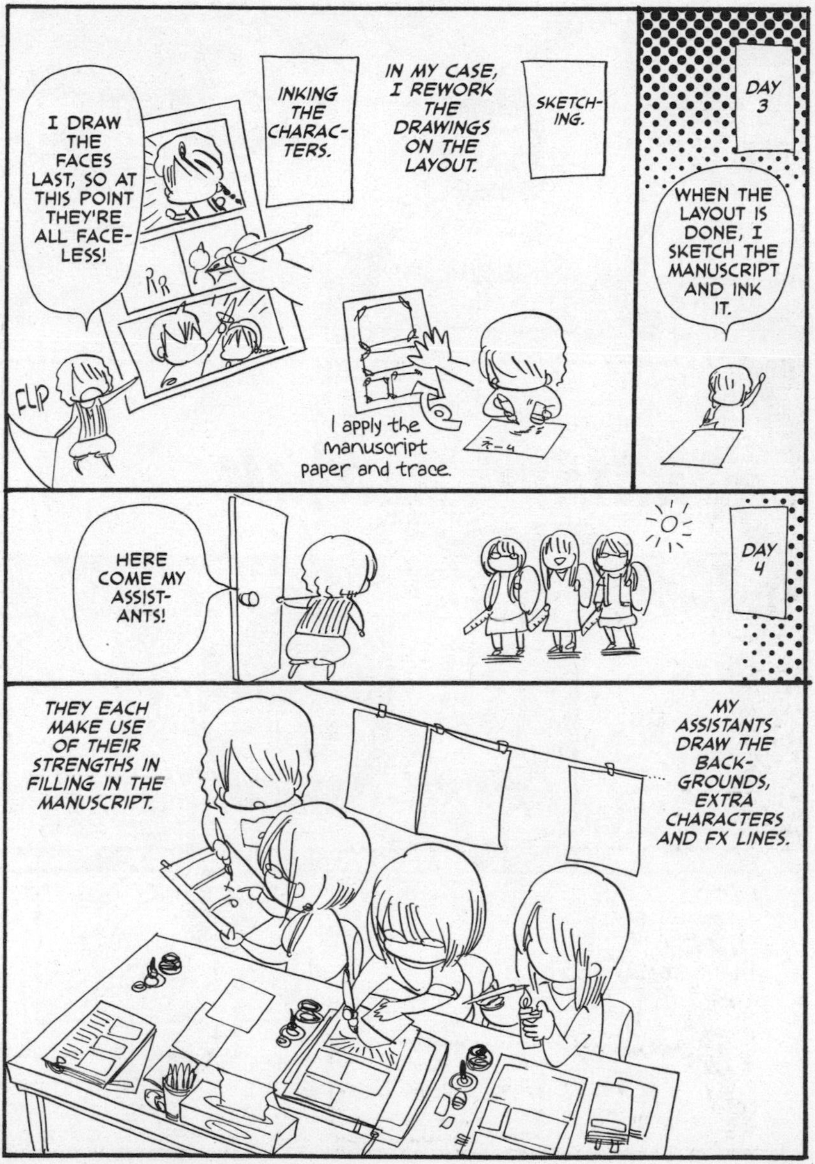
DAY 3
WHEN THE LAYOUT IS DONE, I SKETCH THE MANUSCRIPT AND INK IT.
SKETCH-ING.
IN MY CASE, I REWORK THE DRAWINGS ON THE LAYOUT.
I apply the manuscript paper and trace.
INKING THE CHARAC-TERS.
I DRAW THE FACES LAST, SO AT THIS POINT THEY'RE ALL FACE-LESS!
FLIP
DAY 4
HERE COME MY ASSIST-ANTS!
MY ASSISTANTS DRAW THE BACK-GROUNDS, EXTRA CHARACTERS AND FX LINES.
THEY EACH MAKE USE OF THEIR STRENGTHS IN FILLING IN THE MANUSCRIPT.

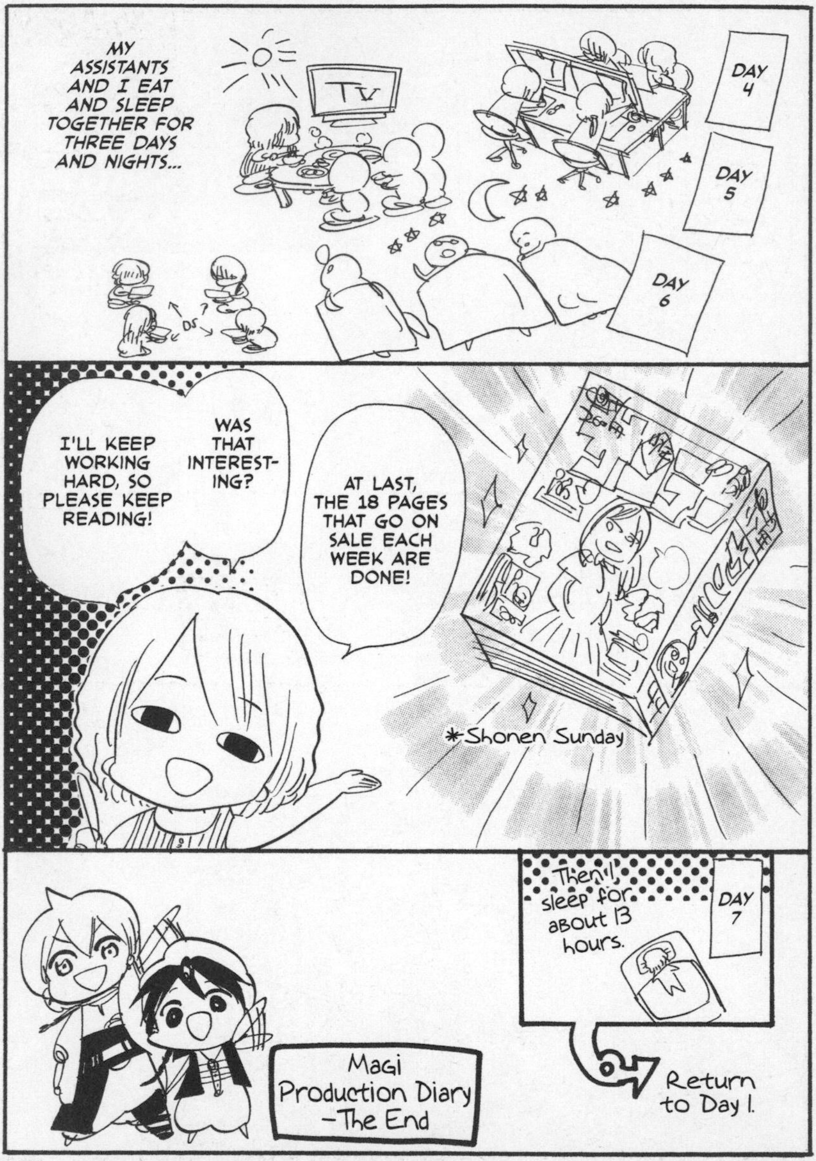
DAY 4
DAY 5
DAY 6
MY ASSISTANTS AND I EAT AND SLEEP TOGETHER FOR THREE DAYS AND NIGHTS...
TV
DS
AT LAST, THE 18 PAGES THAT GO ON SALE EACH WEEK ARE DONE!
*Shonen Sunday
WAS THAT INTERESTING?
I'LL KEEP WORKING HARD, SO PLEASE KEEP READING!
DAY 7
Then I sleep for about 13 hours.
Return to Day 1.
Magi Production Diary —The End

SHINOBU OHTAKA

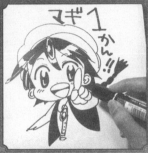

Magi volume 1!!

It's starting!

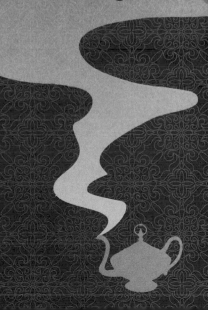

MAGI

Volume 1
Shonen Sunday Edition

Story and Art by
SHINOBU OHTAKA

MAGI Vol.1
by Shinobu OHTAKA
© 2009 Shinobu OHTAKA
All rights reserved.
Original Japanese edition published by SHOGAKUKAN.
English translation rights in the United States of America, Canada,
the United Kingdom, Ireland, Australia and New Zealand arranged with SHOGAKUKAN.

Translation & English Adaptation ◇ John Werry

Touch-up Art & Lettering ◇ Stephen Dutro

Editor ◇ Mike Montesa

Printed in the U.S.A.

Published by VIZ Media, LLC
P.O. Box 77010
San Francisco, CA 94107

10 9 8 7 6 5 4
First printing, August 2013
Fourth printing, September 2015

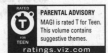

PARENTAL ADVISORY
MAGI is rated T for Teen.
This volume contains
suggestive themes.
ratings.viz.com

WWW.SHONENSUNDAY.COM

www.viz.com

You're reading the
WRONG WAY

MAGI reads from right to left, starting in the upper-right corner. Japanese is read from **right** to **left**, meaning that action, sound effects, and word-balloon order are completely reversed from English order.

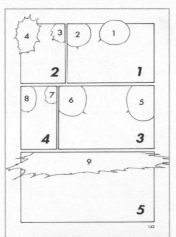

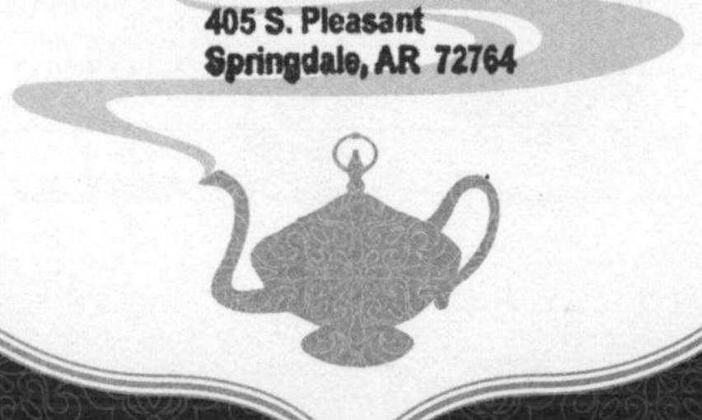

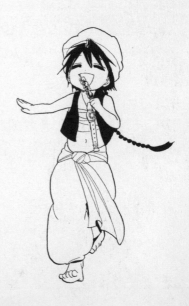